Disaster & Recovery Planning:

A Guide for Facility Managers

5th Edition

Disaster & Recovery Planning:

A Guide for Facility Managers

5th Edition

Joseph F. Gustin

THE FAIRMONT PRESS, INC.

CRC Press
Taylor & Francis Group

Library of Congress Cataloging-in-Publication Data

Gustin, Joseph F., 1947-
    Disaster & recovery planning : a guide for facility managers/by Joseph F. Gustin--5th ed.
        p. cm.
    Includes bibliographical references and index.
    ISBN-10: 0-88173-640-6 (alk. paper)
    ISBN-10: 0-88173-641-4 (electronic)
    ISBN-13: 978-1-4398-4467-0 (Taylor & Francis distribution : alk. paper)
    1. Emergency management--United States. 2. Crisis management--United States. 3. Facility management--United States. I. Title. II. Title: Disaster and recovery planning.

HV551.3.G87 2010
658.4'77--dc22

                                                          2010009537

Published by The Fairmont Press, Inc.
700 Indian Trail
Lilburn, GA 30047
tel: 770-925-9388; fax: 770-381-9865
http://www.fairmontpress.com

Distributed by Taylor & Francis Ltd.
6000 Broken Sound Parkway NW, Suite 300
Boca Raton, FL 33487, USA
E-mail: orders@crcpress.com

Distributed by Taylor & Francis Ltd.
23-25 Blades Court
Deodar Road
London SW15 2NU, UK
E-mail: uk.tandf@thomsonpublishingservices.co.uk

Printed in the United States of America
10 9 8 7 6 5 4 3 2

ISBN-10: 0-88173-640-6 (The Fairmont Press, Inc.)
ISBN-13: 978-1-4398-4467-0 (Taylor & Francis Ltd.)

While every effort is made to provide dependable information, the publisher, authors, and editors cannot be held responsible for any errors or omissions.

THIS BOOK IS DEDICATED TO THE VICTIMS AND SURVIVORS OF SEPTEMBER 11, 2001.

Contents

Foreword

September 11, 2001. Each of us will remember where we were and what we were doing when we heard those first reports. It is a day that inalterably changed our country and changed us as a people.

September 11, 2001. The skyline of the country's premier city, the nation's capital, and a rural field in southwestern Pennsylvania were ravaged by wanton acts of terrorism. With damage estimates in the billions of dollars the real cost cannot be counted. Thousands of human lives were lost.

September 11, 2001. The real tragedy of that fateful day lies among the ruins of the World Trade Center, the Pentagon and that rural field in southwestern Pennsylvania. The thousands of people that were killed and presumed missing are the real tragedy. Their fate and the heroism of their rescuers remain constant reminders to all of us that our lives have changed.

September 11, 2001. The day that American business changed. The degree of complacency that so easily becomes a part of everyday "business-as-usual" approach has changed. It was the day that American business entered an age of awareness.

September 11, 2001.

Preface

A hurricane makes landfall three times along the United States coast and reaches Category 5 at its peak intensity causing an estimated $100 billion plus in damages. Flooding ravages the Midwest. Businesses, homes, farms and property are destroyed. Damages top a billion dollars! An earthquake rips through California causing more that $2 billion in damages. A blizzard ravages the East Coast, taking more than 150 lives and racking up millions of dollars in damages.

Each year, disasters take their toll. Lives are lost and people are injured. Buildings are damaged and property is lost. Business operations come to a grinding halt. As a result, the costs for doing business soar. And everybody—from the boardroom to shareholders to the assembly line to consumers—pays the price for disaster.

But something can be done. Injuries can be limited and the costs of damages can be reduced. And businesses can resume their normal operations more quickly. Each of these "feats" can be accomplished by not only anticipating disasters, but also by effectively planning for the various response measures that can minimize their impact and ensure continuity of operations.

The key to understanding the complexities of disaster preparedness and business continuity lies in focusing upon the issue of prevention and mitigation. As previous editions of *Disaster & Recovery Planning: A Guide For Facility Managers* spoke to these issues, this edition also speaks to the issues of prevention, as well as "controlling" the effects of a disaster on a company's operations.

Disaster & Recovery Planning: A Guide For Facility Managers is written from the perspective of prevention. Its purpose is two-fold. First, it focuses upon identifying those factors and issues that create the potential for hazard. Second, it defines the strategies that all companies can use to address the issues of disaster response and recovery.

While this book is written for facility managers, it also targets other professionals who are charged with the responsibility for designing, installing and maintaining various programs and systems within a company. These include safety compliance officers, risk managers, consultants, engineers, maintenance executives and human resources managers.

Disaster & Recovery Planning can also be used by an organization's highest echelon—CEOs, building owners and their senior staff. It can guide them in heightening their sensitivity to the issues of prevention, as well as assist them in meeting their own specific responsibilities for ensuring the safety and well-being of their employees, tenant-occupants or companies.

As it did in the first four editions, *Disaster & Recovery Planning: A Guide For Facility Managers* presents major aspects of disaster preparedness and recovery planning that are either not well covered, or simply not covered at all in other guides. For example, the role of the media in recovery planning is discussed in detail.

Specific procedures for working with the various forms of media are outlined, so that facility managers are provided with a framework for enlisting the media's assistance in recovery planning.

Disaster and recovery planning is an integral part of a company's long range plan; it supports business operations while ensuring business continuity—and that is where its significance lies. The effective disaster and recovery plan is of strategic importance to employees, occupants, tenants, other business entities, customers and clients and the community in general.

dis-as-ter (di-zäs'ter). *n.* [OFr. *desastre*; It. *disastro* < L. dis- + *astrum* < Gr. *astron* (see ASTRAL), a star; from astrological notions; cf. ILL-STARRED], any happening that causes great harm or damage; serious or sudden misfortune; calamity.

SYN.—disaster implies great or sudden misfortune that results in loss of life, property, etc. or that is ruinous to an undertaking; calamity suggests a grave misfortune that brings deep distress or sorrow to an individual or to the people at large; catastrophe is specifically applied to a disastrous end or outcome; cataclysm suggests a great upheaval, especially a political or social one, that causes sudden and violent change with attending distress, suffering, etc.

—*Webster's New World Dictionary, Dictionary of The American Language, College Edition*

Chapter 1

Disaster Planning and Recovery Issues

Disasters of all kinds can cause loss of life, property and can even cripple companies and institutions. What exactly classifies a disaster? What issues need to be addressed in a disaster response and recovery plan? In this chapter, we will review the most common forms of disaster, then identify the key issues that must be addressed in an effective disaster response and recovery plan.

DISASTER STRIKES

The September 11, 2001 attack on Manhattan's Twin Towers, the Pentagon and a rural field in Shanksville, Pennsylvania, is the most widely known and recognized example of disaster—in the form of terrorism—in history. It is certainly the worst incident of domestic terrorism in United States history. Not only were buildings destroyed, and cities shattered, but the country and the entire global community sat horrified as it watched the grisly scenes of carnage and devastation. Thousands of lives—men and women tending to their business, some with children in tow—are frozen in time. As time passes and wounds heal, we are all left to ponder the events leading up to that fateful September day. While we are all scarred, we adjust and we adapt.

However, if there is any lesson to be learned from the September 11th tragedy, it is to expect the unexpected. Disaster can happen at any time and in any place, whether in New York City, Washington, DC, a rural field, or in Oklahoma City. Disaster planning and preparedness is a responsibility that everyone assumes and that everyone must share, whether the disaster is the result of terrorism or a natural occurrence. It

1

is crucial for the safety and health of everybody from corporate entities to private persons. It is essential for the economic stability and well-being of the country and businesses. And it is important to prevent the images and pictures of disasters' victims from fading into history.

VITALS

According to the Federal Emergency Management Agency (FEMA), there were 59 major disaster declarations in 2009. That year also saw 7 emergency declarations and 49 fire management assistance declarations.

The year 2008 also saw its share of disasters. A total of 75 major disaster declarations, 17 emergency declarations and more than 50 fire management assistance declarations were declared.

In 2007 there were 63 major disaster declarations, 13 emergency declarations and 60 fire management assistance declarations. While hundred of millions of dollars were allocated to disaster relief for these years, the top ten natural disasters ranked by FEMA (1989-2005) resulted in more than $26 billion in disaster relief funding. (See Table 1-1).

While not all emergency situations are disasters, every emergency situation carries the potential for disaster to occur. Effective planning, coupled with ongoing training in emergency response procedures and techniques, provide a blueprint for companies to effectively prepare for crisis situations, thereby minimizing any loss to property—and most importantly, minimizing loss of human life. A well-planned and comprehensive disaster plan leads the way. It is the hallmark of successful business recovery.

CLASSIFYING DISASTERS

Disasters can be classified as either natural, technological, or human-engineered. Natural disasters, or "Acts of God," include floods, earthquakes, hurricanes, tornadoes, wind/rain/snowstorms, etc., along with the concomitant fires, structural collapses, and power and energy failures that oftentimes follow the natural disaster.

Technological, or human-engineered disasters, include terrorism and other forms of crime, including industrial sabotage, as well as occurrences that result from human error—transportation accidents, including road, rail and air accidents, and judgment errors in various work procedures and operations.

Regardless of a disaster's nature, planning that addresses emergency preparedness and response is essential to minimizing the threat to human life, property damage and business operations.

TYPES OF DISASTERS

There are innumerable incidents, events, or situations that fall under the definition of disaster. Any one of these occurrences carries the potential for causing property and business loss, as well as personal injury and loss of life. Examples include:

- Fires.

- Floods.

- Wind/Rain/Snowstorms.

- Earthquakes/Hurricanes/Tornadoes.

- Structural/Roof collapse.

- Power failures.

- Hazardous/Toxic chemical and vapor release.

- Elevator breakdown.

- HVAC failure.

- Telephone/Telecommunications failure.

- Crime/Bomb threats/Terrorism.

- Transportation accidents, including air, rail and road.

- Data and information storage and retrieval collapse.

- Medical/Health emergencies.

And while each of these events demands specific approaches to minimizing its effect, each event must be addressed in terms of the facility's occupant, building and business issues.

Table 1-1. Top Ten Natural Disasters—Ranked by FEMA Relief Costs*, Source: Federal Emergency Management Agency.

Event	Year	FEMA Funding**
Hurricane Katrina (AL, LA, MS)	2005	$7.2 billion*
Northridge Earthquake (CA)	1994	$6.961 billion
Hurricane Georges (AL, FL, LA, MS, PR, VI)	1998	$2.251 billion
Hurricane Ivan (AL, FL, GA, LA, MS, NC, NJ, NY, PA, TN, WVa)	2004	$1.947 billion**
Hurricane Andrew (FL, LA)	1992	$1.813 billion
Hurricane Charley (FL, SC)	2004	$1.559 billion**
Hurricane Frances (FL, GA, NC, NY, OH, PA, SC)	2004	$1.425 billion**
Hurricane Jeanne (DE, FL, PR, VI, VA)	2004	$1.407 billion**
Tropical Storm Allison (FL, LA, MS, PA, TX)	2001	$1.387 billion
Hurricane Hugo (NC, SC, PR, VI)	1989	$1.307 billion

*Amount obligated from the President's Disaster Relief Fund for **FEMA's assistance programs, hazard mitigation grants, federal mission assignments, contractual services and administrative costs as of March 31, 2006.** Figures do not include funding provided by other participating federal agencies, such as the disaster loan programs of the Small Business Administration and the Agriculture Department's Farm Service Agency. **Note:** Funding amounts are stated in nominal dollars, unadjusted for inflation.

** Amount obligated from the President's Disaster Relief Fund for **FEMA's assistance programs, hazard mitigation grants, federal mission assignments, contractual services and administrative costs as of May 31, 2005.** Figures do not include funding provided by other participating federal agencies, such as the disaster loan programs of the Small Business Administration and the Agriculture Department's Farm Service Agency. **Note:** Funding amounts are stated in nominal dollars, unadjusted for inflation

DISASTER PLANNING ISSUES

There are three major issues that must be considered in developing a disaster and recovery plan. These are:

- Occupant issues.
- Building issues.
- Business issues.

Each is critical and must be addressed if the overall objectives of the disaster and recovery plan—which are to minimize the risk of injury and/or loss of human life, as well as to minimize property loss and/or damage—are to be met.

Occupant Issues

Occupants include all people within a facility. Each occupant should be grouped according to his classification as:

- Regular occupant.
- Transient or temporary occupant.

Regular Occupants—Regular occupants include employees of the company or building owner who are assigned to the facility, or who are required to report to the facility on a regular basis. Also included in this category are any of the facility's tenant occupants and their employees.

Temporary Occupants—Temporary, or transient occupants, include various groups of people, or individuals whose presence at the facility is intermittent. Temporary occupants include contractors, subcontractors, vendors, clients, customers and, depending upon the nature of the facility, the general public.

Either category may include people who require special considerations. For example, do not overlook providing for the special needs of people with disabilities.

Occupants with Disabilities—People with disabilities are protected under the provisions of the Americans with Disabilities Act (ADA). The ADA defines a person with a disability as an individual who satisfies one or more of the conditions shown below:

- Has a physical or mental impairment that substantially limits one or more major life activities. According to the Equal Employment Opportunity Commission, major life activities include walking, hearing, lifting, working, speaking, sitting, reading, breathing, standing, seeing, reaching, performing manual tasks and caring for one's self.

- Has a "record" of such an impairment.

- Is regarded as having such an impairment.

- Is associated with an individual who has a disability.

Title I, II and III provisions affect facility managers and will determine, in large part, the approach that facility managers as compliance officers must take to ensure worker safety. People with disabilities may have trouble walking, hearing, seeing or other activities that require special provisions in an emergency action plan. Besides minimizing risk for people with disabilities during an emergency, the Title provisions also seek to minimize risk of injury to other people working or visiting the facility.

The ADA is thorough and comprehensive. As can be seen, its provisions govern virtually all aspects of facility management. For these reasons, it is complex and compliance with its mandates can be difficult. And for these same reasons, ADA compliance must become an integral component of the disaster and recovery plan. For more information about the ADA, see the author's book titled *Safety Management: A Guide For Facility Managers*, a companion volume in the Facilities Management Library. The reader can also refer to *Interiors Management: A Guide For Facility Managers* by Maggie Smith.

Other Occupancy Issues—There are a number of other occupancy issues that must be addressed in the disaster and recovery plan. These other occupant issues are directly related to the nature of the business, or service that is provided.

Hospitals, emergency care centers, as well as nursing homes and other extended care facilities, provide services to both ambulatory and non-ambulatory patients, many of whom require assistance. Depending upon the type of service and care offered to these regular and/or transient patients-occupants, planning initiatives must make provision for them.

Contingent upon the nature and scope of the services provided either by the facility itself or by services that are offered by businesses housed in the facility, the occupant needs of its clients must be identified. For example, many companies now offer on-site child care as a benefit/convenience to their employees. Similarly, there are facilities that provide elder-care services. Identifying the specific requirements of children who attend on-site day care and adults who are enrolled in elder care programs—both of whom may require assistance—are essential considerations that must be addressed in the planning effort.

The range of services that companies, businesses and institutions provide, as well as the functions or purposes that they serve, is almost limitless. Whether a facility serves a specific population, as in the case of a corporate site, school, college, detention center, etc., or whether the facility serves a broader general population, the specific needs of its regular and transient occupants must be identified. By identifying occupant needs, a specific plan of action for meeting those needs can be developed.

Building Issues

Building issues include any and all aspects of the physical structure or site itself. The facility's various component systems, geographic location, neighboring environment, function (single or multiuse), and architectural and structural design and configuration all have a bearing on the planning process and the subsequent disaster and recovery plan.

Structural issues are of critical importance in disaster preparedness. The building's structural integrity must be evaluated in order to properly assess its ability to withstand the various potential disasters that could occur.

For example, resistance to fires, floods, heavy winds, tornadoes, hurricanes, etc. must be determined. Additionally, in those geographic regions that must face the threat of earthquakes, resistance to seismic activity is of paramount importance.

Common Architectural Features—Buildings and facilities vary in architectural design. The physical structures themselves reflect the era or decade in which they were designed and constructed. And while each building has its own unique features that set it apart from other buildings, each shares common features. Some of these common features include:

- Corridors and hallways.
- Stairs, doors and exits.
- Elevators.

- Telephone/Communications centers.
- Electrical supply areas.
- Heating/Boiler/Furnace areas.
- Storage areas, including waste storage.
- Roofs.

Common Building Systems—In addition to sharing these common features, all structures share common building systems that either animate these features or govern their utility.
Some of these common building systems include:

- Interior/Exterior lighting systems.

- HVAC systems.

- Fire and emergency detection systems, including sprinkler systems and various alarm/notification systems.

- Emergency electrical generation systems.

- Security systems, including video surveillance, lock systems, alarms and access control systems.

Each of these features and the systems that govern them must be evaluated in terms of their availability, accessibility, reliability prior to a disaster, as well as their impact upon occupants and business operations during and after the disaster occurrence.

Business Issues

The business nature of the facility, including the nature of tenant business operations (if the building is a commercial rental property), is another factor that must be considered in the planning process. Business issues are operations issues. They drive a company in the direction established by the organization mission, goals and purpose. Their objective is to ensure a business entity's success and financial profitability.

As such, any interruption in these issues can seriously hamper the entity's viability. In many cases, the deleterious effects of a prolonged interruption can cripple a business. From this perspective, the business issues must be addressed in terms of business continuity. For facility managers, who are responsible for the physical site including the continuity of the site's internal operations, the business issues of their own companies and their occupants become particularly significant.

Subsequently, provision must be made for the various business operations that are normally conducted within the facility. This includes site equipment and furnishings, as well as other physical inventory. Financial records—including contracts, other legal and insurance records, employee files, and occupant and customer databases—are crucial to recovery and business continuity/maintenance and must be addressed.

More specifically, the potential impact of disaster on business operations must be assessed in terms of the factors shown below:

- Basic safety and health issues that include hazard detection and prevention.

- Emergency response planning that includes notification and relocation procedures.

- Asset and product retrieval/recovery.

- Telecommunications.

- Vital records recovery.

- Product recovery.

- Emergency access.

- Security.

- Loss prevention.

- Loss documentation.

- Emergency acquisitions.

- Damage control planning.

While not all inclusive, these factors address business continuity concerns. In turn, these concerns identify the strategies required to provide alternatives to interruption.

Addressing The Issues

While each of the above issues serves as the basis for structuring the disaster and recovery plan, ~~each issue must be evaluated in terms of:~~

 Assessing the probability of disaster occurring.

 Assessing the potential impact of disaster.

Identifying limitations and constraints to resource availability.

The prevention of injury and/or loss of human life is, first and foremost, the primary objective of any disaster and recovery plan. Ensuring the safety and well-being of employees and various building occupants supersedes any and all other considerations. Preventing and/or minimizing physical property damage and/or loss is of paramount importance in ensuring business continuity. Any prolonged interruption of site or business operations could have catastrophic consequences for the very survival of a company.

For these reasons, *all potential* disasters must be identified and all potential risk factors associated with a specific type of disaster must be identified.

Assessing the Probability of Disaster—Assessing the probability of disaster, as well as its potential impact in terms of occupant, building and business issues, provides the basic framework for developing the disaster and recovery plan.

Assessing the probability of a disaster involves identifying the various internal and external risk factors that *could* precipitate a disaster. Identification begins with conducting a comprehensive work-site analysis. In its *Handbook for Small Business,* the Occupational Safety And Health Administration (OSHA) provides a detailed checklist that companies of any size may use to identify potential workplace hazards. This checklist (see Appendix II) is invaluable in assessing potential hazards. While not all-inclusive, the *Self-Inspection Checklist* covers a broad range of internal risk factors, as well as pinpoints key considerations for assessing external risks.

External Risk Factors. Assessing the external factors that may pose a potential risk presents another challenge to facility managers. These external risk factors are, oftentimes, less obvious and may appear to have little relevance. However, these less obvious threats can pose a significant risk to a company or business entity. For example, a company located near a highway that is used by chemical transporters could be at greater risk than a facility located directly adjacent to the plant that manufactures chemicals. The odds for a vehicular accident involving a chemical transporter increases the risk potential for that first company.

Other external risk factors that must be included in any risk assessment include:

- The actual physical location of the facility or building (e.g., urban versus suburban geographic location, including land surface and features).

- Climate/weather features that are unique to the geographic location (e.g., hurricanes, tidal waves, tornadoes, etc.).

- Proximity to protective and emergency medical services.

- Proximity to and availability of other site locations that could be used as a "safe site" and/or disaster command headquarters.

Each of these factors, in turn, should be evaluated on the basis of whether any one, or a combination of factors, would either increase or decrease the likelihood of a disaster, or have a negligible effect on the likelihood of a disaster occurring. Once this has been determined, any given potential disaster and its impact on occupant, building and business issues and operations can begin.

Identifying Available Resources—Resource availability is contingent upon the type of disaster occurrence. The single-site disaster occurs at one particular facility or location. On the other hand, an area-based disaster can affect many or all businesses and entities within a given community or region.

In planning for each type of disaster, facility managers must be aware of the availability of resources in either situation. For example, a single-site disaster may have the availability of full access to police and fire support. Emergency and medical support personnel services may also be readily available to assist in the single-site emergency situation.

Area-based disasters that affect a number of businesses and other entities in the community can severely tax protective and medical emergency services. The additional strain imposed on these services in an area-based disaster has an obvious impact on not only the delivery of such services, but also in minimizing the effects that this type of disaster has on the individual site. These effects determine, in large part, the disaster recovery process. Effective disaster and recovery planning, therefore, requires that alternative considerations be made for such service provision.

Disaster Prevention Services. Other resource issues that must be investigated include specific disaster prevention services. The availability of assistance from local and regional police, fire and medical personnel in hazard prevention and emergency service training and education is critical to effective disaster and recovery planning.

Additional resources that are available to businesses, but which are often overlooked, are the local, state and federal regulatory agencies that govern business operations under their jurisdictions. Perhaps because of a perceived fear that contacting these regulatory agencies would lead to inspections, citations and the imposition of penalties, many companies do not request the help that these agencies can provide. These various forms of assistance run the gamut from consultative services to help with emergency planning and preparedness (including training).

Other disaster and emergency planning and preparedness resources include professional associations and industry-specific trade groups, safety product manufacturers/distributors, and organizations such as the American Red Cross, the National Fire Protection Association and the National Safety Council.

Limitations And Constraints. In identifying the availability of resources—whether those resources are community-based or available through regulatory agency support, professional and industry trade association or national safety organizations—it is necessary to consider the limitations to the assistance that each of those resources provides. For example, in the event of a major disaster, government support and aid are not available until 72 hours after the actual disaster occurs.

As described earlier, emergency medical services and personnel, as well as the immediate availability of fire and police service, may be severely limited in the event of a major area or community-based disaster. There are other limitations and constraints, however, that impact upon the disaster recovery process. Each of these constraints must be evaluated in terms of business recovery issues.

DEVELOPING THE RECOVERY PLAN

In the aftermath of a disaster—whether the occurrence is the result of a natural event, or a human-engineered event—attention is focused on returning to "business as usual." And while efforts should be directed to resuming normal business operations as quickly as possible, there are constraints in doing so. For example, any of the various regulatory agencies that govern companies under their jurisdictions, as well as local government enforcement agencies, can determine timing of the actual return to the site and resumption of operations.

This process requires recovery planning, a multiphase process.

Phase I. Identify Business Issues—Phase I begins with identifying those business issues that are necessary to maintain business operations subsequent to the disaster occurrence, as well as resumption of normal business operations. Since business operations issues are vulnerable to significant exposure to damage and/or loss in any kind of disaster or emergency, they must be addressed from a prevention perspective.

To mitigate the effects of damage and/or loss upon business operations, the preventive issues below must be addressed:

- Identifying the recovery team.

- Defining and clarifying roles.

- Developing emergency notification lists.

- Defining control procedures for vital business functions.

- Determining alternate building/departmental/occupant-tenant requirements.

- Securing back-up/alternate site locations.

- Determining time-frames.

- Estimating and documenting loss/recovery costs.

- Securing vital records.

- Defining PR strategies, including damage control plans.

Phase II. Prioritize Critical Business Needs—Phase II involves prioritizing the critical business needs that are necessary for continuing operations, along with those issues identified in Phase I that are necessary to meet those needs. Depending upon the nature of the business/facility (i.e., single- or multiuse), Phase II activities must also consider the basic business operations of the building occupants.

Based upon the information and data obtained from Phase I activities (identifying critical business issues) and Phase II (prioritizing critical business needs) activities, Phase III—the business of developing the recovery plan—can begin.

Phase III. Develop The Recovery Plan—The issues discussed earlier—occupant, building and business issues—may themselves present constraints that can impact actual recovery time. Each of these issues and their implications for the recovery process is discussed below.

Occupant Issues: The Constraints. The odds of injuries sustained as the result of a disaster are determined by the extent and severity of the actual occurrence. Injured employees, some of whom may occupy key positions within the company, as well as "rank-and-file" employees whose services are needed for various production, distribution and service processes, etc., may require extended leaves. Recruiting and training temporary replacement workers may impede the actual business recovery time. In like manner, emotionally injured employees may need the services of professional counselors and/or mental health professionals to come to terms with the disaster. The effects of the occurrence may prevent those people from either returning to work quickly and/or from working to their full capacity. For these reasons, recovery planning must identify both medical services and mental health service providers in advance of the potential disaster.

Building Issues: The Constraints. The nature and severity of a disaster can present many constraints to not only the recovery process, but also to recovery planning. Until an actual event occurs, no one can accurately predict the extent of physical damage to a building. In the event of a major disaster, it may take days, or even weeks for the disaster assessment team to evaluate the full scope and extent of damage.

The building issues, as previously discussed, include various system components. Electrical systems, HVAC systems, water supply systems, etc., will need to be inspected after an occurrence. In many cases, these systems may not be immediately operable or functioning. Accordingly, consideration must be given to the availability of contractors and other service providers who can assist in building recovery operations.

Business Issues: The Constraints. Business recovery issues run the gamut from determining building utility (i.e., total or partial loss) to availability of temporary, or alternate site accommodations for the entity, itself, as well as for tenant-occupants. Business services—including back-up phone and telecommunication systems, computer and networking capabilities, vital records storage, etc.—must be provided for prior to an actual event occurring. Pre-planning and pre-qualifying appropriate site, vendors and service providers are essential to expediting business recovery.

Finally, emergency and/or alternative arrangements with suppliers, distributors and vendors must be provided for prior to an occurrence. Alternative or contingency plans for customer product and order fulfillment are also essential considerations that must be pre-addressed.

Sources

Federal Emergency Management Agency, 2009 Federal Disaster Declarations, January 1 to December 31. 2009.

Federal Emergency Management Agency, 2008 Federal Disaster Declarations, January 1 to December 31. 2008.

Federal Emergency Management Agency, 2007 Federal Disaster Declarations, January 1 to December 31. 2007.

Gustin, Joseph F., *Safety Management: A Guide For Facility Managers*, 2nd ed., Lilburn, GA: The Fairmont Press, Inc., 2008.

United States Department of Labor, Occupational Safety And Health Administration, *OSHA Handbook for Small Businesses*, Small Business Safety and Heath Management Series, OSHA 2209-02R, 2005.

United States Department of Labor, Occupational Safety And Health Administration, Safety And Health Program Management Guidelines: Issuance of Voluntary Guidelines; Notice; *Federal Register*, Part II, Vol. 54, No.16.

United States Equal Employment Opportunity Commission And The United States Department of Justice Civil Rights Division, *The Americans With Disabilities Act: Questions And Answers*, (Updated November 2008).

Chapter 2

Regulatory Influences

Why take the time to develop and implement a disaster response and recovery plan? To protect human life, minimize risk of injury and protect property. Occupants or tenants may demand it. We also want to minimize liability during a period of vulnerability—which is why many insurance carriers require disaster and emergency planning to minimize their own losses. A final important reason is that many of the issues involved are impacted by various regulations and mandates.

COMPLIANCE ISSUES

Compliance with regulatory mandates plays an integral role in the disaster planning and recovery process. Local, state and federal agencies have varying degrees of authority and jurisdiction that oftentimes impact, if not dictate, the planning and recovery effort.

For example, the U.S. Congress passed the *Superfund Amendments And Reauthorization Act* (SARA) in 1986. Part of this legislation included Title III, the *Emergency Planning And Community Right to Know Act*. Title III laid the legislative foundations for each community or state-designated district to develop an emergency response plan to help communities respond effectively to emergency incidents involving hazardous substances. Title III also placed requirements on employers in the community to assist in the planning process and to provide accurate information about the hazardous substances or chemicals they control.

In March, 1989, the Occupational Safety and Health Administration (OSHA) promulgated a final rule on *Hazardous Waste Operations And Emergency Response* (Title 29 Code of Federal Regulations 1910.120). This

17

rule was issued under SARA Title I, "Provisions Relating Primarily to Response And Liability," Section 126, "Worker Protection Standards," and works hand-in-hand with SARA Title III.

The separate goals of the OSHA and SARA regulations issued by the U.S. Environmental Protection Agency (EPA)—workplace emergency preparedness and local community preparedness—are goals for all employers. These goals, according to the U.S. Department of Labor, are "compatible and will go a long way in supporting each other when they are properly attended to by each employer."

The OSHA rule established safety and health requirements for employers and companies involved in hazardous waste operations and response to emergencies concerning hazardous substances, such as requiring employers to have emergency action plans for their workplaces. Subsequently, emergency preparedness is a well-known concept in protecting workers' safety and health.

In 1990, the Clean Air Act Amendments (CAAA) were made into law. Both OSHA and EPA received additional responsibilities for preventing major chemical emergencies. OSHA, as required by the CAAA, promulgated its *Process Safety Management of Highly Hazardous Chemicals* (Title 29 Code of Federal Regulations, Part 1910.119) rule in 1992. The rule expands the emergency planning requirements of OSHA's 1989 regulation and directs employers to establish a process safety management program to prevent or mitigate catastrophic chemical workplace emergencies. The rule requires employers to have an emergency action plan. Similarly, the U.S. EPA requires employers to develop a risk management plan, built on the SARA Title III Program.

Compliance with regulatory mandates plays an integral role in the disaster planning and recovery process. Local, state and federal agencies have varying degrees of authority and jurisdiction that oftentimes impact, if not dictate, the planning and recovery effort.

Literally, hundreds of industry-specific and general industry standards exist. To assist companies, building owners, facility managers and other professionals who are charged with the responsibility for ensuring safety, OSHA has defined emergency response and preparedness requirements. Highlighted below, these requirements set forth by other standard-setting agencies and/or associations—e.g., American National Standards Institute (ANSI) and the National Fire Protection Association (NFPA)—are adopted by reference in Part 1910 and are therefore also mandatory.

General Industry Emergency Response and Preparedness Requirements

Subject And Standard Number	*Emergency Response And Preparedness Requirement*
Employee Emergency Action Plans	
1910.38 (a)(1) and (2)	(a) Emergency Action Plan. (1) Scope And Application. This applies to all emergency action plans required by a particular OSHA standard. The emergency action plans shall be in writing [except as provided in the last sentence of paragraph (a)(5)(iii) of this section] and shall cover those designated actions employers and employees must take to ensure employee safety from fire and other emergencies.

(2) Elements. The following elements, at a minimum, shall be included in the plan:

(I) Emergency escape procedures and emergency escape route assignments.

(ii) Procedures to be followed by employees who remain to operate critical plant operations before they evacuate.

(iii) Procedures to account for all employees after emergency evacuation has been completed.

(iv) Rescue and medical duties for those employees who are to perform them.

(v) The preferred means of reporting fires and other emergencies.

Subject and   *Emergency Response and*
Standard Number   *Preparedness Requirement*

(vi) Names or regular job titles of people or departments who can be contacted for further information or explanation of duties under the plan.

(3) (I) The employer shall establish an employee alarm system which complies with 1910.165.

(ii) If the employee alarm system is used for alerting fire brigade members, or for other purposes, a distinctive signal for each purpose shall be used.

(4) The employer shall establish in the emergency action plan the types of evacuation to be used in emergency circumstances.

(5) (i) Before implementing the emergency action plan, the employer shall designate and train a sufficient number of people to assist in the safe and orderly emergency evacuation of employees.

Process Safety Management
Of Highly Hazardous
Chemicals 1910.119(n)   (n) Emergency Planning and Response. The employer shall establish and implement an emergency action plan for the entire plant in accordance with the provisions of 29 CFR 1910.38(a). In addition, the emergency action plan shall include procedures for handling small releases. Employers covered under this standard may also be subject to the hazardous waste and emergency response provisions contained in 29 CFR 1910.120(a), (p) and (q).

Subject And	Emergency Response And
Standard Number	*Preparedness Requirement*

Hazardous Waste Operations
And Emergency Response

1910.120(b)(2) (b) Safety And Health Program. (2) Organizational structure part of the site program. (I) The organizational structure part of the program shall establish the specific chain of command and specify the overall responsibilities of supervisors and employees. It shall include, at a minimum, these elements:

(A) A general supervisor who has the responsibility and authority to direct all hazardous waste operations.

(B) A site safety and health supervisor who has the responsibility and authority to develop and implement the site safety and health plan and verify compliance.

(C) All other personnel needed for hazardous waste site operations and emergency response and their general functions and responsibilities.

(D) The lines of authority, responsibility and communication.

(ii) The organizational structure shall be reviewed and updated as necessary to reflect the current status of waste site operations.

1910.120 (f)(2) (f) Medical Surveillance. (2) Employees Covered. The medical surveillance program shall be instituted by the employer for the following employees:

(I) All employees who are or may be exposed to hazardous substances or health hazards at or above the permissible exposure limits or, if there is no permissible exposure limit, above the published exposure levels for these substances, without regard to the use of respirators, for 30 days or more a year.

(ii) All employees who wear a respirator for 30 days or more a year or as required by 1910.134.

(iii) All employees who are injured due to overexposure from an emergency incident involving hazardous substances or health hazards.

(iv) Members of HAZMAT teams.

1910.120(I)(1)   (1) Emergency Response By Employees At Uncontrolled Hazardous Waste Sites. Emergency Response Plan. (I) An emergency response plan shall be developed and implemented by all employers involved in hazardous waste cleanup and related activities and employers within the scope of this section to handle anticipated emergencies prior to the commencement of hazardous waste operations. The plan shall be in writing and available for inspection and copying by employees, their representatives, OSHA personnel, and other governmental agencies with relevant responsibilities.

(ii) Employers who will evacuate their employees from the workplace when an emergency occurs, and who do not permit any of their employees to assist in handling the emergency, are exempt from the requirements of this paragraph if they provide an emergency action plan complying with section 1910.38(a) of this part.

Subject And Standard Number	Emergency Response And Preparedness Requirement

1910.120(p)(8)(I)

(p) Certain Operations Conducted Under The Resource Conservation and Recovery Act Of 1976 (RCRA). (8) Emergency Response Program. (I) An emergency response plan shall be developed and implemented by all employers engaged in storing, treating, and disposing of hazardous waste. Such plans need not duplicate any of the subjects fully addressed in the employer's contingency planning required by permits, such as those issued by the U.S. Environmental Protection Agency, provided that the contingency plan is made part of the emergency response plan. The emergency response plan shall be a written portion of the employer's safety and health program required in paragraph (p)(1) of this section. Employers who will evacuate their employees from the worksite location when an emergency occurs and who do not permit any of their employees to assist in handling the emergency are exempt from the requirements of paragraph (p)(8) if they provide an emergency action plan complying with 1910.38(a) of this part.

1910.120(q)(1) and (2)

(q) Emergency Response To Hazardous Substance Releases. This paragraph covers employers whose employees are engaged in emergency response no matter where it occurs except that it does not cover employees engaged in operations specified in paragraphs (a)(1)(i) through (a)(1)(iv) of this section. Those emergency response organizations who have developed and implemented programs equivalent to this paragraph for handling releases of hazardous substances pursuant to section 303 of the Superfund Amendments and Reauthorization

*Subject And
Standard Number*

*Emergency Response And
Preparedness Requirement*

Act of 1986 (Emergency Planning and Community Right-to-Know Act of 1986, 42 U.S.C. 11003) shall be deemed to have met the requirements of this paragraph.

(1) Emergency Response Plan. An emergency response plan shall be developed and implemented to handle anticipated emergencies prior to the commencement of emergency response operations. The plan shall be in writing and available for inspection and copying by employees, their representatives, and OSHA personnel. Employers who will evacuate their employees from the workplace when an emergency occurs, and who do not permit any of their employees to assist in handling the emergency, are exempt from the requirements of this paragraph if they provide an emergency action plan in accordance with 1910.38(a) of this part.

(2) Elements of an Emergency Response Plan. The employer shall develop an emergency response plan for emergencies which shall address, as a minimum, the following to the extent that they are not addressed elsewhere:

(i) Pre-emergency planning and coordination with outside parties.

(ii) Personnel roles, lines of authority, training, and communication.

(iii) Emergency recognition and prevention.

(iv) Safe distances and places of refuge.

(v) Site security and control.

(vi) Evacuation routes and procedures.

(vii) Decontamination.

Subject And Standard Number	Emergency Response And Preparedness Requirement

(viii) Emergency medical treatment and first aid.

(ix) Emergency alerting and response procedures.

(x) Critique of response and follow-up.

(xi) PPE and emergency equipment.

(xii) Emergency response organizations may use the local emergency response plan or the state emergency response plan or both, as part of their emergency response plan to avoid duplication. Those items of the emergency response plan that are being properly addressed by the SARA Title III plans may be substituted into their emergency plan or otherwise kept together for the employer and employee's use.

Permit-Required
Confined Spaces
1910.146(d)(4)(viii)
and (ix), (d)(7) and (9) (d) Permit-Required Confined Space Program. Under the permit-required confined space program required by paragraph (c)(4) of this section, the employer shall:

(4) Provide the following equipment [specified in paragraphs (d)(4)(I) through (d)(4)(ix) of this section] at no cost to employees, maintain that equipment properly, and ensure that employees use that equipment properly:

(viii) Rescue and emergency equipment needed to comply with paragraph (d)(9) of this section, except to the extent that the equipment is provided by rescue service; and

(ix) Any other equipment necessary for safe entry into and rescue from permit spaces.

(7) If multiple spaces are to be monitored by a single attendant, include in the permit program the means and procedures to enable the attendant to respond to an emergency affecting one or more of the permit spaces being monitored without distraction from the attendant's responsibility under paragraph (I) of this section.

(9) Develop and implement procedures for summoning rescue and emergency services, for rescuing entrants from permit spaces, for providing necessary emergency services to rescued employees, and for preventing unauthorized personnel from attempting a rescue.

1910.146(f)(11) and (13) (f) Entry Permit. The entry permit that documents compliance with this section and authorized entry to a permit space shall identify:

(11) The rescue and emergency services that can be summoned and the means (such as the equipment to use and the numbers to call) for summoning those services.

(13) Equipment, such as personal protective equipment, testing equipment, communications equipment, alarm systems, and rescue equipment, to be provided for compliance with this section.

1910.146(I)(4),
(5) and (7)   (I) Duties Of Attendant. The employer shall ensure that each attendant:

(4) Note: When the employer's permit entry program allows attendant entry for rescue, attendants may enter a permit space to attempt a rescue if they have been trained and equipped

Subject And Standard Number	Emergency Response And Preparedness Requirement
	for rescue operations as required by paragraph (k)(1) of this section and if they have been relieved as required by paragraph (I)(4) of this section.
	(5) Communicates with authorized entrants as necessary to monitor entrant status and to alert entrants of the need to evacuate the space under paragraph (I)(6) of this section.
	(7) Summon rescue and other emergency services as soon as the attendant determines that authorized entrants may need assistance to escape from permit space hazards.
1910.146(j)(4)	(j) Duties Of Entry Supervisors. The employer shall ensure that each entry supervisor:
	(4) Verifies that rescue services are available and that the means for summoning them are operable.
1910.146(k)	(k) Rescue And Emergency Services. (1) The following requirements apply to employers who have employees enter permit spaces to perform rescue services.
	(i) The employer shall ensure that each member of the rescue service is provided with, and is trained to use properly, the personal protective equipment and rescue equipment necessary for making rescues from permit spaces.
	(ii) Each member of the rescue service shall be trained to perform the assigned rescue duties. Each member of the rescue service shall also receive the training required of authorized entrants under paragraph (g) of this section.

Emergency Response And
Preparedness Requirement

(iii) Each member of the rescue service shall practice making permit space rescues at least once every 12 months, by means of simulated rescue operations in which they remove dummies, mannequins, or actual people from the actual permit spaces or from representative permit spaces. Representative permit spaces shall, with respect to opening size, configuration, and accessibility, simulate the types of permit spaces from which rescue is to be performed.

(iv) Each member of the rescue service shall be trained in basic first aid and in cardiopulmonary resuscitation (CPR). At least one member of the rescue service holding current certification in first aid and in CPR shall be available.

(2) When an employer (host employer) arranges to have people other than the host employer's employees perform permit space rescue, the host employer shall:

(i) Inform the rescue service of the hazards they may confront when called on to perform rescue at the host employer's facility, and

(ii) Provide the rescue service with access to all permit spaces from which rescue may be necessary so that the rescue service can develop appropriate rescue plans and practice rescue operations.

(3) To facilitate non-entry rescue, retrieval systems or methods shall be used whenever an authorized entrant enters a permit space, unless the retrieval equipment would increase the overall risk of entry or would not contribute to the rescue of the entrant. Retrieval systems shall meet the following requirements.

Subject And   *Emergency Response And*
Standard Number   *Preparedness Requirement*

(i) Each authorized entrant shall use a chest or full body harness, with a retrieval line attached at the center of the entrant's back near shoulder level, or above the entrant's head. Wristlets may be used in lieu of the chest or full body harness if the employer can demonstrate that the use of a chest or full body harness is not feasible or creates a greater hazard and that the use of wristlets is the safest and most effective alternative.

(ii) The other end of the retrieval line shall be attached to a mechanical device or fixed point outside the permit space in such a manner that rescue can begin as soon as the rescuer becomes aware that rescue is necessary. A mechanical device shall be available to retrieve personnel from vertical type permit spaces more than 5 feet deep.

(4) If an injured entrant is exposed to a substance from which a material safety data sheet (MSDS) or other similar written information is required to be kept at the worksite, that MSDS or written information shall be made available to the medical facility treating the exposed entrant.

Fire Brigades
1910.156(b)(1)

(b) Organization. (1) Organizational Statement. The employer shall prepare and maintain a statement or written policy which establishes the existence of a fire brigade; the basic organizational structure; the type, amount, and frequency of training to be provided to fire brigade members; the expected number of members in the fire brigade; and the functions that the fire brigade is to perform at the workplace. The

Subject And   *Emergency Response And*
Standard Number   *Preparedness Requirement*

organizational statement shall be available for inspection by the Assistant Secretary and by employees or their designated representatives.

(2) The employer shall assure that employees who are expected to do interior structural fire fighting are physically capable of performing duties which may be assigned to them during emergencies. The employer shall not permit employees with known heart disease, epilepsy, or emphysema, to participate in fire brigade emergency activities unless a physician's certificate of the employees' fitness to participate in such activities is provided. For employees assigned to fire brigades before September 15, 1980, this paragraph is effective on September 15, 1980. For employees assigned to fire brigades on or after September 15, 1980, this paragraph is effective December 15, 1980.

Hazard Communication
1910.1200 (h)(2)(I)-(iv)   (h) Employee Information and Training. (2) Training. Employee training shall include at least:

(i) Methods and observations that may be used to detect the presence of releases of a hazardous chemical in the work area (for example: monitoring conducted by the employer, continuous monitoring devices, visual appearances or odor of hazardous chemicals when released, etc.);

(ii) The physical and health hazards of the chemicals in the work area;

(iii) The measures employees can take to protect themselves from these hazards, including specific procedures the employer has imple-

Subject And	Emergency Response And
Standard Number	*Preparedness Requirement*

mented to protect employees from exposure to hazardous chemicals, such as appropriate work practices, emergency procedures, and personal protective equipment to be used; and

(iv) The details of the hazard communication program developed by the employer, including an explanation of the labeling system and the material safety data sheet, and how employees can obtain and use the appropriate hazard information.

The significance that OSHA and other regulatory agencies and standard-setting organizations place on emergency preparedness is obvious. Emergency preparedness is a critical component of the disaster and recovery program. And, as such, proper planning for emergencies and disasters is essential to minimize injury, business interruption and property damage and/or loss.

OTHER COMPLIANCE ISSUES

There are other regulatory issues that are not covered by specific standards, but which must be addressed in the disaster and recovery program. Perhaps the most significant of these is the ADA.

The Americans with Disabilities Act

Perhaps no other legislative act in recent history has impacted facility management as much as the ADA. Its scope is far-reaching and pervades every aspect of facility management. From the employment provisions (Title I) of the ADA, to the Public Accommodations and Commercial Facilities provisions (Title III), the ADA defines, in large part, the role of facility manager as compliance officer.

The significance of the Title I employment provisions cannot be underestimated. Title I determines, in large part, the approach facility managers must take to meet their responsibilities to ensuring worker safety and in managing the safety function.

Title II, which governs state and local government operations, as well as Title III, which covers private entities that have been determined to be places of public accommodation or commercial facilities, carry additional responsibilities for facility managers in both the public and private sectors.

These responsibilities include the facility managers' obligations to maintain environments that ensure the safety of people with disabilities, but also minimize risk of injury to those employees who provide services to people with disabilities.

Background—The ADA is a comprehensive civil rights law for people with disabilities. The Equal Employment Opportunity Commission (EEOC) enforces the ADA's Title I employment practices by private entities. The Department of Justice enforces the ADA's requirements in three areas:

Title I: Employment practices by units of state and local governments

Title II: Programs, services and activities of state and local governments

Title III: Public accommodations and commercial facilities of private entities.

The ADA Amendments Act of 2008, which became effective January 1, 2009, affirms the landmark 1990 Act's intent to "...provide a clear and comprehensive national mandate for the elimination of discrimination against individuals with disabilities... ."

Title I: Employment—The ADA was signed into law on July 26, 1990. The employment provisions of the Act, referred to as Title I, became effective on July 26, 1992 for employers with 25 or more employees. July 26, 1994 marked the effective compliance date for employers with 15 to 24 employees.

The ADA prohibits employers from discriminating against *qualified* individuals with a disability who, with or without reasonable accommodation, can perform the *essential* functions of a job. This prohibition extends to:

- The job application process.

- Any term of employment, including hiring, advancement, discharge, compensation, job training, and any and all other terms, conditions and privileges of employment.

Title II: Public Services—Title II provisions of the ADA cover "public entities" which include the "state or local government and any of its departments, agencies, or other instrumentalities."

The specific focus of Title II is on any and/or all activities, services and programs of public entities that include the activities of:

- State legislatures and courts.

- Town meetings.

- Police and fire departments.

- Motor vehicle licensing.

- Employment.

Municipally operated public transportation systems, as well as other state and local government-operated transportation systems are covered by Department of Transportation regulations.

These regulations establish specific requirements for transportation vehicles and facilities, including a requirement that all new buses must be equipped to provide services to people who use wheelchairs.

Title III: Public Accommodations and Services Operated by Private Entities—Referred to as Title III of the ADA, the provisions concerning public accommodations and commercial facilities became effective on January 26, 1992. The significance of Title III is twofold:

1. Title III mandates that public accommodations and commercial facilities be readily accessible to people with disabilities.

2. It directly impacts upon those people who are responsible for the operation and use of facilities, including landlords, tenants, owners, operators and facility managers.

This mandate directly impacts upon facility managers because Title III regulations cover:

• Private entities that own, operate, lease or lease to places of public accommodation.

• Commercial facilities.

• Private entities that offer certain examinations and courses related to educational and occupational certification.

Like the Title I employment provisions and the Title II provisions which regulate programs, services and activities of state and local government, Title III is a civil rights law that prohibits discrimination against individuals with disabilities. Its purpose is to promote the accommodation of people with disabilities in the delivery and receipt of goods and services.

Public accommodations, under the ADA, carry specific obligations, including making reasonable modifications to policies, practices and procedures that are necessary to providing equal goods and services to people with disabilities.

Accordingly, any disaster and recovery plan must include provisions for people with disabilities, including employees and occupants, tenant-occupants, transient occupants and the general public.

Sources

Gustin, Joseph F., *Safety Management: A Guide For Facility Managers*, 2nd ed., Lilburn, GA: The Fairmont Press, Inc., 2008.

United States Department of Justice, Civil Rights Division, Disability Rights Section, *Title II Highlights*.

United States Department of Justice, Civil Rights Division, Disability Rights Section, *Title III Highlights*.

United States Department of Labor, Occupational Safety And Health Administration, "Hazardous Waste Operations And Emergency Response" Title 29, *Code of Federal Regulations*, 1910.120.

United States Department of Labor, Occupational Safety and Health Administration, *Principal Emergency Response And Preparedness Requirements And Guidance*. OSHA 3122-06R, 2004.

United States Department of Labor, Occupational Safety and Health Administration, "Process Safety Management of Highly Hazardous Chemicals," Title 29, *Code of Federal Regulations*, Part 1910.119.

Chapter 3

Emergency Preparedness

The elements of any disaster plan are rooted in the basics of emergency preparedness. As determined by OSHA, emergency preparedness procedures call for certain key elements that are integral to any safety plan and which must be addressed prior to initiating emergency response operations.

KEY ELEMENTS IN EMERGENCY PREPAREDNESS

The six key elements integral to any emergency response plan are:

1. Emergency escape procedures and emergency route assignments.

2. Procedures to be followed by employees who remain to perform (or shut down) critical plant operations before they evacuate.

3. Procedures to account for all employees after emergency evacuation has been completed.

4. Rescue and medical duties for those employees who are to perform them.

5. The preferred means for reporting fires and other emergencies.

6.   Names or regular job titles of people or departments to be contacted for further information or explanation of duties under the plan.

Additionally, employers are required to establish and install an alarm system that provides warning for necessary action as called for in the emergency action plan, or provides reaction time to ensure the safe escape of employees/occupants from the workplace, the immediate work area, or both. If the alarm system is used for alerting fire brigade members, or for other purposes, separate and distinct signals must be used for each purpose.

Finally, before implementing the emergency action plan, the employer must designate and train a sufficient number of people to assist in the safe and orderly emergency evacuation of employees and occupants.

PLANNING FOR POTENTIAL DISASTERS

Emergency preparedness planning should address all potential emergencies and occurrences that can be expected. Therefore, it is essential to perform a hazard audit and worksite or facility analysis to determine potential disasters (see the Self-Inspection Checklist in Appendix II). For example, information on chemicals that are used in the worksite can be obtained from the Material Safety Data Sheets (MSDS) that are provided by the manufacturer or supplier of the chemical. These forms describe the hazards that a chemical may present, list precautions to take when handling, storing or using the substance, and outline emergency and first-aid procedures.

Response Effectiveness And Leadership

The effectiveness of response during any emergency, including a disaster, depends on the amount of planning and training that occurs. Because management must show its active and aggressive support for emergency preparedness and disaster planning, it is management's responsibility to ensure that a program is established and that it is frequently reviewed and updated. The input and support of all personnel within the facility—including company employees and tenant-occupants—*must be obtained* to ensure an effective program. The emergency preparedness plan should be developed locally—i.e., it must be site-specific, and the plan should be comprehensive enough to address all types of emergencies.

Those employees who remain behind to care for essential facility functions until their evacuation becomes necessary must also be provided with specific procedures that detail what actions they must take. These detailed procedures may include monitoring critical power supplies, as well as other essential services that cannot be shut down for every emergency alarm.

In situations that call for emergency evacuation, floor plans and/or workplace maps that *clearly show the emergency escape route and safe areas* must also be included in the plan.

The emergency preparedness and disaster plan must be reviewed with all employees and tenant-occupants:

• When the plan is initially developed.

• Whenever new employees and/or occupants are assigned to the facility.

• Whenever responsibilities under the plan change.

• Whenever the plan itself is changed.

The Chain Of Command

A chain of command should be established to minimize any confusion among employees and tenant-occupants regarding the lines of decision-making authority. Responsible people should be selected to coordinate the work of an emergency response team. Facility managers, by virtue of their critical roles within an organization, are the logical people to be charged with this responsibility. However, it is imperative that additional personnel be designated and trained as back-up support so that the facility is covered, available to implement the plan at all times. The responsibilities of the designated person and back-up support includes:

• Assessing the situation to determine whether an emergency or disaster exists that requires the activation of emergency procedures.

• Directing all site-evacuation efforts to minimize injuries and property loss.

• Ensuring that outside emergency services (i.e., medical, fire and police) are notified when necessary.

• Directing facility/plant operations shutdown, when necessary.

Communications

When an emergency or disaster is determined, it may become necessary to evacuate an entire facility, including offices. In situations involving a fire or explosion, normal utility services, e.g., electricity, gas, heating oil, and water, as well as telephone services may become nonexistent. For this reason, an alternate "safe" site should be considered by companies. A "safe" site not only provides employers with a "central command station" that can be used to coordinate emergency response, but it also provides a centralized reporting location that can be used to expedite employee/personnel/occupant accounting.

Various communications equipment such as portable radio units and systems, public address systems, cellular telephones, auto dialers and other communications transmission systems should be located at the "safe" site for use in an emergency and/or disaster situation.

Alarm systems, as required by various standards and/or codes, must be installed so that employees and tenant-occupants can be alerted to the emergency and/or disaster threat. While the type of alarm system is contingent upon its purpose, alarms should be audible or be seen by all people in the facility. An auxiliary power supply is required in the event that the main power source is interrupted. An alarm sound should be both distinctive and recognizable as a signal to either evacuate the work area or facility, or to take other actions as prescribed in the emergency preparedness plan. Employers who must comply with an OSHA standard that requires emergency employee alarms should note the following OSHA requirements.

Subject And
Standard Number

Employee Alarm
Systems 1910.165(a)

1910.165 (b)

Emergency Employee Alarms:
OSHA Requirements

(a) Scope And Application. (1) This section applies to all emergency employee alarms installed to meet a particular OSHA standard. This section does not apply to those discharge or supervisory alarms required on various fixed extinguishing systems or to supervisory alarms on fire suppression, alarm or detection systems unless they are intended to be employee alarm systems.

(2) The requirements in this section that pertain to maintenance, testing and inspection shall apply to all local fire alarm signaling systems used for alerting employees regardless of the other functions of the system.

(3) All pre-discharge employee alarms installed to meet a particular OSHA standard shall meet the requirements of paragraphs (b)(1) through (4), (c), and (d)(1) of this section.

(b) General Requirements. (1) The employee alarm system shall provide warning for necessary emergency action as called for in the emergency action plan, or for reaction time for safe escape of employees from the workplace or the immediate work area, or both.

(2) The employees' alarm shall be capable of being perceived above ambient noise or light levels by all employees in the affected portions of the workplace. Tactile devices may be used to alert those employees who would not otherwise be able to recognize the audible or visual alarm.

Emergency Employee Alarms:
OSHA Requirements

(3) The employee alarm shall be distinctive and recognizable as a signal to evacuate the work area or to perform actions designated under the emergency action plan.

(4) The employer shall explain to each employee the preferred means of reporting emergencies, such as manual pull box alarms, public address systems, radio or telephones. The employer shall post emergency telephone numbers near telephones, or employee notice boards, and other conspicuous locations when telephones serve as a means of reporting emergencies. Where a communications system also serves as the employee alarm system, all emergency messages shall have priority over all non-emergency messages.

(5) The employer shall establish procedures for sounding emergency alarms in the workplace. For those employers with 10 or fewer employees in a particular workplace, direct voice communication is an acceptable procedure for sounding the alarm provided all employees can hear the alarm. Such workplaces need not have a back-up system.

1910.165 (c)

(c) Installation And Restoration. (1) The employer shall assure that all devices, components, combinations of devices or systems constructed and installed to comply with this standard are approved. Steam whistles, air horns, strobe lights or similar lighting devices, or tactile devices meeting the requirement of this section are considered to meet this requirement for approval.

Subject And
Standard Number

Emergency Employee Alarms:
OSHA Requirements

(2) The employer shall assure that all employee alarm systems are restored to normal operating condition as promptly as possible after each test or alarm. Spare alarm devices and components subject to wear or destruction shall be available in sufficient quantities and locations for prompt restoration of the system.

1910.165 (d)

(d) Maintenance And Testing. (1) The employer shall assure that all employee alarm systems are maintained in operating condition except when undergoing repairs or maintenance.

Additionally, each employee or tenant-occupant should be made aware of the procedures for reporting emergencies, including the use of manual pull box alarms, public address systems, or telephones. Emergency phone numbers should be posted on or near telephones, as well as on employee and tenant-occupant bulletin boards, and in other conspicuous locations. The communications plan should be in writing; all employees and tenant-occupants should be made aware of its purpose and what action(s) should be taken in the event of an emergency or disaster.

Finally, it may be necessary to notify other key personnel such as the facility manager and/or backup person and medical provider during off-duty hours. An updated written priority-call list should be maintained at all times.

Accounting for Personnel

Accounting for personnel is not only a critical issue, it can also be a difficult issue to address. Accounting for people after an emergency site evacuation occurs can be compounded if the evacuation occurs during shift changes, or when other non-site personnel are occupying the building (e.g., contractors, subcontractors, vendors, clients, etc.). For these reasons, a designated member of the facility's emergency response team should be charged with this responsibility. Also, this person should have the additional responsibility and authority to inform the police, fire and appropriate medical personnel of any known or suspected missing people.

The Emergency Response Team

The facility's emergency response team is the first line of defense in emergency and/or disaster situations. Because of the critical role that team members play, each person on the team must be both physically and emotionally capable of performing their assigned duties, which may include:

- Using various types of fire extinguishers.

- Performing first aid procedures, including cardiopulmonary resuscitation, or CPR.

Information Resources Available

Rothstein Associates Inc. offers The Rothstein Catalog on Disaster Recovery that contains hundreds of books, software tools, videos and research reports. For more information, call (203) 740-7444 or fax (203) 740-7401. Visit their website at *www.rothstein.com.*

- Conducting shutdown procedures.

- Implementing evacuation procedures.

- Using a self-contained breathing apparatus, or SCBA.

- Conducting search and emergency rescue procedures.

Since the type and extent of the emergency depends on site operations, the response will vary according to the type of process, materials involved, the actual number of employees and/or tenant-occupants and the availability of outside resources. Emergency response team members should be trained in all the possible emergencies and/or disasters that could occur at the site and in the appropriate response actions that must be performed. For example, team members should be informed about any special hazards that they may encounter during an emergency situation—such as the on-site location and storage of flammable materials, toxic chemicals, water-reactive substances, etc.

Equally important to note is that emergency response team members must also be advised of when not to intervene in an emergency or disaster situation. Certain crisis situations warrant professional firefighters and other professional emergency response personnel. The facility's emergency response team members must be able to determine when a situation is either too dangerous or too threatening to either themselves or others. They must be intellectually astute enough to make those judgment calls that are oftentimes required in emergency and/or disaster situations. In short, all emergency team members must temper enthusiasm and concern with common sense.

Training

Training is the single most important factor in any emergency preparedness and disaster planning effort. Before any plan can be implemented, a sufficient number of people must be trained to assist in the safe and orderly evacuation of the site's personnel and occupants. Training for each type of disaster response is necessary so that emergency response team members know what actions are required.

Additionally, all site employees and tenant-occupants should be trained in:

- Evacuation plans.

Association of Contingency Planners

The Association of Contingency Planners (ACP) is a professional international organization dedicated to "providing the leadership, direction and exchange of information and opportunities to the disaster recovery and contingency planning profession." ACP membership is open to anybody interested in contingency planning and disaster recovery. Members are provided interaction with contingency planners, information, subscription to a newsletter, and access to literature, industry tools and techniques used for contingency planning. For more information, call (800) 445-4ACP. Visit their website at *www. acp-international.com.*

- Alarm systems.

- "Safe-site" reporting procedures.

- Shutdown procedures.

- Types of potential emergencies and/or disasters.

Emergency and/or disaster training should be provided on an annual basis, minimally, and when:

- The plan is initially developed.

- New employees or tenant-occupants are assigned to the facility.

- New equipment, materials, processes, etc., are introduced into the facility.

- Procedures have been updated and/or revised.

- Test drills, rehearsals, etc., demonstrate the need for additional training.

When drills are conducted, it is advisable that they should include groups supplying outside services such as police and fire departments and medical standby facilities.

In addition to training, the company's written emergency control procedures should be made available to all facility employees and tenant-occupants. These control procedures, as well as the actual emergency preparedness/disaster and recovery plan, should be reviewed and updated periodically to maintain its intended objective of program efficiency.

Personal Protection

Effective personal protection is essential for people who may be exposed to potentially hazardous substances. This is particularly true for those members of a facility's emergency response team and/or for those people who remain to perform or shut down critical facility/plant operations before they evacuate.

In an emergency and/or disaster situation, people may be exposed to various hazards, including:

- Chemical splashes or contact with toxic materials.

- Falling objects and flying particles/debris, etc.

- Unknown atmospheres that may contain toxic gases, vapors, mists, etc. or inadequate oxygen to sustain life.

- Fires and electrical hazards.

To adequately protect people in these situations, various types of safety equipment may be required. These are:

- Safety glasses, goggles, or face shields for eye and face protection.

- Hard hats and safety shoes for head and foot protection.

- Respirators for breathing protection.

- Whole body coverings, as well as gloves, hoods and boots for protection from chemicals.

- Body protection for abnormal environmental conditions such as extreme temperatures.

Any safety equipment that is selected, however, should meet the standards set by ANSI and/or various regulatory agencies, including the National Institute for Occupational Safety and Health (NIOSH) and the Mine Safety and Health Administration (MSHA). And, any safety equipment that is, or will be used, should be selected *only after consultation* with safety and health professionals. For example, professional advice will most likely be needed in selecting appropriate respiratory protection. Respiratory protection is necessary for toxic atmospheres of dusts, mists, gases and vapors, as well as for oxygen-deficient atmospheres. There are four basic types of respirators:

1. Air-purifying devices, such as filters, gas masks, and chemical cartridges, which remove contaminants from the air but which cannot be used in oxygen-deficient atmospheres.

2.   Air-supplied devices, such as hose masks, air line respirators, which should not be used in any atmospheres that are immediately dangerous to health or life.

3.   Self-contained breathing apparatus, which are required for unknown atmospheres, oxygen-deficient atmospheres, or atmospheres that are immediately dangerous to life or health (positive-pressure type only).

4.   Escape masks.

Before any member of the emergency response team uses any of the respiratory devices, however, it is imperative that the conditions shown below are satisfied:

1.   A medical evaluation must be made to determine if the people are physically able to use the device(s).

2.   Written procedures detailing the safe use and care of the devices must be developed prior to use.

3.   People who will be using the devices must be trained in the proper use and maintenance of the respirators.

4.   A "fit-test" must be made to determine the proper match between the face piece of the respirator and the face of the wearer. This testing must be repeated periodically. Training must also provide the wearer with opportunities to handle the respirator, have it fitted properly, test its face-piece-to-face seal, wear it in both normal air for a familiarity period and in a test atmosphere.

5.   A regular maintenance program must be installed that includes cleaning, inspecting and testing of all respiratory devices. To ensure that respirators which are used for emergency response are in satisfactory working condition, the devices must be inspected after each use and at least monthly. A written inspection record must also be maintained.

6.   Distribution areas for equipment used in emergencies must be readily *accessible.*

SCBAs offer the best protection to people involved in controlling emergency and/or disaster situations. This apparatus should have a minimum service life rating of 30 minutes. Conditions that require SCBA include:

• Leaking cylinders or containers, smoke from chemical fires, or chemical spills that indicate high potential for exposure to toxic substances.

• Atmospheres with unknown contaminants or unknown contaminant concentrations, confined spaces that may contain toxic substances, or oxygen-deficient atmospheres.

Some emergency and/or disaster situations involve entering confined spaces to rescue people who are overcome by toxic compounds, or who lack oxygen. These confined spaces include tanks, vessels, pits, sewers, pipelines and vaults. Entry into a confined space can expose a person to a variety of hazards, including toxic gases, explosive atmospheres, oxygen deficiency, as well as electrical hazards and hazards that are created by mixers and impellers that have not been deactivated and locked out.

No person should ever enter a confined space under normal circumstances unless the atmosphere within the confined space has been tested for adequate oxygen, combustibility and toxicity. Unless proved otherwise, conditions in a confined space must be considered immediately dangerous to life and health. When a confined space must be entered because of an emergency, the following precautions must be taken:

1. All lines containing inert, toxic, flammable or corrosive materials must be disconnected or "valved-off" before entry.

2. All impellers, agitators, or other moving equipment inside the vessel must be locked out.

3. Appropriate personal protective equipment must be worn by people before they enter the confined space. Mandatory use of safety belts and harnesses must also be stressed.

4. Rescue procedures for each entry must be specifically developed.

When there is an atmosphere that is immediately dangerous to life or health, or a situation that has the potential for causing injury or illness to an unprotected person, a trained standby person should be

DRI Certifications
Providing various levels of certification, DRI, The Institute for Continuity Management is well respected and internationally recognized. They offer several levels of certification and a complete education program. Additional information on certification as well as recertification requirements can be found at *www.drii.org*, or by contacting DRI's Director of Certification at (866) 542-DRII (3744).

present. The standby person should be assigned a fully-charged, positive-pressure, self-contained breathing apparatus with a full face piece. The standby person must also maintain unobstructed life lines and communications to all people within the confined space and be prepared to summon rescue personnel, if necessary. The standby person should not enter the confined space until adequate assistance is present. While awaiting rescue personnel, the standby person may make a rescue attempt utilizing life lines from outside the confined space.

Medical Assistance

In an emergency or disaster situation, time is a critical factor in minimizing injuries. There are a number of requirements that have been outlined by OSHA and which must be met to ensure availability of medical assistance. These requirements are:

1.   In the absence of an infirmary, clinic, or hospital in close proximity to the workplace that can be used for the treatment of all injured employees, the employer must ensure that a person or persons are adequately trained to render first aid.

2.   Where the eye or body of any employee may be exposed to injurious corrosive materials, eye washes or suitable equipment for quick drenching or flushing must be provided in the work area for immediate emergency use. Employees must be trained to use the equipment.

3.   The employer must ensure the ready availability of medical personnel for advice and consultation on matters of employee health. This does not mean that health care must be provided, but rather

that, if medical problems develop in the workplace, medical help will be available to resolve them.

OSHA suggests that the following actions should be considered to fulfill the requirements which apply to all businesses regardless of size:

1. Survey the medical facilities near the place of business and make arrangements to handle routine and emergency cases. A written emergency medical procedure should then be prepared for handling accidents with minimum confusion.

2. If the business is located far from medical facilities, at least one and preferably more employees on each shift must be adequately trained to render first aid. The American Red Cross, some insurance carriers, local safety councils, fire departments, and others may be contacted for this training.

3. First-aid supplies should be provided for emergency use. This equipment should be ordered through consultation with a physician.

4. Emergency phone numbers should be posted in conspicuous places near or on telephones.

5. Sufficient ambulance service should be available to handle any emergency. This requires advance contact with ambulance services to ensure they become familiar with plant locations, access routes and hospital locations.

FEMA Web Site

FEMA hosts a website: http://www.fema.gov.

At this site, FEMA's postings and publications, as well as its library and photo bank, are accessible. Emergency management and planning information can be found at http://www.fema.gov/fema/index.html. FEMA's business publication, *The Emergency Management Guide for Business And Industry*, is also available on-line.

Security

During a disaster, it is oftentimes necessary to secure a facility to prevent unauthorized access and to protect vital records and equipment. An off-limits area must be established by cordoning off the area with ropes and signs. In some situations it may become necessary to notify local law enforcement personnel to secure the area and to prevent the entry of unauthorized people to the facility.

Additionally, certain data may need to be protected, including employee and emergency number files, and legal and accounting files. Companies and their individual facilities normally maintain duplicate copies of such data and information in separate protected locations.

Summary

As incorporated into a company's disaster and recovery plan, these elements should address all potential emergency situations and/ or potential disasters, whether the disaster results from a natural occurrence or through human error or design. These elements are also critical to the effectiveness of response time during an emergency, whether the emergency involves an accidental release of toxic gases, chemical spills, fires, explosions and any personal injury that may be sustained as a result of the occurrence.

Sources

United States Department of Labor, Occupational Safety And Health Administration, *OSHA Handbook for Small Businesses*, Small Business Safety and Health Management Series, OSHA 2209-02R, 2005.
United States Department of Labor, Occupational Safety And Health Administration, *Principal Emergency And Preparedness Requirements in OSHA Standards And Guidance for Safety And Health Programs*, OSHA 3122, 2004 (Rev.).

Chapter 4

The Nature of Disasters

Familiarity with or knowledge of the types of disasters or emergencies that can occur will prepare the facility manager to effectively deal with the disaster or emergency occurrence. While not all emergencies are widespread disasters, there are everyday occurrences that warrant fast thinking and a cool head.

TYPES OF DISASTERS

Disasters and/or emergency occurrences can be classified into two distinct categories: natural or environmental, and human error or technological.

Natural Disasters

Natural disasters include hurricanes, tornadoes, winter storms, floods, fire and earthquakes. Although fire is often the result of arson, it is covered here.

Hurricanes—A hurricane is a tropical storm with winds that have reached a constant speed of 74 miles per hour or more. Hurricane winds blow in a large spiral around a relatively calm center known as the "eye." The "eye" is generally 20-30 miles wide, and the storm may extend outward 400 miles.

As a hurricane approaches, the skies will begin to darken and winds will grow in strength. As a hurricane nears land, it can bring torrential rains, high winds and storm surges. A single hurricane can last for more than two weeks over open waters and can run a path across the entire length of the eastern seaboard.

Areas of the United States vulnerable to hurricanes include the Atlantic and Gulf coasts from Texas to Maine, the territories in the Caribbean and tropical areas of the western Pacific, including Hawaii, Guam, American Samoa and Saipan.

Hurricanes can spawn tornadoes, which add to the destructiveness of the storm. Floods and flash floods generated by torrential rains also cause damage and loss of life. Following a hurricane, inland streams and rivers can flood and trigger landslides.

When a hurricane watch is issued, the best response is to secure the physical property and be prepared to evacuate the area as soon as officials so advise.

In a six-week period from August and September of 2004, four major hurricanes hit Florida, Alabama and the southern U.S., killing more than 160 people. The total damages from the four hurricanes were estimated to exceed $35 billion.

- Hurricane Charley, August 13, Category Four hurricane—34 deaths
- Hurricane Frances, September 5—48 deaths
- Hurricane Ivan, September 16—57 deaths in the U.S., 66 in the Caribbean
- Hurricane Jeanne, September 26—28 deaths.

And in the latter half of 2005, the most active hurricane season in 154 years, Katrina, Rita, Wilma and Zeta hit the southern U.S. including the Caribbean, and Mexico from late August, 2005 through early January, 2006 killing more than 2000 and approximating more than $120 billion in damages.

- Hurricane Katrina, August 25-30, slamming the Gulf Coast with 127 mph winds and major storm surges, destroying hundreds of homes and businesses. There was massive flooding in Mississippi, Alabama. Levees failed in New Orleans. The death toll was approximately 1800 with 1,464 occurring in Louisiana. Katrina was among the most devastating of U.S. hurricanes. While a final dollar count has not been determined, it is estimated that damages from Katrina will exceed $100 billion.
- Hurricane Rita, September 18-30, another Category 5 storm followed soon after Katrina. It made landfall on September 24 on the Texas/Louisiana border as a Category 3 storm. Its 15 foot storm surge caused an estimated $8 Billion in damages. A massive evacu-

ation of the coastal area kept the death toll to 119 storm-related deaths.

- Hurricane Wilma, October 18-24, moved through Haiti killing 11 people, Jamaica, and on to Mexico. The Yucatan peninsula was battered for more than 24 hours before hitting Cuba and southern Florida. Causing extensive damage, Hurricane Wilma left more than six million people without power and killed 35 people. Estimated costs for damage done by Wilma exceeded $10 billion.
- Hurricane Zeta, December 30. 2005 through January 7, 2006, was

---

About Hurricane Katrina

Hurricane Katrina was a long-lived hurricane that made landfall three times along the United States coast and reached Category 5 at its peak intensity. The storm initially developed as a tropical depression in the southeastern Bahamas on August 23, 2005. Two days later, it strengthened into a Category 1 hurricane a few hours before making its first landfall between Hallandale Beach and North Miami Beach, Florida. After crossing the tip of the Florida peninsula, Katrina followed a westward track across the Gulf of Mexico before turning to the northwest toward the Gulf Coast.

Hurricane Katrina made its second landfall as a strong Category 4 hurricane in Plaquemines Parish, Louisiana, on August 29, 2005. Wind speeds of over 140 miles per hour (mph) were recorded in southeastern Louisiana and winds gusted to over 100 mph in New Orleans, just west of the eye. As Katrina made its third and final landfall four hours later along the Mississippi/Louisiana border, wind speeds were approximately 125 mph. Hurricane-force winds extended up to 190 miles from the center of the storm and tropical storm-force winds extended for approximately 440 miles.

The strength and extent of Hurricane Katrina's wind field resulted in a storm surge greater than historical maximums. The combination of a storm surge of up to 30 feet, wave action, and high winds resulted in destruction of buildings and roads in the affected areas. In addition, failure of earthen levees and floodwalls after the storm passed left portions of New Orleans under 20 feet of water. The total number of lives lost, number of injuries sustained, and value of property damaged as a result of Hurricane Katrina are still being tabulated.

the last hurricane of the most active season in more than 150 years.

Previously, in less than a four-week period in 1992, two major hurricanes hit the United States leaving an unprecedented array of devastation. First, Hurricane Andrew pounded parts of Florida and Louisiana to become one of the most expensive natural disasters in United States history with damage estimates in the range of $15 billion to $30 billion. Then, three weeks later, Hurricane Iniki affected three Hawaiian islands resulting in over $1 billion in damage, particularly on Kauai.

Areas of the United States vulnerable to hurricanes include the Atlantic and Gulf coasts from Texas to Maine, the territories in the Caribbean and tropical areas of the western Pacific, including Hawaii, Guam, American Samoa and Saipan.

Even more dangerous than the high winds of a hurricane is the storm surge—a dome of ocean water that can be 20 feet high at its peak and 50-100 miles wide. The surge can devastate coastal communities as it sweeps ashore. Nine out of ten hurricane fatalities are attributable to storm surges.

Tornadoes—Tornadoes are violent windstorms that can occur in any part of the United States but are more frequent in the Midwest, Southeast and Southwest. The states of Alabama, Arkansas, Florida, Georgia, Illinois, Indiana, Iowa, Kansas, Louisiana, Mississippi, Missouri, Nebraska, Oklahoma, South Dakota and Texas are at greatest risk.

Burger King Braves Hurricane Andrew

Hurricanes can have catastrophic effects as witnessed by Hurricane Andrew's 150 mile per hour winds that devastated Florida and Louisiana in 1992. Burger King headquarters in Dade County, Florida sustained $10 million in damages. Almost half of the 700 corporate employees lost their homes.

Burger King's physical corporate headquarters felt the effects of Hurricane Andrew's storm surge. Extensive water damage was sustained as the storm surge knocked out windows and damaged the roof on its devastating path through corporate headquarters. Burger King's disaster plan helped lessen the devastating effect of the storm. Although the physical structure itself sustained $10 million in damages, preplanning saved the database operations which were airlifted before the storm hit to Seattle, Washington. Key people were mobilized immediately and field offices were utilized to handle corporate work. The company established a temporary site which was used as a "Command Center" until alternative arrangements could be made. Interest free loans, clothing, food and other essentials, as well as the establishment of a housing clinic for homeless employees, were some of the efforts Burger King made to its employees left homeless by the storm.

Tornadoes are storms that are characterized by a twisting, funnel-shaped cloud created by thunderstorms. Sometimes tornadoes are spawned by hurricanes. A tornado is produced when cool air overrides a layer of warm air, forcing the warm air to rise rapidly. The damage from a tornado is the result of the high wind velocity and wind-blown debris.

Although short in duration, lasting no more than 20 minutes when they ground, tornadoes are most destructive when they do touch ground. Wind speeds of a tornado may approach 300 miles per hour. One tornado can touch ground several times in different areas. Tornadoes produce the most violent winds on earth.

In November, 1988, 121 tornadoes struck 15 north central states resulting in 14 lives lost and damages reaching $108 million. According to the National Weather Service, about 42 people are killed each year because of tornadoes.

Injuries or deaths related to tornadoes most often occur when buildings collapse, or when people are hit by flying objects, or when they are caught trying to escape the tornado in a car.

The best protection during a tornado is an interior room, away from windows and doors on the lowest level of a building, preferably a basement. Occupants in small buildings should relocate to interior hallways on the lowest floors. Those in high rise buildings should relocate to hallways and interior rooms on the lowest floor available. Rooms constructed with reinforced concrete, brick or block with no windows and a heavy concrete floor or roof system overhead are also considered safe.

Nobody should be permitted to leave the building. Personnel

assigned to modular offices or mobile home-size buildings should be relocated. These structures offer no protection from tornadoes. Auditoriums, cafeterias and gymnasiums that are covered with a flat, wide span roof are not considered safe either.

Tornadoes can occur in any part of the United States but are more frequent in the Midwest, Southeast and Southwest. The states of Alabama, Arkansas, Florida, Georgia, Illinois, Indiana, Iowa, Kansas, Louisiana, Mississippi, Missouri, Nebraska, Oklahoma, South Dakota and Texas are at greatest risk.

Winter Storms—Winter storms can have devastating effects on a business and its operations. The Blizzard of 1993 dumped record amounts of snow across the eastern United States and Canada. Hurricane force winds, killer tornadoes and record snowfall left more than 170 people dead and caused loss of power for many days affecting millions of people and businesses. Property damages were estimated at $1.6 billion.

A winter storm may last for several days and is accompanied by high winds, freezing rain or sleet, heavy snowfall and extremely cold temperatures. It can range from moderate snow over a few hours to blizzard conditions with blinding wind-driven snow that last several days. Some storms may be large enough to affect several states, as in the Blizzard of '93, or a winter storm may affect only a single community.

All winter storms are accompanied by low temperatures and blowing snow which can severely reduce visibility. Heavy snowfall and blizzards can block roads and transportation systems and can cause power outages and structural damage.

Ice storms occur when freezing rain falls from clouds and freezes immediately upon impact. All winter storms make driving and walking extremely hazardous. The leading cause of death during winter storms is from automobile or other transportation accidents. Exhaustion, or heart attacks caused by overexertion, is the second most likely cause of winter storm-related deaths.

The aftermath of a winter storm can impact a community for days, weeks and even months, as evidenced by the Blizzard of '93.

The Blizzard of '93

The Blizzard of '93 dumped record amounts of snow across the eastern United States and Canada. The storm's damage covered an area more than 1,000 miles long and 600 miles wide. Snow, sleet, ice, rain and hurricane-force winds shut down roads, and paralyzed the transportation industry along the eastern seaboard. Syracuse, NY, one of the United States' snowiest cities, received almost three feet of snow. Birmingham, AL, received more snow—13.7 inches—from one storm than it receives in an entire winter. As a result of that blizzard, 50 tornadoes swept through Florida while that state was still trying to recover from the effects of Hurricane Andrew in 1992.

Property damage from the '93 blizzard was staggering. It was one of the most costly United States disasters, tying Hurricane Iniki and exceeding the Loma Prieta Earthquake. Gordon County, GA, just northwest of Atlanta, was particularly hard hit. The roofs of 24 facilities that house carpet mills collapsed from the weight of more than a foot of snow. The collapsed roof of one facility damaged the sprinkler system, saturating stored carpets and damaging work-in-progress. The collapsed roof also damaged manufacturing machinery.

Floods—Floods are the most common and widespread of all natural disasters except for fire. In fact, more than half all presidential disaster declarations over the past forty years resulted from natural phenomenon in which flooding was the major component. In fact, as noted earlier (see Table 3-1), nine of the top ten natural disasters involve flooding. Property damage from flooding now totals over $1 billion each year in the United States.

Flooding can occur after heavy rains, melting snow, tides, storm surges that follow hurricanes or tsunamis that may follow earthquakes. Dam failures, water main breaks and sewer main breaks are some of the human factors or technological factors that contribute to flooding.

Dam failures are usually the result of neglect, poor design or structural damage caused by a major event such as an earthquake. Dam failures are potentially the worst flood events. When a dam fails, a gigantic quantity of water is suddenly let loose downstream destroying anything in its path.

The Flood of '93

The year 1993 witnessed major flooding in the midwestern United States. Hardest hit was Des Moines, Iowa; the city's two rivers overflowed after weeks of torrential rains. Their raging waters burst through levees and containment walls. Although residences and farms were hardest hit, businesses were very much affected when the Des Moines water and sewage treatment plants were flooded. Six feet of sewage water in offices were not uncommon. The flooding of the water treatment plants left businesses without treated water. There was no water for drinking, flushing or piping into sprinkler systems. In addition, flooding at seven electrical substations left approximately 45,000 people without power including the Central Business District. The entire State of Iowa was declared a federal disaster area.

The dollar cost of the storm was staggering—$123 million in damage to business and $700 million in damage to public buildings. In addition agricultural losses amounted to $1 billion and 21,200 homes were damaged, costing $198 million.

Broken water pipes, backed-up sewer lines, clogged drains and open valves are some of the causes of internal flooding or flooding confined to one facility. Most floods, with the exception of flash floods, develop slowly over a period of days. Flash floods are like walls of water that develop in a matter of minutes. Flash floods can be caused by intense storms or dam failures.

Fire—Fire is the most common of all the hazards, causing thousands of deaths and injuries and billions of dollars in property damage each year. It is a threat in any facility—large or small. Preventive measures and occupant training will minimize the ever-present threat. Relocation and evacuation procedures in the event of a fire should be relayed to and understood by all building occupants.

Clearly marked exit signs and clearly defined emergency procedures are all part of a well-organized fire prevention effort.

Earthquakes—An earthquake is a sudden, rapid shaking of the earth caused by the breaking and shifting of rock beneath the earth's surface. This shaking can cause buildings and bridges to collapse as witnessed by the dramatic scenes of the freeway collapse during the

Loma Prieta Earthquake in northern California in October, 1989, which registered 7.1 on the Richter scale and as high as XI on the Mercalli scale. Earthquakes can disrupt gas, electric and phone service. They can sometimes trigger landslides, avalanches, flash floods, fires and tsunamis, which are huge, destructive ocean waves.

Most at risk are buildings with foundations resting on unconsolidated landfill, old waterways, or other unstable soil. Buildings or trailers that are not tied to a reinforced foundation are also at risk. These buildings can be shaken off their mountings during an earthquake. Earthquakes can occur at any time of the year. In the United States, the area west of the Rocky Mountains has the most frequent occurrences of earthquakes, although the central United States historically has had the most violent quakes. All 50 states and all U.S. territories are vulnerable, while 41 states or territories are at moderate to high risk.

The greatest danger exists directly outside buildings, at exits and along exterior walls. Ground movement during an earthquake is seldom the direct cause of death or injury. Most earthquake casualties result from collapsing walls, flying glass and falling objects.

MAN-MADE DISASTERS

Other examples of disasters or emergency occurrences include human error or technological incidents. These include hazardous material accidents, radiological accidents, transportation accidents, bomb threats, civil disturbances and power failure. Note that while fire is of course sometimes created by an act of arson, it is covered above under Natural Disasters.

Hazardous Materials Incidents—Substances that are flammable or combustible, explosive, toxic, noxious, corrosive, oxidizable, an irritant or radioactive are considered hazardous materials. These materials can pose a threat to either life or property, as well as to general health and environmental issues. Hazardous materials incidents could be either internal or external.

Federal laws regulate hazardous materials—the Superfund Amendments and Reauthorization Act (SARA) of 1986; the Resource Conservation and Recovery Act (RCRA) of 1976; the Hazardous Materials Transportation Act (HMTA); the Occupational Safety and Health Act (OSH); the Toxic Substance Control Act (TSCA) and the Clean Air Act.

Three Mile Island

The worst nuclear power plant accident in U.S. history occurred at the Three Mile Island nuclear power plant near Harrisburg, PA, in 1979. A minor mechanical malfunction compounded by human error damaged the nuclear reactor core and threatened to release radioactive materials into the environment. With assistance from government officials and nuclear scientists, a serious release of materials was avoided, although officials were able to detect radiation up to 20 miles from the site.

Title III of SARA regulates the packaging, labeling, handling, storage and transportation of hazardous materials and requires the furnishing of information about the quantities and health effects of materials used. It also requires prompt notification to local and state officials whenever a significant release of those hazardous materials occur.

Radiological Accidents—A radiological accident is an event that involves the release of potentially dangerous radioactive materials into the environment. This release is usually in the form of a cloud or "plume" and could affect the health and safety of anybody in its path. Radiological accidents can occur anywhere that radioactive materials are used, stored or transported. Nuclear power plants, transport of radiological materials and disposal of radioactive waste all pose threats. However, operations of facilities and the transport and disposal of radioactive waste are closely regulated by a variety of federal and local organizations, so the likelihood of an incident is remote.

Radioactive materials are dangerous because of the harmful effect of certain types of radiation on the cells of the body. A radiation accident could allow radiation to contaminate the environment. Radiation cannot be detected by sight, smell or any other sense. Thirty-eight states, particularly those in the eastern half of the contiguous 48 states, as well as the West Coast states, have full-power licensed reactors on site. Nearly 3 million Americans live within 10 miles of an operating nuclear power plant.

Bombings—Bomb threats are the most heinous and serious of all crimes targeted at a facility. A bomb threat interrupts business operations and can cause panic which, in most instances, is the intent of the bomber and/or threat maker.

September 11, 2001
Four commercial airliners were hijacked en route to California from Logan International, Dulles International, and Newark airport. Each of the airlines had a jet fuel capacity of nearly 24,000 U.S. gallons (91,000 liters) or 144,000 pounds (65,455 kilograms). Two o the airliners were flown into the World Trade Center North and South towers, respectively and a third was flown into the Pentagon. The fourth airliner crash landed.

American Airlines Flight 11, a Boeing 767, wide-body aircraft crashed into the north side of the North Tower of the World Trade Center (WTC) at 8:46:30 a.m. (Eastern Daylight Time).

United Airlines Flight 175, a Boeing 767, crashed into the South Tower at 9:02:59 a.m. This event was covered live by television broadcasters from around the world. These broadcasters had their cameras trained on the buildings after the earlier crash.

American Airlines Flight 77, a Boeing 757, crashed into the Pentagon at 9:37:46 a.m.

United Airlines Flight 93, a Boeing 757, crashed in a filed in southwest Pennsylvania just outside of Shanksville, about 150 miles northwest of Washington, D.C. the crash occurred at 10:03:11 a.m. Debris from this crash was found up to eight miles away. The crash in Pennsylvania resulted from the passengers of the airliners attempting to regain control from the hijackers.

The Pentagon was severely damaged during the attack, and 125 lives were lost.

There were 2973 fatalities: 246 on the four planes—no one on board any of the hijacked aircraft survived; 2,602 in New York City in the towers and on the ground, and 125 at the Pentagon. Among the fatalities were 343 New York City Fire Department firefighters, 23 New York City Police Department officers, and 37 Port Authority police officers. An additional 24 people remain listed as missing. The number of fatalities does not include the 19 hijackers involved. A further breakdown shows that in:

New York City
World Trade Center—2602 dead; 24 listed as missing
    American Flight 11-88 dead
    United Flight 175—59 dead
Pentagon
    Building—125 dead
    American Flight 77—59 dead
Shanksville, PA
    United Flight 93—40 dead
Total—2973 dead and 24 remain listed as missing

World Trade Center – 1366 people were at or above the floors of impact in the North Tower (1WTC); according to the 9-11 Commission Report, hundreds were killed instantly by the impact while the rest were trapped and died later.

The report indicated that as many as 600 people were killed instantly or trapped at and above the floors of impact in the South Tower (2WTC). Only about 18 managed to escape in time from above the impact zone and out of the South Tower before it collapsed.

Further, an estimated 200 people jumped to their deaths from the burning towers, landing on the streets and rooftops of adjacent buildings hundreds of feel below. In addition, some of the occupants of each tower above its point of impact made their way upward toward the roof in hope of helicopter rescue. No rescue plan existed for such an eventuality. Fleeing occupants instead encountered locked access doors upon reaching the roof. In any case, thick smoke and intense heat prevented rescue helicopters from landing.

Cantor Fitzgerald L.P., an investment bank on the 101st-105th floors of One World Trade Center, lost 658 employees, considerably more than any other employer. Marsh & McLennan Companies, located immediately below Cantor Fitzgerald on floors 93-101 (the location of Flight 11's impact), lost 295 employees, including one on Flight 175. Additionally, Marsh lost 38 consultants. Approximately 400 rescue workers, most of them of the FDNY, died when the towers collapsed.

Damage

In addition to the 110 floors of the Twin Towers of the , five other buildings at the World Trade Center site, including 7 World Trade Center and the Marriott Hotel, two New York City Subway stations and St. Nicholas Greek Orthodox Church were destroyed or badly damaged. In Manhattan a total of 25 buildings were damaged and all seven buildings of the World Trade Center Complex had to be razed. Two additional buildings were later condemned: the Deutsche Bank Building across Liberty Street from the World Trade Center complex because of the uninhabitable, toxic conditions that existed inside the office tower; and the Borough of Manhattan Community College's Fiterman Hall at 20 West Broadway because of extensive damage from the attacks. As of September, 2006 both these buildings are slated for demolition.

Communications equipment did not escape damage. Broadcast radio, television and two-way radio antenna towers were damaged beyond repair. In Arlington County, a portion of the Pentagon was severely damaged by fire and one section of the building collapsed.

The 1993 World Trade Center Bombing

Like the later Oklahoma City bombing, the World Trade Center bombing in New York City in 1993 shocked Americans across the country and made facility managers everywhere question their own disaster response and recovery plans. Some 180,000 people left the complex unharmed, while 1,000 were injured and about 100 required serious medical care. Six people died. Since the blast, the Twin Towers have beefed up security, instituted ancillary lighting and fluorescent signage, and implemented other measures.

Here are a few perspectives from facility managers on the scene, as reported in *Today's Facility Manager*, October 1993, "After The Blast: Coping At The World Trade Center."

Jackie Todd, Director of Office Services for Brown & Wood, a law firm, felt the vibration of the blast. Todd walked the perimeter of one of Brown & Wood's three floors and detected smoke. Although there was no alarm, Todd ordered an evacuation because of the smoke hazard. Brown & Wood's fire team was dispatched to search the company's floors and get the employees out. The employees were divided into three groups and each group took a stairway that was already packed with people on their way out. After 2-1/2 hours, everybody exited safely and was accounted for. After the disaster, other law firms and clients offered help and the firm moved into two floors of a space recently vacated by a client. Within a month, the company moved back. Counseling was made available to employees still anxious after the bombing. What lessons were learned? Todd realized the value of a good fire team—but realized that Brown & Wood's disaster plan was not as complete as it could have been. Since the bombing, Todd has developed a more thorough plan.

Gwen Bass, Office Services Manager for Fortis, Inc., was close enough to the blast for it to feel like an earthquake. Fortis employees were immediately evacuated. Bass and her team were able to account for all of the employees thanks to a disaster recovery program. Fortis had a phone number set up that everybody called to indicate they were safe and to report where coworkers were. Bass was able to find an employee in an elevator using this method. After evacuation, Fortis employees were moved to the company's Edison, NJ office. The blast occurred on a Friday. After the weekend, with the new offices set up, the employees met in Edison and had a group-counseling session where people shared their experiences. When work resumed on Wednesday, transportation was set up for the New York workers. On April 7, Fortis moved back into the World Trade Center. Since the bombing, Bass has developed an emergency procedures manual.

Preparing for a bomb incident requires careful planning for both the security of the facility and for the actual incident. Contacting the local authorities—police, fire, government agencies and the Bureau of Alcohol, Tobacco And Firearms (ATF)—for help will facilitate the planning for the physical security of the facility and also in the planning and training of the employees involved.

Civil Disturbance—Civil disturbances can be either external or internal. Riots, picketing and demonstrations are external civil disturbances that should be reported to the proper authorities immediately.

Locking of exterior doors that prevent entry of unauthorized personnel into the facility secures the building. Escorts should be provided for all persons needing to enter or exit the building during a civil disturbance. Occupants inside the facility should close all windows and draw all blinds and/or drapes to avoid any direct or indirect confrontation with demonstrators and/or pickets.

Events that occur internally and which can be classified as a civil disturbance, or an internal event which carries the potential for creating a civil disturbance, should be reported to building security and/or the local enforcement authorities.

Power Failure—Power failure within a facility can occur for a variety of reasons and can affect a variety of functions.

A power failure interrupts computers, telecommunications equipment, elevator operations, lighting, HVAC systems, electrical equipment, alarm systems and security systems. When power is restored, power surges can damage the electrical equipment and computer systems.

Power failures can occur because of weather-related incidents—thunderstorms and lightning, ice and hail storms, tornadoes, hurricanes, winter storms, blizzards and extreme heat—causing excess demand on the utility company. Utility company repairs can also be the source of a power failure.

To combat the effects of a power failure, facility managers should have a stock of battery-operated radios and flashlights, and consider emergency standby power supplies (Chapter 11) to keep critical loads operating.

Sources

"After The Blast: Coping At The World Trade Center," *Today's Facility Manager*, October 1993.

Federal Emergency Management Agency, Top Ten Natural Disasters—Ranked by FEMA Relief Costs, June 2009.

Chapter 5

Fire/Life Safety

Of all the potential disasters that can occur, the threat of fire is, perhaps, the most ominous. An ever-present menace, fire can occur at any time and in any facility and with great speed, regardless of the facility's size, its function, or its classification. In this chapter, we will review prevention issues and response measures as well as fire protection systems and building and hazard classifications.

PREVENTION ISSUES AND RESPONSE MEASURES

While fire is a potential threat to any facility, there are measures that can be taken to minimize not only the threat of fire, but also the effects of fire should it occur. These measures should be included in any workplace fire safety program and incorporated into the overall disaster response and recovery plan. While these measures may be classified as preventive, they also serve as the basis for formulating a facility's specific response to fire emergencies.

These preventive and response measures involve assessing the building's general environment and those building components and features that are critical to effective fire protection.

The key points to consider in such an assessment include the:

- Fire protection systems and equipment, including control mechanisms.

- General operating work environment, including building systems and components.

FIRE PROTECTION SYSTEMS

Fire protection systems include fire detection, alarms and communications systems. These systems, which are commonly referred to as protective signaling systems, serve three basic purposes. They are designed and intended to:

- Alert occupants to an emergency situation.

- Notify emergency personnel.

- Maximize "control" of facilities to minimize injury and protect property.

The type of fire detection and alarm system that is installed in a facility is contingent upon a number of factors, including:

- The building's occupancy classification (see Building Classifications later in this chapter).

- The mandatory code(s) established by the authority having jurisdiction.

For example, fire detection and alarm systems that are installed in facilities whose occupants are mobile and whose activities are either not restricted, or very casually monitored (e.g., in a business, retail, or educational occupancy), will have different requirements than detection and alarm systems that are installed in a facility whose occupants are restricted (e.g., hospital or correctional facility). The difference in required detection and alarm systems rests primarily with the degree of dependence upon others for survival. Facilities whose occupants are not restricted are minimally dependent upon other people for survival. Hospital patients who may be sedated, immobile, etc., as well as occupants of correctional facilities whose mobility is restricted are highly and, in many cases, totally dependent upon others for their survival.

However, while the type of required detection and alarm systems may vary, *all such systems* must provide for:

- Signaling (manual and/or automatic).

- Notification that action must be taken in response to a situation.

- Control, which activates the protection systems themselves.

Signaling

Signaling may include either manual fire alarm systems or automatic detection systems. In either case, signaling devices must be properly installed and maintained, as well as routinely inspected to ensure their operability and utility in the event of fire.

Notifying Emergency Personnel

Detection and alarm systems must be equipped to notify both building occupants, fire brigades and other appropriate personnel including local fire departments, that an emergency does, indeed, exist. The facility's occupancy type may determine the appropriate means of notification.

For example, when an emergency situation occurs in a facility whose occupants are dependent upon others for their survival, only those people who are authorized to assist in relocation/evacuation, need to be notified.

While local codes, in conjunction with nationally recognized fire protection standards, determine the acceptability of visual and/or audio notification that is appropriate to occupancy type, another factor comes into play. The ADA determines, in large part, additional requirements for notification. The ADA's requirements, particularly Title III compliance provisions, mandate accommodation for people with disabilities. An occupant who is hearing-impaired, for example, must have accessibility to a notification system other than an audio notification system.

Automatic Notification Systems

When a fire emergency occurs, the municipal fire department must be notified. The authority having jurisdiction, as well as other code requirements (National Fire Protection Association, NFPA 72, National Fire Alarm Code), determines the acceptability of automatic notification systems. According to the NFPA 72, National Fire Alarm Code, there are four acceptable methods of automatic notification delivery. They are:

1. An auxiliary alarm system.

2. A central station connection.

3. A proprietary system.

4. A remote station connection.

Auxiliary Alarm Systems—Auxiliary alarm systems are those which are connected to the municipal fire alarm system. The alarm is transmitted on the same equipment and by the same methods as alarms that are manually transmitted from manual fire alarm boxes.

Central Station Fire Alarm Systems—Central station fire alarm systems are those which receive, record and maintain alarm signals at a central location, and whose personnel take appropriate action. Central station fire alarm systems are operated by companies who furnish, maintain and monitor supervised alarm systems.

Proprietary Fire Alarm Systems—Proprietary fire alarm systems are those which service contiguous and noncontiguous properties under one ownership and whose supervising station is located on-site. These systems are continually staffed by appropriately trained personnel.

Remote Station Fire Alarm Systems—Remote station fire alarm systems are those systems that transmit alarm signals from one or more protected premises to a remote location where appropriate action is taken.

Control Mechanisms

Control mechanisms are those which automatically engage the building system components that are necessary to protect occupants. These automatic control mechanisms include:

• Release of hold-open devices for doors and other openings.

• Automatic door unlocking.

• Stairwell and elevator shaft pressurization.

- Emergency lighting.

- Automatic sprinklers and standpipe systems.

- Other automatic extinguishing systems (e.g., dry chemicals, low expansion foam, carbon dioxide and dry chemical extinguishing systems).

Because these various control mechanisms may not, in any way, impede or impair the operability of the fire detection and alarm components, continual and routine inspection and maintenance must be performed. Requirements for each control mechanism are determined by the authority having jurisdiction in accordance with NFPA code.

Other Control Mechanisms—Other control mechanisms include manual extinguishing equipment. Commonly known as portable fire extinguishers, this type of extinguishing mechanism is considered a universal in basic fire protection. Portable fire extinguishers are used in virtually all facilities and occupancy types. They serve as one of the first lines of defense in fire protection.

Fire Extinguishers

There are four general categories or classes of portable fire extinguishers:

- Class A Extinguishers, which are used on fires involving ordinary combustibles (e.g., paper, cloth or wood).

- Class B Extinguishers, which are used on fires involving flammable liquids (e.g., grease, gasoline and paints).

- Class C Extinguishers, which are used on fires involving electrical equipment.

- Class D Extinguishers, which are used on fires involving combustible materials.

Properly installed, inspected and maintained in accordance with NFPA standards, the effectiveness of portable fire extinguishers has been proved. However, there are several caveats regarding the use of portable fire extinguishers.

First, only those people who have been previously trained in the proper use of extinguishers should attempt to use them in the case of actual fire. Untrained people can lose valuable time if they must stop to read the instructions. This lost time may not only minimize the utility of the portable fire extinguisher in containing the small fire, it may also render the extinguisher useless in many cases. Additionally, any time lost in containing a fire jeopardizes the safety of other building occupants, as well as the safety of the untrained person who attempts to use the portable extinguisher.

Second, if a fire cannot be extinguished quickly, containment efforts should be stopped. The person using the fire extinguisher should leave the fire location and seek refuge. Accordingly, if the fire is extinguished, the person operating the fire extinguisher should remain at the location until the fire department arrives.

Third, portable fire extinguishers should only be used when:

- All notification procedures have been activated.

- Occupant evacuation has begun.

- The fire is confined to a relatively small area.

- The trained person using the extinguisher has a clear escape route should the fire intensify or grow.

Using The Portable Fire Extinguisher—The procedure for using a fire extinguisher is basically the same, regardless of the extinguisher's class. Called the "PASS" procedure, it involves the following steps:

1.   Pulling the pin that unlocks the lever.

2.   Aiming the hose nozzle at the fire's base.

3.   Squeezing the lever to release the contents.

4.   Sweeping the flames from side to side, until they are extinguished.

Assessing Fire Protection Systems

As prevention issues, fire protection systems—including detection, alarm and communications systems—are critical to minimizing the effects of fire on a facility's occupants and on the property itself, as well as its contents.

To ensure the operability of a facility's fire protection system, the following questions should be addressed:

- Are all fire protection systems certified as required by local regulatory code as well as NFPA code?

- Are all fire protection systems, including alarms, tested annually at a minimum?

- If contained on premises, are all interior standpipes and valves tested regularly?

- If located on site property, are outside private fire hydrants flushed at least annually and on a routine preventive maintenance schedule?

- Are all fire doors and shutters in good operating condition?

- Are all fire doors and shutters unobstructed and protected against obstructions, including their counterweights?

- Are all fire door and shutter fusible links in place?

- Are automatic sprinkler system water control valves, air and water pressure checked weekly/periodically as required by code?

- Is the maintenance of automatic sprinkler systems assigned to appropriately trained people or to a sprinkler contractor?

- Are sprinkler heads protected by metal guards when exposed to physical damage?

- Is proper clearance maintained below sprinkler heads?

- Are portable fire extinguishers provided in adequate numbers and types?

- Are all portable fire extinguishers mounted in readily accessible locations?

- Are all portable fire extinguishers recharged regularly and appropriately noted on the inspection tags?

- Are employees periodically trained in the use of portable fire extinguishers and in all fire protection procedures?

- Is the local fire department familiar with the facility and its location and all specific hazards unique to the facility?

These questions serve as a basis for conducting the baseline survey discussed earlier. They are important for determining the effectiveness of the facility's fire protection system. And, in turn, it is a fire protection system's effectiveness that can ensure occupant safety and minimize damage and loss.

GENERAL WORK ENVIRONMENT

Generally speaking, a facility's purpose and function determine its occupancy. And occupancy patterns determine the general work environment. For example, the retail or mercantile facility's work environment is obviously different than the work environment of a hospital, factory, warehouse, or correctional facility. However, while the functions of facilities may vary, there are work environment issues, features, and building system components that are common to any facility regardless of its purpose or occupancy. Some of these common work environment issues include:

- Combustible scrap, debris and waste removal.

- Routine removal of accumulated combustible dust from elevated surfaces including the building's overhead structure.

- Prevention of interior combustible dust suspension through use of vacuum systems.

- Prevention of metallic or conductive dust entering or accumulating on or around electrical enclosures and equipment.

- Use of covered metal containers for paint/chemically-soaked waste.

- Use of flame failure controls on oil/gas fired devices to prevent fuel flow if pilots and/or main burners become inoperable.

These issues, along with the features and building system components that are common to all facilities, are critical fire protection issues. As such, they should be addressed in terms of their effectiveness in the event of fire.

Some of the features and building systems that are common to all facilities include:

• Walkways.

• Floor and wall coverings.

• Stairs and stairways.

• Means of egress.

• Exit doors.

• Electrical system components.

• Flammable/combustible materials.

Walkways

Walkways are the travel paths that may be used in the event relocation and/or evacuation of occupants becomes necessary. Of critical importance during a fire, a walkway's accessibility should be assessed by determining if:

• Aisles and passageways are kept clear and unobstructed.

• Aisles and walkways are appropriately marked.

• Walking surfaces are covered with non-slip materials.

• Holes in floor coverings, walking surfaces are repaired properly.

• Changes in elevations or direction are readily identifiable.

• Adequate headroom is provided for the entire length of the aisle or walkway.

• Standard guardrails are provided wherever aisle or walkway surfaces are elevated more than 30 inches above any adjacent floor, or the ground.

Floor And Wall Openings

Floor and wall openings are critical considerations in the event of fire. Proper maintenance of both kinds of openings must be ensured in order to not only prevent occupant injury during relocation and/or evacuation, but to prevent the spread of fire.

Floor and wall openings should be assessed by determining if:

- Required floor openings are guarded by either a cover, guardrails, or equivalent protection on all sides, except at entrances to stairways or ladders.

- Grates or similar type covers over floor openings such as drains are designed and properly installed to ensure that foot traffic will not be affected by the grate spacing.

- Unused portions of service pits and pits not in use are covered or protected by guardrails or equivalent protection.

- Glass in windows, doors, glass walls, etc. that are subject to human impact are properly installed and maintained.

- Floor or wall openings in fire resistive construction are provided with doors or covers that are compatible with the fire rating of the structure and provided with self-closing features when appropriate.

Stairs And Stairways

When an emergency situation requires the relocation and/or evacuation of occupants, stairs and stairways become one of the key focal points. Assessment of a facility's stairs and stairways includes determining if:

- Standard stair rails or handrails are installed on all stairways having four or more risers.

- All stairways used for purposes of fire escape in existing buildings are at least 22 inches wide.

- Stairs have landing platforms not less than 30 inches in the direction of travel and which extend 22 inches in width at every 12 ft. or less of vertical rise.

- Stair angles are not more than 50 degrees and not less than 30 degrees.

- Stairs of hollow-pan type treads and landings are filled to the top edge of the pan with solid material.

- Step risers on stairs are uniform from top to bottom.

- Steps on stairs and stairways are designed or provided with a surface that renders them slip resistant.

- Stairway handrails are located between 30 and 34 inches above the leading edge of stair treads.

- Stairway handrails have at least 3 inches of clearance between the handrails and the surface on which they are mounted.

- Doors or gates that open directly on a stairway are provided with platforms so that the swing of the door does not reduce the width of the platform to less than 21 inches.

- Stairway handrails are capable of withstanding a load of 200 pounds, applied within 2 inches of the top edge, in any downward or outward direction.

- Stairs or stairways that exit directly into areas of traffic are equipped with adequate warnings designed to prevent occupants from stepping into the path of traffic.

- Stairway landings have a dimension measured in the direction of travel at least equal to the width of the stairway.

- The vertical distance between stairway landings is limited to 12 ft. or less.

Means of Egress

In the event of a fire emergency, a facility's means of egress, or exit, enables occupants to evacuate their immediate work area and move towards safe refuge. Assessing the effectiveness of means of egress includes determining if:

- All exits are marked with an exit sign and illuminated by a reliable light source.

- The directions to exits, when not immediately apparent, are marked with visible signs.

- Doors, passageways or stairways that do not serve as either exits or access to exits but which could be mistaken for exits, are appropriately marked NOT AN EXIT, TO BASEMENT, STOREROOM, etc.

- Exit signs are provided with the word EXIT in lettering at least 6 inches high and the stroke of the lettering at least 3/4-inch wide.

- All exit doors are side-hinged.

- All exits are kept free of obstructions.

- Two means of egress, minimally, are provided from elevated platforms, pits or rooms where the absence of a second exit would increase risk of injury from hot, toxic, corrosive, suffocating, flammable, or explosive substances.

- There are sufficient exits to permit prompt escape.

- The number of exits from each floor of a building and the number of exits from the building, itself, is appropriate for the building occupancy load.

- Exit stairways which are required to be separated from other parts of a building are enclosed by at least 2-hour fire-resistive construction in buildings more than four stories in height and not less than 1-hour fire-resistive construction elsewhere.

- The slope of all ramps used as part of required exiting from a building is limited to 1 ft. vertical and 12 ft. horizontal.

- Any frameless glass doors, glass exit doors, etc. used for exiting are fully tempered and meet all applicable safety requirements and standards for human impact.

Exit Doors

The issue of exit doors is critical in a fire emergency. As an integral component in the relocation and/or evacuation effort, exit doors serve as a primary means for occupant escape. Therefore, the issue of exit doors in a facility should be assessed by determining if:

- The design, construction and installation indicate obvious and direct exit travel.

- Windows which could be mistaken for exit doors are made inaccessible by means of barriers or railings.

- Exit doors can be opened from the direction of exit travel without the use of a key or any special knowledge or effort when the building is occupied.

- Any revolving, sliding or overhead door is prohibited from serving as a required exit door.

- Panic hardware installed on required exit doors will allow opening when a force of 15 pounds or less is applied in the direction of exit travel.

- Adequate barriers and warnings are provided for those exit doors that open directly onto any street, alley, or other area where vehicles are operated.

Electrical System Components

The lifeline of any building is its electrical system. Electricity not only drives building and business components and operations, but electrical systems also control them. Electrical energy carries with it the potential for danger, including the danger of fire.

To assess not only the effectiveness of a facility's electrical system, but also its danger potential, all system components must be routinely inspected and maintained. Evaluating the electrical system's effectiveness, as well as its danger potential, includes determining if:

- Occupants are required to report any obvious hazards in connection with electrical systems and/or components.

- All electrical equipment and tools are either grounded or double-insulated.

- All electrical appliances, including vacuuming systems, polishers, etc., are grounded.

- All extension cords in use have grounding conductors.

- Multiple plug adapters are prohibited, and if so, are they still being used.

- Ground-fault circuit interrupters are installed on each temporary 15 or 20 ampere, 120V AC circuit at locations where construction, demolition, modifications, alterations, or excavations are being performed.

- All temporary circuits are protected by suitable disconnection switches or plug connectors at the junction with permanent wiring.

- Electrical installations present in hazardous dust and vapor areas meet the National Electrical Code® (NEC) for hazardous locations.

- All cord, cable and raceway connections are intact and secure.

- All flexible cords and cables are free of splices and/or taps.

- All interior wiring systems include provisions for grounding metal parts of electrical raceways, equipment and enclosures.

- All disconnecting switches and circuit breakers are labeled to indicate their use, or all unused openings in electrical enclosures and fittings are closed with appropriate covers, plugs, or plates.

- All electrical enclosures (e.g., switches, receptacles, junction boxes, etc.) are provided with tight-fitting covers or plates.

- Disconnecting switches for electrical motors in excess of two horse-power are capable of opening the circuit without exploding, when the motor is stalled.

Flammable And Combustible Materials

Virtually every facility has materials on site that can be classified as either flammable and/or combustible. Ranging from the generic chemical solvents that are used for cleaning, to materials that are used in various office operations (e.g., dry chemicals used for reproduction), and to industry and/or facility specific materials (e.g., chemicals, petro-chemicals, agri-chemicals, etc.), facility managers must be aware of the potential threat to safety that these stored energy sources present.

In order to assess the various levels of protection, as well as the danger potential that these stored contents present, it is necessary to determine if:

- All combustible scrap, debris and waste materials are stored in covered metal receptacles and promptly and properly removed.

- Proper storage is utilized to minimize the risk of fire including spontaneous combustion.

- Only approved containers and tanks are used for the storage and handling of any and all flammable and combustible liquids.

- All connections on drums and combustible liquid pilings, vapors and liquids are tight.

- All flammable liquids are kept in closed containers when not in use.

- Bulk drums of flammable liquids are grounded and bonded to containers during dispensing.

- All storage rooms for flammable and combustible liquids have explosion-proof light fixtures.

- All storage rooms for flammable and combustible liquids have mechanical or gravity ventilation.

- Liquefied petroleum gas that is stored, handled and used is done so in accordance with industry practice, code and standards.

- NO SMOKING signs are posted on liquefied petroleum gas tanks.

- All solvent wastes and flammable liquids are kept in fire-resistant, covered containers until they are removed from the site.

- Vacuuming is used, rather than blowing or sweeping of combustible dust whenever possible.

- Firm separators are placed between containers of combustibles or flammables, when stacked, to assure support and stability.

- Fuel gas cylinders and oxygen cylinders are separated by distance, fire resistant barriers, etc., while in storage.

- Fire extinguishers are selected and provided for the types of materials in areas where they are to be used—i.e., Class A—ordinary combustible material fires; Class B—flammable liquid, gas or grease fires; Class C—energized electrical equipment fires; Class D—combustible metal fires.

- Appropriate fire extinguishers are mounted within 75 feet of outside areas containing flammable liquids, and within 10 feet of any inside storage area for such materials.

- Extinguishers are free from obstructions.

- All extinguishers are serviced, maintained, and tagged at intervals not to exceed one year.

- All extinguishers are fully charged and in their designated places.

- The nozzle heads of permanently mounted sprinkler systems are so directed or arranged that water will not be sprayed into operating electrical switchboards and equipment.

- NO SMOKING signs are posted where appropriate in areas where flammable or combustible materials are used or stored.

- Safety cans used for dispensing flammable or combustible liquids are at a point of use.

- Maintenance procedures call for the immediate clean up of flammable or combustible liquid spills.

- Storage tanks are adequately vented to prevent the development of excessive vacuum or pressure as a result of filling, emptying, or atmosphere temperature changes.

- Storage tanks are equipped with emergency venting that will relieve excessive internal pressure caused by fire exposure.

- NO SMOKING rules are enforced in areas involving storage and use of hazardous materials.

As part of a facility's general work environment, each of these features and building system components becomes critical fire protection issues. As such, they should be assessed in terms of their effectiveness in the event of fire.

BUILDING CLASSIFICATIONS

A facility's classification is determined in large part by jurisdictional code in conjunction with standard-setting organizations. Depending upon its purpose, function and use, as well as its occupancy type, a building can fall into various categories. These categories, or classifications, as defined by the National Fire Protection Association (NFPA), include:

- Assemblies.

- Correctional and detention facilities.

- Education.

- Business.

- Healthcare.

- Mercantile.

- Residential.

- Industrial.

- Storage.

Assemblies

An assembly is a building/facility, or a portion of a building/facility, whose purpose is to accommodate 50 or more people at a given time. Examples of assembly occupancies include:

- Armories.

- Assembly halls.

- Auditoriums (including exhibition halls and gymnasiums).

- Club rooms.

- Conference rooms and college/university classrooms that have an occupant capacity of 50 or more people.

- Courtrooms.

- Dance halls.

- Restaurants, drinking establishments and nightclubs (with a 50+ occupant load).

- Recreation centers.

- Libraries and museums.

- Theaters.

- Places of worship.

- Public transportation facilities and terminals, including air, surface, sub-surface and marine facilities.

Business

Places of business are those which are used for conducting the normal activities of a business, including general operations such as finance, administration, etc. Examples of places of business include:

- Colleges and universities' instructional buildings and classrooms with an occupant load of less than 50 people, and instructional laboratories.

- Professional services including doctors and dentists' offices and outpatient clinics.

- General offices.

- Municipal facilities, including town halls, courthouses, etc.

Correctional and Detention

Correctional and detention facilities are those whose occupants are incarcerated and/or detained. Because the degree of control over occupant activity is extreme, occupants in almost all cases are completely dependent upon others for their safety from fire. Examples of correctional/detention facilities include:

- Adult and juvenile detention facilities.

- Adult and juvenile correctional facilities.

- Adult and juvenile work camps.

- Juvenile training schools.

Education

Educational facilities include buildings or portions of buildings that are used for educational purposes through the 12th grade, by six or more individuals for four or more hours per day, or for more than 12 hours per week. Educational facilities include:

- Academies.

- Kindergartens.

- Nursery schools.

- Elementary and middle schools, junior and senior high schools.

Healthcare

Healthcare facilities are those which are used for providing medical and related services to occupants whose illness, disability or infirmity may make them incapable of protecting themselves in a fire emergency. Examples of healthcare facilities include:

- Hospitals and nursing homes.

- Limited use facilities.

- Ambulatory healthcare centers.

Industrial

Industrial facilities include those that are used for the manufacturing of various products as well as those whose operations include assembling, decorating, finishing, packaging, processing, repairing, etc. Occupants may be exposed to a range of hazardous materials and processes. Examples of industrial facilities include:

- Dry cleaning plants.

- General factories.

- Food processing plants.

- Laundries.

- Power plants.

- Pumping stations.

- Refineries.

Residential

Residential facilities are those which provide sleeping accommodations and include all buildings designed for such purposes. Examples of residential facilities include:

• Hotels, motels and dormitories.

• Apartment buildings.

• Lodging/rooming houses.

• Boarding and care facilities.

Mercantile

Mercantile facilities are those which include stores, markets, etc., and those that are used for the display and sale of merchandise. Examples of mercantile facilities include:

• Auction rooms.

• Department stores.

• Drug stores.

• Shopping centers.

• Supermarkets.

Storage

Storage facilities are those buildings used for storing goods, merchandise, vehicles or animals. Examples of storage facilities include:

• Barns.

• Bulk oil storage.

• Cold storage.

• Freight terminals.

- Grain elevators.

- Parking structures.

- Stables.

- Truck and marine terminals.

- Warehouses.

Since there are different code requirements for each classification, building owners and facility managers should exercise caution in determining the appropriate occupancy classification for their particular site(s). Consulting with the appropriate local jurisdictional authority can prevent any improper classification of building and occupancy type, thus ensuring that fire safety measures are not compromised.

A comprehensive and thorough fire safety plan must also consider other factors. Among the most significant of these factors is hazard classification.

HAZARD CLASSIFICATION

In its *Life Safety Code Handbook*, the NFPA addresses the issue of hazard contents. While the Association's hazard classification is based on the potential threat to life, as that potential is presented by a building's contents, its method of classification is based on life safety. Thus, classification of hazard contents is based on the threat of fire, explosion and other similar occurrences.

The NFPA's classification of hazard contents follows:

Low Hazard—Contents which are of such low combustibility that self-propagating fires cannot occur.

Ordinary Hazard—Contents are those which are likely to either burn with moderate rapidity or which emit considerable smoke.

High Hazard—Contents are those which are most likely to burn with either extreme rapidity or which are most likely to cause explosions.

Despite the fact that the contents of most occupancies are classified as ordinary hazards, there are certain procedures that all building occupants must follow, if and when a fire or other emergency occurs. These procedures which are essential in ensuring the safety of all building occupants and which should be clearly outlined in the occupants' emergency procedures manual include:

- Notifying the facility manager or other appropriate internal contact.

- Notifying the local fire department.

- Activating the manual alarm system.

In addition, specific procedures that outline the steps required for emergency evacuation and/or relocation must be clearly spelled out in the *Occupants' Emergency Manual*. Essential to ensuring the safety of occupants, procedures should include the following "universal" steps:

1. Occupants should be instructed to close but not lock doors behind them as they leave.

2. Doors should be touched prior to being opened. A hot door indicates fire on the opposite side, and the door should not be opened.

3. Stairway doors should be kept closed except when people are moving through them. Holding doors open will cause smoke to be drawn into the stairwell.

4. If smoke is encountered, occupants should breathe through a handkerchief or piece of clothing to reduce smoke inhalation.

5. If caught in heavy smoke, people should drop to their hands and knees and crawl. People should hold their breath as much as possible.

6. If clothing catches fire, people should stop, drop and roll. Attempting to run will only fan the flames and spread the fire.

7.   If people become trapped in a room, the doors should be closed and the door sill should be covered with a towel or other object to limit smoke infiltration. People should attempt to move to a perimeter area and signal for help from a window.

8.   Windows should not be broken out except as a last resort. Breaking a window may cause smoke infiltration from within the building due to pressure differentials or from smoke rising up the side of the building.

Sources

Gustin, Joseph F. *Safety Management: A Guide For Facility Managers,* 2nd ed. Lilburn, GA: The Fairmont Press, Inc., 2008.

Chapter 6

Bomb Threats and Terrorism

Recent terrorist events in the United States underscore the importance of workplace emergency planning efforts. As noted by OSHA, fires or explosions created by arson or an explosive device can be the quickest way for terrorists to affect a targeted business. Planning considerations that help building owners and facility managers reduce their vulnerability to or the consequences of explosive devices must be identified and incorporated into their emergency action plans. It is essential and critical to effective facility planning and preparedness.

THE NATURE OF BOMBS

Bombs can be constructed to look like most any other object. They can be placed or delivered in a number of ways. According to the Bureau of Alcohol, Tobacco and Firearms and Explosives (ATF), the probability of finding a bomb that looks like the "typical" bomb is almost nonexistent. Bombs and incendiary devices can take any shape or form. And whatever form or shape that they do take, they all have one singular purpose—they are intended to explode. Most bombs are home-made. Their design is limited by only two factors: the bomber's imagination and the resources that are available to the bomber.

BOMB THREATS

Bomb threats are delivered in a variety of ways. In most cases, the majority of the threats are called in to the target. On occasion, bomb threats are called in through a third party, or are communicated to the target in writing or by a recording that is sent to the target. There are two logical explanations for reporting a bomb threat.

First, the caller has definite knowledge, or believes that an explosive or incendiary bomb has been placed at the target site and wants to minimize personal injury or property damage. The caller may be either the person who placed the explosive, or somebody who has knowledge that a device has been placed.

Second, the caller wants to create an atmosphere of anxiety as well as panic which, in all likelihood, will disrupt the normal activities at the target site.

Regardless of the motive, though, there will be reactions to the threat. Through effective planning, however, reactions can be controlled and an orderly response to the threat can be accomplished.

Planning For The Bomb Threat

Thorough and comprehensive planning accomplishes several primary objectives. The effective plan:

- reduces the accessibility of a business or building.

- identifies those areas within the facility that can be "hardened" against the potential bomber.

- limits the amount of time lost to conduct a search, if such a determination is made.

- instills confidence in the leadership of the management team, by reinforcing occupants' trust and belief that the persons in charge do care and that every precaution is being taken to ensure their personal safety.

Finally, thorough and comprehensive planning reduces the potential for panic which, in the context of the bomb threat, is the ultimate goal of the caller. Panic which is excessive—unreasoning terror—is the most contagious of all human emotions. Once a state of panic has been reached, the potential for personal injury and property damage is increased.

To effectively prepare for a bomb incident, it is necessary to develop two separate, but interdependent plans—the physical security plan and the bomb incident plan.

The Physical Security Plan

The physical security plan provides for the protection of property, occupants, facilities and material against the unauthorized entry, trespass, damage, sabotage or other illegal or criminal acts. In essence, the physical security plan deals with the prevention and control of access to the facility regardless of any existing security, which may not be designed or equipped to prevent a bomb attack incident.

The Bomb Incident Plan

The bomb incident plan provides the detailed procedures that are to be implemented when a bombing attack is either threatened or actually implemented. In planning for such an occurrence, the bomb incident plan must establish a defined chain of command or line of authority, so that the incident will be handled with the least risk possible. The chain of command also helps to reinforce confidence in management, while minimizing the risk of panic.

Lines of Authority: The Chain of Command—Establishing the lines of authority in the bomb incident plan is complex in both the single occupant organization and in the multi-occupant facility. In such cases, representatives from each floor (in the single occupant organization) and from each tenant-occupant (in the multi-occupant facility) should be involved in the planning process, with one person designated as the team leader/coordinator. All people who serve on the planning team should have a clear understanding of their roles, their direct reporting relationship and the duties they are to perform in the event of a bomb incident.

Planning considerations should also include a designated command center. The command center serves as the hub of activities during the actual bomb incident. The command center itself could be located in the switchboard room, the facility's mailroom or another focal point of telephone and/or radio communications. It should be staffed by the team leader/coordinator and designated members of the team who have the authority to make and execute the necessary decisions. It should also include a current, up-to-date floor plan or blueprint. Lines of communication between the command center and the internal search and evacuation units are of paramount importance. The command center must have the flexibility to maintain ongoing contact with these units and to track their efforts.

Government/Community Resources—In developing the bomb
incident plan, as well as the physical security plan, assistance from the
local police and fire departments may be available. Additionally, local
government agencies, local offices of the ATF and the United States
Postal Service inspectors are available to provide assistance in developing effective strategies.

When possible, representatives from these organizations should
be invited to the facility so that an in-depth survey of the building
may be conducted. Such an on-site survey enables the planning team
to pinpoint possible locations where a bomb could be placed. All possible locations where a bomb could be placed should be listed on a
bomb checklist and retained in the command center. If bomb disposal
units are provided by local enforcement agencies, decisions/agreements
regarding the availability of those units in any search activities can be
determined at that time.

A crucial element of any bomb incident or physical security plan
is training. All personnel, including command center personnel and
particularly the individuals who are assigned to the switch board and
the mail center, must be thoroughly trained in all aspects of responding
to a bomb threat.

SECURITY AGAINST BOMB INCIDENTS

The ATF has outlined various security measures that apply to
"hardening" against the bomb attack. These security measures are discussed below.

Most commercial structures (as well as individual residences) have
some form of security in place, whether planned or unplanned and
whether realized or not. For example, locks on windows and doors,
exterior lighting, etc., are all designed and installed to contribute toward
the security of a facility and the protection of its occupants.

In considering measures to increase a facility's security, the local
police department should be contacted for assistance. Their guidance
is invaluable regarding any security enhancements that may be under
consideration. Additional measures that should be addressed and which
may reduce a building's vulnerability to bomb attacks include the following recommendations:

Building Design—The exterior configuration of a building is, obviously, very important. While, in many instances, its architectural design does not consider the security precautions that must be taken in thwarting bomb attacks, a building's exposure to threat can be minimized by installing additional lighting, fencing and by controlling access.

Bombs that are either delivered by car or which are left in a car are a grave reality. Parking should be restricted, if possible, to 300 feet from the facility. In those situations where restricted parking is not feasible, all employee vehicles should be properly identified and parked closest to the facility itself. Parking for non-employee/occupants should be provided at a distance from the facility.

Landscaping—Landscaping, particularly heavy shrubs and vines, should be maintained close to the ground to minimize either the perpetrator's cover, or "protection" for the bomb. Any ornamental or real window planters/boxes should be removed, unless there is an absolutely essential reason for their presence. Planters and window boxes are the "perfect" hiding places for explosives.

Security Patrols—A highly visible security patrol can be a significant deterrent. Even if security consists of one person, that guard is optimally utilized outside the building. If the guard's services are utilized within the building, the installation of closed-circuit monitoring systems that cover exterior perimeters should be considered.

Burglar alarm systems that are adequate for the building's square foot dimensions are effective deterrents. These systems should be installed by reputable companies that can service and properly maintain the alarm equipments. Signs clearly warning that an alarm system is in place should be posted in very visible locations.

Entrance and Exit Doors—Only entrance and exit doors with interior hinges and hinge pins should be installed. Solid wood or sheet metal-faced doors, as opposed to hollow-core doors, provide additional protection. A steel door frame that properly fits the door is as important as the construction of the door itself.

Window Protection—While the ideal security situation is the building with no windows, there are devices that can be installed which offer added measures of security. These devices include bars, grates, heavy mesh screens and steel window shutters. However, in considering any such enhancement, all local ordinances, including fire safety code, must be researched to ensure appropriateness.

Access Control—Controls should be established for identifying personnel who are authorized access to critical areas within the facility and for denying access to unauthorized persons. These controls should extend to the inspection of all packages and materials that are being taken or "designated" for routing to critical building areas or "key" personnel.

Security and maintenance personnel should be alert for persons who act suspiciously. If any suspicious activity is detected, surveillance should begin. Also, security and maintenance personnel should be instructed to note any and all objects, items, or packages that look "out-of-place" (see Figure 6-1). Such suspicious items should be reported to the appropriate person/authority level for follow up. Any area within a facility where unusual activity has been noted should be inspected, especially potential hiding places for unauthorized personnel such as stairwells, restrooms and unoccupied/empty office spaces.

Doors and other access ways to such areas as computer rooms, boiler rooms, mail rooms, switchboards and elevator control rooms should remain locked when not in use. Procedures for key distribution and retention should be established and maintained by all facilities, regardless of occupancy type or size.

Environmental services, including housekeeping, is another major issue. Trash or dumpster areas should be free of debris and other contents. Bombs can be easily concealed in these areas. All combustible materials should be properly disposed of or protected if further use is anticipated.

Where feasible, detection devices should be installed. Placed at all entrances, as well as in those areas previously identified as likely places where a bomb may be placed, these detection devices serve as effective deterrents.

Heightened security measures should also be instituted in many of the buildings that are open to the public. Despite the minimal inconvenience to the public that "signing-in" and "signing-out" would incur, this kind of policy would add an extra measure of safety to all building occupants.

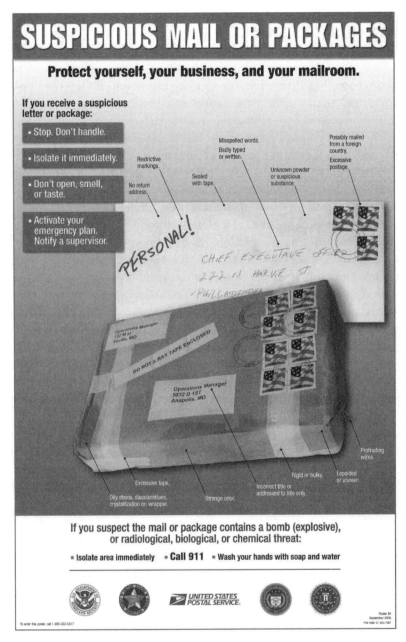

Figure 6-1. Suspicious Mail/Packages
Source: United States Postal Service (USPS)

MAIL CENTER SECURITY

Security is extremely important to mail room operations in both large and small facilities. Lack of security can result in theft of supplies, postage and mail. More importantly, sensitive mail that may contain critical information concerning the company/facility may be threatened. Also the facility's mail room could be subject to both mail bombs and biological, chemical and radiological threats, including anthrax.

The mail room is the focal point for a facility. But oftentimes it is also the most overlooked when applying security policies and procedures. A comprehensive and effective mail room security program should include policies and procedures to reduce risks and losses and should be included in the comprehensive emergency response plan.

The key to a successful and effective mail room screening program is to have a comprehensive bomb threat response plan that addresses mail bombs, bomb threats, and suspiciously placed devices. When properly planned and implemented, a bomb threat response plan will prevent any such incident from creating panic or inflicting physical harm to the occupants/tenants or to the facility itself.

The United States Postal Service, the leading experts in mail bomb detection and investigation, offers suggestions to use when formulating a comprehensive bomb threat response plan. This bomb threat response plan addresses both bomb threats and placed devices. Postal inspectors have devised a mail bomb screening program that can be adapted to virtually any mail center operation, regardless of the size of the firm. To be successful, the mail bomb-screening program depends on a well-trained mail center staff, good communication with the firm's management, security and mail center, and the cooperation of employees at every level.

This mail bomb screening procedure is designed to guide the mail center manager, security manager or facility manager through the steps necessary to establish a mail/privately delivered package bomb screening program (see Table 6-1).

Vulnerability

The vulnerability of a company/facility depends upon a variety of factors—both internal and external. A sound assessment of the company's/facility's vulnerability is critical to the preparation of a bomb

Table 6-1. Mail Screening Program

1. Perform a vulnerability assessment to determine if the facility/company or a particular employee or tenant is a potential target.

2. Appoint a mail center security coordinator and an alternate to be assigned responsibility for and to ensure compliance with the developed plan.

3. Establish direct lines of notification and communication among the mail center security coordinator, management and security office.

4. Develop specific screening and inspection procedures for all incoming mail or package deliveries and train employees in those procedures.

5. Develop specific mail center handling techniques and procedures for items identified through screening as suspicious and dangerous.

6. Develop verification procedures for confirming the contents of suspicious packages encountered through the screening process.

7. Designate an isolation area for use with suspicious packages encountered through the screening process. Establish a safety zone around the isolation area.

8. Construct a holding container for suspicious packages.

9. Conduct training sessions for mail center, security and management personnel to validate the practicality of all phases of the mail bomb screening program.

10. Conduct unannounced tests for all mail center personnel.

threat response plan.

Potential sources of vulnerability include:

- Foreign terrorism—Does the company have foreign officers, suppliers, or outlets? If so, in what countries? Does the company do business in countries where there is political unrest or civil strife?

- Domestic hate groups—Is the company/facility a high-profile organization whose services, research, or products are the subjects of public controversy?

- Workplace Violence—Has the company/facility experienced down-sizing, take-over or reorganization? Has an employee complained of being physically abused, harassed, or of being "stalked"? Has an employee made threats to harm any other employee or the firm in general?

Motivation

According to the United States Postal Service (USPS) and law enforcement agencies, revenge is the most common motivation for making bomb threats or placing mail bombs.

Targets of those seeking revenge include:

- Jilted spouse/partners

- Former/current business associates/partners

- Former employees

- Persons who have experienced layoffs and/or terminations due to downsizing, etc.

- Law enforcement officers

- Members of the judiciary

- Potential witnesses

As such, United States Postal Service inspectors found that bomb threats may target either individuals or organizations. However, while mail bombs generally target specific individuals, placed devices are intended to disrupt organizations and injure indiscriminately.

If these risk factors apply to the workplace/facility and cannot be eliminated, the company/facility's vulnerability to a terrorist incident may be greater than that of other workplaces. To further assess the potential threat and consequences of a terrorist incident at or near the company/facility, local law enforcement, the local office of the FBI, the Bureau of Alcohol, Tobacco, Firearms, and Explosives (ATF), and/or the Local Emergency Planning Committee (LEPC) should be consulted. Information from these agencies should be utilized to complete the company/facility's risk assessment and determine which of the three risk zones noted below best characterizes the facility/company workplace.

DEVELOPING THE BOMB THREAT RESPONSE PLAN

As noted earlier, the bomb threat response plan should be part of an overall corporate disaster/emergency recovery management plan. The plan should include provisions for both mailed bombs and placed bombs; and address planning team issues and command center issues.

The Planning Team—The planning team should include individuals from corporate management and security. Postal inspectors recommend that a facility's mail center manager, or a designee, be included in the planning stage. Most likely the Mail Center Security Coordinator would assume responsibility for the mail bomb-screening program.

While some persons would serve as active members, with others serving advisory capacities, input from all functional areas within the company should be obtained. These other areas include:

- upper management
- line management
- labor
- human resources
- engineering and maintenance
- safety, health and environmental affairs
- public relations/information
- security
- community relations
- sales and marketing
- legal
- finance and purchasing

The Command Center—The command center member in charge should have authority to make important decisions regarding the company's or facility's response to any bomb threat situation, including the site evacuation of the company/facility.

Location—The location of the command center should be at or near the communications center of the company/facility. As noted earlier, the command center should be equipped with:

• A current updated copy of the bomb threat response plan.

• A list of the current members of the command center working group.

• Telephone numbers for police, postal inspectors, the Bureau of Alcohol, Tobacco and Firearms and Explosives (ATF), the fire department, and emergency medical services.

• A tenant/employee roster that includes all current telephone numbers, including home, office, pagers and cellular telephones of employee/building occupants.

• Current copies of the company's/facility's floor plans or building blueprints.

Evacuation

Evacuation routes and alternate routes can be adopted from fire escape routes. It is recommended, however, that actual fire escape routes not be used. There is the possibility that a bomber would target such routes, such as stairwells and/or emergency exits, normally used during a fire evacuation.

Supervisors should be furnished with these evacuation routes. In addition to the evacuation route, a separate and distinct alarm, designated only for emergency bomb response evacuation threats, should be sounded. It is recommended that fire alarms not be used.

BOMB THREAT RESPONSE PLAN— CONSIDERATIONS

There are a number of considerations regarding a facility's bomb threat response plan. These considerations include the following:

1. The bomb threat response plan should complement the overall physical security plan. In other words, are the premises secured against unauthorized entry? In order to answer this question, a vulnerability assessment must be conducted.

2. The command center staff should include corporate management, security and the facility's mail center security coordinator.

3. The command center staff must have the authority to deal with any threat received. It must also have the authority to order an evacuation.

4. The command center must be equipped with telephone numbers of police, fire department, medical emergency services and all employees. As noted above, copies of the facility's floor plans and/or blueprints must be maintained at the command center as well.

5. Review local jurisdictional and/or enforcement policy conducting bomb threat searches.

6. If needed, organize and train search teams of volunteer employees familiar with areas to be searched.

7. Equip search teams with basic tools, such as flashlights, screwdrivers, pry bars and keys to all offices and storage areas.

8. Train telephone operators and receptionists to remain calm if receiving a threat, as well as to gather additional information.

9. Establish policy requiring all mailed and privately delivered parcels to undergo screening in the facility's mail center.

10. Train mail center employees to recognize suspicious parcel and mail bomb characteristics during screening.

11. Advise all employees to contact the facility's mail center if they receive a parcel they are not expecting and/or which cannot be explained

Postal inspectors recommend including the facility's mail center manager, or a designee, in the planning group. That person, as Mail Center Security Coordinator, will be responsible for the mail bomb-screening program.

Command Center Organization

As mentioned earlier, representatives from corporate management, security and the mail center should form the nucleus of the command center. This working group should address any emergency where bombs or bomb threats must be confronted. Members of the command center working group, and their alternates, should be specified by name and title. Most importantly, command center members should have authority to make important decisions as to how the firm will respond to any bomb threat situation, including evacuation of company facilities.

Preparation should include planning for evacuation routes and alternates, easily adapted from fire escape routes, and evacuation signals. Evacuation routes should be furnished to all supervisors. Again, it is recommended that fire alarms not be used to signal an emergency bomb response evacuation. The possibility exists that a bomber would target routes, such as stairwells and/or emergency exits, normally used during a fire alarm.

Local police and fire departments should be contacted about their respective bomb search policies. In the event of a threat, will they help conduct the search? If so, what will they need from the command center?

The bomb threat response plan must also include provisions to ensure that non-postal deliveries (except commercial shipments) are channeled through the mail center. Since all organizations receive mail and other parcel deliveries, a mail bomb-screening program through which all parcel deliveries are channeled is an essential component of this process.

Telephone threats received by company receptionists, or others, should be brought to the attention of the security officer and then relayed to the mail center manager, who needs to be informed of any specific information which would assist the mail bomb screening process.

Lastly, the bomb threat response plan should encompass all facilities at the site, including outbuildings, and parking lots or garages immediately adjacent to buildings occupied by tenants/employees. If the firm maintains offices at multiple sites, security officers at each site must be included in the communications loop.

It is highly recommended that discussions, meetings and/or consultations with security experts knowledgeable in terrorist tactics and vulnerability assessment be held.

Physical Security—Placed Bombs v Mailed Bombs

Since the majority of explosive devices are placed and not mailed, it is imperative that the security plan include control over physical accessibility to the facility, as well as to the immediate surroundings. Such steps can minimize risk potential.

Suggestions for physical security include:

- security guards greeting all visitors and examining personal belongings being brought into the building or office area.;

- restricting access to the facility or office through locked or guarded entryways;

- keeping storage rooms, boiler rooms, telephone & utility closets, and similar hiding places locked or "off-limits" to visitors;

- using easily distinguishable identification badges for staff personnel and for visitors;

- requiring visitors to be accompanied by staff employees to and from the office or facility entrance;

- requesting visitors to display identification to security personnel when they sign in. A detailed log on all visitors' times of arrival and departure should be maintained, as well; and

- consider using the services of a Certified Protection Professional to conduct a detailed evaluation of a facility's or company's personnel and physical security safeguards.

RESPONDING TO BOMB THREATS

A company's bomb threat response plan must address the possibility of receiving bomb threats in writing or by telephone. While all threats should be taken seriously, a firm's response may depend on the circumstances present at any given time.

Each bomb threat presents three basic options:

1. evacuate everyone immediately and search;

2. evacuate some employees while a search is undertaken; or

3. evacuate no one and search.

A fourth option, to ignore the threat, is not generally considered viable. If the company policy is to evacuate all employees and shut down operations when any threat is received, this will probably result in false alarms placed by employees anxious to exploit the policy. It is better to judge the credibility of each threat individually. The decision to evacuate all or part of the facility should be made by the command center-working group. Whatever the policy, it should not be publicized.

Written Threats

Written threats provide physical evidence which must be protected from contamination. Written threats and any envelopes in which they are received, should be placed under clear plastic or glassine covers. Further, unnecessary handling should be avoided. All efforts must be made to retain evidence such as fingerprints, hand/typewriting, paper and postal marks. This kind of evidence proves essential in tracing the threat and in identifying the writer. The circumstances of their receipt should be recorded.

Telephone Threats

Telephone threats offer an opportunity to obtain more detailed information, perhaps even the caller's identity. For that reason, telephone receptionist or others who take calls from the public should be trained to remain calm and to solicit as much information as possible. They should keep the caller on the line. The caller should be asked several times in an attempt to gather as much additional information as possible.

Telephone receptionists should ask the following questions while remaining calm:

• What kind of bomb is it?

• What does it look like? Please describe it.

- Where is it located? Can you give us the office and floor number and building location?

- What will cause it to detonate?

- Many innocent people may be hurt. Why are you doing this?

- What is your name and address?

The bomber's intentions may be to damage property, not injure or kill anyone. If so, the person receiving the call may be able to obtain useful information before the caller ends the conversation. Under no circumstances should the person taking the call hang up if the caller is still on the line.

The person taking the call should write down the threat verbatim, in the caller's own words, and record any additional information. Once the threat has been received, corporate security and management must decide on the proper response such as evacuation procedures. Police and fire departments should be notified immediately.

Searches may be conducted by individuals from within the firm who have volunteered for such duty, but extensive training must be provided. Police agencies often will not conduct searches of private facilities. Since management and employees know the facility, they are more likely to observe unusual items that police and fire personnel could overlook.

Search Team Deployment

If the local police and fire departments will not assist in the search for an explosive device, company search teams will have to be deployed. Teams may consist of managers only or teams of managers and employees.

For best results, the individuals conducting the search should be very familiar with all the sights, sounds and smells of the area to be searched.

The ideal search team usually consists of two volunteer employees and a supervisor. The employees conduct the search under the direction of the supervisor, who communicates the progress of the search to the command center. Volunteers should be trained in basic search and building clearance techniques by private security professionals.

Search techniques should be kept confidential and training should be limited to employees with a "need to know."

Search teams should be outfitted beforehand with a few elementary tools, such as screwdrivers, crescent wrenches, pry bars, and flashlights. Also needed are the keys to open storage rooms, boiler rooms, telephone, and utility closets. If the keys are not made available, then the custodian or a member of the facility department should accompany the team.

A complete building search should begin with the areas most accessible to the public. Typically, this means beginning with the building's exterior and moving indoors through the main entrance or lobby to waiting rooms, rest rooms, stairwells, and elevators.

Once inside, a two-employee team should begin its search at the same point and work in opposite directions around the room or office back to the center of the room.

They should begin at floor level and work their way up in four-foot increments. The search patterns should overlap somewhat. This process should be repeated in a methodical manner from office to office and from floor to floor throughout the facility. If a suspicious item is found, the area should be cordoned off and the police called. Once cleared, the search should continue throughout the facility until the entire area is declared safe for re-entry. This precaution is necessary because a bomber may plant more than one device.

Under no circumstances should volunteers attempt to handle or remove suspicious devices. Authorities should be contacted as soon as possible once a device has been located.

For suspicious items found placed on company property, it is important to note that the suspicious device must not be touched; doing so may "trigger" a detonation. Further, the

- situation must be reported immediately to the company's security office;

- immediate area be evacuated and cordoned off to prevent inadvertent exposure to the danger. Vibration from movement near the suspicious item may cause an explosion, or a timing mechanism may be set to activate the device within minutes of placement;

- windows must be opened whenever possible to minimize the effect of any injuries caused by detonation.

BOMB SCREENING PROGRAM

Vulnerability Assessment

The security officer and top management should meet to evaluate the probability of the organization or its personnel becoming targets for mail bombs and bomb threats. As previously noted, the vulnerability of a company or facility and/or its employees, tenants, officers or owners must be assessed. As such, the following questions can be used to develop any information that would help to identify bombing targets:

- Does the company/facility provide products, materials, technical assistance, or operate facilities within any country involved or connected with current terrorist activity or any government suffering domestic unrest?

- Has the company/facility refused to do business with, withdrawn from, or failed to successfully negotiate business contracts with companies, organizations, or governments within the last two years that are affiliated with current terrorists or represent countries suffering domestic unrest?

- Does the company/facility manufacture or produce weapons or military support items for international arms trade that would normally bear markings identifying the organization as the manufacturer?

- Does the company/facility support political or social causes that would make it a likely target for radical domestic "hate" groups?

- Has any member of the company's/facility's management made public statements or authored papers on any facet of current terrorist activity or topics, or taken any controversial public position?

- Have any employees and/or tenants/occupants advised the company that they have been the target of physical violence or harassing activities such as threatening phone calls or physical threats?

- Has any current or former employee threatened violence against either the organization or another employee in connection with a real or alleged grievance?

Care must be given not to violate individual employees' privacy, and all information should be treated as extremely sensitive. This information should be shared with the mail center security coordinator in the event a suspicious package is received, but should not be disseminated to other employees.

The Mail Center Security Coordinator

Management should ensure that the mail center security coordinator and an alternate are mature, responsible, and emotionally stable. This selection should be made from those persons already participating and trained in the overall bomb threat response plan.

The responsibilities/duties of the mail center coordinator include:

- Overseeing the mail bomb screening process, including:
  — Ensuring that all deliveries are channeled to the mail center,
  — Training employees in detecting suspicious packages, verifications, safe handling, and
  — Close and effective communication with security and management in any crisis.

- Assuming command of the situation when a suspicious package is identified by mail center employees in the screening process.

- Ensuring that personnel who have detected the suspicious postal item have placed sufficient distance between themselves and the suspicious item.

- Preventing employees from clustering around the suspicious item.

- Notifying management directly and providing management with specific details of the item.

• Implementing the remaining steps of the plan under the direction of management and security.

Lines of Communication

Direct channels of communication among the mail center security coordinator, senior management and security are vital.

A "command center" comprised of management and security representatives should be the focal point of communications when the bomb threat response plan is operational. The mail center security coordinator must be able to communicate directly with managers in this command center.

Security must receive prompt notification when a suspicious package is identified or a threat is received in the mail center. Additional verification may be required of corporate security, or notification may be given to the supporting police, postal inspector, and bomb squad disposal units.

These channels of communications will also be of significant help when a package clears the screening process and is delivered and is declared suspicious by the recipient. Information concerning that parcel should be relayed back to the mail center in the event other similar parcels are being processed.

Screening Procedures

Incoming mail to a facility/company generally follows the same pattern. Bags or bundles of mail, and other courier deliveries are delivered to a centralized mail center for distribution. In fact, the United States Postal Service recommends that if this centralized receiving procedure is not currently in operation, steps should be taken to institute such a program. The initial sorting of the mail for delivery to units, divisions, or individuals in the facility/organization must be done by hand. Each item then, is picked up, its address read, the item then placed into its proper distribution box for delivery.

It is at this point the screening of incoming mail for suspicious items should occur. This screening should be done by the person who normally handles this mail at the sorting area. Why? Because it is the individual who sorts mail on a regular basis who is most likely to notice packages or mail that is out of the ordinary. Incoming mail should be screened per the recognition points identified by the United States Postal Service. These recognition points can be found on the postal services' "Letter and Package Bomb Indicators." This poster should be displaced in the facility's mail room. See Figure 6-1.

General screening procedures of incoming mail and packages are not foolproof. Many times it is the recipient who ultimately detects a suspicious package. Therefore, the poster entitled "Letter and Package Bomb Indicators" should be distributed facility/company wide to all tenants/occupants and employees in order to increase their sensitivity to this threat.

Mail and placed bombs are becoming more sophisticated. Fewer of the devices can be readily identified by merely examining the exterior of the package. Employees should be told

- to be suspicious if they are not expecting a package.

- to check the return address, if they do not recognize the return address they should contact the security office. The security office when will attempt to contact the sender; and

- NOT TO OPEN *the package* until it is determined to be harmless.

SUSPECTED MAIL BOMBS—
SCREENING RESPONSE PROCEDURES

As outlined by the USPS, the response procedures for suspected mail bomb encountered during screening include the following:

A.   Upon notification that a suspicious package has been found, the mail center coordinator should:

1.   Ask the employee to write down the specific recognition point(s) in the screening process that caused the alert such as: excessive postage, no return address, rigid envelope, lop-sided, or a strange odor.

2.   Alert the other employees/building occupants that a suspicious package has been found. The employees should also be alerted to the following:
     - the nature of the suspicious package; and
     - to distance themselves from the area.

SUSPICIOUS MAIL GUIDELINES

Upon receipt of a suspicious letter or package:
Handle with care. Don't shake or bump.
Do not open, smell, touch, or taste.
Isolate it immediately.
Treat it as suspect. Call local law enforcement authorities.

If a letter or parcel is opened and/or a bomb threat is identified...
For a Bomb:
Evacuate immediately.
Call police.
Contact postal inspectors.
Call local fire department/HAZMET unit.

For Radiological Threats the following apply:
Limit exposure—do not handle.
Distance (evacuate area).
Shield yourself from object.
Call police.
Contact postal inspectors.
Call local fire department/HAZMET unit.

For Biological or Chemical Incidents
Isolate—do not handle
Wash your hands with soap and warm water.
Call police.
Contact postal inspectors.
Call local fire department/HAZMET unit.

3. Place the suspicious item in reinforced container and take it to the isolation area.

4. Record all the available information from each side of the item—name/address of addressee and of sender, postmark, cancellation date, types of stamps and any other markings or labels found on the item. Note: *all information should be copied using exact spelling.*

5. Inform management and security that a suspicious item has been detected through the screening process.

6. Contact the police and postal inspectors. All required information must be given to the authorities.

B. When management or security receives notification from the mail center coordinator, their actions should, in general, follow these guidelines:

1. Accurately record all information pertaining to the suspicious item in an incident log.

2. If possible, dispatch a security officer with a Polaroid camera to photograph all sides of the suspicious item once it is in the holding container. *The package should not be moved.* The bomb scene officer then has the exact details of the markings needed for use.

3. Contact the addressee of the suspicious package for verification of the item by asking specific questions (see Table 6-2).

4. Attempt to resolve the verification by contacting the "sender" as indicated on the suspicious package's return address.

5. If the return address/addressee proves to be fictitious, or the sender cannot be located within a reasonable period of time, the police and postal inspectors should be notified that a suspicious package has been detected through the mail screening process. The authorities should also be notified

---

SUSPICIOUS LETTER/DOCUMENT—CHARACTERISTICS

Have any powdery substance on the outside.

Are unexpected or from someone unfamiliar to the recipient.

Have excessive postage, handwritten or poorly typed address, incorrect titles or titles with no name, or misspellings of common words.

Are addressed to someone no longer with the organization or are otherwise outdated. Have no return address or have an address that cannot be verified as legitimate.

Are or unusual weight, given their size, or are lopsided or oddly shaped.

Have an unusual amount of tape on them.

Are marked with restrictive endorsements, such as "Personal" or "Confidential."

Have strange odors or stains.

---

that the suspicious package has been placed in the holding container in the isolation area. The responders then should be notified of the specific location of the holding area and the name of mail center coordinator or security officer.

6.   Notify appropriate management level personnel of the detection, through mail screening, of a suspicious package.

7.   Stand by to offer in-house assistance to the police and postal inspectors upon their arrival.

Package Verification
Before calling the police, security personnel should attempt to

find out if the addressee of the suspicious package has any knowledge of the item or its contents. If the addressee can positively identify the suspicious item, it may be opened by security with relative safety. However, if the sender must be contacted to identify the item and contents, management must make the decision whether to open the parcel.

Table 6-2 lists sample questions to ask the addressee or sender during the verification process.

Table 6-2. Package Verification Questions

- Is the addressee familiar with the name and address of the sender?

- Is the addressee expecting package from the sender? If so, what is the approximate size of the item?

- Ask the sender to fully explain the circumstances surrounding the sending of the parcel and to describe the contents. At this point, management and security must make a decision whether to proceed to open the parcel or not.

- If the sender is unknown, is the addressee expecting any other business correspondence from the city, state, or country of origin of the package?

- Is the addressee aware of any friends, relatives, or business acquaintances currently on vacation or on business trips in the area of origin?

- Has the addressee purchased or ordered any merchandise from any business concern whose parent organization might be located in the city, state, or country of origin?

If the verification process determines that the sender is unknown at the return address, or the return address is fictitious, consider that the parcel may be dangerous.

Suspicious Package Isolation Area

When the mail screening process identifies a suspicious item, it is essential to rapidly remove personnel from the area and the potential bomb from the workplace. The potential bomb should be placed in an area of isolation. Security personnel and the mail center coordinator should select a space or area near the mail center which offers a degree

---

HANDLING OF SUSPICIOUS PACKAGES OR ENVELOPES

Do not shake or empty the contents of any suspicious package or envelope.

Do not carry the package or envelope, show it to others or allow others to examine it.

Put the package or envelope down on a stable surface; no not sniff, touch, taste, or look closely at it or at any contents which may have spilled.

Alert others in the area about the suspicious package or envelope. Leave the area, close any doors, and take actions to prevent others from entering the area. If possible, shut off the ventilation system.

WASH hands with soap and water to prevent spreading potentially infectious material to face or skin. Seek additional instructions for exposed or potential exposed persons.

If at work, notify a supervisor, a security officer, or a law enforcement official. If at home, contact the local law enforcement agency.

If possible, create a list of persons who were in the room or area when this suspicious letter or package was recognized and a list of persons who also may have handled this package or letter. Give this list to both the local public health authorities and law enforcement officials.

---

of isolation. Suspicious mail and/or parcels may be placed in this area pending verification and/or the arrival of the authorities. The USPS recommends the following general guidelines for selecting and creating the isolation area are as follows:

- The isolation area should be easily accessible from the mail screening area and located where the least number of people will be impacted during transfer.

- Access to the isolation area should not involve the opening of doors, climbing of stairs, or passage through areas of clutter or poor illumination.

- The total distance from the mail screening area to the isolation area should not exceed 50 yards.

- The isolation area should be located outdoors and sheltered from the elements in a covered loading dock or an open shed area. This serves as protection for the elements.

RECEIVING SUSPICIOUS MAIL

Do not try to open the mail piece.

Isolate the mail piece.

Evacuate the immediate area.

Call a postal inspector to report that a letter/parcel has been received that may contain biological or chemical substances.

Holding/Carrying Containers

The holding container should be constructed of heavy wood or exceptionally strong plastic. It should also be light enough for one or two individuals to carry. It should not be constructed of metal. Although the container is *not* intended to contain an explosion it would, nevertheless, help to direct the force of any explosion away from other employees, flammables, or windows. The container must be well ventilated. And again, it should be placed away from high traffic areas where other employees are working. It is advised that local authorities and/or security firms be contacted in order to determine the best type of container.

Testing The Plan

Testing should involve mock suspicious parcels placed in the mail center or elsewhere in the facility. These tests should be conducted in such a manner so that employees will not be alarmed. They should be considered "dress rehearsals" designed ensure that the lines of communication function and are understood.

Conducting scheduled tests is an excellent way to test the efficiency of an emergency contingency plan. Hold post-testing meetings to go over problems and resolve them before the next test.

BIOLOGICAL
AND CHEMICAL THREATS

Biological, chemical and radiological threats are considered weapons of mass destruction. The Federal Criminal Code defines these weapons as those that

- are designed or intended to cause death or serious bodily injury through the release, dissemination, or impact of toxic or poisonous chemical, or their precursors; such as mustard gas, nerve agents, and sarin gas (chemical);

- involve a disease organism, such as small pox botulinum toxin and anthrax (biological);

- are designed to release radiation or radioactivity at a level dangerous to human life (radiological).

ANTHRAX

Anthrax is an acute bacterial infection of the skin, lungs, or gastrointestinal tract. Infection occurs most commonly via the skin. It is caused by *Bacillus Antricus*—a bacterium that forms spores. Anthrax occurs in domesticated and wild animals, including goats, sheep, cattle, horses and deer. There are three types of anthrax:

- cutaneous (skin)

- inhalation (lungs)

- gastrointestinal (digestive).

The cutaneous or skin form occurs most frequently on the hands and forearms of persons working with infected livestock or contaminated animal products and represents 95% of cases of human anthrax. It is initially characterized by a small solid elevation of the skin, which progresses to a fluid filled blister with swelling at the site of infection. The scab that typically forms over the lesion can be black as coal, hence the name anthrax—Greek for coal. With treatment, the case fatality rate is less than 1% among people who get the skin form of the disease. The fatality rate for untreated inhaled or intestinal anthrax is over 90%.

The inhaled form of anthrax is contracted by inhalation of the spores, occurring mainly among workers handling infected animal hides, wool, and furs. Under natural conditions, inhaled anthrax is exceedingly rare, with only 18 cases reported in the United States in the 20th century.

The gastrointestinal form is ingested when raw or undercooked contaminated meat has been ingested. It has an incubation period of one to seven days. (See Table 6-3.)

Anthrax can be used as a weapon—as discovered in the United States in 2001. It was deliberately spread through the United States postal system. Letters were sent with powder containing anthrax, resulting in 22 cases of anthrax infection and one fatality.

Anthrax is categorized by the Centers for Disease Control as a Category A agent. Category A agents are those that:

- Pose the greatest possible effect on the health of the public.
- May spread across a large area or need for public awareness
- Need a great deal of planning to protect the health of the public.

The symptoms (warning signs) of anthrax are different depending on the type of the disease:

- *Cutaneous*: The first symptom is a small sore that develops into a blister. The blister then develops into a skin ulcer with a black area in the center. The sore, blister and ulcer do not hurt.

- *Inhalation*: The first symptoms of inhalation anthrax are like cold or flu symptoms and can include a sore throat, mild fever and muscle aches. Later symptoms include cough, chest discomfort, shortness of breath, tiredness and muscle aches.

- *Gastrointestinal*: The first symptoms are nausea, loss of appetite, bloody diarrhea, and fever.

After an incubation period of 1-7 days, the onset of inhalation anthrax is gradual. Symptoms can appear within 7 days of coming into contact the all three types of the anthrax bacteria. For inhalation anthrax, symptoms can appear within a week or up to 42 days (see Table 6-3).

THE TREATMENT FOR ANTHRAX

Treatment with antibiotics beginning one day after exposure has been shown to provide significant protection against death in tests with monkeys, especially when combined with active immunization. Penicillin, doxycycline, ciproflaxin, are all effective against most strains of the disease. Penicillin is the drug of choice for naturally occurring anthrax. If untreated, inhaled anthrax is fatal.

A vaccine is available and consists of a series of 6 doses over 18 months with yearly boosters. This vaccine, while known to protect against anthrax acquired through the skin, is also believed to be effective against inhaled spores.

Effective decontamination can be accomplished by boiling contaminated articles in water for 30 minutes or longer and using some common disinfectants. Chlorine is effective in destroying spores and vegetative cells. Anthrax spores are stable, able to resist sunlight for several hours and able to remain alive in soil and water for years.

MEDIA RELATIONS

The issue of handling the media is of paramount importance in any bomb incident. All contacts with the media, including official responses should be coordinated through a designated spokesperson. All other persons should be instructed not to discuss the situation with outsiders, especially the news media.

The purpose of this provision is to furnish the news media with

Table 6-3. Types of Anthrax Infections

Type	Exposure	Transmittal and Characteristics	Symptoms
Cutaneous	Skin	Cutaneous anthrax is the most common naturally occurring type of infection.	Skin infection begins as a raised bump that resembles a spider bite. Within 1 to 2 2 days, the infection develops into a blister and then a painless ulcer, with a characteristic black necrotic (dying) area in the center.
		Cutaneous anthrax usually occurs after skin contact with contaminated meat. wool, hides, or leather from infected animals.	
		The Incubation period ranges from 1 to 12 days.	The lesion is usually painless, but patients also may have fever, malaise, and headache.
		Infection is introduced through scratches or abrasions of the skin.	Lymph glands in the adjacent area may swell.
Inhalation	Inhalation	Anthrax spores must be aerosolized to cause inhalational anthrax.	Inhalation anthrax resembles a viral respiratory illness. Initial symptoms include sore throat, mild fever, muscle aches, and malaise.

	Inhalation anthrax is contracted by inhalation of the spores. It occurs mainly among workers handling infected animal hides, wool, and fur.	Symptoms may progress to respiratory failure and shock with meningitis.
	The number of spores that cause human infection is unknown.	After an incubation period of 1 to 7 days, the onset of inhalation anthrax is gradual.
	The incubation period of inhalational anthrax among humans is unclear, but it is reported to range from 1 to 7 days, possibly ranging up to 60 days.	
Gastro-intestinal	Ingestion	Gastrointestinal anthrax usually follows the consumption of raw or undercooked contaminated meat and has an incubation period of 1 to 7 days.	Gastrointestinal anthrax is characterized by acute inflammation of the intestinal tract.
		Initial signs are nausea, loss of appetite, vomiting, fever followed by abdominal pain, vomiting of blood, and severe diarrhea.

Source: United States Postal Service

LIMITING PHYSICAL EXPOSURE

Identify single point of contact to open mail.

If possible, DO NOT open mail in area where other personnel are present.

Have appropriate gloves available for individual use.

Screen all mail for suspicious packages.

---

accurate information and to see that additional bomb threat calls are not precipitated by irresponsible statements from uniformed sources.

SUMMARY

Addressing the issue of bomb threats involves developing two separate but interdependent plans—the physical security plan and the bomb incident plan. Attention must be directed to those strategies that are designed to protect occupants and property. The physical security plan addresses the issue of prevention and access control. The bomb incident plan provides the detailed procedures that must be employed when the bomb threat or actual bomb incident occurs.

Sources
Centers for Disease Control and Prevention, Emergency Preparedness and Response, February, 2006

Gustin, Joseph F., *Disaster & Recovery Planning: A Guide for Facility Managers*, 4th ed., Atlanta: The Fairmont Press, 2007.

United States Postal Service, "Mail Center Security Guidelines," Publication 166, September, 2002.

Chapter 7

Dirty Bombs

BACKGROUND

Recent terrorist events have raised concern about the possibility of a terrorist attack that would involve the release of radioactive materials. The most common means of such an attack would, in all probability, involve the use of a "dirty bomb."

As defined by the United States Nuclear Regulatory Commission (NRC), a dirty bomb, or Radiological Dispersion Device (RDD), combines conventional explosives such as dynamite with radioactive materials in the solid, liquid or gaseous form. The bomb, itself, is intended to disperse radioactive material into a small, localized area around the explosion. This could possibly cause people and buildings to be exposed to the radioactive material contained in the bomb. The main purpose of a dirty bomb is to frighten people and to contaminate the targeted buildings or land. As such, the buildings or land would be rendered untenable for a long period of time.

It is believed that the conventional explosive, itself, would be more lethal than the radioactive material. At the levels created by most probable sources, not enough radiation would be present in a dirty bomb to kill people or to cause severe illness. For example, radioactive material is used in hospitals for the diagnosis or treatment of cancer. This radioactive material itself is sufficiently benign so that approximately 100,000 patients a day are released from hospitals with this radioactive material in their bodies.

However, there are other radioactive materials that could cause problems. For example, these radioactive materials, once dispersed in the air could contaminate several city blocks. One of the objectives of the terrorist is to cause public fear and possible panic. The release of a dirty bomb and its contents would cause a disruption to a company's normal business operations as well as to incur costly cleanup efforts.

A second type of RDD might involve a powerful radioactive source hidden in a public place. A trash receptacle in a busy train or subway station, trash receptacles or decorative planters in front of buildings, any area or location where large numbers of people pass through or congregate are potential sources for the housing of a RDD. Any dispersal of radioactive material in these areas carries the potential for people who pass by or congregate in these areas to get a significant dose of radiation.

It is important to note that a dirty bomb is not similar to a nuclear weapon. As noted previously, the major impact of a dirty bomb is produced by the blast and the resulting panic and fear that will ensue. While they are explosive devices that are used to spread radioactive materials, RDDs are not particularly effective means for exposing large numbers of people to lethal doses of radiation. They are likely to affect relatively small areas. Because the materials will disperse as a result of the explosion, only the areas near the blast will be contaminated. The level or degree of contamination will depend upon how much radioactive materials were in the bomb, as well as the weather conditions at the time of the blast.

A nuclear detonation, on the other hand, is a catastrophic event. In addition to the concomitant nuclear fallout and associated damage to structures, such a detonation would severely disrupt civil authority and the infrastructure. Evacuation procedures would be both complicated and compromised, as would the resumption of normal operations within the country.

THE IMPACT OF DIRTY BOMBS

In addition to creating fear and requiring costly cleanup, the primary impact from a dirty bomb containing low-level radioactive sources would be the blast, itself. Promptly detecting the kind of radioactive material used in the bomb would assist local authorities in advising the affected population of what protective measures to take. Such measures would include leaving the immediate area, or going inside until further directed. Gauging how much radiation is present would be difficult to do when the sources of the radiation are unknown. However, there would not be enough radiation in a dirty bomb to cause severe illness from exposure to radiation at the levels created by most of these probable sources.

It is important to note, though, that certain radioactive materials dispersed in the air could conceivably contaminate several city blocks. The extent of the local contamination would depend on a number of variables. These variables include the size of the explosive device, the amount and type of radioactive materials used in the device, and the weather conditions at the time of the attack.

SOURCES OF RADIOACTIVE MATERIAL

There is wide-spread speculation regarding terrorist accessibility to the various radioactive materials that could be placed in a dirty bomb. The most harmful radioactive materials are found in nuclear power plants and nuclear weapons sites. However, increased security at these facilities makes obtaining such materials much more difficult.

Because of the danger and difficulty involved in obtaining high-level radioactive materials from a nuclear facility, there is a greater chance that the radioactive materials used in dirty bombs would come from low-level radioactive sources. Such low-level radioactive sources are found in hospitals, on construction sites and at food irradiation plants. The sources in these areas are used to diagnose and treat illnesses, sterilize equipment, inspect welding seams and irradiate food to kill harmful microbes.

WHAT TO DO FOLLOWING
A DIRTY BOMB EXPLOSION

Radiation cannot be seen, felt or tasted by humans. Subsequently, if people are present at the scene of an explosion, they will not know whether radioactive materials were involved at the time the explosion occurred. If people are not too severely injured by the blast and they are not directed to return to the building site, there is a series of steps that should be taken. According to the United States Department of Health and Human Services/Centers for Disease Control and Prevention (CDC), people who are present at the time of a dirty bomb blast should:

- Leave the immediate area on foot. People should not panic. Nor should they take public or private transportation such as buses,

For more information about radiation and emergency response, see the Centers for Disease Control and Prevention's website at: http://www.bt.cdc.gov or contact the following organizations:

- The CDD Public Response Source at 1-888-246-2675
- The Conference of Radiation Control Program Directors [http://www.crcpd.org/]
- The Environmental Protection Agency [http://www.epa.gov/radiation/rert/]
- The Nuclear Regulatory Commission [http://www.nrc.gov/]
- The Federal Emergency Management Agency (FEMA) [http://www.fema.gov/]
- The Radiation Emergency Assistance Center/Training Site [http://www.orau.gov/reacts/]
- The U.S. National Response Team [http://www.nrt.org/production/nrt/home.nsf]
- The U.S. Department of Energy (DOE) [http://www.energy.gov] at 1-800-dial-DOE

For more information on other radiation emergency topics, visit www.bt.cdc.gov/radiation or call the CDC public response hotline at (888) 246-2675 (English), (888) 246-2857 (Español), or (866) 874-2646 (TTY).

subways or cars. If radioactive materials were involved, taking public/private transportation could contaminate cars or the public transportation system.

- Go inside the nearest building. Doing so will reduce exposure to any radioactive materials that may be present at the scene.

- Remove clothing as soon as possible; clothing should be placed in a plastic bag and the bag sealed. By removing the clothing, most of the contamination caused by external exposure to radioactive materials will be removed.

- Save the contaminated clothing. This will allow for testing for exposure without invasive sampling.

- Take a shower or wash as best they can. Since washing reduces the amount of radioactive contamination on the body the effects of total exposure are effectively reduced.

- Be on the lookout for information. Once emergency personnel can assess the scene and the damage, they will be able to tell people whether radiation was involved.

Note that the CDC advises that by listening to television and/or radio broadcasts, people will be told if radiation was involved. If radioactive materials were released, people would be told where to report for radiation monitoring and blood testing. This monitoring and blood testing would be used to determine whether people were exposed to the radiation, as well as what steps would need to be taken to protect their health. Being at the site where a dirty bomb explodes does not necessarily guarantee that people will be exposed to radioactive materials. Until doctors are able to check people's skin with sensitive radiation detection devices, it will be uncertain whether they were exposed. Doctors will be able to assess risks after the exposure level has been determined.

It is important to note that even if people who were present at the time of a dirty bomb blast do not know whether radioactive materials were present, following these steps would be helpful in reducing any possible injury from other chemicals that may have been present in the blast.

Sources
Department of Health and Human Services, Centers for Disease Control and Prevention. CDC Fact Sheet, *Dirty Bombs*, July, 2003.

U.S. Nuclear Regulatory Commission, Office of Public Affairs. Fact Sheet, *Dirty Bombs*, March, 2003.

Chapter 8

Chemical, Biological and Radiological Weapons and the Facility Manager— An Overview

INTRODUCTION

Terrorism, as defined by the United States Federal Bureau of Investigation (FBI), is the "unlawful use of force or violence committed by a group or individual against persons or property to intimidate or coerce a government, the civilian populations, or any segment thereof, in furtherance of political or social objectives."

In recent years, the world has witnessed countless acts of terrorism. Over the past decade alone, numerous and wanton terrorist acts have occurred. And the United States has not been exempt. The most notable examples of terrorism include the first bombing of the World Trade Center in 1993, the bombing of the Murrah Federal Building in Oklahoma City in 1995, and the September 11, 2001 attacks. Following the September 11th attacks, terrorist activities took a new turn as evidenced by the sending of anthrax-laced mail to various locations and targets. U.S. interests were being attacked with a "new" and more insidious weapon.

GOALS

Because of its goals, a terrorist attack can occur with or without warning. The goal or purpose of an attack is to cause disruption of routine, economic loss, loss and/or disruption of critical resources and

129

vital services, loss of life and emotional devastation. Certainly, in each
of the cases listed above, the terrorist goals were met.

WEAPONS CLASSIFICATION

Generally speaking, terrorist weapons can be classified into the
following basic types:
• Explosive
• Incendiary
• Biological
• Chemical
• Nuclear

Explosives
According to the United States Department of Transportation
(DOT), an explosive can fall into either of the following definitions:

• A substance or article, including a device that is designed to explode (e.g., an extremely rapid release of gas and heat); or

• Any substance or article, including a device, which by chemical
reaction within itself, can function in a similar manner even if the
substance or article in question is not designed to explode.

Incendiaries
Incendiary devices are any mechanical, electrical or chemical devices that are used intentionally to ignite combustion and start a fire.
Whether the devices are mechanical, electrical or chemical, they are
comprised of three basic components—a fuse/igniter; the body of the
device (e.g., container); and the filler. Depending on its intended use
the body, or container, is made of glass, metal, plastic or paper. If the
device contains chemicals it will be usually made of metal, or some
other non-breakable material. A liquid accelerant will usually be placed
in a breakable container such as glass.

Biological Weapons
Humans are exposed daily to biological agents. Natural resistance
to these agents, inoculations, good hygiene and nutrition help ward off

any ill-effects or harm that these biological agents may pose. However, since these biological agents are found in nature, they are easily accessible, have the potential for rapid spread and can be contagious.

Several biological agents can be adapted and used as terrorist weapons. These include anthrax which is found in hoofed animals, tularemia (rabbit fever), and the pneumonic plague, which is sometimes found in prairie dog colonies, and botulism, which is found on food products. According to the United States Department of Health and Human Services Centers for Disease Control (CDC), biological agents of the greatest concern are:

- anthrax
- smallpox
- plague
- tularemia
- botulism, and
- viral hemorrhagic fevers.

These agents can be easily transmitted from person to person. As such, they can result in high mortality rates and have an impact on public health.

Routes of Exposure

The way biological agents make their way into a human's system is through inhalation, ingestion and skin absorption/contact. Exposure to a biological incident may not be detected readily because the onset of some symptoms may take days to weeks. Since biological agents are usually odorless and colorless, typically there will be no characteristic symptoms to signal an incident. Therefore, the number of victims and the geographical areas affected may be greater than the initial area. Because the infected persons are not aware of their exposure they travel to their homes infecting other people. On the other hand, some effects may be very rapid, producing symptoms in as little as four to six hours.

Differences Between Agents

Chemical, biological and radiological material, as well as industrial agents, can be introduced into humans through the following ways:

- In the air that is breathed
- The water that is drunk, or
- Physical contact on surfaces

These chemical, biological and radiological materials can be dispersed in a number of ways ranging from simple to complex methods. These methods include placing a container in a heavily used area; opening that container; using conventional garden/commercial spray devices to disperse the contents of that container; or detonating an improvised explosive device.

Chemical incidents are characterized by the rapid onset of medical symptoms—minutes to hours—and easily observed signatures. These easily observable signatures include: colored residue, dead foliage, pungent odor, and dead insect and animal life. (See Table 8-1).

Biological incidents, however, are slower to detect. The onset of symptoms requires days to weeks and typically there will be no characteristic signatures. Also, the affected area may be greater because contaminated individuals—not aware of their contamination—may move beyond the affected area. This movement beyond an affected area has implications for infecting a greater number of people or a wider area. (See Table 8-2).

Radiological incidents also are slower to detect. Days to weeks are required for the onset of symptoms and again, as with the case of biological incidents, there are typically no characteristic signatures. Radiological materials are colorless and odorless and therefore, are not recognizable by the senses. And, with the case of biological incidents, contaminated individuals, not aware of their contamination, may move beyond the affected areas, thereby affecting a greater number of people, or a wider geographic area. (See Table 8-3.)

Chemical Agents

Chemical agents that might by used by terrorists range from warfare agents to toxic chemicals commonly used in industry. The CDC identifies the following nerve agents that pose a threat as chemical weapons:

- VX
- Sarin
- Tabun
- Soman
- Vesicants or blistering agents such as sulfur mustard
- Toxic chemicals such as:

Table 8-1. Indicators of a Possible Chemical Incident

Dead animals/birds/fish	Numerous animals—wild/domestic, small/large—birds and fish in the same area.
Lack of insect life	If normal insect activity—ground, air, and/or water—is missing, then check the ground/water surface/shoreline for dead insects. If near water, check for dead fish/aquatic birds.
Physical symptoms	Numerous individuals experiencing unexplained water-like blisters, wheals—like bee stings—, pinpointed pupils, choking, respiratory ailments and/or rashes.
Mass casualties	Numerous individuals exhibiting unexplained serious health problems ranging from nausea to disorientation to difficulty in breathing to convulsions and death.
Definite pattern of casualties	Casualties distributed in a pattern that may be associated with possible agent dissemination methods.
Illness associated with confined geographic area	Lower attack rates for people working indoors versus outdoors, or outdoors versus indoor.
Unusual liquid droplets	Numerous surfaces exhibit oily droplets/film; numerous water surfaces have an oily film—with no recent rain.
Areas that look different in appearance	Not just a patch of dead weeds, but trees, shrubs, bushes, food crops, and/or lawns that are dead, discolored, or withered—with no current drought.
Unexplained odors	Smells may range from fruity to flowery to sharp/pungent to garlic/horseradish-like to bitter almonds/peach kernels to new mown hay. It is important to note that the particular odor is completely out of character with its surroundings.
Low-lying clouds	Low-lying cloud/fog-like condition that is not explained by its surroundings.
Unusual metal debris	Unexplained bomb/munitions-like material, especially if it contains a liquid—with no recent rain.

Source: United States Central Intelligence Agency.

Table 8-2. Indicators of a Possible Biological Incident

Unusual numbers, of sick or dying people or animals	As a first responder, strong consideration should be given to calling local hospitals to see if additional casualties with similar symptoms have been observed. Casualties may occur hours to days or weeks after an incident has occurred. The time required before symptoms are observed is dependent on the radioactive material used and the dose received. Additional symptoms likely to occur include unexplained gastrointestinal illnesses and upper respiratory problems similar to flu/colds.
Unscheduled and unusual spray being disseminated	Especially if outdoors during periods of darkness.
Abandoned spray devices	Devices will have no distinct odors.

Source: United States Central Intelligence Agency.

Table 8-3. Indicators of a Possible Radiological Incident

Unusual numbers, of sick or dying people or animals	As a first responder, strong consideration should be given to calling local hospitals to see if additional casualties with similar symptoms have been observed. Casualties may occur hours to days or weeks after an incident has occurred. The time required before symptoms are observed is dependent on the radioactive material used and the dose received. Additional symptoms include skin reddening and, in severe cases, vomiting.
Unusual metal debris	Unexplained bomb/munitions-like material.
Radiation symbols	Containers may display a radiation symbol.
Heat emitting material	Material that seems to emit heat without any sign of an external heating source.
Glowing material/particles	If the material is strongly radioactive, then it may emit a radio luminescence.

Source: United States Central Intelligence Agency.

— Cyanide, and
— Ricin

Criteria for determining priority chemical agents include:
- Chemical agents already known to be used as weaponry;
- Availability of chemical agents to potential terrorists;
- Chemical agents likely to cause major morbidity or mortality;
- Potential of agents for causing public panic and social disruption; and
- Agents that require special action for public health preparedness.

Other categories of chemical agents include:
- Nerve agents
  — Tabun
  — Sarin
  — Soman
  — GF
  — VX
- Blood agents
  — Hydrogen cyanide
  — Cyanogen chloride
- Blister agents
  — Lewisite
  — Nitrogen and sulfur mustards
  — Cyanogen chloride

- Heavy metals
  - Arsenic
  - Lead
  - Mercury
- Volatile toxins
  - Benzene
  - Chloroform
  - Trihalomethanes
- Pulmonary agents
  - Phosgene
  - Chlorine
  - Vinyl chloride
- Incapacitating agents
  - BZ
- Pesticides: persistent and non-persistent
- Dioxins: furans and polychlorinated biphenyls (PCBs)

Chemical agents fall into the following classes:
- Nerve agents
- Blister agents
- Blood agents
- Choking agents
- Irritants

Nerve agents disrupt nerve impulse transmissions. The victims of a nerve agent attack will experience uncontrolled salivation, lacrimation (tears), muscle twitching and contraction. Nerve agents resemble a heavy oily substance. Aerosols are the most efficient distribution. Small explosions and spray device equipment to generate mists may be used. Nerve agents kill insect life, birds and other animals as well as human beings. Many dead animals at the scene of an incident may be an outward warning sign or detection clue that a nerve agent attack has occurred.

Blister agents, also called vesicants, cause redness and is possibly followed by blisters. They are similar in nature to other corrosive materials. Blister agents readily penetrate layers of clothing and are quickly absorbed into the skin.

These agents are heavy, oily liquids dispersed by aerosol or vaporization. As such, small explosions may occur or spray equipment may be used to disperse the agents. In a pure state, they are nearly colorless and odorless. Slight impurities, however, give them a dark color and an odor suggesting mustard, garlic or onions. Outward signs of blister agents include complaints of eye and respiratory irritation along with reports of a garlic-like odor.

Blood agents interfere with the ability of blood to transport oxygen. The ultimate result is asphyxiation. Common blood agents include hydrogen cyanide (AC) and cyanogen chloride (CK). Cyanide and cyanide compounds are common industrial chemicals. CK can cause tearing of the eyes and irritate the lungs. All blood agents are toxic at high concentrations and lead to rapid death. Affected persons require removal to fresh air and respiratory therapy.

Under pressure, blood agents are liquids. In pure form, they are gases. All forms have the aroma of burned almond or peach kernel. They are common industrial chemicals and are readily available.

Choking agents cause stress to respiratory system tissues. Severe distress causes edema (fluid in the lungs) which can result in asphyxiation. This type of asphyxiation resembles drowning. Chlorine (CL) and phosgene (CG), common industrial chemicals, are choking agents. Clinical symptoms of chlorine and phosgene include severe eye irritation and respiratory distress (coughing and choking). The choking agent chlorine has the easily recognizable odor of chlorine. Phosgene has the odor of newly cut hay. Since both are gases, they must be stored and transported in bottles or cylinders.

Irritants cause respiratory distress and tearing. They are designed to incapacitate. They can cause intense pain to the skin, especially in moist areas of the body. Irritants are also called riot control agents or tear gas. Generally speaking they are not lethal. However, under certain circumstances they can result in asphyxiation. Common irritants are Mace® (CN), tear gas (CS) and capsicum/pepper spray. Table 8-4 is a quick reference that describes the biological agents, their characteristics and their implications. Table 8-5 is a quick reference that describes the chemical agents, their characteristics and their implications.

Nuclear Weapons

Humans are exposed daily to low levels of radiological substances—sun, soil, X-rays. It is the exposure to an uncontrolled and massive dose of radioactive material that threatens life and well-being. Nuclear material, used in conjunction with explosives, is called a dirty bomb.

Table 8-4. Biological Agent Quick Reference

Biological Agents				
AGENT	**INCUBATION**	**LETHALITY**	**PERSISTENCE**	**DISSEMINATION**
Bacteria				
Anthrax	1-5 days	3-5 days fatal	Very stable	Aerosol
Cholera	12 hours-6days	Low with treatment High without	Unstable Stable in saltwater	Aerosol Sabotage of water
Plague	1-3 days	1-6 days fatal	Extremely stable	Aerosol
Tularemia	1-10 days	2 weeks moderate	Very stable	Aerosol
Q fever	14-26 days	Weeks?	Stable	Aerosol Sabotage
Viruses				
Smallpox	10-12 days	High	Very stable	Aerosol
Venezuelan Equine Encephalitis	1-6 days	Low	Unstable	Aerosol Vectors
Ebola	4-6 days	7-16 days fatal	Unstable	Aerosol Direct contact
Biological Toxins				
Botulism toxins	Hours to days	High without treatment	Stable	Aerosol Sabotage
Staphylococcal enterotoxin B	1-6 days	Low	Stable	Aerosol Sabotage
Ricin	Hours to days	10-13 days fatal	Stable	Aerosol Sabotage
Tricothecene mycotoxins (T2)	2-4 hours	Moderate	Extremely stable	Aerosol Sabotage

Source: hld.sbccom.army.mil; http://usamriid.army.mil/education/bluebook.html

The possible sources of radiation are the nuclear bomb, a dirty bomb, or a material release.

There are three types of radiation emitted from nuclear material:
* Alpha
* Beta
* Gamma

Alpha particles are the heaviest and most highly charged of the nuclear particles. Alpha particles, however, cannot travel more than a few inches in air. They are completely stopped by an ordinary sheet of paper or the outermost layer of dead skin that covers the body. However, if ingested through eating, drinking, or breathing, they become internal hazards and cause massive internal damage.

Table 8-5. Chemical Agent Quick Reference

Chemical Agents			
AGENT	SIGNS, SYMPTOMS	DECONTAMINATION	PERSISTENCE
Nerve Agents			
Tabun (GA)	Salvination Lacrimation	Removed contaminated clothing.	1-2 days if heavy concentration
Sarin (GB)	Urination Defecation Gastric	Flush with a soap and water solution for patients. Flush with large amounts of	1-2 days; will evaporate with water
Soman (GD)	disturbances Emesis	5% bleach and water solution for objects.	Moderate, 1-2 days
V Agents (VX)			High; lasts 1 week high concentration As volatile as motor oil
Vesicants (Blister Agents)			
Sulfur Mustard (H)	Acts first as a cell irritant, then as a cell poison. Conjunctivitis, reddened skin, blisters, nasal irritation, inflammation of throat and lungs.	Remove contaminated clothing; Flush with soap and water solution for patients; Flush with large amounts of a 5% bleach and water solution for objects.	Very high, days to weeks
Distilled Mustard (HD)			
Nitrogen Mustard (HN1,3)			
Mustargen (HN2)			Moderate
Lewisite (L)	Immediate pain; blisters later		Days, rapid hydrolysis with humidity
Phosgene Oxime (CX)	Immediate pain; blisters later; necrosis equivalent to second & third degree burns		Low, 2 hours in soil
Chemical Asphyxiants (Blood agents)			
Hydrogen Cyanide(AC)	Cherry red skin or 30% cyanosis. Gasping for air. Seizures prior to death. Effect similar to asphyxiation, but more sudden	Remove contaminated clothing. Flush with a soap & water solution for people; large amounts of 5% bleach and water solution for objects.	Extremely volatile, 1-2 days
Cyanogen Chloride(CK)			Rapidly evaporates & disperses
Arsine(SA)			Low

Source: hld.sbccom.army.mil; http://usamriid.army.mil/education/bluebook.html

Beta particles are smaller and travel much faster than alpha particles. Typical beta particles can travel several millimeters through tissue. Generally speaking, they do not penetrate far enough to reach vital organs. External exposure (i.e., outside the body) to beta particles is normally thought of as a slight danger.

Prolonged exposure of the skin to large amounts of beta radiation however, may result in skin burns. Beta-emitting contamination enters the body from eating, drinking, breathing and unprotected open wounds. Like alpha particles, they are primarily internal hazards.

Gamma rays are a type of electromagnetic radiation transmitted through space in the form of waves. These rays are pure energy and are the most penetrating type of radiation. Gamma rays can travel great distances and penetrate most material. Gamma rays can affect all human tissue and organs as they pass through the body. Gamma radiation has instinctive and short-term symptoms such as skin irritation, nausea, vomiting, high fever, hair loss and dermal burns. Acute radiation sickness occurs when an individual is exposed to a large amount of radiation within a short period of time. Materials used to shield gamma rays and X-rays include such thick materials as lead, steel or concrete.

THE RISKS

As seen from the descriptions of the various weapons, the risks associated with explosive and incendiary devices are more obvious. On the other hand, biological, chemical or nuclear (radiological) agents are less obvious. For example, in terms of a facility's immediate surroundings, the odor of an accelerant used in incendiary devices is obvious. However, the release of mists, liquids or vapor clouds is less obvious. Table 8-6 is a hazards checklist that outlines the types of facility sites and the potential hazards that are present in these facilities. Other examples of less obvious "occurrences" or "events" may include:

- Explosions that seem to destroy only the package, but which may release biological contaminants, radiation or chemicals;

- Unscheduled spraying or abandoned spraying devices, which may indicate a release of biological or chemical contaminants;

- Hazardous materials/lab equipment that are not site specific, indicating a possible biological, nuclear (radiological) or chemical contamination;

- Numerous sick/dead animals, fish, birds, indicating a possible biological or chemical dispersion in the area.

While unattended packages left in high-risk areas may be indicative of incendiary or explosive devices, those untended packages may also contain biological, nuclear or chemical contaminants.

Personal/Physical Signals

The consequences of these less obvious contaminations on the population can be manifested in various ways. For example, chemical contamination can result in persons reporting unusual tastes/odors; persons salivating, tearing or having uncontrolled muscle spasms. Impaired breathing and redness of skin are also indicative of chemical contamination. Mass casualties without obvious trauma, as well as distinct patterns of casualties with common symptoms, can also be the result of chemical contamination. Biological contamination can produce large numbers of people seeking medical attention with symptoms that are uncharacteristic of the season.

In either case, however, knowing what to do when such obvious or less obvious events occur becomes of paramount importance.

IMPLICATIONS FOR THE FACILITY MANAGER

Recent terrorist threats and the use of biological and chemical agents against civilians have exposed our vulnerability to terrorist acts. As such, it highlights the need to enhance our capacity to detect and control these acts of terrorism.

In the past, most planning for emergency response to terrorism has been concerned with overt acts such as bombings. Other overt terrorist acts include the use of chemical agents. Since chemical agents are absorbed through inhalation or through the skin or mucous membrane, their effects are usually immediate and obvious. Such overt acts require immediate response.

On the other hand, attacks with biological agents are more likely to be covert. Biological attacks present different challenges and require an additional dimension to the emergency planning process. The effects of biological attacks do not have an immediate impact because of the delay between exposure and onset of illness. As such, the likelihood

Table 8-6. Hazards Checklist Structural Alarms

If these sites are involved:	Look for these hazards:
Hospitals, medical labs or clinics	Biological waste
	Infectious patients or lab animals
	Radioactive materials
	Compressed and anesthetic gases
	Cryogenic liquid oxygen
	Syringes, sharp instruments
	Ethylene oxide
	Nitrous oxides
	Radioisotopes
Manufacturing and processing	Resins (alkyds, vinyls)
	Pigments (dry metallic powders)
	Compressed gases
	Ammonia refrigerant
	Lubricating and cooking oils
	Dusts and cotton fibers
	Aerosols
	Radioisotopes, radioactive materials
Retail and commercial	Flammable gases & liquids
	Corrosives
Business offices	Cleaning products
	Copy chemicals
Residences and hotels	Gasoline & solvents
	Pesticides & fertilizers
	Pool products
	Paint
	Cleaning supplies
	Illegal drug labs
Schools	Pool products
	Laboratory chemicals
Farms	Pesticides
	Oxidizers
	Anhydrous ammonia
Construction	Ammonium nitrate fuel oil mixture
	Compressed gases
	Solvents
	Radioisotopes
Mining	Methane
	Cola dust & metal sulfide ores
	Radioactive materials (uranium)

Source: U. S. Department of Health and Human Services, Centers for
Disease Control and Prevention (CDC)

for a disease to be disseminated through the population by person-to-person contact increases.

Certain chemical agents can also be disseminated through contaminated food or water. The Centers for Disease Control (CDC) reported that the vulnerability of the food supply was illustrated in Belgium in 1999, when chickens were unintentionally exposed to dioxin-contaminated fat used to make animal feed. Because the contamination was not discovered for months, the dioxin, a cancer-causing chemical that does not cause immediate symptoms in humans, was probably present in chicken and eggs sold in Europe in 1999. This dioxin episode demonstrates how a covert act of food-borne biological or chemical terrorism could affect not only human or animal health, but industrial commerce as well. This incident underscores the need for prompt diagnoses of unusual or suspicious health problems in animals as well as in humans. And this lesson was demonstrated by the outbreak in New York City in 1999 of mosquito-borne West Nile virus in birds and humans.

Detection, diagnosis and mitigation of illness and injury caused by biological and chemical terrorism is a complex process. It involves numerous partners and additional activities. Meeting this challenge adds a new dimension to the emergency planning process. As such, building owners and facility managers will need to work closely with their employees and building occupants so that all individuals are aware of potential hazards. Also, building owners and facility managers will need to work in concert with their local police and fire departments, as well as with local healthcare providers and agencies. By doing so, the strategies required to prevent and/or mitigate illness or injury caused by biological and chemical acts can be developed.

Sources

Gustin, Joseph F. *Disaster and Recovery Planning: A Guide for Facility Managers,*4th ed., Lilburn, GA: The Fairmont Press, Inc., 2007.

Gustin, Joseph F. *The Facility Manager's Handbook,* Lilburn, GA: The Fairmont Press, Inc., 2003.

Gustin, Joseph F. *Safety Management: A Guide for Facility Managers,* 2nd ed., Lilburn, GA: The Fairmont Press, Inc., 2008.

United States Department of Health and Human Services, Centers for Disease Control and Prevention (CDC), *Biological and Chemical Terrorism: Strategic Plan for Preparedness and Response, Recommendations of the CDC Strategic Planning Workgroup,* April 21, 2000/49(RR04); 1-14.

Chapter 9

Evacuation

When a natural disaster occurs, a fire breaks out or somebody calls in a bomb threat, it may be necessary to evacuate the building. Orderly and complete evacuation of all occupants and visitors requires careful provision for egress routes and accounting for all individuals after the evacuation. With planning that takes into account all factors, quick and orderly evacuations can be achieved with minimal problems.

EVACUATIONS

While the nature of the specific disaster as well as the potential threat to occupant safety are the prime consideration that determine the order to evacuate.

A written evacuation plan is essential for two reasons. First, a written plan provides all building occupants with specific information on procedures for orderly evacuation in the event of a disaster or emergency. In addition, a written evacuation plan satisfies the mandate of the General Duty Clause of the OSH Act of 1970—to provide a safe and healthful working environment for all workers.

Means of Egress

Means of egress is the continuous and unobstructed way of travel from any point in a building or structure to a public way consisting of three separate and distinct components. These components are the:

143

- Exit access

- Exit

- Exit discharge

Exit Access—The exit access is that component of a means of egress that leads to an exit. For example, an exit access includes rooms and the building spaces that people occupy, as well as doors, corridors, aisles, unenclosed stairs and enclosed ramps that must be traveled to reach an exit.

Exit—An exit is that component of the means of egress that is separated from all other spaces of a building by either construction—which must have the minimum degree of fire resistance—or equipment so that a protected way of travel to the point of exit discharge is provided. Exits include exterior exit doors, exit passageways, separated exit stairs and separated exit ramps.

Exit Discharge—The third component that comprises a means of egress is the exit discharge, or the path of travel from the termination of an exit to a public way. Since some building exits do not discharge directly into a public way, the path of travel may be within the building itself or outside the building. In either case, the purpose is to provide building occupants with the means for reaching safety.

Each of these components comprise the means of egress which must be provided from every location within the facility. Accordingly, all means of egress within the facility must be routinely inspected and regularly maintained to ensure maximum operability and utility by occupants seeking safety.

Types of Evacuation

There are two types of evacuation—partial evacuation and total, or complete, evacuation. While the nature of the disaster/emergency, as well as the potential threat to the safety of building occupants, determines the type of evacuation undertaken, the *immediacy* of the threat must also be considered.

Partial Evacuation—In a partial evacuation, occupants who are immediately affected, or whose safety may be jeopardized by the occurrence, are relocated from the endangered area to a safe or secured area. This secured area may be either located within the facility itself or away from the building. For example, when fire is detected in a multistory facility or high-rise building, occupants on the floors immediately above and below the origin of the fire are evacuated.

Total Evacuation—In a total or complete evacuation, all occupants are required to vacate the site premises with the possible exception of the disaster/emergency team members. In some situations, again depending upon the nature and immediacy of the disaster or emergency, team members may remain behind to ensure that all other occupants have vacated the site and/or to secure the building proper and critical building contents.

Evacuation Factors

There are several factors that must be considered in determining which type of evacuation must be undertaken. These factors are:

- The nature of the disaster/emergency occurrence.

- The potential threat to occupant safety, as determined by the severity of the occurrence.

Each of these factors, in turn, determines the immediacy of the evacuation need.

Evacuation: The Issue of Immediacy—Facilities located in the Atlantic and Gulf coastal regions of the continental United States, as well as in the coastal areas of Hawaii and the Caribbean, are threatened by hurricanes. And while the losses incurred by hurricane damage can run into the hundreds of millions of dollars, the advance notice of hurricanes that is provided to the affected areas precludes, in many cases, personal injury.

The National Weather Service's forecasting and tracking systems are able to identify and predict a hurricane's path and the storm's level of intensity with a fairly high degree of accuracy (see Table 9-1 for Hurricane Scale). Based upon the available data received from these tracking systems, the National Weather Service issues notices to all areas within the storm's path, so that these areas have a fairly reasonable amount of preparation time. Oftentimes, notice of an impending hurricane is provided so far in advance that a "formal" occupant evacuation becomes unnecessary. The "luxury" of this advance notice, therefore, provides facility managers and members of the disaster planning team with time to prepare for securing the building and its contents. Once an actual hurricane warning is issued by the National Weather Service, occupants should be instructed to leave the facility's premises by a given time, provided that such time is adequate for occupants to seek refuge on an individual basis. In situations such as these—where advance notice can be provided—the immediate need to evacuate is less urgent.

These notices usually take the form of "watches" and "warnings."

Watch Versus Warning—A watch is defined by those weather conditions that carry the potential for threat to safety. The warning, on the other hand, is defined in terms of actual conditions that exist and that threat is imminent. For example, a tornado warning may prompt an immediate partial evacuation of building occupants to pre-designated "safe" areas of refuge within the facility itself.

In the event of fire, either a partial or total evacuation may be ordered. While the floors immediately above and below the fire's location are generally evacuated first, there are occasions when all building occupants will be required to evacuate.

Table 9-1. Hurricane scale. Source: National Weather Service.

Category	Wind Speed	Storm Surge
I	74 - 96 mph	4 - 5 ft.
II	96 - 110 mph	6 - 8 ft.
III	111 - 130 mph	9 - 12 ft.
IV	115+ mph	18+ ft.

Other Evacuation Factors—There are a number of other critical factors related to evacuation that must be addressed in developing evacuation strategies. These factors include determining:

- Internal authority/responsibility levels for ordering and supervising the evacuation. Depending upon the nature and severity of the occurrence, the evacuation order may be made by either the designated site person, the local fire department and/or other jurisdictional authority, or both.

- Timing of the order. Depending upon the potential threat to occupant safety, any decision to evacuate may need to be made immediately.

- Various types of assistance that will be made available to persons with disabilities. Assistance may come in the form of trained in-house personnel and/or fire and emergency services personnel, in assisting in the evacuation of occupants with disabilities.

Another critical factor that must be addressed in developing a facility's evacuation strategies is the threat of bombs and explosives-related violence.

BOMB THREATS

The most serious of all decisions is whether to order an evacuation in the event of a bomb threat. According to the ATF, there are three options available to a company's management team when a bomb threat is received. Facility managers may:

1. Ignore the threat.

2. Order an immediate and total evacuation.

3. Search and evacuate if necessary.

Option 1: Ignore The Bomb Threat

Ignoring a bomb threat completely can result in some problems. While a statistical argument can be made that few bomb threats are real, the fact that bombs have been located in connection with threats cannot be overlooked. If building occupants learn that bomb threats have been received and ignored, it could result in morale problems and have a long-term adverse effect on business operations. In addition, there is the possibility that if the bomb threat callers feel that they are being ignored, they may actually go beyond the threat and, in fact, plant the bomb.

Option 2: Order An Immediate Evacuation

Ordering an immediate and total building evacuation on every bomb threat received is, at face value, the preferred response. However, there are negative factors inherent in this option that must also be considered. For example, any immediate and total evacuation disrupts business operations. If bomb threat callers know that a company's policy is to evacuate each time a bomb threat is received, they are likely to continue calling with the intention of bringing the facility's operations to a virtual standstill. Additionally, disgruntled or dissatisfied employees who know that their company's policy is to order an immediate and total evacuation, may call in such threats in order to close the facility down. In doing so, the disgruntled employee is able to "exact revenge," or "set things straight." Another possible scenario is the student who wishes to cancel classes, avoid tests, etc., may call in a bomb threat. In addition, bombers who wish to cause personal injuries could place the explosive device near exits that are used for evacuation.

Option 3: Search and Evacuate

Initiating a search after a bomb threat is received and then ordering the evacuation after finding a suspicious package or device is, perhaps, the most viable of all options, because it is not as disruptive as the immediate and total evacuation. It does satisfy the requirement to do something when the threat is received. Additionally, if an explosive device is discovered, an evacuation can be accomplished expeditiously while avoiding the potential danger areas of the bomb.

EVACUATION AND SEARCH UNITS

In developing evacuation strategies for their own particular properties, facility managers and other members of the disaster response and recovery planning team should consider forming internal evacuation and search units. Comprised of selected management and supervisory personnel, this team's internal evacuation unit can direct the orderly evacuation and relocation of building occupants when such action becomes necessary. An evacuation unit that is well-trained in evacuation procedures becomes particularly important in the event of a bomb threat incident. Specific, bomb-incident evacuation training is usually provided by local police, fire and other jurisdictional authorities, as well as various community-based resources.

Evacuation And Search Unit Training

In the event of a bomb threat, priority of evacuation becomes critical. The expeditious evacuation of occupants from the floor levels above and below the targeted or suspected area is necessary to remove occupants from danger.

There are specific site-search techniques that also comprise bomb incident training. This type of training, which is provided to members of the team's search unit, includes detection and location methods and procedures. Additional training that is provided to members of the team's search unit includes the proper procedures for marking and taping a room after that room or a particular area has been searched, and proper reporting procedures.

Once the bomb or incendiary device has been detected, it is imperative that any direct contact with the bomb be avoided. Its location should be well marked and a route back to the device should be noted. Indeed, one aspect of training that should *not* be included is techniques used to neutralize, remove or directly contact the explosive device. Only authorized enforcement officials with specialized knowledge in explosives should ever attempt to move, dismantle, or disengage a bomb.

For obvious reasons, only people who are thoroughly familiar with all aspects of a facility's floor plan should be recruited for the evacuation and search team. For a search to be effective, members of the search unit must have a thorough knowledge of hallways, restrooms, false ceilings and so on as well as any and all other site locations where explosive or incendiary devices may be planted or concealed. In many cases, local police and firefighters will be unfamiliar with the actual layout of the facility and will need to rely upon members of the search unit for building specifics.

ADDITIONAL CONSIDERATIONS

There are several other considerations regarding evacuation that must be addressed in the disaster plan. These include the location to

NO SCALE

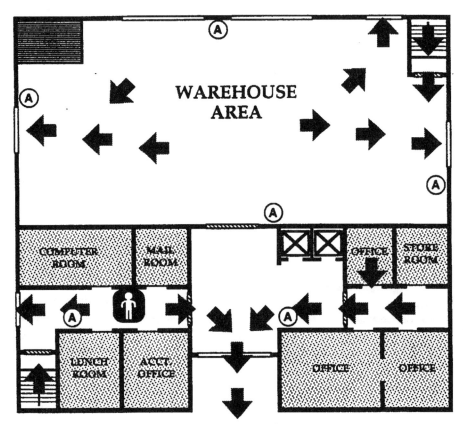

YOU ARE HERE

Ⓐ Fire Alarm (Looks like, Sounds like)

FIRE DEPARTMENT: **911** or (7-Digit Number)

CAUTION: IN CASE OF FIRE USE STAIRWAY
DO NOT USE ELEVATORS

Figure 9-1a. Sample building evacuation plan. Courtesy: Los Angeles
City Fire Department. Reprinted from *Fire Protection: A Guide For
Facility Managers* by David Wagner, UpWord Publishing, Inc., 1996.

NO SCALE

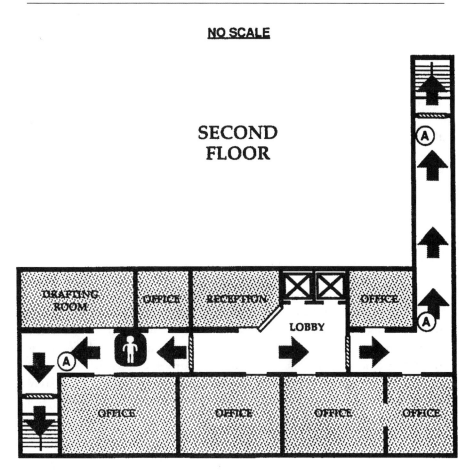

SECOND
FLOOR

 YOU ARE HERE

Ⓐ Fire Alarm (Looks like, Sounds like)

FIRE DEPARTMENT: **911** or (7-Digit Number)

CAUTION: IN CASE OF FIRE USE STAIRWAY
DO NOT USE ELEVATORS

Figure 9-1b. Sample building evacuation plan. Courtesy: Los Angeles City Fire Department. Reprinted from *Fire Protection: A Guide For Facility Managers* by David Wagner, UpWord Publishing, Inc., 1996.

which occupants will report upon completion of the partial or total evacuation; confirmation of successful evacuation; and maintenance of evacuation routes.

Reporting Locations

Regardless of the type of evacuation that may be ordered, a reporting location must be identified. In those situations that warrant a partial evacuation, consideration must be given to which area within the facility itself will be made available for evacuated occupants. Areas within the facility that have controlled or limited access for security reasons are not logical choices. Neither are any business operations areas that may be disturbed by a sudden influx of additional personnel. The evacuation strategy must address location issues so that unnecessary problems do not crop up during an actual occurrence.

The evacuation strategy must also address the issue of total building evacuation. An off-site location must be identified. The location itself should provide safety from the disaster site and should be large enough to accommodate the total number of evacuees. Without an identified destination, the safety of evacuees could be jeopardized. Falling debris from the disaster site could seriously injure evacuees left standing or milling about the street. Additionally, the effectiveness of fire and emergency rescue services could be compromised by large numbers of people congregating outside the disaster site.

Confirming Evacuation

Essentially, there are two methods by which an evacuation can be confirmed—the roll-call (or head count) method, and the search method. Each has its own distinct advantages depending upon occupancy type and facility size.

The Roll-call Method—For those facilities that house a relatively small number of regular occupants, the roll-call method is an effective means for verifying evacuation. The evacuation supervisor, or designee, can either count heads against the occupant list, or require a voice count against the occupant list to ensure that all occupants successfully evacuated.

The Search Method—In larger facilities that house a relatively large number of occupants, the roll-call method is often not practical.

LOOK FOR STAIRWAY SIGNS -and- KNOW WHICH STAIRWAY PERMITS ROOF ACCESS

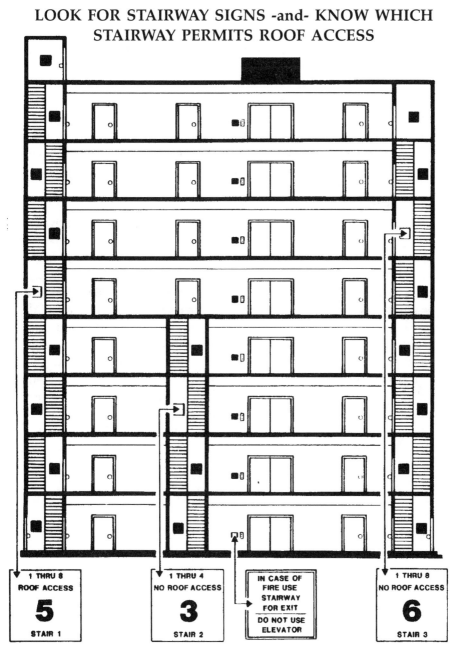

Figure 9-2. Signs are an invaluable tool in ensuring an orderly evacuation. The signs shown here clearly indicate which signs offer roof access. Courtesy: Los Angeles City Fire Department. Reprinted from *Fire Protection: A Guide For Facility Managers* by David Wagner, UpWord Publishing, Inc., 1996.

In a total evacuation of these facilities wherein large numbers of regular occupants are either tenanted, or in those occupant types that include transients—i.e., mercantile, assembly occupancies—it becomes almost impossible to account for each person. In these instances, the search method is most effective.

Upon authorization from the appropriate jurisdictional agency to re-enter an evacuated site, the search method can be undertaken to determine successful evacuation. In those instances where authorization to re-enter an evacuated site is not immediately given, the jurisdictional agency may be called upon to conduct the post-evacuation search.

Maintaining The Evacuation Route

A final, but no less important consideration, is the issue of evacuation route maintenance. As part of a facility's routine inspection and maintenance program, special attention must be given to designated evacuation routes.

Essential from a regulatory standpoint, all routes designated and used in evacuation must be properly maintained. Additionally, all building components must be operable and ready for use in the event that an order to evacuate becomes necessary. These building components include lighting and emergency lighting systems, elevators, smoke and fire resistant ceilings and walls, and stair pressurization systems. And, finally, as previously discussed, all components that comprise the means of egress—the exit access, exit and exit discharge—must be properly maintained so that their utility can be ensured and that occupants can reach a point of safety.

Sources

The Occupational Safety And Health Act of 1970 (December 29, 1970), PL91-596, 29 USC 651.

Wagner, David, *Fire Protection: A Guide for Facility Managers.* New York: UpWord Publishing, Inc., 1996.

Chapter 10

Earthquakes

In the event of an earthquake, the greatest risk to a facility, its operations and its occupants is the damage caused to and by its nonstructural components. For this reason, it is important for facility managers and the disaster and recovery planning team to assess the vulnerability of the building's nonstructural components, and to identify those preventive measures that will be taken to minimize injury and physical property damage.

THE NATURE OF EARTHQUAKES

An earthquake is a sudden, rapid shaking of the earth caused by the breaking and shifting of rock beneath the earth's surface. This shaking can cause buildings and bridges to collapse, as evidenced by the dramatic scenes of the freeway collapse during the 1989 earthquake in northern California.

However, the area west of the Rocky Mountains is not the only region in the United States vulnerable to earthquakes. While the West Coast states have the most frequent occurrences,, the central United States historically has had the most violent earthquakes. All 50 states and all U.S. territories are vulnerable. In fact, more than 40 states or territories are at moderate to high risk of experiencing earthquakes (see Figure 10-1).

Moderate Risk	High Risk	Very High Risk
• Alabama	• American Samoa	• Alaska
• Colorado	• Arizona	• California
• Connecticut	• Arkansas	• Commonwealth of
• Delaware	• Illinois	Northern Mariana
• Georgia	• Indiana	Islands
• Maine	• Kentucky	• Guam
• Maryland	• Missouri	• Hawaii
• Massachusetts	• New Mexico	• Idaho
• Mississippi	• Puerto Rico	• Montana
• New Hampshire	• South Carolina	• Nevada
• New Jersey	• Tennessee	• Oregon
• New York	• Utah	• Virgin Islands
• North Carolina		• Washington
• Ohio		• Wyoming
• Oklahoma		
• Pennsylvania		
• Rhode Island		
• Texas		
• Vermont		
• Virginia		
• West Virginia		

Figure 10-1. Earthquake Risk by State and Territory. Courtesy: U.S. Department of Homeland Security/Federal Emergency Management Agency.

STRUCTURAL VERSUS NONSTRUCTURAL COMPONENTS

The structural components of any building are those which resist gravity, wind, earthquakes and other types of loads. Structural components include a building's foundation, as well as its columns, beams, braces, floor and roof sheathings, slabs and decking, and load-bearing walls (see Figure 10-2).

The nonstructural components of a building include, but are not necessarily limited to, the following contents and parts of the facility itself:

• Ceilings and windows.

• Computers.

• Office equipment.

- Inventory/supplies, etc., that are stored on shelving.
- File cabinets.
- HVAC equipment.
- Electrical equipment.
- Furnishings and lighting.

Because a building's nonstructural components cannot resist various pressures and force loads, they carry significant risk exposure. Note the following examples of nonstructural earthquake damage reported by FEMA:

- More than 170 campuses in the Los Angeles Unified School District suffered damage—most of it nonstructural—during the 1994 Northridge earthquake. At Reseda High School, the ceiling in a classroom collapsed and covered the school desks with debris. The acoustic ceiling panels fell in relatively large pieces, approximately 3 ft. or 4 ft. square, accompanied by pieces of the metal ceiling runners and full-length sections of strip fluorescent light fixtures. Because the earthquake occurred at 4:31 a.m., when the building was unoccupied, none of the students were injured.

- A survey of elevator damage following the 1989 Loma Prieta earthquake revealed 98 instances where counterweights came out of the guide rails and 6 instances where the counterweight impacted the elevator cab, including one case where the counterweight came through the roof of the cab. Fortunately, no injuries were reported.

- One hospital patient on a life-support system died during the 1994 Northridge earthquake because of failure of the hospital's electrical supply.

- During the 1993 Guam earthquake, the fire-rated nonstructural masonry partitions in the exit corridors of one resort hotel were extensively cracked, causing many of the metal fire doors in the corridors to jam. Hotel guests had to break through the gypsum wallboard between rooms in order to get out of the building, a process that took as long as several hours. Fortunately, the earthquake did not cause a fire in the building, and no serious injuries were reported.

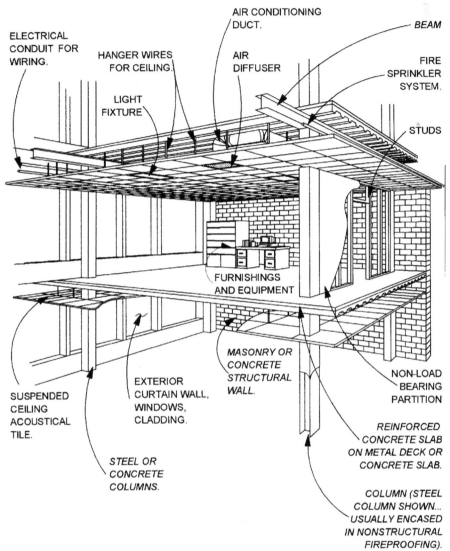

ELECTRICAL
CONDUIT FOR
WIRING.

HANGER WIRES
FOR CEILING.

LIGHT
FIXTURE

AIR CONDITIONING
DUCT.

AIR
DIFFUSER

BEAM

FIRE
SPRINKLER
SYSTEM.

STUDS

FURNISHINGS
AND EQUIPMENT

SUSPENDED
CEILING
ACOUSTICAL
TILE.

EXTERIOR
CURTAIN WALL,
WINDOWS,
CLADDING.

*MASONRY OR
CONCRETE
STRUCTURAL
WALL.*

NON-LOAD
BEARING
PARTITION

*STEEL OR
CONCRETE
COLUMNS.*

*REINFORCED
CONCRETE SLAB
ON METAL DECK OR
CONCRETE SLAB.*

*COLUMN (STEEL
COLUMN SHOWN...
USUALLY ENCASED
IN NONSTRUCTURAL
FIREPROOFING).*

KEY
NONSTRUCTURAL ITEMS (STANDARD TEXT)
STRUCTURAL ITEMS (ITALICS)

Figure 10-2. Nonstructural and structural components of a typical
building. Courtesy: Federal Emergency Management Agency.

Causes of Nonstructural Damage

According to FEMA, earthquakes have three primary effects on the nonstructural elements of buildings. They are:

1. Inertial or shaking effects on the nonstructural elements.

2. Distortions imposed on nonstructural components when the structure sways.

3. Pounding or movement across separation joints between adjacent structures.

Inertial Forces—When a building is shaken during an earthquake, the building's base moves in unison with the ground. The building and building contents above the base, however, will experience inertial forces. For example, when unrestrained items are shaken by an earthquake, inertial forces may cause those items to slide, swing, overturn, or strike other objects, including people. Items such as file cabinets, emergency power-generating equipment, free-standing bookshelves, office equipment and items stored on racks and shelves, can all be damaged. Even very large and heavy objects are vulnerable. For example, during an earthquake, inertial forces are directly proportional to the mass or weight of an object. Therefore, a heavily loaded file cabinet requires stronger restraints to prevent it from sliding or overturning than a lighter cabinet with the same dimensions (see Figure 10-3).

Building Distortion—During an earthquake, structures will distort, or bend, from side to side in response to the earthquake forces. For example, the top of a tall building may lean over several feet in each direction during an earthquake. The *distortion* over the height of each story is known as "story drift." While the story drift might range from 1/4 inch to several inches, depending on the size and intensity of the quake and the building's structure, the nonstructural components (e.g., windows, partitions, etc.) will distort the same amount. Subsequently, when the gaps close and the building structure pushes directly on the nonstructural components, glass, plaster/drywall, etc., will crack. Most components are damaged by building distortion, rather than by ground shaking or inertial forces.

Building Separation—A third source of nonstructural damage involves pounding, or movement across separation joints between adjacent structures. A separation joint is the distance between two different building structures, often two wings of the same facility, that allows the structures to move independently. A seismic gap is a separation joint that can accommodate relative lateral movement during an earthquake. In order to provide functional continuity between the separate wings, utilities must often extend across the building separations, while architectural finishes must be detailed to terminate on either side.

For base-isolated buildings that are mounted on seismic shock absorbers, a seismic isolation gap occurs at the ground level, between the foundation and the base of the structure. The separation joint may be an inch or two in older buildings, or as much as a foot in newer construction, depending on the expected horizontal movement or seismic drift. Subsequently, all piping, flashing, fire sprinkler lines, partitions, flooring, HVAC ducts, etc., have to be detailed to accommodate the seismic movement expected at these locations when the two structures move either closer together, or farther apart. Damage to items that cross these seismic gaps is a common type of earthquake damage. If the size of the gap is insufficient, pounding between the adjacent structures may result in damage to structural components. Oftentimes, serious damage is caused to the nonstructural components such as parapets, veneer or cornices on the facades of older buildings.

Methods For Reducing Nonstructural Hazards

According to FEMA, there are several methods that can reduce the potential risks associated with earthquake damage to nonstructural components. These methods include:

- Conducting a facility survey.

- Identifying common sense measures.

- Upgrading details.

- Developing organizational planning programs.

Conducting a Facility Survey—Nonstructural hazards may be present in any type of facility. In order to determine what measures should be taken to minimize the impact of these hazards, a site survey should be conducted to identify the nonstructural components that carry the potential for loss. Undertaking a comprehensive base-line survey will not only increase awareness of potential hazards within the facility,

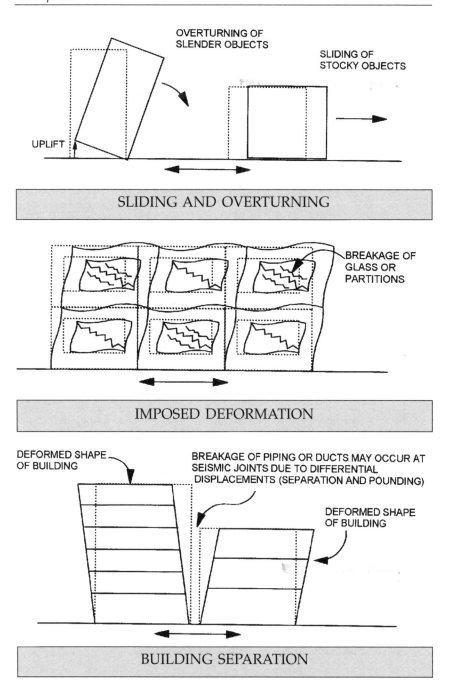

Figure 10-3. Effects of earthquakes on nonstructural components. Courtesy: Federal Emergency Management Agency.

but it will also increase understanding of the level of risk of nonstructural earthquake damage.

Common Sense Measures—The site survey may identify many items that represent a high or moderate risk in their present location, but which could be relocated. Answers to the following questions may also help identify common sense measures that can be used to reduce potential risks:

- Where do building occupants spend most of their time?

- Are there heavy, unstable items near desks that could be moved?

- What is the probability that someone could be injured by falling objects?

- Which areas of the facility have a higher occupant load, thereby creating a potentially higher safety risk?

- Are there items that are no longer useful that can be removed?

- What items can be relocated to prevent possible injury and which do not need to be anchored to prevent damage or loss?

- If something slides or falls, in what direction is it likely to go?

While the answers to these questions are not always obvious, it may be useful to rearrange furniture and move tall or heavy objects to where they cannot block doors or exits. Shelved items might be rearranged so that heavier items are placed at or near the bottom and lighter ones near the top of the shelving. Additionally, chemicals can be moved to prevent contact if their containers break. Any excess supplies could be stored in original shipping containers in order to reduce the possibility of breakage.

Upgrading Details—There are a number of techniques available to reduce potential nonstructural earthquake damage. FEMA lists the following upgrade measures:

- Using anchor bolts to provide rigid anchorage to a structural floor, or wall bracing items to structural walls or floors.

- Providing tethers or safety cables to limit the range of movement if items fall or swing.

- Providing stops or bumpers to limit the range of movement if items slide.

- Providing flexible connections for piping and conduit where they cross seismic joints or connect to rigidly mounted equipment.

- Attaching contents to a shelf, desktop, or counter top.

- Providing base isolation or seismic shock absorbers for individual pieces of vital equipment.

While some of these methods are designed to protect the functional integrity of particular items, others are designed to reduce the consequences of failure. FEMA suggests that it is important to understand the applicability and limitations of the various upgrade schemes and select the appropriate scheme for a particular item in a particular context.

Critical and expensive items warrant specialized attention. For essential facilities in areas where severe shaking is anticipated, the Agency suggests that any or all of the following elements may be needed in order to provide an appropriate level of nonstructural protection:

- Specialized engineering expertise.

- Higher design forces than those required by code.

- Experienced specialty contractors.

- Special construction inspection.

- Load-rated hardware.

- Vendor-supplied equipment that has been tested on a shaking table.

- Special design details such as base isolation for individual pieces of equipment.

- Larger seismic gaps to prevent pounding between adjacent structures; and/or stiffer structural systems such as shear walls to avoid excessive distortion of structural framing.

Developing Organizational Planning Programs—In an organizational setting, an effective program to reduce nonstructural earthquake hazards may have to be integrated with other organizational functions. These functions include:

Earthquake Info Available

The Earthquake Engineering Research Institute is a national, nonprofit, technical society of engineers, geoscientists, architects, planners, public officials, and social scientists. EERI members include researchers, practicing professionals, educators, government officials, and building code regulators. In its mission statement, EERI's objective is to reduce earthquake risk by:

1. Advancing the science and practice of earthquake engineering
2. Improving understanding of the impact of earthquakes on the physical, social, economic, political, and cultural environment
3. Advocating comprehensive and realistic measures for reducing the harmful effects of earthquakes.

More information is available at www.eeri.org

- Earthquake preparedness.

- Emergency response.

- Facilities maintenance.

- Procurement.

- Long-term planning.

- Facilities development.

While some organizations may opt for an ambitious program that calls for anchoring all of their existing equipment and contents, other companies may concentrate on new facilities and new equipment. In either case, there are many possible implementation strategies. Additionally, programming designed to develop employee awareness, as well as to provide emergency training, is rooted in the basics of emergency planning.

EMERGENCY PLANNING GUIDELINES

FEMA addresses the various issues related to nonstructural damage in its emergency planning guidelines.

The first step is to develop a valid picture of the probable post-earthquake state of the facility. Conducting a comprehensive baseline survey and vulnerability analysis will indicate what types of items are present and provide an approximate assessment of their earthquake resistance. The better this survey and analysis are, the more likely it is that the envisaged post-earthquake conditions will actually materialize. Less expert assessments will be more likely to either overestimate or underestimate damage. Even with the most thorough of analyses, however, there is still great uncertainty in the process of estimating earthquake performance.

One approach to this uncertainty is to assume the worst. This conservative approach is not warranted and is prohibitively expensive for purposes of allocating construction money to upgrade items, but in the initial stage of the emergency response planning process, it may be inexpensive to at least briefly consider the impact of severe damage to each nonstructural item on the list. What would be the emergency planning implications if each particular nonstructural item were to be severely damaged?

For example, what would be the consequences if an emergency power generator were damaged or if its support services rendered inoperative. This will provide the worst-case scenario.

A particular generator may be anchored to the concrete slab with adequate bolts; it may have an independent fuel supply; the batteries may be restrained; and the cooling water system, if any, may be braced or anchored. The owner or operator may test the generator monthly and may be confident that it will work after an earthquake. However, out of 100 very well-protected generators such as the one described above, at least a few would probably fail to run after a large earthquake. The probable outcome is that the generator will work properly, but there is still an outside chance that it won't. In the 1994 Northridge earthquake, a number of facilities, including more than one major hospital that was designed and constructed under the State of California's Hospital Seismic Safety Act, had temporary emergency power outages.

If there are inexpensive backup measures that can be included in the plan or in the training program or exercises, then this may be a form of inexpensive insurance. Such inexpensive measures might include: switching off all electricity except where it would be dangerous to occupants or deleterious to equipment testing battery-powered exit lights; buying a supply of flashlights and batteries; maintaining a list of local suppliers of rental generators; and exploring whether recreational vehicle generators could supply power to run some essential functions and, if so, including the idea as a backup tactic in the earthquake plan (employees could be quickly queried to see whether some RVs might be available for use by the company or organization).

After the worst-case outcome has been considered with regard to each nonstructural item, it will then be necessary to consider the probable-case scenario. Because emergency planning resources are limited, extensive effort cannot be devoted to every conceivable problem. Once a facility survey has been completed, the estimated vulnerabilities indicated on the nonstructural inventory form can be used as a guide.

Human Response

As protection against almost all types of nonstructural damage, the common advice to take cover beneath a desk or table is generally valid. Taking refuge in a doorway is not recommended, since lintel beams over doorways provide little protection from falling debris, which can occur in and near doorways, particularly in exterior walls of buildings. Taking refuge under a desk or table is a simple measure to undertake, but this advice requires some training and exercises if the technique is to work. Some people may have an immediate impulse to try to run outdoors if the shaking is severe or lasts for more than a few seconds. Many adults will feel embarrassed about crawling under a table. The quarterly earthquake drills for school students, now required by law in both public and private schools in California, appear to be very successful in getting students to take cover quickly and follow instructions during earthquakes. Similar drills, if only annual, are necessary if adult office workers, salespeople, or government employees are to be expected to respond quickly and protect themselves when the need arises.

In settings where there are no desks or tables, occupants should get down beside the next best thing. In an auditorium or public assembly setting, kneeling down between the seats is the best advice. It may be possible to move away from obvious hazards, such as items on tall industrial storage racks, and to put oneself in a safer position at the other side of a room, but in a very severe earthquake it may be impossible to stand up or walk.

Earthquake Plans

The following points relating to nonstructural damage should be addressed in an earthquake plan.

Pre-Earthquake Tasks—The plan should describe the identification and upgrading of nonstructural items and the procedures for routinely checking to see that protective measures are still effective. If emergency training for employees is anticipated, then that should be written into the plan also.

Earthquake Emergency Response Tasks—What tasks must be accomplished immediately after an earthquake? The tasks can be made contingent upon the severity of the earthquake and the amount of damage that is immediately seen to have occurred. If the structure of the building is obviously damaged—if there are sizable cracks in concrete walls, floors, or columns; if the building is leaning out of plumb; or if any portion of it has pulled apart or collapsed—then evacuation of the building will obviously be in order. This is not the time for a thorough survey of nonstructural damage. If there is no apparent structural damage, a survey of the mechanical equipment, elevators, and so on, could be listed as the appropriate response. Hazardous material storage areas should be quickly checked for spills.

Responsibilities—For each task, somebody must be assigned responsibility. If no responsibility is assigned in the plan, it is likely that nobody will carry out the task. Because the earthquake may happen at any time and will have roughly a 75 percent chance of happening outside normal work hours, backup positions for responsibilities should be listed.

To minimize the obsolescence of the plan, it is preferable to list positions rather than individuals' names, but in any event, someone must have responsibility for the plan itself and for keeping it current. Figure 10-5 provides a blank form for use in collecting information that may be helpful in formulating an earthquake plan.

Training

How should a company establish an earthquake training program? Ironically, the best advice may be to avoid establishing a separate train-

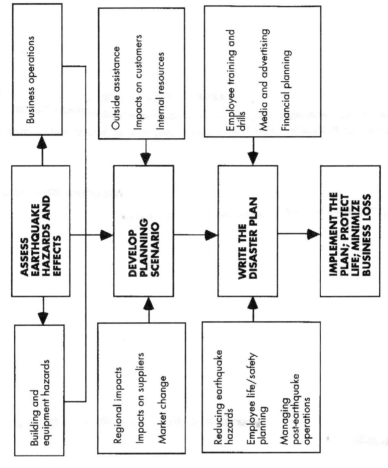

Figure 10-4. Sample earthquake response planning process. Courtesy: California Seismic Safety Commission.

ing program and, instead, to integrate earthquake training tasks into other ongoing training programs. Because of the infrequency of earthquakes, even the best earthquake training program may slowly lose its effectiveness or completely die out. In addition, a training program that requires its own separate funding will probably have a relatively low priority in the overall ranking of training concerns. But it may be possible to find ways of slightly expanding existing training programs—at small cost—to deal with the problems unique to earthquakes.

Fire safety is typically the most common of hazards on which hazard training is based. In the process of instructing employees about extinguishers, alarms, notification procedures, safe storage methods, exiting, and other fire-related topics, it may be possible to incorporate an earthquake safety training unit at the same time. It is essential to have procedures for controlling leaks from fire sprinklers and other pipe lines. Security staffs should be trained in the process of responding to earthquakes at the same time they are familiarized with other emergency plans for theft, fire, or other hazards. Maintenance personnel must be trained in certain upkeep and operational aspects of the HVAC system, elevators, plumbing, lights, sprinkler system, and so on, and many of these items are precisely the components of a building that will require attention in an earthquake hazard reduction or response plan. Workplace safety training sessions are ideal forums for dealing with earthquake safety.

To minimize the number of earthquake training requirements, consider the unique aspects of earthquake problems that are not already covered by preparations for other hazards. For example, the fact that the phones may not work is one of the key ways in which earthquake response differs from that for fire or other hazards. If an emergency plan addresses building evacuation, it should identify gathering points that are at a safe distance from falling hazards adjacent to other buildings. Individual emergency plans may contemplate a telephone outage, an electrical outage, the need to evacuate the building, traffic disruption, injury, pipe leakage, or window breakage, but it is unlikely that the response plan for any other hazard will consider that all these events may occur simultaneously. At a minimum, having an earthquake backup plan for reporting injuries or fires in the event that the telephones are inoperable is one essential feature to include.

The nearest fire station should be located and indicated on a street map so that aid can be quickly summoned in person if the

Information Gathering Checklist:
Organizational Characteristics

1. **Facility/Organization name**

2. **Address**

3. **Building:** ___ owned by occupant, ___ leased by occupant

4. **Organization:** ___ company, ___ government agency, ___ other

5. **Organizational structure** (overall organizational chart)

6. **Functional responsibilities**
   Who has responsibility for:
   > Authorization for earthquake program, budgeting?
   > Detailed administration of earthquake program?
   > Safety training courses?
   > Posters, brochures, memos, newsletters?
   > Workplace safety, compliance with safety regulations?
   > Fire brigades, emergency response team?
   > First aid, health care?
   > Personnel: Absenteeism, help with personal problems?
   > Insurance?
   > Risk management, risk control?
   > Facilities management: New construction and remodeling?
   > Facilities management: A&E contracts?
   > Facilities management: Maintenance?
   > Facilities management:
   >   Operation of mechanical/electrical systems?
   > Facilities management: Post-earthquake safety inspections?
   > Security?
   > Operational authority for evacuations, building closing?
   > Public relations, press statements?
   > Communications?
   > Food service?
   > Transportation: Personnel, cargo?

7. **Relationship to off-site portions of the organization.** Which communication/transportation/interaction links are the most essential?

8. **Relationship to other organizations.** Which links are essential?

9. **On-site functions.** Which are essential?

Figure 10-5. Information-gathering checklist: Organizational characteristics. Source: Federal Emergency Management Agency.

phones are out. Even if emergency medical services are not provided by the fire department, the radio equipment available at fire stations will allow for communication with other agencies.

In addition to adding earthquake training to other ongoing training programs, it may be reasonable to occasionally devote brief training sessions exclusively to earthquake preparedness. An annual training schedule can easily be coordinated with an annual exercise schedule, as discussed below.

Exercises

A comprehensive site survey can provide estimates of nonstructural vulnerability. These estimates can be used to compile a list of nonstructural damage situations for inclusion in an earthquake scenario to be used for an exercise.

The list of nonstructural damage events may grow lengthy and may include contingencies that would be very costly and disruptive to simulate. For example, full-scale evacuations of high-rise buildings without the use of the elevators are rarely conducted; rather, one or two floors are evacuated periodically. Turning the electricity off will accurately simulate an earthquake-caused power outage and the attendant problems of visibility in windowless office areas, lack of air conditioning, and so on, but this may be too disruptive, or in some cases unsafe, to do throughout an entire office building. In a large company or government office, one department, one wing, or one work area of the building could be included in a more realistic simulation of effects while employees in the remainder of the facility are allowed to function normally or simply participate in a brief "take cover" exercise.

Employees with specialized earthquake response tasks—such as the maintenance personnel who check for water or gas leaks, supervisors who are responsible for checking on the well-being of employees in their areas, and safety or security officers responsible for communications within the building or with outside emergency services—should have more frequent training and exercises. A brief annual exercise, such as having people take cover beneath desks and reminding them not to use elevators after earthquakes, is probably adequate for most employees, whereas more frequently brief drills may be warranted for employees with specialized tasks. An important test of preparedness for nonstructural damage is to check to see whether the responsible personnel can quickly identify which valves to shut in order to control water pipe leakage in any part of the facility.

Personal Emergency Kits

Each employee should be encouraged to have their own Personal Emergency Kit containing a supply of necessary medical prescriptions, a flashlight, portable battery powered radio, a water bottle or soft drink, and an energy bar or some snack food. For women who wear high heels, it may also be useful to keep a pair of flat shoes handy, since evacuation procedures often require women to remove their high heels. Other items like a jacket, mittens, hat, or thermal blanket might be useful depending upon the local climate.

Master Earthquake Planning Checklist

The checklist in Figure 10-6 provides an overview of the tasks involved in establishing an earthquake protection program to address nonstructural components.

Sources

Federal Emergency Management Agency, *Reducing The Risks of Nonstructural Earthquake Damage: A Practical Guide,* Third Edition, FEMA 74/September, 1994 by Wiss, Janney, Elstner Associates, Inc., for the Federal Emergency Management Agency (FEMA) under the National Earthquake Technical Assistance Contract (NETAC) EMW-92-C-3852.

Murphy, Peter, "The Hidden Threat: Earthquakes Can Shake Up Your Facility with Nonstructural Damage," *Today's Facility Manager,* June 1993.

Master Nonstructural Earthquake Protection Checklist

1. **Task:** Establish executive policy requiring a nonstructural evaluation, and allocate funds for initial work.
   Responsibility: Chief Executive Officer, Board of Directors, Executive Committee.
2. **Task:** Survey the facility for nonstructural vulnerabilities.
   Responsibility: Outside consultant or in-house engineering, maintenance, safety or other department.
3. **Task:** Analyze the conditions, and estimate future earthquake effects.
   Responsibility: Same as for No. 2.
4. **Task:** Develop a list of nonstructural items to be upgraded, with priorities and cost estimates. (If a facilities development guideline document is to be produced, coordinate performance criteria to be used on future new construction and upgrade standards.)
   Responsibility: Same as for No. 2; may include bids from contractors.
5. **Task:** Decide what items will be upgraded, how the work will be done, and by whom.
   Responsibility: Same as for No. 1, with input from No. 2.
6. **Task:** Implement the upgrade program.
   Responsibility: In-house staff or contractors, with administration of contracting or tasking by No. 2 or in-house construction administrators.
7. **Task:** Develop an earthquake response plan that contemplates nonstructural damage, with pre-emergency, during, and post-emergency earthquake tasks and responsibilities itemized.
   Responsibility: Consultant or in-house safety or other department, with general policy and budgeting, same as for No. 1.
8. **Task:** Train personnel in accordance with the plan in No. 7.
   Responsibility: Training, safety or other department.
9. **Task:** Plan and implement exercises that will test the training of No. 8 and the planning of No. 7.
   Responsibility: Same as for No. 7 or No. 8.
10. **Task:** Evaluate the performance of the above program, preferably within one year after inception or according to the deadlines set in an implementation schedule, and annually thereafter.
    Responsibility: Same as for No. 1 in smaller organizations, or same as for No. 7.

Figure 10-6. Master nonstructural earthquake protection checklist.
Source: Federal Emergency Management Agency.

Chapter 11

Violence
In The Workplace

Homicides, robberies, beatings, sexual assaults—sounds like crime stories on life in an urban America broadcast on the News at 11, right? These are also the types of violent acts that occur in the workplace far too often. Although a well-planned and carefully developed violence prevention program cannot address every potentially violent incident, facility managers can minimize the risk of violence and its serious consequences.

CRIME IN THE WORKPLACE: AN OVERVIEW

The Bureau of Labor Statistics (BLS) reports that workplace homicides have declined over 50% since 1994. And while that figure shows significant improvement, homicide is still one of the four most frequent causes of workplace fatality. (See Table 11-1).

A specific category of violent crime, workplace violence is more than a physical attack. According to the FBI, homicide, as well as other physical assaults, is on a continuum that includes domestic violence, stalking, threats, harassment and bullying. Emotional abuse, intimidation and other forms of conduct that create anxiety, fear or a climate of distrust in the workplace falls into this definition.

Categories of Workplace Violence

The FBI classifies workplace violence into four broad categories:

1. Violence committed by criminals who enter to commit robbery or another crime and who have no connection with the workplace;

2. Violence directed at employees by customers, clients, patients, etc., for whom an organization provides service;

3. Violence against co-workers, supervisors or managers by a present or former employee; and,

4. Violence committed in the workplace by someone who is personally involved with an employee such as an abusive spouse, domestic partner, boyfriend or girlfriend, etc.

A closer look provides a clearer understanding of which occupations or employee groups are most at risk.

Category 1. Violence by criminals otherwise unconnected to the workplace accounts for nearly 80 % of workplace homicides. In these incidents the motive is usually theft, and in many cases the criminal is carrying a gun or other weapon which increases the likelihood that the victim will be killed or seriously wounded. Occupational groups that are more vulnerable to the category 1 are taxi drivers, late-night retail or gas station clerks and others who are on duty at night who work in isolated locations or dangerous neighborhoods and who, in fact, carry cash or have access to cash.

Preventive strategies for this category emphasize physical security measures, special employer or company policies in employee training. The FBI notes that reasons for the decline in workplace homicides since the early 1990's is due to the safety and security measures adopted by companies or businesses that may be particularly vulnerable.

Category 2. This violence involves assaults on employees by either customers, patients or someone who is receiving a service. Violence usually occurs while the employees are performing their normal jobs. Dealing with dangerous people is part and parcel of certain occupations, e.g., police, corrections personnel, security guards, or mental health workers. However, violence can erupt anywhere or anytime when a customer or patient is angry at the quality of service, denial of service, or a delay in provision of service.

The largest numbers of these assaults are those who work in health care—doctors, nurses and aides, as well as emergency medical response teams. Also included are those hospital employees who work in admissions, emergency rooms, crisis and acute care units.

Table 11-1. The four most frequent work-related fatal events, 1992-2008*

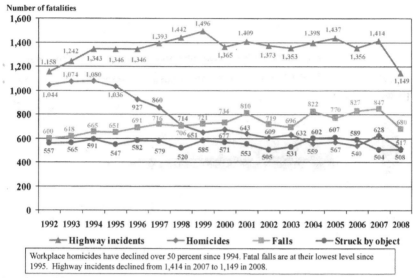

Number of fatalities

—▲— Highway incidents —◆— Homicides —■— Falls —●— Struck by object

Workplace homicides have declined over 50 percent since 1994. Fatal falls are at their lowest level since 1995. Highway incidents declined from 1,414 in 2007 to 1,149 in 2008.

*Data for 2008 are preliminary. Data for prior years are revised and final.
NOTE: Data from 2001 exclude fatalities resulting from the September 11 terrorist attacks.
SOURCE: U.S. Bureau of Labor Statistics, U.S. Department of Labor, 2009.

Categories 3 and 4. These incidents involve forms of violence committed by past or present employees as well as violent acts committed by domestic abusers or by stalking. Violence in these categories is equally as dangerous or damaging as any other form of violent act. However, when these types of violence comes from either employees or someone close to the employee there is a greater chance that warning signs have already presented themselves. This knowledge along with an appropriate prevention training program can mitigate the potential for the violence.

WORKPLACE VIOLENCE—THE COST

Preliminary statistics provided by the Bureau of Labor Statistics show that in 2008 there were a total of 517 workplace homicides of which 413 were the results of shootings.

These alarming statistics have sobering consequences for everyone.

Most significant, of course, is the needless loss of human life. Companies and their employees are thrown into a tailspin when senseless acts of violence occur. From an economic perspective, companies lose millions of dollars in lost productivity and downtime. A study of the effects of workplace violence conducted by the U.S. Department of Justice revealed that workplace violence costs employers millions of lost workdays each year. These lost workdays translate into millions of dollars of lost wages. Also impacted by workplace violence are the legal and security costs, medical costs, and worker's compensation costs.

From a human perspective, the toll is even more exacting. Employees who are the victims of violence, as well as their co-workers, can and often do ride an emotional roller coaster. Reaction to violence in the workplace can manifest itself in various ways.

Workers can and often do experience heightened anxiety as well as depression. Anger—itself a significant factor in violence, nightmares, sleeplessness, withdrawal, paranoia and, in some cases, substance abuse—is a common response to violence-induced stress.

EMPLOYER RESPONSE

Since the issue of workplace violence is first and foremost a safety issue, facility managers must be prepared to assist employers in responding to the issue. However, before a response can be prepared, several questions need to be answered.

Since there is an Occupational Safety and Health Administration (OSHA) requirement that employers are required to provide to provide "a safe and healthful working environment" for their employees the question is—what are employers required to do in order to provide this "safe and healthful working environment"?

What can employers do to prevent violence from occurring?

What should employers do to assist employees—victims as well as co-workers—to cope with the after-effects of the violent act?

Employer Requirements

There are no specific regulatory standards that govern workplace violence. Two significant "actions," however, have taken place. The Secretary of Labor has directed OSHA to study the issue of workplace violence to determine why more than 8,000 workers have been killed since 1980. And OSHA has issued safety and security guidelines for health care and community services workers.

These guidelines can suggest the possible direction that employers will be required to take regarding workplace violence. *The Guidelines for Security and Safety and Health Care and Community Service Workers* stresses the need for a written program for job, safety, health and security.

The Written Safety Program

A written safety program should be developed and incorporated into the Disaster and Recovery Plan. This written safety program, depending upon the size of the company, begins with a planning group. This planning group should evaluate the company's current capability to response to incidents of workplace violence. Once evaluated, recommendations for response improvement should be defined.

Who should be included in this planning group? Again, depending upon the size of the company, representatives from management, Employee Relations, Employee Assistance, Facility, Security, Public Relations, Employee Unions and Personnel should be involved. In smaller companies, the Facility manager alone may be responsible. In any event, the company's legal department should also be consulted once recommendations are finalized.

Once the planning group is formed, what are the steps involved in the planning process? The General Services Administration suggests:

1. Analyze the company's current ability to handle potentially violent situations.
2. Fill the skills gap.
3. Develop an employee-reporting procedure.
4. Develop a response plan.

The written safety program, which begins with analyzing the worksite, includes reviewing a company's client type, physical facility/site, staffing levels, lighting, accessibility to the physical facility and prior security problems. According to the GSA, a written safety program has several advantages including:

• Informing employees what the policy covers;
• Encouraging employees to report incidents;
• Informing employees whom to call; and

- Demonstrating senior management's commitment in dealing with reported incidents.

The program's effectiveness is further enhanced by securing top management and employee commitment and involvement. Other core components of the written safety program include involving law enforcement agencies and the ongoing training and education of all employees.

The Policy Statement
The workplace violence policy statement should include the following:

- The types of offenses that contribute to workplace violence: physical violence, harassment, intimidation and other disruptive behavior;
- The types of incidents involving individuals: employee to employee, and client/customer/non-employee to employee incidents;
- The responsibility of employees for maintaining a safe work environment;
- The company response to all reported incidents;
- The company actions to stop inappropriate behavior; and
- The assurance of management support.

The success of the violence prevention program rests with all employees—management as well as "rank and file"—to recognize the potential for violence and knowing how to respond to the violent act.

Recognizing the Warning Signs of Violence
There are certain behavioral characteristics that people with a propensity towards violence share. Given the "right" setting, individuals who fit the "profile" of a violence-prone individual may react to a situation, or set of circumstances, violently. While analyzing past incidents of workplace violence, The Federal Bureau of Investigation's (FBI's) National Center for the Analysis of Violent Crime (NAVC), Profiling and Behavior Assessment Unit identified some of the indicators of increased risk of violent behavior. These include:

• Direct or veiled threats of harm;

• Intimidating, belligerent, harassing, bullying, or other inappropriate and aggressive behavior;

• Numerous conflicts with supervisors and other employees;

• Bringing in a weapon to the workplace, brandishing a weapon in the workplace; making inappropriate references to guns, or fascination with weapons;

• Statements made by individuals:
  — Showing fascination with incidents or workplace violence;
  — Indicating approval of the use of violence to resolve a problem;
  — Indicating identification with perpetrators of workplace homicides;
  — Indicating desperation (over family, financial, and other personal problems) to the point of contemplating suicide;

• Drug/alcohol abuse; and

• Extreme changes in behavior.

An employee facing such problems as a job layoff or termination, stressful family situations such as a death, divorce, etc., or an employee suffering from mental illness or who is in therapy, are also indicators that can lead someone into physical violence.

However, it is important to keep in mind that employers should not automatically presume that a person "fitting" the profile will commit a violent act. About 20 percent of individuals who fit the profile are not any more likely to be violent than most people.

Workplace Violence Prevention—Responsibilities

Who is responsible for the safety of employees and staff of a company/industry? All employees involved share in the responsibility for maintaining a safe work environment. The following section, outlined by the United States Department of Agriculture (USDA), provides a more detailed description of the responsibilities of various persons or offices including:

- Employees.
- Managers and Supervisors.
- Department Heads.
- Human Resources Staff.
- Employee Assistance Program Counselors.
- Union Employee Organizations.
- Facilities Staff.
- Security Staff.
- Law Enforcement Staff.
- Conflict Resolution Offices.

Employee Responsibilities

- Be familiar with the company policy regarding workplace violence.
- Be responsible for securing their own workplace.
- Be responsible for questioning and/or reporting strangers to supervisors.
- Be aware of any threats, physical or verbal, and/or any disruptive behavior of any individual and report such to supervisors.
- Be familiar with the procedures for dealing with workplace threats and emergencies.
- Do not confront threatening individuals.
- Take all threats seriously.

Manager and Supervisor Responsibilities

- Inform employees of company policies and procedures.

- Ensure that employees know specific procedures for dealing with workplace threats and emergencies including how to contact police, fire and other safety and security personnel.

- Ensure that employees with special needs are aware of emergency evacuation procedures and have assistance (as necessary) regarding emergency evacuation situations.

- Respond to potential threats and escalating situations by utilizing proper resources from the following: local law enforcement and medical services, human resources staff and the Employee Assistance Program, if available.

• Take all threats seriously.

• Check prospective employees' background prior to hiring.

Department Head Responsibilities

• Develop a policy statement reflecting that the company will not tolerate violent or disruptive behavior and that all reported incidents will be taken seriously.

• Ensure that the company's workplace prevention policy is available to employees.

• Ensure that employees are aware of the policies, procedures and instructions in the company policy.

• Ensure that safety and law enforcement personnel have completed an on-site review of the safety and security of the building and offices.

• Provide adequate resources for employee training and awareness.

• Ensure that performance standards of appropriate staff reflect the importance of workplace safety and security.

• Provide for briefings on workplace violence at staff meetings.

Human Resources Staff Responsibilities

• Provide for supervisory training which includes basic leadership skills such as:
— Setting clear standards of conduct and performance.
— Addressing employee problems promptly.
— Using the probationary periods, performance counseling, discipline, and other management tools conscientiously.

• Provide technical expertise and consultation to help supervisors determine what course of administrative action is most appropriate in specific situations.

• Determine whether disciplinary action should be taken.

- Help supervisors determine proper reasonable accommodation.

Employee Assistance Program Counselor Responsibilities

- Provide short-term counseling and referral services to employees at no cost.

- Help in the prevention of workplace violence through:
  — Early involvement in organizational change.
  — Training employees in dealing with angry co-workers and customers; conflict resolution and communication skills.
  — Training supervisors to deal with problems as soon as they surface without diagnosing the employee's problem.
  — Consultation with supervisors to identify specific problem areas, develop action plans to resolve problems in the early stages, and encourage employees to contact the EAP, if available, for individual counseling.
  — Consultation with incident response teams when a potential for violence exists or an actual incident is reported.
  — Participation on critical incident stress debriefing teams in the event of a violent situation.

Union/Employee Organization Responsibilities

- Be familiar with and actively support policy and contract language on workplace violence prevention.

- Stay alert to security issues and potential threats.

- Be aware of procedures for addressing workplace threats and emergencies.

- Be aware of the Employee Assistance Program including the procedures/policy regarding the ability of designated union officials to make employee referrals to the EAP.

- Work closely with all levels of management to ensure that employees are up-to-date on company workplace violence prevention policy and procedures.

- Participate fully with management in all phases of workplace violence prevention and response, including membership on threat assessment and incident response teams.

Facilities Staff/Securities Staff Responsibilities

- Serve as the liaison with law enforcement as well as the company expert on security matters.

- Conduct regular threat assessment survey of the facility to determine the level of security preparedness and any gaps in the security posture.

- Serve as the facility security expert, keeping management advised of the risk of violence, the security gaps identified by threat assessments, and the means to close these gaps, including the latest technologies.

- Work with facility personnel to improve the security levels of the buildings, grounds, parking lots, etc.

- Train facility personnel in security measures and violence prevention techniques.

Facilities personnel should work closely with security staff to ensure that the buildings, areas and grounds are safe for employees and visitors. This includes not only keeping buildings and grounds well maintained but participating with security personnel in threat assessment surveys, keeping management informed of the status of the physical plan, and providing budget request with justification for security upgrades.

Law Enforcement Staff Responsibilities

- Identify in advance the types of situations that may occur and when and how law enforcement should be notified of an incident.
- Indicate whether law enforcement officers have jurisdictional restrictions and identify alternative law enforcement agencies that may be able to provide assistance.
- Indicate whether law enforcement officers have arrest authority.
- Provide threat assessment personnel who can assist the company in determining the best way to protect personnel.
- Suggest safety and security measures that need to be implemented.
- Arrange for all-employee briefings or training on specific workplace violence issues.

Workplace Violence Prevention—Employee Training

An effective workplace violence prevention training program that emphasizes management's commitment to employee safety is an important component of a company's disaster prevention plan. The training program must emphasize that management will take a proactive approach to reported incidents of threats, intimidation, harassment, etc. The training program should inform employees that:

• Management will take reports of threats seriously;

• Incidents should be reported; and

• Management is committed to deal with the reported incidents.

The training program should also emphasize that:

• All employees should know how to report incidents of violent, intimidating, threatening and other disruptive behavior.

• All employees should know the procedures for reporting incidents, including the phone number of the appropriate personnel during a crisis or an emergency.

• Additionally, workplace violence prevention training for employees may also include the following topics:
    — Explanation of the company's workplace violence policy;
    — Encouragement to report incidents;
    — Ways of preventing or diffusing volatile situations or aggressive behavior;
    — How to deal with hostile persons;
    — Managing anger;
    — Techniques and skills to resolve conflicts;
    — Stress management, relaxation techniques, wellness training;
    — Security procedures, e.g., the location and operation of safety devices such as alarm systems.

• Supervisory training for workplace violence prevention may also include:
    — Ways to encourage employees to report incidents in which they feel threatened for any reason by anyone inside or outside the organization;

— Skills in behaving compassionately and supportively towards employees who report incidents;
— Skills in taking disciplinary actions;
— Basic skills in handling crisis situations;
— Basic emergency procedures, and
— How to ensure that appropriate screening of pre-employment references has been done.

Workplace Violence Checklist

Table 11-2 can be used to identify and evaluate workplace security hazards. Please note that **"TRUE" indicates a potential risk for serious security hazards.**

Handling Threats

Employees should be encouraged to report any and all threats made against them to their supervisor. Threats, no matter how innocuous or trivial they may appear, carry the potential for violence. Therefore, prompt response to a reported threat should be a priority for management.

When appropriate, management should consult with their legal department for the best course of action to take.

Employee Relations Considerations

Knowledge of employee relations plays an integral role in the prevention and response to potentially violent workplace actions. The Employee Relations Department can:

- Help in coordinating effective responses;

- Determine the administrative options available for the removal of potentially dangerous employees;

- Determine what resources are needed depending upon the situation;

- Ensure that disciplinary actions are taken for violent, threatening, harassing, and other disruptive behavior;

- Draft a response to an employee who raises the issue of a medical condition and/or disability as a defense against the behavior;

Table 11-2. Workplace Violence Checklist. Source: Occupational Safety and Health Administration (OSHA).

T	F	This industry frequently confronts violent behavior and assaults of staff.
T	F	Violence has occurred on the premises or in conducting business.
T	F	Customers, clients, or coworkers assault, threaten, yell, push, or verbally abuse employees or use racial slurs or sexually explicit remarks.
T	F	Employees are **NOT** required to report incidents or threats of violence, regardless of injury or severity to the employer.
T	F	Employees have **NOT** been trained by the employer to recognize and handle threatening aggressive or violent behavior.
T	F	Violence is accepted as "part of the job" by some managers, supervisors, and/or employees.
T	F	Access and freedom of movement within the workplace are **NOT** restricted to those persons who have a legitimate reason for being there.
T	F	The workplace security system is inadequate—i.e., door locks malfunction, windows are not secure, and there are no physical barriers or containments systems.
T	F	Employees or staff members have been assaulted, threatened, or verbally abused by clients and patients.
T	F	Mediation and counseling services have **NOT** been offered to employees who have been assaulted.

Table 11-2. (*Continued*)

T	F	Alarm systems such as panic alarm buttons, silent alarms, or personal electronic alarm systems are **NOT** being used for prompt security assistance.
T	F	There is no regular training provided on correct response to alarm sounding.
T	F	Alarm systems are **NOT** tested on a monthly basis to assure correct function.
T	F	Security guards are **NOT** employed at the workplace.
T	F	Closed circuit cameras and mirrors are **NOT** used to monitor danger areas.
T	F	Metal detectors are **NOT** available or **NOT** used in the facility.
T	F	Employees have **NOT** been trained to recognize and control hostile and escalating aggressive behaviors, and to manage assault behavior.
T	F	Employees **CANNOT** adjust work schedules to use the "Buddy system" for visits to clients in areas where they feel threatened.
T	F	Cellular phones or other communication devices are **NOT** made available to field staff enabling them to request aid.
T	F	Vehicles are **NOT** maintained on a regular basis to ensure reliability and safety.
T	F	Employees work where assistance is **NOT** quickly available.

- Order and offer psychiatric examinations;

- Provide information on appeals of disciplinary actions.

Security Measures

Maintaining a physically safe workplace is part of any good prevention program. There are a variety of security measures to help ensure safety. These include:

- Employee photo identification badges;

- On-site guard services and/or individually coded card keys for access to buildings and areas within buildings according to individual needs; and

- Assistance in registering, badging and directing visitors in larger facilities.

Workplace Security

Whether a company has its own in-house security staff, contracts with private security firms, or depends upon local law enforcement, a plan should be in place for a workplace violence prevention program involving the coordination of all these units. Planning a program for the prevention of workplace violence begins by working with and coordinating the services of the various law enforcement organizations

Meeting with the local police department can help establish a procedure regarding law enforcement response in the event of an incident or potential incident. Once a plan has been formulated and coordinated between the company and local law enforcement, open lines of communication should exist to avoid later misunderstandings of which department—in-house, off-site or local law enforcement—is responsible when an incident occurs.

In the initial planning stage, the following can be determined by the law enforcement/security officers:

- Identify the types of situations they can address and when and how notification of an incident takes place;

- Indicate whether their officers have arrest authority;

- Identify jurisdictional restrictions;

- Identify alternative law enforcement agencies that can provide assistance;

- Identify threat assessment professionals who can assist in the protection of threatened employees;

- Explain anti-stalking laws;

- Explain how and when to obtain restraining orders;

- Suggest security measures to be taken for specific situations;

- Advise on what evidence is necessary and how it can be collected/ recorded;

- Arrange for supervisory employee briefings or training on specific workplace violence issues such as:
  — Personal safety and security measures;
  — Types of incidents to report to law enforcement/security;
  — Types of measures law enforcement/security may take to protect employees;
  — Suggestions on how to react to an armed attacker;
  — Suggestions for dealing with angry customers or clients;
  — Suspicious packages;
  — Bomb threats;
  — Hostage situations and;
  — Telephone harassment and threats.

The Violence Protection Program: A Basic Action Plan

One major component of any workplace violence program is prevention. This section will focus on additional measures that can be taken to reduce the risk of violent behavior.

Incorporating OSHA's *Guidelines for Security and Safety of Health Care and Community Service Workers* into a company-specific violence prevention program includes four basic action-planning steps: coordinating a team effort; developing emergency notification procedures; defining employee counseling procedures and developing communications strategies.

The primary safety officer of the company, often the facility manager, needs to assemble a "crisis management team." With top management representation and participation, the team should be comprised of key managers including internal and external safety and security personnel, medical personnel, legal counsel, human resources staff, employee assistance professionals, employee representatives and public relations support.

The specific responsibilities of the company's crisis management team are to:

1. Determine how the issue of workplace violence will be addressed in the company.

2. Develop procedures for notifying team members, internal security, local law enforcement, other employees, the general public and family members, when an emergency arises.

3. Define procedures for providing counseling to employees in terms of:
    a. What services will be provided to employees within the crucial 24-48 hours following the incident, as well as long-term services.
    b. Where will counseling services be provided (i.e., on site versus alternate location).

4. Develop communications strategies for addressing manager and employee concerns regarding return-to-work and pay issues. A generic press release must also be predeveloped, along with specific criteria that detail what to say and what not to say to the media. Damage control strategies that are designed to protect the company's name and reputation must also be defined.

WORKPLACE VIOLENCE AS A LIABILITY ISSUE

Because employers are required to provide a safe working environment, the question of liability takes on a special significance when a violent incident occurs. When an employee commits a violent act that injures a co-worker or third party, the employer can be held liable. The key to determining employer liability rests with the issue of negligence. Negligence in either hiring a new employee or in retaining persons with a propensity towards violence assumes a violation of the employer's general duty to provide a safe working environment. Therefore, it is necessary to take precautions in hiring a new person, and in monitoring current employee behavior.

Hiring New Workers

The human resources department, which pre-screens job applicants before referring then to the hiring manager, can also arrange for pre-employment tests, as well as medical examinations when and where appropriate, and only in conjunction with criteria established by the spectrum of employment law (e.g., ADA).

Department and division managers, and facility managers also have an additional mechanism in place to assist them. The introductory or probationary period is the most opportune time to closely scrutinize new employees and to terminate them when necessary and when it is appropriate to do so.

Retaining Employees

Retaining employees is contingent, of course, upon performance. However, other factors come into play as well. Employee behavior, adhering to policies, procedures and work practices are also taken into consideration. Any deviation from the established "norms" should be addressed quickly and aggressively.

While disciplining employees is never easy, it is essential to maintaining business and department operations, and doing so in a safe environment. Documenting an employee's poor performance and/or inappropriate behavior is the key to effective discipline. Consistency in application is the corner stone of an equitable disciplinary policy.

Limiting Exposure to Liability

OSHA's *Safety And Health Program Management (Voluntary) Guidelines*, as well as *The Voluntary Guidelines for Health Care And Community Service Workers* discussed earlier in this chapter, emphasizes the importance of training.

In all matters related to safety management, including violence prevention, training is of paramount importance. Training that addresses the issue of discipline, recognizing "troubled employees," diffusing the hostile situation and ensuring ADA compliance, should be provided routinely to managers and supervisors.

Training that focuses on employee responsibilities to maintain a safe working environment includes:

- Policy and safe work practices and procedures.
- Employer notification of real and potential problems.
- Appropriate behavior response in potentially violent situations.
- Emergency evacuation (and self-removal) procedures.

Employee training should be conducted regularly and incorporated into the overall employee training program.

Recovery After An Incident

Planning for workplace violence protection is a necessary part of the disaster/recovery plan. It cannot, however, stop someone determined to commit violence from committing that violent act. Therefore, management should be prepared for the recovery aspect of a violent incident. Listed below are several steps management can take initially when a violent incident occurs:

- Ensure that there is a management presence in the worksite.
- Share information with employees.
- Include union leadership.
- Bring in crisis response professionals.
- Support informal debriefing.
- Support care-giving within work groups.
- Handle critical sites with care.
- Buffer those affected from post-event stresses.
- Help employees face feared places or activities.
- Remember the healing value of work.

Ensure a management presence in the worksite. When management is visible, it sends a signal to employees that management is concerned for employee welfare and well-being and will answer any question/concerns that employees may have.

Share information with employees. Communication between management and employees should be open—employees will have questions that need to be answered to help resolve the effects of the incident in their own minds. When information becomes available to management, management should pass that information on to employees simply and directly. "Hotlines," message boards, etc., are some effective ways to disseminate basic information. Individuals who have questions should be provided with a user-friendly system to answer those questions.

Include union leadership. Union representatives can help reassure employees as well as get information to them.

Use crisis response professionals. Mental health professionals from either the company's Employee Assistance Program and/or the community should be brought in as soon as possible. These counselors would offer such services as debriefing, defusing and informal counseling.

Support informal debriefing. Employees should be provided with opportunities to talk informally even after the formal debriefing process. These informal debriefings could occur during break times.

Support care-giving within work groups. Employees should not be isolated from their normal support groups at work. Employees generally will need to support and care for one another.

Handle critical sites with care. The site of a violent incident will most likely be secured as a crime scene. Once the crime scene becomes "un-secured," every effort should be made to clean up the affected site without making it sterile.

Buffer those affected from post-event stresses. To reduce the pressure of the media from the vulnerable employees/family members, management should coordinate information to the media and provide timely dissemination of information.

Help employees face feared places or activities. Having a friend or loved one at the site, or being supported by close work associates, may make returning to the site easier for the employee.

Remember the healing value of work. Returning to a sense of normalcy by getting back to work can help the healing process. The return to work should also be tempered with respect for the deceased, injured and/or traumatized.

Sources

Gustin, Joseph F., *Safety Management: A Guide For Facility Managers*, 2nd ed., Lilburn, GA: The Fairmont Press, Inc., 2008.

May, Barry, *Security Management: A Guide for Facility Managers*, New York: The Facilities Management Library, UpWord Publishing, Inc., 1996.

United States Department of Agriculture, *The USDA Handbook On Workplace Violence Prevention And Response*. AD-1135. October, 2001.

United States Department of Labor, Bureau of Labor Statistics, *Census of Fatal Occupational Injuries 2008*.

United States Department of Justice, Federal Bureau of Investigation, Critical Incident Response Group, National Center for the Analysis of Violent Crime, *Workplace Violence: Issues in Response*. 2002.

United States Office of Personnel Management, Office of Workforce Relations, *Dealing With Workplace Violence, A Guide for Agency Planners*. OWR-09, February, 1998.

Chapter 12

Computer and Data Protection

Many organizations depend upon computer systems for continuity of their operations. With the possible exception of the smallest of business enterprises, computers and electronic data processing systems serve as a company's "lifeline." It is not surprising, then, that computer and electronic data systems protection becomes a high priority for many companies.

COMPUTER AND EDP SYSTEMS PROTECTION

The most serious threat to a facility's computer/EDP system is fire. Whether a fire originates within the area that houses the system (e.g., the data center), or whether fire originates outside the area, the potential loss to the facility can have a deleterious effect on the continuity of operations.

Fire Hazards

In assessing potential fire hazards, attention should focus on the various components that comprise the system, as well as the system's environment.

Mainframe equipment, as well as auxiliary system equipment, is encased in sheet metal housing and does not necessarily present a fire hazard. However, cables and wiring, printed and integrated circuitry, transistors, as well as various insulators used in the systems, are combustible. Additionally, smaller equipment is encased in rigid plastics. Plastics, regardless of composition, density and/or tensile strength, are combustible. When plastics burn, the vapors that are emitted may combine with oxygen and moisture, causing electronic circuitry to corrode. The corrosion may be exacerbated by increased temperatures at the source of the fire. Smoke and its residue (i.e., soot) can settle on equipment and components, causing damage and malfunctioning of equipment and components. Additionally, water from fire suppression/sprinkler systems that falls on circuits may cause the circuitry to malfunction or short-circuit.

Other fire hazards, which can be described as content hazards, include the various forms of media used in computer operations. Disks, reels, magnetic tapes and cassettes can readily fuel a fire, while also serving as a ready source of vapor release.

Additional content hazards include the various kinds of paper supplies, materials and office products that are typically stored in a facility's data center. Furnishings, whether of wood, plastic or composite construction—as well as wall, floor and ceiling coverings, insulation, lighting fixtures, ventilation systems and ductwork—are core considerations in assessing fire hazards in the data center.

External Hazards

Data center operations are vulnerable to external factors that present the potential for hazards, as well. Some of these external factors include:

- The energized electrical equipment that is not part of data operations, but which can create exposure to computer systems, when such other equipment malfunctions.

- Electrical power system interruptions, overloading, power surges, etc., can create conditions that can fault circuits and pave the way for ignition.

- Fires that originate in other areas of the facility, as well as smoke that travels to the data center from those fires, can damage computers and peripheral equipment.

Risk Assessment

In assessing the potential risk to computer and electronic data processing functions, facility managers and the planning team must consider the factors that are critical to data center operations. These factors include:

- Building and data center site design.

- Contents and furnishings.

- Fire and smoke detection systems.

- Fire and smoke suppression systems.

- Response measures.

- Maintenance.

- Recovery.

Building and Data Center Design—Ideally, a company's data center should be located in a separate fire-resistant facility. However, the data center operations of many companies share tenancy with other business functions of the company. When this is the case, the data center should be located in areas that are:

- Both smoke-tight and protected by fire-resistant walls (minimum of one-hour fire resistance).

- Equipped with doors which have a fire-resistance rating equal to that of the walls.

- Located away from any business function whose operations involve the use, handling, transport or storage of hazardous and combustible materials.

Additionally, installation of any wall-intrusive cables, wiring, etc. should be plugged or sealed with appropriate fire-resistant materials.

Provision should also be made for a dedicated ventilation system, and air pressure within the data center should be maintained at slightly higher levels to prevent any smoke/fumes from reaching the area.

Contents and Furnishings—Any systems that are used to store various data center media and vital records should also have a fire-resistant rating of one hour.

Furnishings such as desks, chairs, filing systems, etc., that are located in the data center, should be constructed of non-combustible materials.

Fire and Smoke Detection Systems—Fire and smoke detection systems are prerequisite loss-prevention considerations. Upon detection, such systems can activate alarms, disengage electrical current to mainframes and other computer systems and peripheral equipment. Additionally, such systems can engage, or activate fire suppression systems.

Fire Suppression Systems—Fire suppression systems play a critical role in data center loss prevention. The traditional approach to fire suppression involved the use of halons (specifically, Halon 1301) as an extinguishing agent in computer centers and other vital records areas (e.g., a hospital's medical records department). However, since halons were determined to be agents that deplete the earth's ozone layer, production was halted as of January 1, 1994, the result of an international agreement known as the Montreal Protocol.

An alternative gaseous suppression system is a carbon dioxide system. Its use, however, must be restricted to areas within the data center that are either unattended, or which operate on a delayed activation basis. The time-delay is essential because carbon dioxide systems are oxygen depleting. Personnel must be provided with "lead time" to vacate the area.

Like other gaseous suppression systems, a carbon dioxide system is particularly effective when the area/material to be protected is vitally crucial to an organization. Carbon dioxide systems have very rapid extinguishing capabilities. Provided that the data center is "tightly" constructed (in order to prevent escape of the gas), a fast build-up of gas occurs, quickly extinguishing fire and smoke.

Unlike heat-sensitive systems that are activated only after certain temperatures are reached, the gaseous suppression system quickly engages at the early stages of a fire. Hence, damage from smoke is minimized, preventing serious loss to the data system and to the various media used by the data system.

Response Measures—There are a number of response measures that are available to a company in the event of a data center-located fire. Any of these response measures, however, are contingent upon well-trained personnel who are not only familiar with data center operations, but who are also familiar with the methods and procedures of emergency response. These basic methods and procedures include:

- Using the portable extinguishing equipment that serves as a first-line defense in fighting the localized fire.

- Ensuring that automatic suppression systems are operating.

- Turning off power sources.

- Notifying the local fire department and appropriate facility personnel.

All of these response measures, however, are only effective if personnel are properly and thoroughly trained in procedures and methods use.

Maintenance—As with any other aspect of disaster and emergency preparedness, regular inspection and maintenance of fire protection systems must be routinely conducted. Fire protection systems, including portable extinguishers, must be properly charged with the appropriate agent. An actual fire is not the most opportune time to find out that the extinguisher has not been filled.

After each use, automated sprinkler/extinguishing systems should be checked and cleaned to ensure utility and full operability when and if such systems are needed again. Routine inspection, as part of a company's regularly scheduled maintenance program, ensures maximum effectiveness of the systems.

Recovery—Because of the critical role that computers and data operations play in an organization, recovery efforts take on a particular significance.

As part of planning for recovery, specialists in data/equipment/media/records restoration should be identified in order to ensure their availability when disaster strikes. Following an occurrence, restoration specialists can be deployed to begin data salvage and recovery measures.

In addition to measures performed by restoration specialists, company personnel should undertake the various measures that are required to limit exposure to water and smoke damage. Some of these measures may include covering stationery equipment, removing portable equipment, files, media, work-in-progress, and ensuring that power sources are de-energized.

Response measures such as these can minimize the impact of a data center fire on company operations and can expedite the recovery process.

TELECOMMUNICATIONS PROTECTION

Below are a few tips to improve telecommunications protection, some of which are based on an article by Les Baxter (a technical manager) and Massod Shariff (a systems engineer) of AT&T Bell Laboratories in Middletown, NJ, published in the May 1994 issue of *Today's Facility Manager*:

Star Network Configuration—A telecommunications or data system's "topolog" indicates the arrangement of the input/output devices. The designer has three choices—star, ring and linear bus. Telephone systems and some local area networks (LANs) are of the star configuration. Star configurations are most advantageous in disaster situations. In a star configuration, all input/output devices are connected to a main hub. Cables branch off to isolated work areas. With this configuration, a power outage to one or more work areas will not affect the others.

Ring Network Configuration—Ring configurations, as the name implies, are where input/output devices at individual work areas are linked in a circle. Therefore, the chain is only as strong as its weakest link. If a ring configuration is in use, consider adding another ring as a back-up, a design called "dual-ring architecture." If the ring in use fails, the back-up ring will ensure continuity of operations.

Redundancy—The redundancy feature discussed above in Ring Configuration can be duplicated for other aspects of the telecommunications infrastructure. Network cables that enter the building can be duplicated to enter the building at another location. Cables within the building that connect floors can be duplicated to enter each floor at a different location.

Firestopping—Holes through walls and floors to permit wiring and cabling to connect distant work areas are fire-stopped during installation—that is, they are sealed to resist fire coming through the holes. Make sure that when new cables and wires are installed between floors, that they are also fire-stopped.

Automation—The routing system can be automated so that if a failure occurs, appropriate data links can be rerouted immediately and automatically.

ELEMENTS OF COMPUTER SECURITY

An effective computer security program consists of physical security, administrative security and technical protections. Technical security alone cannot protect sensitive or proprietary company information. Controls need to be in place to limit physical access to the facility. In addition, the facility's climate and its power issues also affect the information systems. Therefore, to protect the information system most fully the following areas need to be addressed:

- Physical access.
- Climate.
- Fire safety/suppression.
- Electrical power and
- Data.

Physical Access Controls

Physical access controls restrict the entry and exit of personnel and help protect the disappearance of equipment and media from a facility. These controls need to address the elements required for the operation of the system including: the location of the system hardware, the locations of the peripheral or system support wiring, supporting services, back-up media, etc.

Once these controls are put into place it is important to periodically test the effectiveness of these controls in each of the affected areas. These tests should be conducted at varying times including both occupied and unoccupied times.

Climate

Computer systems are sensitive to high temperatures and also generate significant amounts of heat. Therefore the climate control of the data center becomes a major area of concern. Climate control units should be appropriate for the size of the data center room. These units should also be appropriately sized for the heat output of the computer systems located in the room. Ideally, these units should have a built-in notification system that activates if the temperature of the room is not normal or if a failure of the system occurs.

Another area of climate concern in the data center is the water that condenses around HVAC systems. This water should be removed from the room, since computers are also in danger from water.

Fire Safety/Suppression

Building fires are a serious security threat. Fires pose the risk to human life, the potential destruction of hardware and data and the damage caused from smoke and corrosive gases. As previously discussed, smoke, corrosive gases and high humidity from a localized fire can damage systems throughout an entire building. Also, water from fire suppression/sprinkler systems falling on circuits and/or equipment may cause that circuitry or equipment to malfunction or short-circuit. Therefore, only non-water suppression systems should be used in data centers.

Failure of Supporting Utilities

Power spikes, HVAC malfunctions, plumbing leaks, sewage overflows, and other utility failures can cause system interruptions and may damage the computer hardware.. Facility managers should ensure that these utilities, including their many elements, function properly.

Plumbing Leaks—Plumbing leaks, although infrequent, can be seriously disruptive. The facility manager should take care to note the location of plumbing lines that might endanger system hardware and take the necessary steps to reduce risk (e.g., moving hardwire, relocating plumbing lines, and identifying shutoff valves).

Structural Collapse—A building may be subjected to a load greater than it can support. Earthquakes, snow loads on a roof, explosions, or a fire that weakens structural elements all contribute to a structural collapse.

Data Interception

Interception of data poses serious threats to the organization. Owners, management, facility managers and other company personnel should be aware that there are three routes of data interception: direct observation, interception of data transmission, and electromagnetic interception. Mobile and portable systems such as laptop computers, hand-held computers, palm pilots, etc., are especially vulnerable since they may contain proprietary information. Accidents, theft, unauthorized access are some of the risks posed by mobile and portable units. Procedures should be in place for the use of company-owned mobile and portable systems including:

- Secure storage of laptop computers when not in use.
- Encryption of data files on stored media.

Computer Room Example

There are basic elements that are necessary for the proper function of basic security in the computer room. Table 12-1 lists some of these necessary basic elements.

Physical and Environmental Protection

Security measures are taken to protect systems, buildings, and related supporting infrastructures against threats associated with their physical environment. Table 12-2 lists some of elements that are part of the computer security program.

Sources

Gustin, Joseph F., *Disaster and Recovery Planning: A Guide for Facility Managers*, 4th ed., Lilburn, GA: The Fairmont Press, Inc., 2007.

United States Department of Commerce, National Institute of Standards and Technology, *Contingency Planning Guide for Information Technology Systems: Recommendations of the National Institute of Standards and Technology*, Special Publication Number 800-34, June, 2002. Washington, DC: U.S. Government Printing Office.

United States Department of Commerce, National Institute of Standards and Technology, *Generally Accepted Principles and Practices of Securing Information Technology Systems*, Special Publication Number 800-14, September, 1996. Washington, DC: U.S. Government Printing Office.

Table 12-1. Sample Computer Room Controls

Physical/Environment Controls for Computer Room

In Place
Card keys for building and work-area entrances
Twenty-four hour guards at all entrances/exits
Cipher lock on computer room door
Raised floor in computer room
Dedicated cooling system
Humidifier in tape library
Emergency lighting in computer room
Four fire extinguishers rated for electrical fires
One B/C-rated fire extinguisher
Smoke, water, and heat detectors
Emergency power-off switch by exit door
Surge suppressor
Emergency replacement server
Zoned dry pipe sprinkler system
Uninterruptible power supply for LAN servers
Power strips/suppressors for peripherals
Power strips/suppressors for computers
Controlled access to file server room

Planned Plastic sheets for water protection
Closed-circuit television monitors,

Source: National Institute of Standards and Technology

Table 12-2. Physical and Environmental Security Checklist

	Policy	Procedure	Implement	Tested	Complete	Risk Based Decision Made	Notes	Initials
Physical &Environmental Protection								
Physical Access Control								
Critical Element: Have adequate physical security controls been implemented that are commensurate with the risks of physical damage or access?								
Is access to facilities controlled through the use of guards, identification badges, or entry devices such as key cards or biometrics?								
Is there a regular review of the personnel list with access to sensitive areas?								
Are deposits/withdrawals of tapes & other library storage media authorized & logged?								
Are keys or other access devices needed to enter the computer room & tape media library?								
Are unused keys or other entry devices secured?								
Do emergency exit/re-entry procedures ensure that only authorized personnel are allowed to re-enter after fire drills, etc.?								
Are visitors to sensitive areas signed in & escorted?								
Are entry codes changed periodically?								
Are physical accesses monitored?								
Are any apparent security violations investigated?								
Is action taken when a security breach is found?								

Table 12-2. (*Continued*)

Is suspicious access activity investigated & action taken?								
Are checks in place for the authentication of visitors/contractors & maintenance personnel?								
Fire Safety Factors								
Are appropriate fire suppression & prevention devices installed & in working order?								
Are fire ignition sources reviewed periodically for electronic device & wiring failure, improper storage materials & possibility of arson?								
Supporting Utilities								
Are HVAC systems regularly maintained?								
Is there a redundant air-cooling system?								
Are electric power distribution, heating plants, water sewage, etc., periodically reviewed for risk of failure?								
Are building plumbing lines known & do not endanger system?								
Has an uninterruptible power supply or backup generator been provided?								
Have controls been implemented to mitigate other disasters, such as floods, earthquakes, etc.?								
Interception of Data								
Critical Element: Is data protected from interception?								
Are computer monitors located to eliminate viewing by unauthorized persons?								
Is physical access to data transmission lines controlled?								
Mobile and Portable Systems								
Critical Element: Are mobile/portable systems protected?								
Are sensitive data files encrypted on all portable systems?								
Are portable systems securely stored?								

Source: National Institute of Standards and Technology

Chapter 13

Standby Power Systems

*Standby power is often necessary to keep critical operations such as computer-based activities and telecommunications moving during a power outage that may accompany a disaster. In this chapter, provided by **Mohammad Qayoumi, Ph.D.**, author of **Electrical Systems: A Guide For Facility Managers** (a companion volume in the Facilities Management Library), we will review standby power options.*

EMERGENCY PREPAREDNESS AND STANDBY POWER SYSTEMS

An important measure of an organization's strength is its ability to respond successfully to emergencies—particularly if the loss of human life and property is possible. It is true that no amount of preparation and backup systems can totally eliminate the risk posed by emergencies, but innovative design and careful planning can significantly reduce their impact. Disasters occur infrequently, of course, but when they do, they can destroy a company, so the same attitude that is given to the necessity of buying a strong insurance policy should be given to effective emergency design and planning.

Effective emergency response starts with having a system design based on sound engineering principles. But although this is a necessary requirement, it is not altogether sufficient. An effective operational plan is also needed. Such a plan should be comprehensive enough to give adequate guidelines for action, yet flexible enough to be adaptable to sudden changes and varying demands. A good plan not only protects human lives, but also reduces exposure to liability—namely, the accountability for actions or lack thereof in view of one's authority and responsibility.

In addition to a sound electrical system and an emergency response plan, emergency and standby power supplies may need to be installed to keep critical processes and equipment moving during the emergency.

The ideal would be a seamless transition between normal and standby power. In real situations, however, it may not be an economical choice. Therefore, compromises must be accepted.

Determining Standby Power Requirements

The first step in determining the standby power requirement is to determine what kind of power interruption can be tolerated. Based on this criterion, electrical loads fall in one of the following categories:

- If a load cannot be interrupted for more than half a cycle (i.e., 1/120 of a second for a 60 Hz system), it is called a critical load.

- If a load cannot be interrupted for more than 10 seconds, it is called an essential load.

- If a load can be interrupted for the duration of the normal power failure, it is called a non-essential load.

Of course, the standby power requirement for each category is different.

System Types

Based on the source of electric power, standby and emergency systems are categorized into four types:

Batteries—Batteries are an effective means of providing an emergency power source for fire alarms, emergency communication, exit signs, protective relays and emergency lighting. These loads are connected to a bank of batteries. A battery charger, connected to normal AC power supplies, charges the batteries. According to the National Electrical Code® (NEC®), the system should be capable of maintaining the load for 90 minutes without dropping below 87.5 percent of normal voltage. These systems are simple, reliable and robust. The maintenance requirements also are minimal, although since batteries have a finite life they must be replaced.

Generators—An electric generator is the most common source of standby power. The engine is powered by natural gas, gasoline or diesel.

The load is coupled to normal power and the emergency generator through the transfer switch. Under normal conditions, the transfer switch connects the load with the utility power source. When there is loss of utility power, the generator will start running and the transfer switch will connect the load to the generator. This process takes about 10 seconds. When the utility power is restored, the load is transferred to normal AC power after 15 minutes. The advantage of a generator is that it can serve the load for an extended period as long as there is an adequate supply of fuel. Since during a power interruption there is a 10-second delay before the generator can service the load, the load must have more than a 10-second ride-through.

A number of factors must be taken into account when a generator is specified. The type of fuel is important. For example, natural gas generators are efficient and easy to maintain. From a pollution point of view, the flue gas does not constitute a significant problem. But natural gas generators are not considered true emergency systems, because if there is an interruption from the utility gas supply, the unit will be useless in an emergency. That is why certain agencies such as the Joint Commission for Accreditation of Hospitals does not consider a natural gas unit as a true emergency generator.

In light of this, for critical loads, gasoline- or diesel-powered generators are considered appropriate. Normally, for small-sized units, gasoline is more appropriate. For larger units, diesel is preferable due to its lower operating cost, lower maintenance requirements and safety. This is because diesel fuel has a high flash point and low volatility.

Alternate Power Source—Another method of providing standby power is serving a load by more than one source with a double-ended or triple-ended power station. This technique will be effective as long as both feeders are powered by different and independent sources. Such an arrangement will provide redundancy for feeder cables, transformers and circuit breaker failures for the primary systems. The transfer to the alternate feeder can be manual or automatic. Similar to a standby generator, there will be a momentary power interruption of about 10 seconds during the transfer.

Uninterruptible Power Supplies (UPS)—A UPS is used where continuous power is required. A UPS also protects the load from systems power disturbances such as harmonics, transients and voltage surges and sags.

There are generally two types of UPS systems: rotary and static.

A rotary system consists of a motor-generator set which isolates the critical load from normal power. During an interruption, the motor-generator set can continue to provide power to the load for at least 100 milliseconds by its kinetic energy. This can be extended to many seconds with the addition of a flywheel. However, for an extended power outage, an auxiliary energy source (i.e., batteries or a generator) is needed. In most cases, a bypass circuit is provided. This will enable the system to operate with normal power if the UPS malfunctions. Transfer to the by-pass circuit can be manual or automatic.

A static UPS utilizes a rectifier and inverter module in connection with backup batteries. The rectifier circuit converts normal AC power to DC which charges the batteries and supplies the inverter section. The inverter converts DC power back to AC. During an interruption, the batteries will continue to supply the inverter until they are drained or the normal power is restored. Normally, the batteries must be large enough to last a minimum of 20 minutes.

Determining the Appropriate System

Determining the appropriate standby power system is, in principle, no different than any other managerial decision. That is, given a set of constraints, how can a system that will ensure an optimum solution be selected?

One of the first elements for consideration is the quality of service and frequency of utility power failure. This will depend on the particular utility company, the geographical location and the time of the year. It is important to gather data for the average duration as well as the range of these failures. Obviously, if the reliability of the utility service is not high or if the average power outage is long then it will influence the type and size of the standby power. Moreover, if the quality of utility power is not satisfactory, a UPS will address these concerns as well.

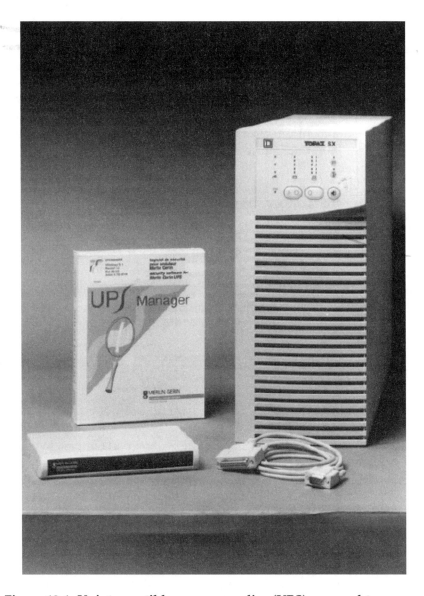

Figure 13-1. Uninterruptible power supplies (UPS) are used to ensure a seamless transition from normal power to standby power for critical loads such as data centers, industrial network servers, SCADA equipment, computers, telephone equipment and mission critical systems. Courtesy: Square D Company.

The next step is to classify the loads into three functional categories to determine whether the load is supporting people, equipment or the entire building.

The people category consists of loads associated with human safety such as life support systems in a hospital, air-traffic control systems, etc. In these cases, a UPS is required.

The equipment category consists of systems such as data processing centers, industrial processes, etc. that are needed to operate an overall system.

The building category consists of all support systems in a building such as lighting, HVAC, elevators, communication systems, security systems, fire alarm systems, etc.

For the last two categories, only equipment such as a data processing center will utilize UPS, while the rest typically use a battery or emergency generator for backup. Batteries are normally used for smaller loads such as lighting, alarms, control circuits, telephones, fire protection systems and security alarms. For larger loads such as HVAC, elevators and other essential devices, a standby generator is used.

SUMMARY

The primary motivation for providing a standby power source is to improve the overall reliability of the system. As every system is made of many parts, the reliability of individual parts impact the overall system reliability. An important rule for having a robust system is simplicity and reducing the number of system parts (especially moving elements) to a minimum. In addition, critical elements that have a major impact on system performance must be determined.

With a standby generator, for example, the transfer switch plays a critical role because it has to operate correctly during normal power and emergency power. If the transfer switch malfunctions, it might transfer to generator power unnecessarily—thus causing an unneeded power interruption—or it will not transfer during a power failure. Precautions should be taken, and that entails maintenance and testing of the equipment in addition to good equipment records.

With a UPS, if the anticipated utility outages are longer than the capacity of the batteries, an auxiliary generator can be used to charge the batteries.

After design and installation, another important aspect of standby power is having an effective maintenance program, as mentioned above. This way, the system will operate when it is needed. An essential element of preventive maintenance is periodic testing of the total system. In many cases with generator maintenance, scheduling becomes a big challenge because power will have to be shut down and that means downtime.

Maintenance requirements differ widely depending on the equipment. For instance, batteries simply need to be checked for water level, tight leads and the specific gravity of the acid. For a backup generator, the maintenance consists of checking the engine, the generator, the transfer switch and the control circuitry. The maintenance procedure for a UPS is more involved because of more sophisticated electronic parts. Manufacturers' recommendations should be followed.

When deciding on standby power, a cost/benefit analysis is required to determine the need for such a system. The motivation for standby power is either a code requirement; protection of life, property and profits; or any combination of these. For code requirements, refer to the appropriate sections of ANSI/NFPA, ANSI/IEEE, ANSI/UL or ANSI/NEMA for details.

All other standby power decisions can be based on economic considerations. This means what kind of power interruptions can be tolerated, what is the initial cost of a standby system, what are its operating and maintenance costs, and what combination of decisions will give us an optimum solution.

Finally, it should be recognized that the presence of a standby source only improves the reliability of the system on a statistical basis. It can never guarantee that one will still not experience a service interruption.

Sources

Qayoumi, Mohammad, Ph.D., P.E. *Electrical Systems: A Guide For Facility Managers.* New York: UpWord Publishing, Inc., 1996.

Chapter 14

Loss Prevention Strategies

Contingency planning is the process of developing site-specific strategies that are necessary to ensure the continuation of a company's essential business functions. It involves identifying those preventive measures and actions that must be taken to minimize exposure to a disaster occurrence, as well as minimizing the effects of a disaster on a company's vital business operations.

DEVELOPING YOUR STRATEGY

In developing site-specific strategies, several key considerations must be addressed. These considerations include:

- The scope of the disaster
- The nature of site operations
- Time frames
- Cost

Scope of the Disaster

In planning for the measures and actions to be taken in the event of disaster, the planning team must first determine what constitutes a disaster. Determining the criteria for a disaster is based upon two factors:

1. The impact of a potential occurrence upon the entity's *essential business functions* and operations.

2. The specific measures that must be taken to prevent the disaster from occurring.

217

Nature of Business Operations

The nature of the business entity itself is a factor that must be considered in contingency planning efforts. A total electrical system failure, for example, could have catastrophic consequences for a hospital. Life support systems would shut down, monitoring devices would be cut off, various medical and surgical procedures, etc., would be interrupted. These situations are *critical loads*; emergency power systems must be readily available and activated when necessary (see Chapter 10).

On the other hand, a total electrical system failure would have minimal impact upon the essential business operations of a car rental company. While employees and customers would be temporarily inconvenienced, automobile reservations could be manually logged for the duration of the electrical shutdown and keyed-in when the electrical service is restored and the data system is reactivated. A primary concern for the car rental company, however, would be the potential loss of its fleet in the event of a natural disaster. In terms of significant damage and loss, car rental companies with offices in the southeast United States, or in the Caribbean, would be particularly vulnerable to the impact of a hurricane.

Time Frames

Determining the appropriate contingency strategies also involves determining the acceptable level(s) of "downtime." Once the scope of the disaster and its potential impact upon the essential business functions has been determined, an estimation of acceptable maximum "downtime" must be arrived at. Downtime is defined in terms of the acceptable time periods for using alternate procedures to maintain a company's essential functions.

For example, if a garment manufacturer's facility is rendered untenable because of a fire, that company's planning team must determine how long the essential functions can be maintained in an alternate facility with less space and limited fabric storage capabilities.

Cost

The cost of activating contingency plans and procedures is another factor that must be considered by the planning team. Emphasis must be placed on developing alternative solutions that are cost-effective. Yet, these solutions must not compromise the recovery effort.

Identifying and prioritizing functions and their related operations that are essential to business, continuation, is the first step in determining recovery costs. However, any reasonable cost projection cannot be made until the other considerations have also been addressed. These other considerations are:

- Determination of the nature of a potential disaster and its impact upon those business functions which have been determined to be essential.

- Establishment of the maximum acceptable time frames for alternate procedures to be used in continuation of business operations.

Each of these considerations is interrelated and each is necessary for defining the strategic approaches a company or entity must take in developing contingency plan.

LOSS PREVENTION

The purpose of loss prevention programming is twofold. First, it involves taking those actions that can reduce the chances of a disaster occurring (particularly important when the potential disaster is technological in nature). Second, it includes taking those actions that can minimize potential exposure if the disaster should occur. As such, loss prevention strategies form the basis for business continuity or contingency planning.

Designing strategies that meet the definitional purposes of loss prevention involves a series of basic steps. These steps are:

- Develop a loss prevention policy.
- Identify and evaluate all hazards and risk exposures.
- Determine recovery priorities.
- Develop contingent programming that minimizes potential losses.

Develop the Loss Prevention Policy

Loss prevention begins with developing and writing a loss prevention and control policy. The policy itself must be more than a statement of management concern; the document must reflect the active commitment of management to an aggressive program of loss prevention. This commitment, endorsed by the highest level of the business entity, must be communicated to all levels within the organization, as well as to all support and ancillary personnel, including outside contractors.

Elements of The Policy Statement—In clear concise terms, the policy statement should include the following elements:

• Identification of all areas of loss prevention.

• Identification of key levels of responsibility and authority for developing and implementing loss prevention programming in each identified risk area.

• Definition and outline of enforcement procedures and/or disciplinary procedures for non-compliance.

Identify and Evaluate Hazards

Once the loss prevention policy has been developed, those people who are responsible for each loss prevention area should begin the systematic identification and evaluation of hazards within their respective areas. Since many disasters occur as a result of human behavior (e.g., failure to comply with required work procedures in handling of hazardous materials; disregarding basic work safety procedures; failure to routinely inspect and maintain fire protection systems, etc.). This type of potential disaster must also be included in the facility-wide audit.

Some of the risk areas include:
• Fire protection systems and equipment.
• Hot work.
• Maintenance.
• Construction.
• Housekeeping.
• Smoking.
• Surveillance.
• Insurance regulations and recommendations.
• Staff and occupant training.
• Hazardous materials evaluation.

Determine Recovery Priorities

Companies, entities and their facilities vary. While at times product and service lines may tend to blur, each business is different. An organization's mission, structure, nature and function, as well as its various methods of operation, determine even the most subtle differences between and among companies. And because they are different, each entity has its own unique set of operational requirements which must be maintained if the entity is to continue.

As part of a company's loss prevention approach, these operational requirements must be identified and prioritized in order to ensure continuity of operations through the duration of the disaster recovery period. These critical business priorities must also be maintained until all facets of normal operations are restored.

One of the most critical issues that must be addressed in terms of supporting a company's essential business functions in the wake of disaster is the issue of vital records recovery and management. As such, the effective loss prevention strategy must also focus on—and provide for—contingent records maintenance programming.

Vital Records Management—The records of a company that are generally considered vital to business continuity include those documents that define the company in terms of its structure, organization and financial status. Specifically, these records include any documents that describe the entity as a:

- Private versus public enterprise.
- As a corporation, partnership, limited partnership or sole proprietorship, as well as other issues of governance.

Other records that define an entity include documents that outline the terms and recitals of:
- All legal records.
- Business affiliation agreements.
- Current and pending vendor/sales/customer and client contracts.
- Licenses and permits.
- Insurance policies.
- Tax and financial data, including accounts receivable/payable.
- Personnel/employee records, including employment contracts and payroll/benefit/medical records.
- Building specifications, including blueprints, floor plans, etc.
- Regulatory/compliance documents.

While many companies have backup, as well as off-site storage provisions for many of these cited examples, there are numerous records and documents that are maintained at the primary worksite. These documents, reports and paperwork that comprise a company's "work-in-progress" should be addressed in the records management contingency plan.

Develop the Loss Prevention Program

The last step in developing company-wide loss prevention strategies involves designing contingent programs for each of the identified risk areas.

In determining the appropriateness of loss prevention programming, a number of factors must be considered. These factors include:

• The nature of the disaster that could occur (natural versus technological).

• The vulnerability of a particular risk area to the impact of a potential disaster, regardless of its nature.

In turn, each of these factors is determined by various levels of prevention and defined within the context of a facility's recovery priorities, as well as the regulatory components that govern facility operations.

Levels of Prevention—The levels of prevention that must be undertaken to maintain risk are contingent upon the nature of the particular disaster. For example, natural disaster occurrences such as weather or climatic events (e.g., floods, earthquakes, hurricanes, tornadoes, high winds, snow and winter freeze) cannot be prevented. Regardless of any planning team effort, these natural events will occur. In preparing for the natural disaster occurrence, the focus of planning efforts must be on mitigating the effects of the natural occurrence on occupants, buildings and business components.

Disaster occurrences that result from either human error or design require the development and installation of different levels of prevention and training. For example, in those companies and businesses whose operations include the use of hazardous materials, emphasis on employee training takes on an expanded importance as a loss prevention measure. In addition to the normal fire safety and evacuation training that is provided to all employees (as part of their new-hire orientation, and as part of their ongoing training), specific skills training in procedures for proper handling, use and disposal of toxic materials must be provided to all affected employees.

CONTINGENCIES FOR DATA/SYSTEM AVAILABILITY

Quick restoration of IT resources is the goal of a well-planned, thorough contingency plan.

Recovery Options

*   Off-site Storage.
*   Formal Backup Policy.
*   Formal Testing Program.
*   System Configuration.
*   Compatibility.
*   Selection of Backup Media.

Off-site Storage. If possible, critical data should be backed up and stored at an off-site facility that is secure and environmentally controlled. The stored data should also include information on data content, structure and any relevant licensing and vendor information. See Figure 14-1.

Formal Backup Policy. A formalized backup policy specifies frequency of backup; frequency of reuse and methods of disposal. Included in the formal backup policy would be the procedures for the retrieval and identification of the data from the off-site storage location, how restoration is to be accomplished and procedures for the return to storage. Ideally, once a backup is made it should be sent to the off-site location within a day.

Formal Testing Policy. A policy for timeline of frequency of testing the policy for system and data recovery should be determined; i.e., weekly, monthly, quarterly, etc. A complete test should be done at least once a year. The testing could include simulations of real events including hacker attacks, insider attacks and denial of service attacks.

In addition, patch levels, and the applications and version currently running on the computer, etc., aids in system recovery. Also, any changes/upgrades to the hardware and software, including system addition/system removal should be documented the same way.

System Configuration. System recovery depends upon the care taken when a new system is first used. Documentation of such items as the operating system and version, patch levels, and the applications and versions that are running the computer, etc., aids in system recovery.

Compatibility. Any backup devices used in system recovery should be compatible with the operating systems and applications of the computer system.

Selection of Backup Media. The amount of data for backup, its frequency and required retention, the recovery and transport requirements, the restoration and elimination procedures, availability, and cost determines the type of backup media that will be used. Backup media includes diskettes, tape cartridges, zip drives, compact disks, network storage devices such as networked disks, or server backup. Internet backup or on-line backups are also an alternative but the issue of confidentiality proves necessary when using Internet backup options.

Backup Options

Backup of data is an important part of the contingency plan. There are different types of system backups including:

- Full.
- Incremental.
- Differential.
- Redundant Array of Interactive Devices (RAID).
- Disk Replication.

Full Backup. As the name suggests, a full backup stores all the files selected for backup. Large storage capacity and lengthy recording time distinguish a full backup.

Incremental Backups. Files that are created or modified since the last backup are incremental backups. In terms of recovery, restoration from an incremental backup may require more time since restoration depends upon the time of the last full backup.

Differential Backups. A differential backup stores files that were created or modified since the last full backup. Restoration requires only the full backup tape and the last incremental tape. Therefore, this approach is less time consuming to complete that a full backup and requires fewer storage units than an incremental approach.

Redundant Array of Interactive Devices (RAID). Provides disk redundancy and fault tolerance for data storage and decreases mean time between failure. It is used to mask disk drive and disk controller failures.

Disk Replication. Data is written to two different disks—a protected server and a replication server—so that two valid copies of data are available.

Figure 14-1. Off-Site Storage/Vendor Considerations. Source: National Institute of Standards and Technology.

When selecting an off-site storage facility and vendor, the following criteria should be considered:

- Geographic area-the distance from the organization and the probability of the storage site being affected by the same occurrence event as the organization.

- Accessibility-the length of time necessary to retrieve the data from storage and the storage facility's operating hours.

- Security-the security capabilities of the storage facility and employee confidentiality, which must meet the data's sensitivity and security requirements.

- Environment-the structural and environmental conditions of the storage facility-temperature, humidity, fire prevention, and power management control.

- Cost-the cost of shipping, operational fees, and disaster response/recovery services.

LOSS PREVENTION TECHNIQUES

While natural disaster occurrences can run the full gamut of climatic events, technological or human-engineered disasters include fires and explosions, hazardous materials spills, fire protection systems and equipment failures, riots and civil disturbances, sabotage and bomb threats. Additionally, other technological or human-engineered occurrences include exploitation of computer vulnerabilities, disgruntled employees and cyber attacks. Any and all measures taken to counter the effects of these occurrences on a company must be structured in ways that provide a framework for achieving an optimal level of quality, production and operations despite the occurrences. These optimal levels of quality, production and operations are, in turn, what define business continuity initially and full business recovery ultimately.

As a planning and prevention technique, mitigation involves taking those actions that will reduce the impact of a disaster occurrence on occupants, the building itself and the various business components. Determining which exposures present the greatest risk, as well as determining which of those exposures can and cannot be controlled, provides the basis for developing loss prevention strategies that lead to recovery.

Flood Loss

Floods and flash flooding occur within all 50 states. Areas at particular risk are those located in low-lying areas, near water, or downstream from a dam. According to FEMA, floods are the most widespread of all disasters, with the exception of fire. Most communities in the United States can expect to experience some kind of flooding after spring rains, heavy thunderstorms, or winter snow thaws. Floods can be slow, or fast rising, but generally develop over a period of days.

Dam failures are potentially the worst flood event. A dam failure is usually the result of neglect, poor design, or structural damage caused by a major event such as an earthquake. When a dam fails, a gigantic quantity of water is suddenly let loose downstream, destroying anything in its path.

Flood waters can be extremely dangerous. According to FEMA, the force of six inches of swiftly moving water can knock people of their feet. Flash flood waters move at very fast speeds and can roll boulders, uproot trees, destroy buildings and obliterate bridges. In fact, walls of water can reach heights of 10 to 20 ft. and generally are accompanied by a deadly cargo of debris. The Big Thompson River near Denver, Colorado, overflowed after an extremely heavy storm. The July, 1976, flood created a way of water 19 ft. high. Roaring down the Big Thompson Canyon where many people were camping, the torrent killed 140 people and caused millions of dollars in property loss.

As previously noted, flooding occurs for a variety of reason. While flooding can occur within a building or outside the building, it can cause significant damage to the physical property as well as to building contents. Flooding poses a particular threat to occupant safety.

For example, in situations where flooding originates within the facility, certain measures can be taken to reduce the risk and minimize dollar loss. Once the flood source within a building has been located, procedures for electrical system shutdown within the affected area can be initiated. Affected contents within the area can be relocated.

Oftentimes, in situations where flooding is caused by natural occurrences such as hurricanes, heavy rains, spring thaws, etc., advance warning is provided. These advance warnings, which come in the form of advisories issued by the National Weather Service, include flood watches and warnings.

Watches Versus Warnings—A flood watch advisory is issued when flooding is possible within an area. A flood warning advisory is issued when a flood is in progress or when flooding is imminent. When flood warnings are issued, immediate preventive measures should be initiated.

Forecasts such as those issued by the National Weather Service not only enable facility managers to anticipate problems, but such advance warnings provide adequate time to initiate any preventive measures needed to minimize the effects of the impending flood. These measures may include actions such as relocating building contents to areas within the facility that are above predicted flood levels, initiating electrical system shutdown procedures, readying evacuation procedures, and even intentionally flooding below-grade areas. (When severe flooding is predicted, it is sometimes necessary to intentionally flood the below-grade areas. Such action can minimize structural damage/loss, because intentional flooding reduces the pressure of invasive flood waters.)

Post Flood Assessment—Subsequent to flooding and when determination has been made for safe building re-entry by either internal authority or regulatory/enforcement authority, immediate damage assessment should take place. This post-flood assessment should include inspecting:

- All fire protection equipment and systems to determine operability.
- The building structure, with particular attention to foundation damage.
- Any damage caused by floating debris, including waste products.
- Any damage to worksite records, documentation and other types of "work-in-progress."

Finally, all equipment, including electric motors and switchgears, must be cleaned and dried and then tested for operability and utility.

However, regardless of a flood's origin, systematic planning efforts that define the measures and procedures to be taken in the event of a flood occurrence must be included in the loss prevention strategy so that damage and dollar loss can be minimized.

Records Recovery—For example, the courses of action that a company will take to protect its work-in-progress and other on-site data from water damage should be identified. The various processes involved in vital records restoration and reclamation, as well as the internal and external personnel who will be involved in the recovery efforts, should be clearly detailed. Records recovery issues that should be addressed include:

- Post-flood records access.
- Damage assessment.
- Salvage planning.
- Removal and packing of water-damaged records and data.
- Records/data disposal.
- Vacuum and freeze drying processes.
- Storage.

A well-organized records recovery plan not only reduces the costs of salvage and restoration, it also minimizes the impact on those functions that are essential to business continuity.

Hot Work Losses

One of the most critical risk areas is "hot work." Hot work—which involves brazing, grinding, pipe thawing, soldering/welding, and cutting—requires the use of various torches that produce open flames. Careless use of torch equipment, including disregarding or failure to comply with proper work/safety procedures, and negligent housekeeping are just some of the causes for explosions and fires in facilities. And, whether the losses incurred by a company are caused by employees or outside contractors, the fact remains that human failure in either the work operations or in the supervision of the work operations is the contributing factor.

In assessing the risk of hot work, several issues come into play. These issues are:

- The location where the hot work is to be performed.
- The building components and contents within the location where the hot work is to be performed.
- Regulatory components governing hot work.

Each of these issues should be addressed in the policy statement as outlined above, and reinforced in written procedures. These written procedures should be communicated to not only those facility employees whose job involves hot work, but to outside contractors who are engaged to perform the hot work. Additionally, disciplinary measures/actions that will be taken by company/building management when employees or contractors are found to be in non-compliance with the policy and procedures, must also be communicated to all people involved in hot work operations.

Location—The location of any proposed hot work must be inspected to ensure that the area and its component features are as "fireproof" as possible. For example, the fire resistance of walls should be checked to determine that any heat generated by the hot work does not ignite any combustible materials that may be stored on the other side. Ceiling, floors and openings should be properly covered and/or plugged with appropriate fire-resistant materials to prevent sparks from igniting areas within the openings, or combustible materials that may be present in those openings. Any exposed ductwork should also be covered with appropriate fire-resistant materials to minimize not only the danger of flying sparks, but also to minimize heat conduction which could cause ignition of any dust particles contained in or circulated by the ductwork.

Contents—The contents of any location or area targeted for hot work should be removed. Any flammable or combustible liquids should be sealed and relocated to another area within the facility. The location should also be pre-tested for any residual vapors, or similar contaminants, before the work is actually started. When possible, machinery and equipment should be removed. If it is not feasible to do so, such machinery and equipment should be covered with appropriate fire-resistant materials to reduce the risk of spark/heat contact with any oil/grease and lint/dust that is present on all machinery and equipment.

Storage racks should be cleared of contents as well, whether the hot work is scheduled to be done on the racks or on other contents.

Finally, all hot work performed by either employees or outside contractors must be supervised. An assigned person trained in basic fire prevention techniques, including the use of extinguishers, should be present during the hot work operations. This assigned person is responsible for monitoring the progress of the work, inspecting adjoining areas and testing for any combustible gas accumulation prior to the initiation of the work, as well as during and after the work is completed. Subsequent to the completion of the hot work, the work site and adjoining areas should be checked for any smoldering fires or other unusual conditions.

Regulatory Components—The maze of regulations that governs the workplace includes hot work activities. Examples of such regulations include the following OSHA standards covering emergency response and preparedness requirements for general industry and the construction and shipyard industries.

General Industry Emergency Response and Preparedness Requirements 29 CFR Part 1910, Subpart Q

Subject and Standard Number	Emergency Response Preparedness Requirement
Welding, Cutting and Brazing	
1910.252 (d)(2)(iii)	(d) Fire Prevention and Protection. (2) Special Precautions. (iii) Fire Watch.
	(a) Fire watches shall be required whenever welding or cutting is performed in locations where other than

a minor fire might develop, or any of the following conditions exist:

(1) Appreciable combustible material, in building construction or contents, closer than 35 ft. to the point of the operation.

(2) Appreciable combustibles are more than 35 ft. away but could easily be ignited by sparks.

(3) Wall or floor openings within a 35 ft. radius expose combustible material in adjacent areas including concealed spaces in walls or floors.

Subject and Standard Number	*Emergency Response Preparedness Requirement*
	(4) Combustible materials are adjacent to the opposite side of metal partitions, walls, ceilings, or roofs and are likely to be ignited by conduction or radiation.

(b) Fire watchers shall have fire extinguishing equipment readily available and be trained in its use. They shall be familiar with facilities for sounding an alarm in the event of a fire. They shall watch for fires in all exposed areas, try to extinguish them only when obviously within the capacity of the equipment available, or otherwise sound the alarm. A fire watch shall be maintained for at least a half hour after completion of welding or cutting operations to detect and extinguish possible smoldering fires.

1910.252 (f)(13)	(f) Health Protection. (13) First-Aid Equipment. First-aid equipment shall be available at all times. All injuries shall be reported as soon as possible for medical attention. First aid shall be rendered until medical attention can be provided.

Subject and Standard Number	*Emergency Response Preparedness Requirement*

Construction Industry Emergency Response and Preparedness Requirements
29 CFR Part 1926, Subpart J

Fire Prevention

1926.352 (d) and (e)	(d) Suitable fire extinguishing equipment shall be immediately available in the work area and shall be maintained in a state of readiness for instant use.

(e) When the welding, cutting or heating operation is such that normal fire prevention precautions are not sufficient, additional personnel shall be assigned to guard against fire while the actual welding, cutting, or heating operation is being performed, and for a sufficient period of time after completion of the work to ensure that no possibility of fire exists. Such personnel shall be instructed as to the specific anticipated fire hazards and how the fire fighting equipment provided is to be used.

Subject and *Emergency Response*
Standard Number *Preparedness Requirement*
Shipyard Industry Emergency Response and Preparedness Requirements
29 CFR Part 1915, Subpart D
Fire Prevention
1915.52   (a) Paragraph (a) applies to ship repairing, shipbuilding and shipbreaking, and paragraph (b) applies to ship repairing and shipbuilding only.

(1) When practical, objects to be welded, cut, or heated shall be moved to a designated safe location or, if the object to be welded, cut or heated cannot be readily moved, all movable fire hazards including residues of combustible bulk cargoes in the vicinity shall be taken to a safe place.

(2) If the object to be welded, cut or heated cannot be moved and if all the fire hazards including combustible cargoes cannot be removed, positive means shall be taken to confine the heat, sparks, and slag, and to protect the immovable fire hazards from them.

(3) When welding, cutting, or heating is performed on tank shells, decks, overheads, and bulkheads, since direct penetration of sparks or heat transfer may introduce a fire hazard to an adjacent compartment, the same precautions shall be taken on the opposite side as are taken on the side on which the welding is being performed.

(4) In order to eliminate the possibility of fire in confined spaces as a result of gas escaping through leak-

ing or improperly closed torch valves, the gas supply to the torch shall be positively shut off at some point outside the confined space whenver the torch is not to be used or whenever the torch is left unattended for a substantial period of time, such as during the lunch hour. Overnight and at the change of shifts, the torch and hose shall be removed from the confined spaced. Open end fuel gas and oxygen hoses shall be immediately removed from confined spaces when they are disconnected from the torch or other gas consuming device.

(b) The provisions of this paragraph shall apply to ship repairing and shipbuilding only.

Subject and Standard Number

Emergency Response Preparedness Requirement

(1) No welding, cutting, or heating shall be done where the application of flammable paints or the presence of other flammable compounds or of heavy dust concentrate creates a hazard.

(2) Suitable fire extinguishing equipment shall be immediately available in the work area and shall be maintained in a state of readiness for instant use. In addition, when hot work is being performed aboard a vessel and pressure is not available on the vessel's fire system, an auxiliary supply of water shall be made available where practicable, consistent with avoiding freezing of the lines or hose.

(3) When the welding, cutting, or heating operation is such that normal fire prevention precautions are not sufficient, additional personnel shall be assigned to guard against fire while the actual welding, cutting, or heating operation is being performed and for a sufficient period of time after completion of the work to insure that no possibility of fire exists. Such personnel shall be instructed as to the specific anticipated fire hazards and how the fire fighting equipment provided is to be used.

(4) Vaporizing liquid extinguishers shall not be used in enclosed spaces.

(5) Except when the contents are being removed or transferred, drums, pails and other containers which contain or have contained flammable liquids shall be kept closed. Empty containers shall be removed to a safe area apart from hot work operations, or open flames. (c) In all cases, suitable fire extinguishing equipment shall be immediately available in the work area and shall be maintained in a state of readiness for instant use. Personnel assigned to contain fires within controllable limits shall be instructed as to the specific anticipated fire hazards and how the fire fighting equipment provided is to be used. The provisions of the paragraph shall apply to shipbreaking only.

CONTINGENCY PLANNING

Contingency planning involves more than planning for a move off-site after a disaster destroys a facility. It also addresses how to keep an organization's critical functions operating in the event of disruptions, large and small. Table 14-1 summarizes essential key points in an effective contingency planning program.

Contingency planning directly supports an organization's goal of continued operations. It addresses the issues of operating a company's critical business functions during an emergency. Computer support is critical to the organization's disaster recovery/business continuity plan.

Business Plan. In a company business plan business-critical functions are identified and prioritized. A contingency plan with clearly defined and prioritized functions will keep a business running during a occurrence.

Resources. Once resources are identified, their priorities can be assigned. Resources cross a company's territorial areas—department functions, department managers, etc.

Common Resources. There are resources that are common to most organizations. These include:

• People.
• Processing Capability—mainframes, personal computers.
• Data and Applications.

Table 14-1. Contingency Planning. Source: National Institute of Standards and Technology

	Policy	Procedure	Apply	Test	Complete	Risk Based Decision Made	Notes	Initials
Have critical, sensitive operations & supporting computer resources been identified?								
Are critical data files & operations identified?								
Is the frequency of file backup documented?								
Are supporting critical operations resources identified?								
Have processing priorities been established & approved?								
Has a comprehensive contingency plan been developed & documented?								
Is the plan approved?								
Are recovery responsibilities assigned?								
Are there policies for operations restoration?								
Is there an alternate processing site; & a contract in place?								
Is the location of stored backups identified?								
Are backup files created on a prescribed basis & rotated off-site?								
Is system & application documentation maintained at the off-site location?								
Are system defaults reset from a backup restoration?								
Are the backup storage & alternate sites physically protected?								
Has the contingency plan been distributed to personnel?								
Are tested Contingency/ Disaster recovery plans in place?								
Is an up-to-date copy of the plan stored securely off-site?								
Are employees trained in their roles & responsibilities?								
Is the plan periodically tested and readjusted as appropriate?								

- Physical Infrastructure.
- Documentation.

Develop Scenarios

An organization should anticipate potential contingencies for unplanned cyber occurrences. Possible scenarios should help an organization develop a plan to address the wide range of things that can go wrong. Anticipating what can go wrong can sometimes prevent that wrong from happening. The scenarios should address those elements that affect the above resources—people, processors, data and applications, physical infrastructure, etc.

Develop Strategies

Practical considerations should be part of a company's contingency planning strategy. For example, an alternate site for data storage, as well as materials storage, may prove more feasible than the purchase and maintenance of an alternate on-site Uninterruptible Power System (UPS).

The contingency planning strategy has several elements in common. These are:

- Emergency Response.
- Recovery.
- Resumption.
- Implementation.
- Testing and Revision.

Emergency Response. As in any other emergency response, the critical actions that are taken are done so as to minimize loss.

Recovery. In the recovery mode the steps needed to continue critical functions are taken.

Resumption. Resumption determines the requirements needed for a return to normal business functions.

Implementation. Once the strategies have been determined, the implementation phase sets in. Preparation, documentation and training are part of the implementation phase.

Testing and Revision. Contingency plans should be tested and revised when necessary.

Computer Security Responsibilities

Developed by the NIST, there is a seven step process to develop and maintain a viable contingency planning program for a company's IT system. These steps are designed to be integrated into each stage of the system development life cycle for the various Information Technology (IT) systems. These steps are defined as follows.

1. **Develop a contingency planning policy.** A formal company organization policy provides the authority and guidance necessary to develop an effective contingency plan.
2. **Conduct a business impact analysis (BIA).** A BIA plan helps to identify and prioritize critical IT systems and components.
3. **Identify preventive controls.** Measures taken to reduce the effects of system disruptions can increase system availability and reduce contingency life-cycle costs.
4. **Develop recovery strategies.** Thorough recovery strategies ensure that the system may be recovered quickly and effectively following a disruption.
5. **Develop a contingency plan.** The contingency plan should contain detailed guidance and procedures for restoring a damaged system.
6. **Test the plan and train personnel.** Testing the plan identifies planning gaps, whereas training prepares recovery personnel for plan activation. Both activities improve the plan's effectiveness and overall agency preparedness.
7. **Maintain the plan.** The plan should be a living document that is updated regularly to remain current with system enhancements.

This is a sample format for developing an IT contingency plan. As with any successful plan it should be incorporated into the company's business continuity/disaster and recovery plan. Following a system disruption there are three phases that govern actions. These phases include the:

- **Notification/Activation Phase.** This phase describes the process of notifying recovery personnel and performing a damage assessment.

- **The Recovery Phase** discusses actions taken by recovery teams and personnel to restore IT operations at an alternate site or using contingency capabilities.

• **The Reconstitution Phase** is the final phase. This phase outlines the actions taken to return the system to normal operating conditions.

Alternate Sites

Plans must also be made for relocation if a system cannot be recovered at the original site. In most cases the system must be relocated to an alternate site for temporary processing. The plan should discuss various types of alternate sites and their respective capabilities. The following list some alternate sites that may be used:

• Cold sites.
• Mobile sites.
• Warm sites.
• Hot sites.
• Mirrored sites.

• *Cold Site*—A backup facility that has the necessary electrical and physical components of a computer facility, but does not have the computer equipment in place. The site is ready to receive the necessary replacement computer equipment in the event that the user has to be moved from the main computing location to an alternate site.

• *Mobile Site*—A self-contained, transportable shell custom-fitted with the specific IT equipment and telecommunications necessary to provide full recovery capabilities upon notice of a significant disruption.

• *Warm Site*—An environmentally conditioned workspace that is partially equipped with IT and telecommunications equipment to support relocated IT operations in the event of a significant disruption.

• *Hot Site*—A fully operational off-site data processing facility equipped with both hardware and system software to be used in the event of a disaster.

- *Mirrored Site*—A fully redundant, real-time information facility identical to the original site.

Several strategies or techniques are common to all IT systems. Some common contingency strategies include the following:

- **Off-site storage.** System information should be backed up regularly and stored off-site in a protected environment. Operating systems, applications, and application data should be backed up based on system and data criticality. Software licenses, system configurations, and other vital records should be stored off-site with the backup data.

- **Interoperability.** Providing standard platforms and configurations assist system recovery and reduce expenses associated with procuring replacement equipment.

- **Redundancy.** Redundant data storage, communications paths, power sources and system components reduce the likelihood of system failure. The costs of implementing redundant capabilities should be weighed against the risks of system outage.

- **Coordination with security controls.** Contingency planning cannot exist alone. Planning should be coordinated with existing and proposed technical management. Planning should also be coordinated with operational security controls in order to reduce system risks and ensure viable contingency capabilities.

Plan Testing, Training and Exercises

Plan testing is a critical element of a viable contingency plan. Benefits of plan testing include identifying and addressing deficiencies; evaluating the ability of recovery staff to quickly and effectively implement the plan. In addition, each element of the contingency plan should be tested. Testing each element of the plan confirms the accuracy of individual recovery procedures and its overall effectiveness. The following areas should be addressed in a contingency test:

- System recovery on an alternate platform from backup tapes.
- Coordination among recovery teams.
- Internal and external connectivity.

- System performance using alternate equipment.
- Restoration of normal operations.

NIST recommends that to derive the most value from the test, explicit test objectives and success criteria should be identified. For example, one test objective might be the recovery of a database, database server, and operating system at an alternate site within eight hours and database recovery with no errors. The use of test objectives and success criteria enables the effectiveness of each plan element and the overall plan assessment. Test results and lessons learned should be documented and reviewed by test participants and other personnel as appropriate. Information collected during the test and post-test reviews that improve plan effectiveness should be incorporated into the contingency plan.

Training for personnel with contingency plan responsibilities should complement testing and should be provided at least annually. However, new hires who will have plan responsibilities should receive training shortly after they are hired. Ultimately, contingency plan personnel should be trained to the extent that they are able to execute their respective recovery procedures without aid of the actual document. This is an important goal in the event that paper or electronic versions of the plan are unavailable due to the extent of the occurrence. Recovery personnel should be trained on the following plan elements:

- Purpose of the plan.
- Cross-team coordination and communication.
- Reporting procedures.
- Security requirements.
- Team-specific processes including activation/notification, recovery, and reconstitution phases

COMPUTER SECURITY INCIDENT HANDLING

A computer security incident can be the result of a computer virus, other malicious code, a system intruder, or a cyber-attack. The definition of a computer security incident is somewhat flexible and may vary by organization and computing environment. However, regardless of definition, a quick response to an incident is imperative for continuity of business operations. An organized and definitive incident handling or incident response plan mitigates the loss of time in handling the incident. Time lost can result in compromised information, lost business or negative publicity.

An incident response plan should include the following:

- Responsibilities.
- Reporting procedures.
- Training.
- Testing.

Responsibilities. The plan should spell out, or indicate the key personnel who are responsible for handling computer incidents. Valuable time will not be lost if employees do not have to search for the "right" person to call.

Reporting Procedures. The plan should include detailed information on what "constitutes" an incident; the time line for reporting an incident; the way to report an incident, what assistance will be provided and a "hotline" number to call.

Training. The training of employees in the incident handling response is an essential component in the plan. Employees should know what constitutes an incident, how to recognize an incident and how to report an incident.

Testing. An incident response plan should be tested periodically, with a minimum of once a year, more often if feasible. Testing should be both announced and unannounced. Unannounced tests should include simulations of real intrusions.

SUMMARY

Loss prevention strategies include those actions that are designed to minimize any potential exposure if a disaster should occur, as well as to reduce the chances of a disaster actually occurring. Both sets of actions include evaluating those building systems and features that carry the potential for risk.

Evaluating these features or components involves assessing the vulnerability or risk "level" of each. Since no single building system, feature or function operates independently, each must be measured in terms of its utility to and with other system components and functions. Only in this way can a company's loss prevention strategies identify optimal solutions of minimizing risk levels and monitoring results.

Sources

Federal Emergency Management Agency, Emergency Preparedness Backgrounds and Fact Sheets: Floods. Document No. 15091

Gustin, Joseph F, *Disaster and Recovery Planning: A Guide for Facility Managers,* 4th ed., Lilburn, GA: The Fairmont Press, Inc., 2007.

United States Department of Commerce, National Institute of Standards and Technology, *Contingency Planning Guide for Information Technology Systems: Recommendations of the National Institute of Standards and Technology,* Special Publication Number 800-34, June, 2002. Washington, DC: US. Government Printing Office.

United States Department of Commerce, National Institute of Standards and Technology, *Computer Security Incident Handling Guide: Recommendations of the National Institute of Standards and Technology,* NIST Special Publication Number 800-61, Washington, DC: US. Government Printing Office. January 2004.

United States Department of Labor, Occupational Safety and Health Administration, Construction Industry Emergency Response Preparedness Requirements, 29CFR1926, Subpart J.

United States Department of Labor, Occupational Safety and Health Administration, Construction Industry Emergency Response Preparedness Requirements, 29CFR1910, Subpart Q.

United States Department of Labor, Occupational Safety and Health Administration, Construction Industry Emergency Response Preparedness Requirements, 29CFR1915, Subpart D.

Chapter 15

Crisis Planning and Damage Control

It is important for any company or facility to develop strategies for dealing with the media. Essential from a public relations perspective, a company must be able to respond to calls, questions and, at times, on-site visits from both the print (newspapers and magazines) and the broadcast (television and radio) media. In this chapter, we will discuss techniques for effectively dealing with the media and using the media during a disaster.

CRISIS PLANNING

Failure to respond to media queries through avoidance, or the very questionable "No Comment" response (which presumes either guilt or cover-up), will not prevent a company's disaster occurrence from being told. Since the "story" will ultimately and oftentimes quickly find its way into the homes, cars and offices of a company's customers, clients, suppliers, distributors, employees and competitors, it is critically important that only valid and responsible information be conveyed to the various audiences.

For these reasons, a well-developed crisis/damage control plan can assist an organization in its business continuity efforts and expedite the recovery process.

The Crisis Plan

The crisis plan is designed to deal with any unexpected crisis situation, including disasters, that may occur at a company or facility. If properly developed and communicated, the plan and its procedures can:

243

- Effectively counter any negative rumors or news stories which could adversely impact upon business continuity and recovery.

- Ensure a minimum of confusion at a time when confusion is least appreciated.

Because the nature of a disaster as well as its potential impact determine a company's specific response strategies, the crisis plan should be generic enough to accommodate different disaster occurrences. The key elements that should be included in a company's crisis plan include:

- Contact chart that identifies key departmental managers (corporate)/
key occupant representatives (multitenant facility); this chart should include contact phone numbers (office and emergency) of key persons. The contact chart should also include the names and phone numbers of key customers and clients, distributors, suppliers, etc.

- Staff/Occupant relations guidelines.

- Media relations guidelines.

- Prepared public relations materials that include generic press releases, generic scripts for radio and television "spots," scripts for telecommunications/automated voice mail responses and a defined budget for contingency advertising purchase.

Contact Chart—There are two general purposes for developing a contact chart. First, it is intended to identify the key personnel in either the corporate, or single-tenant setting, and key occupant representatives in multitenanted facilities who must be contacted in the case of an emergency occurrence. Second, it serves as the basis for establishing a chain of communications that not only provides appropriate information to affected persons, but also provides a vehicle for receiving information from those persons.

Because of the crucial role it plays in damage control and in the entire disaster and recovery planning process, the contact chart should be maintained and updated on a regular basis. As new managers and tenant occupants move in or out of the organization/facility, their "vitals" should be added or deleted.

Staff Relations Guidelines—In the event of a disaster (or any crisis situation, for that matter), the possibility of negative publicity always exists. Inaccurate or misleading information paves the way for rumors that, if allowed to circulate within the community, can irreparably damage a business' recovery efforts. A well-developed damage control plan, with clearly detailed procedures for all personnel within an entity's structure, can prevent any negative or misleading information from being disseminated.

The primary purpose of the damage control plan is to leave the audience—readers, viewers, listeners—with the assurance that the crisis situation is under control. The governing principle in any damage control plan is to identify only those persons within a company who can effectively respond to media questions and concerns and who can serve in the capacity of official company spokesperson. While these individuals—the primary spokesperson and back-up—do not necessarily require a media background, both individuals must be able to think and respond quickly and accurately in high pressure situations, regardless of the nature of those situations. When a crisis or disaster occurs, tensions run high. These tensions and accompanying stress can be exacerbated under the glaring lights of television cameras' news crews, reporters and their newspads, and the television/radio microphone.

Upon notification that a crisis situation is underway, the official company spokesperson, in consultation with the company's president/building owner, and the disaster and recovery planning team leader, must make the decision to activate either all or part of the Damage Control Plan.

Media Relations Guidelines—The media—both print and broadcast—can play a pivotal role in business continuity and recovery. As part of a company's regular business operations, many entities have established relationships with their local media and work hard to cultivate those relationships. By the same token, many companies, especially smaller ones, do not have formal media relations departments or programs. In either case, however, one thing is almost certain. When disaster strikes, the media will cover the "story." Questions will be asked, statements and interviews will be requested. For this reason, companies, through their appointed spokespersons, must know what to do, how to do it and what to say to the media.

Equally important is the fact that an entity's spokesperson should know how to enlist the media's help in conveying the message that, despite the business interruption, the company will survive.

Procedures for Working with the Media—In the event of an emergency or disaster situation, or at some point during or subsequent to the actual occurrence, the affected company may be contacted by the media for either a statement or interview. When calls such as these are received, they should be immediately directed to the designated spokesperson. In large companies, the public relations director or marketing manager is the authorized spokesperson. Smaller entities must pre-determine who will serve as the official public relations officer. Once the determination has been made, the following key points should be included in the company's media contact procedures:

A.   MEDIA CALLS

All press inquiries should be directed to the designated spokesperson. All employees should be directed to refer all media calls to that person.

B.   QUESTIONS TO ASK BEFORE RESPONDING

Before responding to any calls, the designated spokesperson should ask the following questions:

- Who is the reporter?

- What is the newspaper/station/channel?

- What is the deadline?

- What is the subject of the interview?

- When will the news story be published/aired?

Establish at the outset that in talking with the press the discussion will be directed to customers, prospective customers, the community at large, etc.

Treat the subject with low-key, matter-of-fact answers/responses that sap the subject of its "scare" potential.

Clear, concise and understandable language should always be used (i.e., industry and technical jargon should be avoided).

All questions should be answered with total candor.

If answers cannot be provided, the authorized spokesperson should say so. The reporter should be informed that the information will be provided after it is obtained. (Once the information is obtained, the reporter must be contacted. Any promise made should be kept!) No one should be pressured into responding to a question that they are not qualified or prepared to give. The company spokesperson should always assume that any response will find its way into print.

With television and radio responses, brevity is essential. Information is more likely to be quoted—and quoted correctly—if it can be provided within a 20- or 40-second "burst."

C. DISCUSSION POINTS

The designated spokesperson should be prepared to discuss:

- The nature of the occurrence.

- The impact of the occurrence on business operations.

- What actions the company is taking or will take to minimize the impact of the occurrence on employees, customers, the community, etc.

D. PROTOCOL

The following protocol should be followed at all times by the official company spokesperson:

- Important facts should be stated at the beginning of the interview.

- Fairness and accuracy should be ensured at all times.

- "Off-the-record" comments should never be made.

- Facts should never be exaggerated.

- Always be truthful with the media.

- Requests or demands for "approval" of a report should never be made. If inaccuracies occur, the media does want it brought to their attention. However, the inaccuracies should be important enough to merit a complaint.

- Pressure tactics should never be used in an attempt to get something printed or broadcast, or kept out of print, or off the air.

Finally, if requests for site interviews, "spot" reports, etc., are made, and if it is feasible to do so, specific site areas should be designated. Having reporters, microphones, cameras, etc., in these designated locations can minimize any possible disruptions to recovery efforts/business operations.

THE MEDIA'S ROLE IN RECOVERY EFFORTS

Crisis planning and damage control are integral components of the disaster and recovery planning process. Like the disaster and recovery process itself, which anticipates potential disasters and the impact of those occurrences on a company or facility, damage control strategies anticipate the need for addressing media concerns. The effective crisis planning and damage control effort also anticipates the need for working with the media to assure existing business relationships, including clients, customers, the community and the competition, of its viability.

The media as a resource can effectively "promote" a company's recovery efforts if "newsworthy" information is available.

Newsworthy information can be provided to the media in various forms, including: press releases and news conferences, as well as purchasing newspaper ads and broadcast time to deliver important messages. Each of these should be considered in the overall damage control planning effort.

Press Releases

A press release is a written "report" of any current activity in a company, entity or organization. It can describe new products, services, senior staff appointments or changes, or any topic currently receiving attention, including a disaster occurrence.

In the event of a disaster occurrence, the press release can be used to notify, update, inform and reassure a company's public (e.g., employees, customers, clients, distributors, suppliers and the competition) about the business' continued operations in the wake of disaster. A positively written yet truthful statement released to a company's public through the media can place the company in a pro-active position, contingent, of course, upon the activation of all other preparedness components.

There are several general guidelines for writing a press or news release. They include:

- Type in single space the company name, the name of the appropriate company spokesperson, or contact, and the telephone number of the contact in the upper left corner of the first page. (By providing a phone number, the newspaper can reach the company spokesperson with any questions regarding the story should it become necessary to do so.) Since newspapers and reporters do not follow a standard "9 to 5" routine, also include an "after-hours" number where the company contact can be reached.

- Indicate the release date of the story, per the following example: FOR RELEASE: Tuesday, April 27, 2010. Unless there is a specific reason to do so, the release date should be the day the release is sent.

- The actual copy—without a headline—should be started about a third down the page. The space above should be kept blank for the headline—which is always written by the editor—and editor notes.

- The copy should be double-spaced.

- Only one side of the paper should be used.

- The story should be kept brief.

- If the release must be continued on another page, do not end the page in the middle of a paragraph. If the page cannot accommodate an entire paragraph, start that paragraph at the beginning of the next page.

- If the release has more than one page, write "more" at the end of page one. At the top of the next page, write Page 2.

- End the release with "###" or "-30-," which tells the editor that the story is over (see Figure 15-1 for a sample press release).

While these guidelines "speak" to press releases that are geared towards paper and scissors editing, they are nevertheless appropriate for the computer/video editing systems that are currently used by the media. If a company's press release is accepted, it will be processed electronically.

Radio And Television "Spots"

There are occasions which may call for broadcast coverage, particularly when the broadcast media wants to do a follow-up story on an event that impacts upon a community and its citizens. For example, if a facility is forced to relocate to an alternate site, the media (both print and broadcast) may want to do an interview at the alternate site to report on the "progress" of the recovery efforts. Such an interview can provide a sense of closure to an event, particularly if the event in question has major implications for a community and its citizens. Often, this sense of closure is important for its psychologically "healing" effects. It can and oftentimes does signify new beginnings, re-birth and a moving forward.

Since not all situations are necessarily "media events," it may be important for the company to "feed" its public with positive information on business operations. Utilizing the media can be an effective means for doing so. However, a note of caution is in order. A company or entity should never attempt to manipulate the media. Any and all media efforts that are undertaken must be done so genuinely, ethically and judiciously.

Writing The Broadcast Script—The key to effectively writing the broadcast script is to remember that the copy must be written as if it were intended to be spoken. Unlike the printed word, the broadcast audience cannot reread a sentence or a paragraph. Therefore, the script must be written for the ear and not the eye. Also, broadcast style dictates that remarks be attributed at the beginning of the "spot."

For example, when a company wants to announce the return to its original facility which was gutted by fire, the copy should read:

"John Whyte, President of XYZ Castings, announced today that the company is 'coming home'."

XYZ Castings, Inc.

CONTACT: John Smith, Facility Manager
XYZ Castings, Inc.
123 Main Street
Anytown, NY 10010
555-9300
555-4321 (Home)

FOR RELEASE: TUESDAY, APRIL 27, 2010

XYZ CASTINGS REOPENS DOORS

John Whyte, President of XYZ Castings, will be on hand to welcome the public to the reopening of the company's facility at 23 Elm Street on Saturday, May 1, 2010.

When the roof of the 100,000-square-foot facility was destroyed in the February 10th blizzard, the company was forced to move its operations to a temporary location.

Joining Whyte in welcoming the public to the noontime reopening will be the company's 60 employees, all of whom assisted in the company's recovery efforts. The noon event will include a tour of the facility followed by a reception. According to Whyte, "This is our way of saying thanks to the community for its support during our disaster recovery period."

For more information call the company at 555-9800.

# # #

Figure 15-1. Sample press release.

All broadcast copy must be accompanied by "pronouncers," which are used by the news announcer to ensure the correct pronunciation. Using the example above, the copy would be submitted to the radio/television station as follows:

"John Whyte (pronounced wit), President of XYZ Castings, announced today that the company is coming home."

Radio and television stations will edit and rewrite copy. However, the less editing/rewriting they have to do to the submitted material, the better the chance that it will be used and that the meaning of the copy will not be inadvertently altered.

Automated Voice Mail/Telephone Answering Devices

In the event that a disaster occurrence forces the relocation of a company to an alternate site, the company's after-hours voice mail response should announce the entity's "new," albeit temporary, location. A calm, pleasant and reassuring voice should identify the company, and mention normal working hours of the new location. The suggestion to leave name, number and brief message should be included in the response to the after-hours caller.

All calls should be promptly returned the next business day or as soon as possible, so that customers, clients, etc., are assured that their needs will be met, despite the disaster occurrence. An appropriate voice mail response might say:

"Thank you for calling XYZ Castings. Our normal business hours are from 8:00 a.m. to 5:00 p.m. at our new, temporary location—123 Main Street, Anytown, NY. Please call again, or leave your name, phone number and a brief message. Your call will be returned. We are here to handle all your business needs. Thank you for calling XYZ Castings."

Remember that telephone answering devices also can be used to locate and account for all employees after a disaster occurrence. As part of the disaster response and recovery plan, employees can be trained to call in with their whereabouts and the whereabouts of colleagues.

Chapter 16

Mitigation

Disasters are events that can cause loss of life and property. They occur when hazards impact people and property. The damage caused to companies in terms of human loss—injury/death—and economic loss, can be prevented, or at the least minimized. To better structure the way in which potential disasters are managed, we look to the basic tenets of emergency management previously discussed.

For approximately the last fifty years the focus of emergency management planning was on the response to and recovery from nuclear attack by foreign enemies. During the 1990's this emphasis shifted to address natural disasters such as hurricanes, earthquakes, tornadoes and floods.

However, there is now a need to incorporate new threats into emergency management planning. The threats of terrorism and technological disasters loom in the forefront of business mitigation/planning and recovery. The September 11, 2001 attacks on New York City, Washington, D.C., and the field in Shanksville, Pennsylvania, demonstrate that very need to mitigate the threat from man-made sources.

In addition to these violent acts of terrorism, there are other man-made incidents that demonstrate the need for prevention and diligence—the bombing of the 1996 Summer Olympics, the 1995 bombing of the Oklahoma City Murrah Federal Building, the 1993 World Trade Center bombing, and the numerous Internet cyber attacks are just a few examples. See Table 16-1 for FEMA's Event Profile for Terrorism and Technological Hazards.

Mitigation

As defined by the Federal Emergency Management Agency, FEMA, mitigation is any sustained action taken to reduce or eliminate long-term risk to life and property from a hazard event. Mitigation encourages long-term reduction of hazards vulnerability. The goal of mitigation is to decrease the need for response as opposed to simply increasing the response capability. Mitigation can save lives and reduce property damage. When done cost-effectively, mitigation reduces the cost of disasters to property and building owners. When planned and practiced by communities, mitigation can protect critical community facilities, reduce exposure to liability, and minimize disruption to the community.

The Disaster Mitigation Act of 2000

The Disaster Mitigation Act of 2000 (DMA 2000) is legislation designed to improve the planning process for state and local governments. This legislation reinforces the importance of mitigation planning and emphasizes planning for disasters before they occur. The pre-Disaster Mitigation Act of 2009 also reinforces the planning process.

Preparedness

Preparedness includes those plans and preparations made to save lives. Preparedness also facilitates response operations.

Response

Response includes those actions taken to provide emergency assistance, save lives, minimize property damage and speed recovery immediately following a disaster.

Recovery

Recovery includes those actions taken to return to a normal or improved operating condition following a disaster.

While every accident or deliberate attack cannot be prevented, mitigation can reduce the occurrence of an incident or the effects of an incident. A well thought-out mitigation (disaster/recovery) plan works for both natural and man-made or technological incidents. The process of dealing with natural disasters as well as all forms of terrorism (cyber, bio-, agri-, etc.), and/or hazardous materials accidents, is essentially the same. The steps used in mitigation/disaster/recovery planning are:

1. Identify and organize resources.
2. Conduct a risk assessment.
3. Develop a mitigation plan.
4. Implement the actions.

1. **Identify resources**. The resources of a company, as previously discussed, include: personnel; equipment; the facility itself; the facility's supporting systems; the organization's capabilities—training, evacuation plan and employee support system; and the company's backup systems.

2. **Conduct a risk or threat assessment and estimate potential losses.** When conducting a risk assessment, a number of factors come into play. These include company plans/policies (e.g., evacuation/fire protection plans, etc.), as well as the identification of man-made hazards. These hazards include both terrorism and technological hazards. See Table 16-2.

3. **Identify mitigation actions that will reduce the effects of the hazards.** When developing the mitigation plan, several core elements form the basic components of the plan. These include the executive summary; emergency management elements; response procedures; support documents; and resource lists. To determine the specific goals and milestones that must be achieved, a list of tasks to be performed should be developed and prioritized. In addition, identification of the personnel who will perform the tasks and the time frame that the tasks will be performed is necessary. Finally, developing procedures for addressing the problem areas and the resource shortfalls identified is also necessary.

5. **Implement the actions; evaluate the results; keep the plan up-to-date.** Mitigation plan implementation means acting on recommendations made during the vulnerability analysis; integrating the plan into company operations; and training employees. An effective plan integrates all the components—natural disasters, technological and human-engineered—into one comprehensive plan.

Table 16-2 Man-made Hazards—Terrorist and Technological. Source: Federal Emergency Management Agency (FEMA)

Terrorism	Technological Hazards
Bombs/explosive devices	Industrial accident (fixed facility)
Biological agent	Industrial accident (transportation)
Chemical agent	
Nuclear bomb	
Radiological agent	
Arson/incendiary attack	
Armed attack	
Cyber-terrorism	
Agri-terrorism	
Intentional hazardous material release	

SUMMARY

As with any effective disaster/recovery plan, disaster mitigation utilizes much pre-planning. An effective hazard mitigation/disaster and recovery plan is the critical first step in making the company/facility/community more disaster resistant.

Hazard Mitigation Planning and Disaster/Recovery Planning involves the coordination of actions taken to reduce injuries, deaths, property damage, economic losses, and degradation of natural resources due to natural or human-caused hazards events. The actions of an effective Hazard Mitigation Plan, and/or Disaster/Recovery Plan have long-term benefits.

Table 16-1. Event profiles for terrorism and technological hazards. Source: Federal Emergency Management Agency.

Hazard	Application Mode	Hazard Duration	Extent of Effects; Static/Dynamic	Mitigating and Exacerbating Conditions
Conventional Bomb/ Improvised Explosive Device	Detonation of explosive device on or near target; delivery via person, vehicle, or projectile.	Instantaneous; additional "secondary devices" may be used, lengthening the time duration of the hazard until the attack site is determined to be clear.	Extent of damage is determined by type and quantity of explosive. Effects generally static other than cascading consequences, incremental structural failure, etc.	Overpressure at a given standoff is inversely proportional to the cube of the distance from the blast; thus, each additional increment of standoff provides progressively more protection. Terrain, forestation, structures, etc. can provide shielding by absorbing and/or deflecting energy and debris. Exacerbating conditions include ease of access to target; lack of barriers/shielding; poor construction; and ease of concealment of device.
Chemical Agent *	Liquid/aerosol contaminants can be dispersed using sprayers or other aerosol generators; liquids vaporizing from puddles/ containers; or munitions.	Chemical agents may pose viable threats for hours to weeks depending on the agent and the conditions in which it exists.	Contamination can be carried out of the initial target area by persons, vehicles, water and wind. Chemicals may be corrosive or otherwise damaging over time if not remediated.	Air temperature can affect evaporation of aerosols. Ground temperature affects evaporation of liquids. Humidity can enlarge aerosol particles, reducing inhalation hazard. Precipitation can dilute and disperse agents but can spread contamination. Wind can disperse vapors but also cause target area to be dynamic. The micro-meteorological effects of buildings and terrain can alter travel and duration of agents. Shielding in the form of sheltering in place can protect people and property from harmful effects.

Table 16-1 (Continued)

Arson/ Incendiary Attack	Initiation of fire or explosion on or near target via direct contact or remotely via projectile.	Generally minutes to hours.	Extent of damage is determined by type and quantity of device/accelerant and materials present at or near target. Effects generally static other than cascading consequences, incremental structural failure, etc.	Mitigation factors include built-in fire detection and protection systems and fire-resistive construction techniques. Inadequate security can allow easy access to target, easy concealment of an incendiary device and undetected initiation of a fire. Non-compliance with fire and building codes as well as failure to maintain existing fire protection systems can substantially increase the effectiveness of a fire weapon.
Armed Attack	Tactical assault or sniping from remote location.	Generally minutes to days.	Varies based upon the perpetrators' intent and capabilities.	Inadequate security can allow easy access to target, easy concealment of weapons and undetected initiation of an attack.
Biological Agent *	Liquid or solid contaminants can be dispersed using sprayers/aerosol generators or by point or line sources such as munitions, covert deposits and moving sprayers.	Biological agents may pose viable threats for hours to years depending on the agent and the conditions in which it exists.	Depending on the agent used and the effectiveness with which it is deployed, contamination can be spread via wind and water. Infection can be spread via human or animal vectors.	Altitude of release above ground can affect dispersion; sunlight is destructive to many bacteria and viruses; light to moderate wind will disperse agents but higher winds can break up aerosol clouds; the micro-meteorological effects of buildings and terrain can influence aerosolization and travel of agents.

Table 16-1 (*Continued*)

Hazard	Application Mode	Hazard Duration	Extent of Effects; Static/Dynamic	Mitigating and Exacerbating Conditions
Cyber-terrorism	Electronic attack using one computer system against another.	Minutes to days.	Generally no direct effects on built environment.	Inadequate security can facilitate access to critical computer systems, allowing them to be used to conduct attacks.
Agriterrorism	Direct, generally covert contamination of food supplies or introduction of pests and/or disease agents to crops and livestock.	Days to months.	Varies by type of incident. Food contamination events may be limited to discrete distribution sites, whereas pests and diseases may spread widely. Generally no effects on built environment.	Inadequate security can facilitate adulteration of food and introduction of pests and disease agents to crops and livestock.
Radiological Agent **	Radioactive contaminants can be dispersed using sprayers/aerosol generators, or by point or line sources such as munitions, covert deposits and moving sprayers.	Contaminants may remain hazardous for seconds to years depending on material used.	Initial effects will be localized to site of attack; depending on meteorological conditions, subsequent behavior of radioactive contaminants may be dynamic.	Duration of exposure, distance from source of radiation, and the amount of shielding between source and target determine exposure to radiation.

Table 16-1 (Continued)

Nuclear Bomb **	Detonation of nuclear device underground, at the surface, in the air or at high altitude.	Light/heat flash and blast/shock wave last for seconds; nuclear radiation and fallout hazards can persist for years. Electromagnetic pulse from a high-altitude detonation lasts for seconds and affects only unprotected electronic systems.	Initial light, heat and blast effects of a subsurface, ground or air burst are static and are determined by the device's characteristics and employment; fallout of radioactive contaminants may be dynamic, depending on meteorological conditions.	Harmful effects of radiation can be reduced by minimizing the time of exposure. Light, heat and blast energy decrease logarithmically as a function of distance from seat of blast. Terrain, forestation, structures, etc. can provide shielding by absorbing and/or deflecting radiation and radioactive contaminants.
Hazardous Material Release (fixed facility or trans-portation)	Solid, liquid and/or gaseous contaminants may be released from fixed or mobile containers.	Hours to days.	Chemicals may be corrosive or otherwise damaging over time. Explosion and/or fire may be subsequent. Contamination may be carried out of the incident area by persons, vehicles, water and wind.	As with chemical weapons, weather conditions will directly affect how the hazard develops. The micro-meteorological effects of buildings and terrain can alter travel and duration of agents. Shielding in the form of sheltering in place can protect people and property from harmful effects. Non-compliance with fire and building codes as well as failure to maintain existing fire protection and containment features can substantially increase the damage from a hazardous materials release.

* Source: *Jane's Chem-Bio Handbook*
** Source: FEMA, *Radiological Emergency Management* Independent Study Course

Chapter 17

Assessing and
Managing Risk

The terrorist attacks of September 11, 2001 clearly demonstrated
that our institutions and our infrastructure have been targeted.
The terrorist's weapons of mass destruction can include biologi-
cal, chemical, radiological, nuclear, or high explosive weaponry.
And, while terrorist groups would have to overcome significant
technical and operational challenges to make and release many
chemical and biological agents of a sufficient quality and quan-
tity to kill large numbers of people, it has been tried.

Examples of terrorist activity, both at home and abroad, include the
incidents of anthrax-laced letters sent to public and high-profile citizens
following the September 11th attacks. In the release of the nerve agent
sarin in a Tokyo subway in 1995, 12 people were killed and thousands
were injured. In 1984, a religious cult in Oregon contaminated salad bars
in local restaurants with salmonella bacteria in order to prevent people
from voting in a local election. Although there were no fatalities as a
result of this terrorist attack, hundreds of people were diagnosed with
food-borne illness.

As both private and public sector organizations become more
aware of their vulnerability to terrorist attacks, they are also becoming
acutely aware of the need to increase security measures. In order to better prepare against terrorism and other threats, facility managers and
building owners are reviewing their policies and procedures with an eye
toward risk management.

Risk Management

Risk management is the systematic, analytical process that considers the likelihood of a threat harming individuals or physical assets. Risk management identifies actions that reduce the risk and mitigate the consequences of an attack or event. Risk management acknowledges that risk generally cannot be eliminated but risk can be reduced by enhancing protection from known or potential threats. These risk management principles

• Identify weaknesses in a company, system or organization

• Offer a realistic method for making decisions about the expenditure of scarce resources and the selection of cost-effective countermeasures to protect assets

• Improve the success rate of a company/organization's security efforts by emphasizing the communication of risks and recommendations to the final decision-making authority

• Assist facility managers, building owners and security professionals as well as other key decision makers answer the question "How much security is enough?"

Since risk is a function of assets, threats and vulnerabilities, risk management

• allows organizations and companies to determine the:

• magnitude and effect of potential loss;

• likelihood of such loss actually happening; and finally,

• countermeasures that could lower the probability or magnitude of the loss.

As defined by the National Infrastructure Protection Center (NIPC), risk is the potential for some unwanted event to occur. Examples of such unwanted events include loss of information and money, as well as organizational reputations, or someone gaining unauthorized access to the company's physical property, data systems, etc. As such, risk is the function of the likelihood of the unwanted event occurring and its consequences. Therefore, it is obvious that the higher the probability and the greater the consequences, the greater the risk to the company or organization.

The likelihood of the unwanted event occurring depends upon threat and vulnerability. Threat is the capability and the intention of a terrorist to undertake actions that are detrimental to a company or organization's interests. Threat is a function of the terrorist only. It cannot be controlled by the owner or the user of the asset, i.e., building owner, facility/property manager, etc. However, the intention of terrorists to exploit their capability may be encouraged by vulnerability in the company or organization's assets. Or conversely, the intention of the terrorist may be discouraged by the owner's countermeasures.

Vulnerability is any weakness in an asset that can be exploited by a terrorist to cause damage to the company/organization's interest. The level of vulnerability and level of risk can be reduced by implementing appropriate security countermeasures.

An asset is anything of value. Assets include:

- people
- information
- hardware
- software
- facilities
- company reputation
- company operations

In other words, assets are what a company or organization needs to get the job done. Consequently, the more critical the asset is to a company or organization, and the more critical the asset is to meeting company goals, the greater the effect of damage and/or destruction to the asset.

Risk Assessment

The first step in the process of assessing risk to a terrorist attack is to identify the relative importance of the people, business activities, goods and facilities involved in order to prioritize security actions. This applies to both new and existing facilities. The Federal Emergency Management Agency (FEMA) recommends the following actions:

- Define and understand the core functions and process of the business or institutional entity
  — Identify critical business infrastructure:
  — Critical component—people, functions and facilities
  — Critical information systems and data
  — Life safety systems and safe haven areas
  — Security systems

- Assign a relative protection priority such as high, medium or low to the occupants, business functions or physical components of the facility:
  — High Priority—loss or damage of the facility would have grave consequences such as loss of life, severe injuries, loss of primary services or major loss of core processes and functions for an extended period of time.
  — Medium Priority—loss or damage of the facility would have moderate to serious consequences such as injuries or impairment of core functions and processes
  — Low Priority—loss or damage of the facility would have minor consequences or impact, such as a slight impact on core functions and processes for a short period of time.

Threat Assessment

A terrorist threat comes from people with the intent to do harm, who are known to exist, have the capability for hostile action, and have expressed the intent to take hostile action.

Threat assessment is a continual process of compiling and examining information concerning potential threats. Information should be gathered from all reliable sources. The assessment process consists of:

- Defining threats and
- Identifying likely threat event profiles and tactics.

Defining Threats

Defining threats involves analyzing the following information regarding terrorists:

- Existence
- Capability
- History
- Intention
- Targeting

Existence is the assessment of who is hostile to the organization.
Capability is the assessment of what weapons have been used in carrying out past
attacks.
History is the assessment of what the potential terrorist has done in the past and
how many times.
Intention is the assessment of what the potential terrorist hopes to achieve.
Targeting is the assessment of the likelihood that a terrorist performing surveillance on a particular facility, nearby facilities, or facilities that have much in common with a particular organization.

Identifying Likely Threat Event Profiles and Tactics

To identify the likelihood of specific threats and tactics, the following variables should be evaluated:

- attack intentions
- hazard event profiles
- the expected effects of an attack on the facility/organization.

Table 17-1 presents general event profiles for a range of possible forms of terrorist attacks. The profiles describe the mode, duration and extent of the effects of an attack, as well as any mitigating and exacerbating conditions that may exist. These descriptions can be used to identify threats of concern to individual organizations.

Assigning a Threat Rating

A threat rating should be assigned to each hazard of concern to a particular organization. The threat rating, like protection priority, is based on expert judgment. For purposes of simplicity the ratings may read high, medium or low:

Table 17-1. Event Profiles for Terrorism and Technological Hazards

Hazard/Threat	Application Mode	Hazard Duration	Extent of Effects; Static/Dynamic	Mitigating and Exacerbating Conditions
Agriterrorism	Direct, generally covert contamination of food supplies or introduction of pests and/or disease agents to crops and livestock.	Days to months.	Varies by type of incident. Food contamination events may be limited to discrete distribution sites, whereas pests and diseases may spread widely. Generally no effects on built environment.	Inadequate security can facilitate adulteration of food and introduction of pests and disease agents to crops and livestock.
Armed Attack - Ballistics (small arms) - Stand-off weapons (rocket propelled grenades, mortars)	Tactical assault or sniping from remote location.	Generally minutes to days.	Varies, based upon the perpetrators' intent and capabilities.	Inadequate security can allow easy access to target, easy concealment of weapons, and undetected initiation of an attack.

Source: FEMA

- **High Threat.** Known terrorists or hazards, capable of causing loss and/or damage to a facility exist. One or more vulnerabilities are present and the terrorists are known or are reasonably suspected of having intent to attack the facility.

- **Medium Threat.** Known terrorists or hazards that may be capable of causing loss of or damage to a facility exists. One or more vulnerabilities may be present. However, the terrorists are not believed to have intent to attack the facility.

- **Low Threat.** Few or no terrorists or hazards exist. Their capability of causing damage to a particular facility is doubtful.

These ratings may be changed over time. What may be a high threat in the present may, over time, be lessened to a medium or low threat depending upon the conditions at a particular time.

Alternative Approach

Assessing terrorist threats is the most difficult aspect of planning to resist terrorist attacks. This is particularly true for those building own-

Table 17-1. Event Profiles for Terrorism and Technological Hazards (*Continued*)

Hazard/Threat	Application Mode	Hazard Duration	Extent of Effects; Static/Dynamic	Mitigating and Exacerbating Conditions
Arson/Incendiary Attack	Initiation of fire or explosion on or near target via direct contact or remotely via projectile.	Generally minutes to hours.	Extent of damage is determined by type and quantity of device /accelerant and materials present at or near target. Effects generally static other than cascading consequences, incremental structural failure, etc.	Mitigation factors include built-in fire detection and protection systems and fire-resistive construction techniques. Inadequate security can allow easy access to target, easy concealment of an incendiary device and undetected initiation of a fire. Non-compliance with fire and building codes as well as failure to maintain existing fire protection systems can substantially increase the effectiveness of a fire weapon.
Biological Agents - Anthrax - Botulism - Brucellosis - Plague - Smallpox - Tularemia - Viral hemorrhagic fevers - Toxins (Botulinum, Ricin, Staphylococcal Enterotoxin B, T-2 Mycotoxins)	Liquid or solid contaminants can be dispersed using sprayers/aerosol generators or by point or line sources such as munitions, covert deposits, and moving sprayers.	Biological agents may pose viable threats for hours to years, depending on the agent and the conditions in which it exists.	Depending on the agent used and the effectiveness with which it is deployed, contamination can be spread via wind and water. Infection can be spread via human or animal vectors.	Altitude of release above ground can affect dispersion; sunlight is destructive to many bacteria and viruses; light to moderate winds will disperse agents but higher winds can break up aerosol clouds; the micro-meteorological effects of buildings and terrain can influence aerosolization and travel of agents.

Source: FEMA

ers and facility managers who have not had any experience in doing so. An effective alternative approach may be to select a level of desired protection for a business operation based on management decision making, and then proceeding to a vulnerability assessment. Various federal agencies along with the U.S. Department of Defense correlate "levels of protection" with potential damage and expected injuries. The following levels are based on Department of Defense definitions:

Table 17-1. Event Profiles for Terrorism and Technological Hazards (Continued)

Hazard/Threat	Application Mode	Hazard Duration	Extent of Effects; Static/Dynamic	Mitigating and Exacerbating Conditions
Chemical Agents - Blister - Blood - Choking/lung/pulmonary - Incapacitating - Nerve - Riot control/tear gas - Vomiting	Liquid/aerosol contaminants can be dispersed using sprayers or other aerosol generators; liquids vaporizing from puddles/containers; or munitions.	Chemicals agents may pose viable threats for hours to weeks, depending on the agent and the conditions in which it exists.	Contamination can be carried out of the initial target area by persons, vehicles, water, and wind. Chemicals may be corrosive or otherwise damaging over time if not remediated.	Air temperature can affect evaporation of aerosols. Ground temperature affects evaporation of liquids. Humidity can enlarge aerosol particles, reducing inhalation hazard. Precipitation can dilute and disperse agents, but can spread contamination. Wind can disperse vapors, but also cause target are to be dynamic. The micro-meteorological effects of buildings and terrain can alter travel and duration of agents. Shielding in the form of sheltering in place can protect people and property from harmful effects.
Conventional Bomb - Stationary vehicle - Moving vehicle - Mail - Supply - Thrown - Placed - Personnel	Detonation of explosive device on or near target; via person, vehicle, or projectile.	Instantaneous; additional secondary devices may be used, lengthening the time duration of the hazard until the attack site is determined to be clear.	Extent of damage is determined by type and quantity of explosive. Effects generally static other than cascading consequences, incremental structural failure, etc.	Energy decreases logarithmically as a function of distance from seat of blast. Terrain, forestation, structures, etc., can provide shielding by absorbing and/or deflecting energy and debris. Exacerbating conditions include ease of access to target; lack of barriers/shielding; poor construction; and ease of concealment of device.
Cyberterrorism	Electronic attack using one computer system against another.	Minutes to days.	Generally no direct effects on built environment.	Inadequate security can facilitate access to critical computer systems, allowing them to be used to conduct attacks.

Source: FEMA

Table 17-1. Event Profiles for Terrorism and Technological Hazards (*Continued*)

Hazard/Threat	Application Mode	Hazard Duration	Extent of Effects; Static/Dynamic	Mitigating and Exacerbating Conditions
Hazardous Material Release (fixed facility or transportation) - Toxic Industrial Chemicals and Materials (Organic vapors: cyclohexane; Acid gases: cyanogens, chlorine, hydrogen sulfide; Base gases: ammonia; Special cases: phosgene, formaldehyde)	Solid, liquid, and/or gaseous contaminants may be released from fixed or mobile containers.	Hours to days.	Chemicals may be corrosive or otherwise damaging over time. Explosion and/or fire may be subsequent. Contamination may be carried out of the incident area by persons, vehicles, water, and wind.	As with chemical weapons, weather conditions will directly affect how the hazard develops. The micro-meteorological effects of buildings and terrain can alter travel and duration of agents. Shielding in the form of sheltering in place can protect people and property from harmful effects. Non-compliance with fire and building codes as well as failure to maintain existing fire protection and containment features can substantially increase the damage from a hazardous materials release.
Nuclear Device	Detonation of nuclear device underground, at the surface, in the air or at high altitude.	Light/heat flash and blast/shock wave last for seconds; nuclear radiation and fallout hazards can persist for years. Electromagnetic pulse from a high-altitude detonation lasts for seconds and affects only unprotected electronic systems.	Initial light, heat and blast effects of a subsurface, ground or air burst are static and are determined by the device's characteristics and employment; fallout of radioactive contaminants may be dynamic, depending on meteorological conditions.	Harmful effects of radiation can be reduced by minimizing the time of exposure. Light, heat, and blast energy decrease logarithmically as a function of distance from seat of blast. Terrain, forestation, structures, etc., can provide shielding by absorbing and/or deflecting radiation and radioactive contaminants.
Radiological Agents - Alpha - Beta - Gamma	Radioactive contaminants can be dispersed using sprayers/aerosol generators, or by point or line sources such as munitions, covert deposits, and moving sprayers.	Contaminants may remain hazardous for seconds to years, depending on material used.	Initial effects will be localized to site of attack; depending on meteorological conditions, subsequent behavior of radioactive contaminants may be dynamic.	Duration of exposure, distance from source of radiation, and the amount of shielding between source and target determine exposure to radiation.

Source: FEMA

Table 17-1. Event Profiles for Terrorism and Technological Hazards (*Continued*)

Hazard/Threat	Application Mode	Hazard Duration	Extent of Effects; Static/Dynamic	Mitigating and Exacerbating Conditions
Hazardous Material Release (fixed facility or transportation) - Toxic Industrial Chemicals and Materials (Organic vapors: cyclohexane; Acid gases: cyanogens, chlorine, hydrogen sulfide; Base gases: ammonia; Special cases: phosgene, formaldehyde)	Solid, liquid, and/or gaseous contaminants may be released from fixed or mobile containers.	Hours to days.	Chemicals may be corrosive or otherwise damaging over time. Explosion and/or fire may be subsequent. Contamination may be carried out of the incident area by persons, vehicles, water, and wind.	As with chemical weapons, weather conditions will directly affect how the hazard develops. The micro-meteorological effects of buildings and terrain can alter travel and duration of agents. Shielding in the form of sheltering in place can protect people and property from harmful effects. Non-compliance with fire and building codes as well as failure to maintain existing fire protection and containment features can substantially increase the damage from a hazardous materials release.
Nuclear Device	Detonation of nuclear device underground, at the surface, in the air or at high altitude.	Light/heat flash and blast/shock wave last for seconds; nuclear radiation and fallout hazards can persist for years. Electromagnetic pulse from a high-altitude detonation lasts for seconds and affects only unprotected electronic systems.	Initial light, heat and blast effects of a subsurface, ground or air burst are static and are determined by the device's characteristics and employment; fallout of radioactive contaminants may be dynamic, depending on meteorological conditions.	Harmful effects of radiation can be reduced by minimizing the time of exposure. Light, heat, and blast energy decrease logarithmically as a function of distance from seat of blast. Terrain, forestation, structures, etc., can provide shielding by absorbing and/or deflecting radiation and radioactive contaminants.
Radiological Agents - Alpha - Beta - Gamma	Radioactive contaminants can be dispersed using sprayers/aerosol generators, or by point or line sources such as munitions, covert deposits, and moving sprayers.	Contaminants may remain hazardous for seconds to years, depending on material used.	Initial effects will be localized to site of attack; depending on meteorological conditions, subsequent behavior of radioactive contaminants may be dynamic.	Duration of exposure, distance from source of radiation, and the amount of shielding between source and target determine exposure to radiation.

Source: FEMA

Table 17-1. Event Profiles for Terrorism and Technological Hazards (*Continued*)

Hazard/Threat	Application Mode	Hazard Duration	Extent of Effects; Static/Dynamic	Mitigating and Exacerbating Conditions
Surveillance - Acoustic - Electronic eavesdropping - Visual	Stand-off collection of visual information using cameras or high powered optics, acoustic information using directional microphones and lasers, and electronic information from computers, cell phones, and hand-held radios. Placed collection by putting a device "bug" at the point of use.	Usually months.	This is usually the prelude to the loss of an asset. A terrorist surveillance team spends much time looking for vulnerabilities and tactics that will be successful. This is the time period that provides the best assessment of threat as it indicates targeting of the facility.	Building design, especially blocking lines of sight and ensuring the exterior walls and windows do not allow sound transmission or acoustic collection, can mitigate this hazard.
Unauthorized Entry - Forced - Covert	Use of hand or power tools, weapons, or explosives to create a man-sized opening or operate an assembly (such as a locked door), or use false credentials to enter a building.	Minutes to hours, depending upon the intent.	If goal is to steal or destroy physical assets or compromise information, the initial effects are quick, but damage may be long lasting. If intent is to disrupt operations or take hostages, the effects may last for a long time, especially if injury or death occurs.	Standard physical security building design should be the minimum mitigation measures. For more critical assets, additional measures, like closed circuit television or traffic flow that channels visitors past access control, aids in detection of this hazard.

Source: FEMA

- **High Protection.** Facility superficially damaged; no permanent deformation of primary and secondary structural members or non-structural elements. Only superficial injuries are likely.

- **Medium Protection.** Damaged, but repairable. Minor deformations of non-structural elements and secondary structural members and no permanent deformation in primary structural members. Some minor injuries, but fatalities are unlikely.

- **Very Low Protection.** Heavily damaged, onset of structural collapse. Major deformation of primary and secondary structural members, but progressive collapse is unlikely. Collapse of non-structural elements. Majority of personnel suffer serious injuries.

There are likely to be a limited number—10 percent to 25 percent—of fatalities.

Note that the "very low" level is not the same as doing nothing. No action could result in catastrophic building failure and high loss of life.

Vulnerability Assessment

A terrorism vulnerability assessment evaluates any weaknesses that can be exploited by a terrorist. It evaluates the vulnerability of facilities across a broad range of identified threats/hazards and provides a basis for determining physical and operational mitigation measures for their protection. It applies both to new building programming and design as well as to existing building management and renovation over the service life of a structure.

A vulnerability rating can also be assigned to the appropriate aspects of building operations and systems to the defined threats for the particular facility. These ratings can also be assigned as high, medium or low:

- **High Vulnerability.** One or more significant weaknesses have been identified that make the facility highly susceptible to a terrorist or hazard.

- **Medium Vulnerability.** A weakness has been identified that makes the facility somewhat susceptible to a terrorist or hazard.

- **Low Vulnerability.** A minor weakness has been identified that slightly increases the susceptibility of the facility to a terrorist or hazard.

The Building Vulnerability Assessment Checklist located in Appendix IV compiles a list of questions to be addressed in assessing the vulnerability of facilities to terrorist attack. The following is useful in the initial screening of existing facilities to identify and prioritize terrorism risk reduction needs.

Initial Vulnerability Estimate

The initial vulnerability estimate provides a quick, qualitative assessment of the vulnerability of existing buildings to terrorist attack. Three means of data collection using a simple scale of high, medium and low ratings may provide useful information. The data collection is based upon three criteria:

- Visual inspection
- Document review
- Organization and management procedures review

Visual Inspection—When visually inspecting the condition of the property, an evaluation of the site and all the facility systems is performed. This includes the architectural, structural, building envelope, utility, mechanical, plumbing and gas, electrical, fire alarm, communications and information technology systems. Equipment operations and maintenance procedures and records, security systems, and planning and procedures should also be evaluated. The inspection may need to go beyond the site to determine the vulnerability of utility and other infrastructure systems.

Document Review—The planning team, which includes the building owner and the facility manager, should review all necessary plans, specifications and related construction data in terms of terrorism vulnerability. Equipment operation, maintenance procedures and records, as well as security procedures, should be included in this review.

Organization and Management Procedures Review—The planning team should review business and operations practices and procedures to identify opportunities that can reduce exposure to attack. This review also includes tenant operations.

Vulnerability Estimate Screening

Tables 17-2 through 17-10 from FEMA provide guidance for initial vulnerability assessment. The goal of this assessment is to distinguish facilities of high, medium or low vulnerability to terrorist attack. The implication is that high vulnerability facilities should receive more detailed analysis. Specific strategies for risk reduction should be developed.

For this initial assessment, subjective ratings by building owners, facility managers and other qualified professionals who are familiar with the facility, are appropriate. Assigning a "high," "medium" or "low" vulnerability rating to the responses to vulnerability questions for each building system, will provide a preliminary basis for estimating the overall vulnerability of a particular facility to terrorist attack. The responses will also indicate areas of opportunity for mitigation actions to reduce terrorism risk.

Site Questions

Vulnerability assessment of the "site" examines surrounding structures, terrain, perimeter controls, traffic patterns and separations, landscaping elements/features, and lines of sight.

"Site" questions focus primarily on visual inspection to develop ratings. The questions emphasize vulnerability to moving vehicle, stationary vehicle, and covert entry tactics. Vulnerability to blast is the primary concern addressed.

Architectural Questions

Assessing "architectural" vulnerability investigates tenancy, services, public and private access, access controls, activity patterns and exposures.

"Architectural" questions focus equally on visual inspection and evaluation of organizational and management procedures to develop ratings. The questions emphasize vulnerability to moving vehicle, stationary vehicle and covert entry tactics. Vulnerability to blast is a primary concern.

Structural and Building Envelope Questions

A vulnerability assessment of "structural" systems examines construction type, materials, detailing, collapse characteristics and critical elements. An assessment of the "building envelope" examines strength, fenestration, glazing characteristics/detailing and anchorage.

These questions rely on a review of construction documents and visual inspection to develop ratings. Vulnerability to blasts is the primary concern.

Utility Systems Questions

A vulnerability assessment of "utility" systems examines the full range of source and supply systems serving the facility including water, fuel and the electricity supply, as well as the fire alarm and suppression systems and communication systems.

Table 17-2. Site Systems Vulnerability Estimate

	Vulnerability Rating (H, M, L)	Visual inspection	Document review	Org/Mgmt procedure	Moving vehicle	Stationary vehicle	Covert entry	Mail	Supplies	Blast effects	Airborne (contamination)	Waterborne (contamination)
What major structures surround the facility?	□	●	●									
What critical infrastructure, government, military, or recreation facilities are in the local area that impact transportation, utilities, and collateral damage (attack at this facility impacting the other major structures or attack on the major structures impacting this facility)?	□	●	●	●								
What are the adjacent land uses immediately outside the perimeter of this facility?	□	●	●									
What are the site access points to the facility?	□	●			●		●					
What is the minimum distance from the inspection location to the building?	□	●			●		●				●	
Is there any potential access to the site or facility through utility paths or water runoff?	□	●	●				●					
What are the existing types of vehicle anti-ram devices for the facility?	□	●			●						●	
What is the anti-ram buffer zone standoff distance from the building to unscreened vehicles or parking?	□	●			●							
Are perimeter barriers capable of stopping vehicles?	□	●	●		●							
Does site circulation prevent high-speed approaches by vehicles?	□	●			●							
Is there a minimum setback distance between the building and parked vehicles?	□	●				●				●		
Does adjacent surface parking maintain a minimum standoff distance?	□	●				●				●		
Do site landscaping and street furniture provide hiding places?	□	●					●					

LEGEND: □ = Determine high, medium, or low vulnerability rating.   ● = Applicability of factor to question.

Source: FEMA

These questions rely on information obtained from visual inspection, review of construction documents and organizational/management procedures to develop the ratings. Vulnerability to waterborne contaminants is the primary consideration.

Mechanical Systems

A vulnerability assessment of mechanical systems examines air supply and exhaust configurations, filtration, sensing and monitoring,

Disaster & Recovery Planning

Table 17-3. Architectural Systems Vulnerability Estimate

	Vulnerability Rating (H, M, L)	Visual inspection	Document review	Org/Mgmt procedure	Moving vehicle	Stationary vehicle	Covert entry	Mail	Supplies	Blast effects	Airborne (contamination)	Waterborne (contamination)
What major structures surround the facility?	□	●	●	●								
Do entrances avoid significant queuing?	□	●		●								
What are the adjacent land uses immediately outside the perimeter of this facility?	□	●		●								
Are public and private activities separated?	□	●					●					
Are critical assets (people, activities, building systems and components) located close to any main entrance, vehicle circulation, parking, maintenance area, loading dock, or interior parking?	□	●	●	●	●	●	●				●	
Are high-value or critical assets located as far into the interior of the building as possible and separated from the public areas of the building?	□	●	●	●							●	
Is high visitor activity away from critical assets?	□		●				●					
Are critical assets located in spaces that are occupied 24 hours per day?	□			●								
Are assets located in areas where they are visible to more than one person?	□			●								
Do interior barriers differentiate level of security within a facility?	□	●	●	●								
Are emergency systems located away from high-risk areas?	□	●	●	●								

LEGEND: □ = Determine high, medium, or low vulnerability rating. ● = Applicability of factor to question.

Source: FEMA

system zoning and control, and elevator management.

These questions and ratings rely on information obtained from review of construction documents and visual inspection. Vulnerability to airborne contaminants is the primary concern, including contamination from chemical, biological and radiological attack.

Plumbing and Gas Systems

A vulnerability assessment of plumbing and gas systems examines the liquid distribution systems serving the facility including water and fuel distribution, water heating and fuel storage.

Table 17-4. Structural and Building Envelope Systems Vulnerability Estimate

	Vulnerability Rating (H, M, L)	Visual inspection	Document review	Org/Mgmt procedure	Moving vehicle	Stationary vehicle	Covert entry	Mail	Supplies	Blast effects	Airborne (contamination)	Waterborne (contamination)
What type of construction?	□	●	●							●		
Is the column spacing minimized so that reasonably sized members will resist the design loads and increase the redundancy of the system?	□	●	●							●		
What are the floor-to-floor heights?	□	●	●							●		
Is the structure vulnerable to progressive collapse?	□	●	●							●		
Are there adequate redundant load paths in the structure?	□	●	●							●		
What is the designed or estimated protection level of the exterior walls against the postulated explosive threat?	□		●							●		

LEGEND: □ = Determine high, medium, or low vulnerability rating. ● = Applicability of factor to question.

Source: FEMA

These questions rely on information from a review of construction documents to develop ratings. Vulnerability to waterborne contaminants is the primary concern.

Electrical Systems

A vulnerability assessment of electrical systems examines transformer and switchgear security, electricity distribution and accessibility, as well as emergency systems.

These questions rely on information from visual inspection and a review of construction documents to develop ratings. No particular attack mechanism is emphasized.

Fire Alarm Systems

A vulnerability assessment of fire alarm systems examines detection sensing and signaling, system configurations, accessibility of controls and redundancies.

These questions rely on information obtained from the review of the construction documents, as well as a review of organizational/man-

Table 17-5. Utility Systems Vulnerability Estimate

	Vulnerability Rating (H, M, L)	Visual inspection	Document review	Org/Mgmt procedure	Moving vehicle	Stationary vehicle	Covert entry	Mail	Supplies	Blast effects	Airborne (contamination)	Waterborne (contamination)
What is the source of domestic water? (utility, municipal, wells, lake, river, storage tank)	□	•	•									•
How many gallons and how long will it allow operations to continue?	□	•	•	•								•
What is the source of water for the fire suppression system? (local utility company lines, storage tanks with utility company backup, lake, or river)	□	•	•									
Are there alternate water supplies for fire suppression?	□	•	•	•								
Are the sprinkler and standpipe connections adequate and redundant?	□	•	•									
What fuel supplies do the facility rely upon for critical operation?	□	•	•	•								
Where is the fuel supply obtained?	□			•								
Are there alternate sources of fuel?	□			•								
Can alternate fuels be used?	□		•	•								
What is the normal source of electrical service for the facility?	□	•	•									
What provisions for emergency power exist? What systems receive emergency power and have capacity requirements been tested?	□	•	•	•								
By what means does the main telephone and data communications interface the facility?	□	•	•	•								

LEGEND: □ = Determine high, medium, or low vulnerability rating.   • = Applicability of factor to question.

Source: FEMA

agement procedures to develop ratings. No particular attack mechanism is emphasized.

Communications and Information Technology Systems

A vulnerability assessment of communications and information technology systems examines distribution, power supplies, accessibility, control, notification and backups.

These questions rely on information from visual inspection, a review of construction documents, as well as a review of the organizational/management procedures to develop ratings. No particular attack mechanism is emphasized.

As companies and organizations increase their security measures

Table 17-6. Mechanical Systems Vulnerability Estimate

	Vulnerability Rating (H, M, L)	Visual inspection	Document review	Org/Mgmt procedure	Moving vehicle	Stationary vehicle	Covert entry	Mail	Supplies	Blast effects	Airborne (contamination)	Waterborne (contamination)
Where are the air intakes and exhaust louvers for the building? (low, high, or midpoint of the building structure)	□	●	●									●
Are there multiple air intake locations?	□	●	●									●
How are air handling systems zoned?	□	●	●									●
Are there large central air handling units or are there multiple units serving separate zones?	□		●									●
Are there any redundancies in the air handling system?	□		●	●								●
Where is roof-mounted equipment located on the roof? (near perimeter, at center of roof)	□	●										

LEGEND: □ = Determine high, medium, or low vulnerability rating. ● = Applicability of factor to question.

Source: FEMA

Table 17-7. Plumbing and Gas Systems Vulnerability Estimate

	Vulnerability Rating (H, M, L)	Visual inspection	Document review	Org/Mgmt procedure	Moving vehicle	Stationary vehicle	Covert entry	Mail	Supplies	Blast effects	Airborne (contamination)	Waterborne (contamination)
What is the method of water distribution?	□	●										●
What is the method of gas distribution? (heating, cooking, medical, process)	□	●										
What is the method of heating domestic water?	□	●	●	●								
Are there reserve supplies of critical gases?	□		●	●								

LEGEND: □ = Determine high, medium, or low vulnerability rating. ● = Applicability of factor to question.

Source: FEMA

Table 17-8. Electrical Systems Vulnerability Estimate

	Vulnerability Rating (H, M, L)	Visual inspection	Document review	Org/Mgmt procedure	Moving vehicle	Stationary vehicle	Covert entry	Mail	Supplies	Blast effects	Airborne (contamination)	Waterborne (contamination)
Are there any transformers or switchgears located outside the building or accessible from the building exterior?	□	●										
Are they (transformers or switchgears) vulnerable to public access?	□	●										
Are critical electrical systems located in areas outside of secured electrical areas?	□	●	●	●								
Does emergency backup power exist for all areas within the facility or for critical areas only?	□	●	●									

LEGEND: □ = Determine high, medium, or low vulnerability rating.   ● = Applicability of factor to question.

Source: FEMA

Table 17-9. Fire Alarm Systems Vulnerability Estimate

	Vulnerability Rating (H, M, L)	Visual inspection	Document review	Org/Mgmt procedure	Moving vehicle	Stationary vehicle	Covert entry	Mail	Supplies	Blast effects	Airborne (contamination)	Waterborne (contamination)
Is the fire alarm system stand-alone or integrated with other functions such as security and environmental or building management systems?	□		●	●								
Is there redundant off-premises fire alarm reporting?	□		●	●								

LEGEND: □ = Determine high, medium, or low vulnerability rating.   ● = Applicability of factor to question.

Source: FEMA

and attempt to identify vulnerabilities in critical assets, they are looking for a mechanism to ensure an efficient investment of resources to counter threats. One such mechanism is a risk management model that will

- assess assets, threats and vulnerabilities; and

- incorporate a continuous assessment feature.

Table 17-10. Communication and its Systems Vulnerability Estimate

	Vulnerability Rating (H, M, L)	Visual inspection	Document review	Org/Mgmt procedure	Moving vehicle	Stationary vehicle	Covert entry	Mail	Supplies	Blast effects	Airborne (contamination)	Waterborne (contamination)
Where is the main telephone distribution room and where is it in relation to higher risk areas?	□	●	●	●								
Where are communication systems wiring closets located? (voice, data, signal, alarm)	□	●	●									

LEGEND: □ = Determine high, medium, or low vulnerability rating.   ● = Applicability of factor to question.

Source: FEMA

The questions listed above provide a framework for such a model. By reviewing these ratings, a preliminary determination can be made of where the major vulnerabilities and threats could occur in a facility. Additionally, a preliminary determination can be made regarding which risks require immediate attention. As noted, however, the ratings (low, medium, high) are subjective and as a result may not be exact. A more detailed and quantitative evaluation is required. This detailed evaluation involves a significantly more thorough review of information in all areas, including additional information that concerns:

- Equipment Operations and Maintenance (up-to-date drawings, manuals and procedures, training, monitoring, etc.);

- Security Systems (perimeter and interior sensing, monitoring and control, security system documentation and training, etc.); and

- The Security Master Plan (currency, responsibilities, etc.).

A complete list of detailed questions can be found in Appendix IV. These questions should be considered in fully evaluating vulnerability to terrorist threats. The means of data collection that should be employed and the particular tactics and attack mechanisms addressed by each question are identified in the appendix. This is done so that specialized checklists can be created to assess vulnerability to terrorist tactics of particular concern to an individual company or organization. By following such a model, organizations are able to "tailor" their management of risk to the current situation, as well as to assess future risks.

Sources

Federal Emergency Management Agency (FEMA), *Risk Management Series: Insurance, Finance, and Regulation Primer for Terrorism Risk Management in Buildings*, FEMA 429. December 2003.

Federal Emergency Management Agency (FEMA), *Risk Management Series: Primer for Design of Commercial Buildings to Mitigate Terrorist Attacks*, FEMA 427. December 2003.

Gustin, Joseph F., *Bioterrorism: A Guide for Facility Managers*, Lilburn, GA: The Fairmont Press, Inc., 2005.

Gustin, Joseph F., *Cyber Terrorism: A Guide for Facility Managers*, Lilburn, GA: The Fairmont Press, Inc., 2004.

Gustin, Joseph F. *Disaster and Recovery Planning: A Guide for Facility Managers*, 4th ed., Lilburn, GA: The Fairmont Press, Inc., 2007.

National Infrastructure Protection Center (NIPC). *Risk Management: An Essential Guide to Protecting Critical Assets*, November 2002.

Chapter 18

Putting the Plan Together

As discussed earlier, disaster and recovery planning is rooted in the basics of emergency preparedness. As such, each key element of emergency preparedness is integral to preparing for, mitigating, responding to and recovering from an emergency or disaster occurrence. In this chapter, we will review the steps involved in developing and implementing a successful disaster and recovery plan.

PUTTING IT TOGETHER

The steps involved in putting the disaster and recovery plan together include:

1. Establishing the planning team.
2. Analyzing capabilities and hazards.
3. Developing the plan.
4. Implementing the plan.

However, in order for the disaster and recovery effort to be successful, the support of a company's senior management is required. The chief executive sets the tone by authorizing planning to take place and directing senior management to get involved. When presenting the case for disaster and recovery planning, it is important for facility managers to focus on the benefits to the company. These benefits include:

- Assisting companies to fulfill their moral, legal and ethical responsibilities to protect employees, occupants, the community and the environment.

- Facilitating compliance with the various regulatory requirements of federal, state and local enforcement agencies.

- Enhancing a company's ability to recover from financial loss, regulatory fines, loss of market share, and damages to equipment/products or business interruption.

- Reducing exposure to civil or criminal liability in the event of an incident.

- Enhancing a company's image and credibility with employees, occupants, customers, suppliers and the community.

- Reducing a company's insurance premiums.

STEP 1: ESTABLISH A PLANNING TEAM

There must be an individual or group in charge of developing the disaster and emergency recovery management plan. The following provides guidance for formulating the planning team.

Form the Team

The size of the planning team will depend on the facility's operation, requirements and resources. Involving a group of people is particularly effective because it:

- Encourages participation and gets more people invested in the process.

- Increases the amount of time and energy participants are able to give.

- Enhances the visibility and stature of the planning process.

- Provides for a broad perspective on the issues.

While some persons will serve as active members and others will serve in advisory capacities, input from all functional areas within the company should be obtained. These other areas include:

- Upper management.
- Line management.
- Labor.
- Human resources.
- Engineering and maintenance.
- Safety, health and environmental affairs.
- Public relations/information.
- Security.
- Community relations.
- Sales and marketing.
- Legal.
- Finance and purchasing.

Regardless of the role they serve, all planning team members should be appointed in writing by upper management. Their job descriptions could also reflect their assignment.

Establish Authority

Demonstrate management's commitment and promote an atmosphere of cooperation by authorizing the planning group to take the steps necessary to develop a plan. The group should be led by the chief executive or the plant manager. Establish a clear line of authority between group members and the group leader, though not so rigid as to prevent the free flow of ideas.

Issue A Mission Statement

The company's chief executive or plant manager should issue a mission statement to demonstrate the organization's commitment to the disaster recovery effort. The statement should:

- Define the purpose of the plan and indicate that it will involve the entire organization.

- Define the authority and structure of the planning group.

Establish A Schedule and Budget

A work schedule and planning deadlines should be established. Time lines can be modified as priorities become more clearly defined.

An initial budget should be developed to cover the costs incurred by research, printing, seminars, consulting services and other expenses that may be necessary during the development process.

STEP 2: ANALYZE CAPABILITIES AND HAZARDS

The second step in developing the comprehensive emergency management program entails gathering information about the entity's current capabilities, as well as possible hazards and potential emergencies. This information serves as the basis for conducting a vulnerability analysis to determine the facility's capabilities for handling disasters and emergencies.

Where the Company Stands

In analyzing a company's capabilities, a review of all internal plans and policies should be conducted. The review should include the following documents:

- Evacuation plan.
- Fire protection plan.
- Safety and health program.
- Environmental policies.
- Security procedures.
- Insurance programs.
- Finance and purchasing procedures.
- Plant closing policy.
- Employee manuals.
- Hazardous materials plan.
- Process safety assessment.
- Risk management plan.
- Capital improvement programs.
- Mutual aid agreements.

Outside Resources

Outside groups are a necessary and invaluable component of the planning process. Meetings with government agencies, various community organizations and utility companies should be arranged. Discussions should focus on potential emergencies and plans, as well as the resources that are available for responding to the emergency occurrence.

Outside groups and sources of information include:

- Community emergency management office.
- Mayor or community administrator's office.
- Local emergency planning committee (LEPC.)
- Fire department.
- Police department.
- Emergency medical services organizations.
- American Red Cross.
- National Weather Service.
- Public works department.
- Planning commission.
- Telephone companies.
- Electric utilities.
- Neighboring businesses.

Identify Codes and Regulations

Plan development must include identifying all applicable federal, state and local jurisdictional codes and regulations, including: Federal Occupational Safety and Health Administration (OSHA) standards; State Occupational Safety and Health Administration standards for those entities whose business operations are located in states known as State Plan States (a state that has its own federally approved safety and health plan); environmental regulations; fire codes; seismic safety codes; transportation regulations; zoning regulations and corporate policies.

Identify Critical Products, Services and Operations

The information obtained from identifying critical products, services and operations is important to assess the impact of potential disasters and emergencies and to determine the need for backup systems. Areas that should be reviewed include:

- Company products and services and the facilities and equipment needed to produce them.

- Products and services provided by suppliers, especially sole-source vendors.

- Lifeline services such as electrical power, water, sewer, gas, telecommunications and transportation.

- Operations, equipment and personnel vital to the continued functioning of the facility.

Identify Internal Resources and Capabilities

The internal resources and capabilities that may be needed in the event of an emergency occurrence should be identified. These resources include:

1. **Personnel**, including fire brigade; hazardous materials response team; emergency medical services; security, emergency management group; evacuation team and public information officer.

2. **Equipment**, including fire protection and suppression equipment, communications equipment, first-aid supplies, emergency supplies, warning systems, emergency power equipment and decontamination equipment.

3. **Facilities**, including emergency operating center, media briefing area, shelter areas, first-aid stations and sanitation facilities.

4. **Organization Capabilities**, including training, evacuation plan and employee support systems.

5. **Backup Systems**, including arrangements with other facilities to provide for:

   - Payroll.
   - Communications.
   - Production.
   - Customer services.
   - Shipping and receiving.
   - Information systems support.
   - Emergency power.
   - Recovery support.

Identify External Resources

There are many external resources that could be needed in a disaster or emergency. In some cases, formal agreements may be necessary to define the facility's relationship with the following entities:

* Local emergency management office.
* Fire department.
* Hazardous materials response organization.
* Emergency medical services.
* Hospitals.
* Local and state police.
* Community service organizations.
* Utilities.
* Contractors.
* Suppliers of emergency equipment.
* Insurance carriers.

Insurance Review

Any and all policies governing company/facility operations, property/contents coverage, as well as liability coverage (product, pollution, etc.), should be reviewed with insurance carriers to ensure adequate protection from exposure/loss, as well as to determine appropriate/adequate coverage for projected recovery costs, etc.

Conduct A Vulnerability Analysis

Assessing the vulnerability of a facility involves determining the probability and the potential impact of each disaster and emergency on the facility itself. Consideration should be given to emergencies that could occur within a specific facility (i.e., site-specific), and those emergencies that could occur within the community that could impact upon a facility's operations. Additionally, emergency occurrences that have been identified by the local emergency management office should also be included in the overall analysis. Other factors to consider include historical, geographic, technological, human engineered, physical and regulatory.

Historical Factors

In evaluating the historical factors that may affect a particular facility, it is necessary to review the types of disaster and emergencies that have occurred in the facility itself, as well as in other businesses and within the community. Historical factors include:

- Fires.
- Severe weather.
- Hazardous materials spills.
- Transportation accidents.
- Earthquakes.
- Hurricanes.
- Tornadoes.
- Terrorism.
- Utility outages.

Geographic Factors

In assessing the geographic factors, the planning team must consider those potential events that could occur as a result of its location. Some of these geographic factors include:

- Proximity to flood plains, seismic faults and dams.

- Proximity to companies that produce, store, use or transport hazardous materials.

- Proximity to major transportation routes and airports.

- Proximity to nuclear power plants.

Technological Factors

Technological factors that must be considered in the assessment include the consequences of a process or system failure caused by:

- Fire, explosion, hazardous materials incidents.
- Safety system failure.
- Telecommunications failure.
- Computer system failure.
- Power failure.
- Heating/cooling system failure.
- Emergency notification system failure.

Human Error Factors

Many disaster and emergency situations are caused by human error. In fact, human error is the single largest cause of workplace emergencies. Some of the causes of the human error-induced emergency include:

- Poor training.
- Poor maintenance.
- Carelessness.
- Misconduct.
- Substance abuse.
- Fatigue.

Physical Factors

Assessing those factors that carry the potential for contributing to a disaster or emergency include:

- The physical construction of the facility.
- Hazardous processes or byproducts.
- Facilities for storing combustibles.
- Layout of equipment.
- Lighting.
- Evacuation of routes and exits.
- Proximity of shelter areas.

Regulatory Factors

In assessing factors that could impact upon a facility and its operation, consideration must be given to the regulatory issues that govern the business, industry and the facility. Each potential disaster or emergency must be assessed in terms of:

- Restricted or prohibited access to the site.
- Loss of electrical power.
- Downed communication lines.
- Ruptured gas mains.
- Water damage.
- Smoke damage.
- Structural damage.
- Air/water contamination.
- Explosion.
- Building collapse.
- Trapped occupants.
- Chemical releases.

Estimating Probability

Once each of the potential disasters and emergencies have been identified and assessed in terms of these contributing factors, the probability of a potential occurrence should be determined.

Assessing Potential Impact

An assessment of the impact on occupants, in terms of potential injury or death, must be determined. Additionally, the impact on building and business operations must be assessed in terms of property losses and damages and the potential loss of market share, respectively.

Property issues must be evaluated in terms of potential replacement costs, repair costs and temporary replacement costs. Business issues must be assessed in terms of:

- Business interruption.
- Employees unable to report to work.
- Customers unable to reach the facility.
- Violation of contractual agreements.
- Imposition of fines/penalties and/or legal costs.
- Interruption of critical supplies.
- Interruption of product distribution.

Each of the potential disasters/emergencies must be viewed against the company's internal response capabilities and the available external response capabilities. If these are inadequate, consideration should be given to:

- Developing additional disaster/emergency procedures.
- Conducting additional training.
- Acquiring additional equipment.
- Establishing mutual aid agreements.
- Establishing agreements with specialized contractors.

When assessing the availability of external resources, particularly community emergency resources—police, firefighters and paramedics—it is important to remember that they will focus their response where the need is greatest. In an area-wide disaster, for example, community emergency resources may not be available to respond immediately to a particular site.

STEP 3: DEVELOPING THE PLAN

The basic components of the disaster and emergency management plan include the executive summary, emergency management elements, response procedures, support documents and resource lists.

Executive Summary

The executive summary gives management a brief overview of the plan; the facility's disaster/emergency management policy; authorities and responsibilities of key personnel; the types of disasters and emergencies that could occur; and where response operations will be managed.

Emergency Management Elements

This section of the plan briefly describes the facility's approach to the core elements of disaster/emergency management, which are:

- Direction and control.
- Communications.
- Life safety.
- Property protection.
- Community outreach.
- Recovery and restoration.
- Administration and logistics.

These elements, which are described in detail in Chapter 17, are the foundation for the procedures that a facility should follow to protect occupants and equipment and resume operations.

Response Procedures

The procedures spell out how the facility will respond to disasters and emergencies. Whenever possible, these procedures should be developed as a series of checklists that can be quickly accessed by senior management, department heads, response personnel and employees. These procedures should detail the actions that would be necessary to 1) assess the situation, 2) protect employees, customers, visitors, equipment, vital records and other assets, particularly during the first three days, and 3) get the business back up and running.

Specific procedures might be needed for any number of situations, including bomb threats or tornadoes, and functions such as:

- Warning employees and customers.
- Communicating with personnel and community responders.
- Conducting an evacuation and accounting for all persons in the facility.
- Managing response activities.
- Activating and operating a disaster/emergency operations center.
- Fighting fires.
- Shutting down operations.
- Protecting vital records.
- Restoring operations.

Support Documents

Documents that could be needed in a disaster and/or emergency include:

- Emergency call lists (wallet size, if possible) of all persons on and off site who would be involved in responding to a disaster/emergency, their responsibilities and their 24-hour telephone numbers.

- Building and site maps that indicate:

  - Utility shutoffs
  - Water main valves
  - Gas main valves
  - Electrical cutoffs
  - Storm drains
  - Floor plans
  - Fire extinguishers
  - Exits
  - Designated escape routes
  - High-value items
  - Location of each building (including building name, street address)

  - Water hydrants
  - Water lines
  - Gas lines
  - Electrical substations
  - Sewer lines
  - Alarms and enunciators
  - Fire suppression systems
  - Stairways
  - Restricted areas
  - Hazardous materials (including cleaning supplies and chemicals)

Resource Lists

Resource lists contain information that could be needed in the event of a disaster or emergency. These lists provide information that identifies major resources (i.e., equipment, supplies, services), as well as any mutual aid agreements with other companies and government agencies.

The Development Process

The development process includes 1) identifying challenges and prioritizing activities, 2) writing the plan, 3) establishing a training schedule, and 4) coordinating activities with outside organizations.

Identifying Challenges and Prioritizing Activities

To determine the specific goals and milestones that must be achieved, a list of tasks to be performed must be developed. Additionally, the persons who will perform the tasks, as well as when they will perform them, should also be identified. Procedures for addressing the problem areas and resource shortfalls that were identified in the vulnerability analysis should also be developed.

Writing the Plan

Each member of the planning team should be assigned a specific section of the plan to write. Aggressive time lines with specific goals should be predetermined. The schedule should outline realistic time frames that include target dates for the first draft, review, second draft, tabletop exercise, final draft, printing and distribution.

Establishing A Training Schedule

A specific person or department should be assigned the responsibility for developing the facility's training schedule.

Coordinating With Outside Agencies

Periodic meetings with appropriate local government agencies and organizations should be held. While their official approval may not be required, they will likely have valuable insights and information to offer.

Determining federal, state and local requirements for disaster or emergency reporting should be incorporated into the procedures, as should determining protocols for turning control of response over to outside agencies. Some of the issues that may need to be addressed are:

- Which gate or entrance responding units will use.
- Where and to whom they will report.
- How they will be identified.
- How facility personnel will communicate with outside responders.
- Who will be in charge of response activities.

An additional issue that must be determined is building reentry during a disaster or emergency. The kind(s) of identification that authorities require of key facility personnel who may need to reenter the building must be defined.

Provision must be made for the needs of disabled persons and non-English speaking personnel as well. For example, a blind employee could be assigned a partner in case an evacuation is necessary. The ADA defines a disabled person as anyone who has a physical or mental impairment that substantially limits one or more major life activities, such as seeing, hearing, walking, breathing, performing manual tasks, learning, caring for oneself or working. The emergency planning priorities may be influenced by government regulation. To remain in compliance, the planning team may be required to address specific emergency management functions that might otherwise be a lower priority activity for that given year.

Maintaining Contact with Other Corporate Offices

It is necessary to communicate with other offices and divisions in a company to identify their disaster and emergency notification procedures; the conditions where mutual assistance would be necessary; how offices will support each other during an emergency; and the names, telephone/pager numbers of key personnel.

When all of the necessary information has been incorporated into the procedures, the initial draft of the emergency plan is ready for review and/or revision. The review process itself allows for identifying any areas of confusion that may need to be clarified and/or modified, prior to implementing the plan.

Plan Approval and Distribution

The written approval of the entity's chief executive precedes plan distribution. Each person who receives a copy of the approved plan should be required to sign for it and to assume responsibility for all subsequent changes. The final plan should be distributed to the company's:

- Chief executive and senior management.
- Key members of the company's emergency response organization.
- Company headquarters.
- Community emergency response agencies (appropriate sections).

Additional copies should be made available to key company personnel who should be instructed to keep a back-up copy at their homes in the event that an emergency situation should render their office copies untenable.

STEP 4: IMPLEMENTING THE PLAN

Disaster/emergency plan implementation means more than simply exercising the plan during an occurrence. It means acting on recommendations made during the vulnerability analysis, integrating the plan into company operations and training employees.

Integrating the Plan into Company Operations

Disaster/emergency planning must become part of the corporate culture. Opportunities must be provided to build awareness; to educate and train personnel; to test procedures; to involve all levels of management/departments and the community in the planning process; and to make disaster/emergency management part of what personnel do on a day-to-day basis. To determine how completely the plan has been integrated into the organization's culture can be accomplished by asking the following questions:

1. How well does senior management support the responsibilities outlined in the plan?

2. Have disaster/emergency planning concepts been fully incorporated into the facility's accounting, personnel and financial procedures?

3. How can the facility's processes for evaluating employees and defining job classifications better address disaster/emergency management responsibilities?

4. Are there opportunities for distributing disaster/emergency preparedness information through newsletters, manuals or employee mailings?

5. What kinds of safety posters or other visible reminders would be helpful?

6. Do personnel know what they should do in an emergency?

7. How can all levels of the organization be involved in evaluating and updating the plan?

Conducting Training, Drills and Exercises

Everybody who works at or visits the facility requires some form of training. This could include periodic employee discussion sessions to review procedures, technical training in equipment use for disaster/emergency responders, evacuation drills and full-scale exercises. The basic considerations for developing a training plan follow.

Planning Considerations—Training considerations should include the training and information needs of employees, contractors, visitors, managers, as well as those persons with a disaster response role identified in the plan itself. Based on a 12-month period, the training should address:

*   Who will be trained.
*   Who will conduct the training.
*   What specific training activities will be used.
*   When and where will each session take place.
*   How the training will be evaluated and documented.

Training Activities. Training activities can take many forms. Some of the specific activities include orientation/education sessions, tabletop exercises, walk-through drills, functional drills, evacuation drills and full-scale exercises.

Orientation and Education Sessions. These are the regularly scheduled discussion sessions to provide information, answer questions and identify needs and concerns.

Table Exercise. Members of the emergency management group meet in a conference room setting to discuss their responsibilities and how they would react to emergency scenarios. This is a cost-effective and efficient way to identify areas of overlap and confusion before conducting more demanding training activities.

Walk-Through Drill. The disaster/emergency management group and response teams actually perform their emergency response functions. This activity generally involves more people and is more thorough than a tabletop exercise.

Functional Drills. These drills test specific functions such as medical response, emergency notifications, warning and communications procedures and equipment, though not necessarily at the same time. Personnel are asked to evaluate the systems and identify problem areas.

Evacuation Drill. Personnel walk the evacuation route to a designated area where procedures for accounting for all personnel are tested. Participants are asked to make notes as they go along of what might become a hazard during an emergency; e.g., stairways cluttered with debris, smoke in the hallways. Plans are modified accordingly.

Full-scale Exercise. A real-life disaster or emergency situation is simulated as closely as possible. This exercise involves company disaster/emergency response personnel, employees, management and community response organizations.

Employee Training—General training for all employees should address the following topics:

- Individual roles and responsibilities.
- Information about threats, hazards and protective actions.
- Notification, warning and communications procedures.
- Means for locating family members in an emergency.
- Disaster/emergency response procedures.
- Evacuation, shelter and accountability procedures.
- Location and use of common emergency equipment.
- Disaster/emergency shutdown procedures.

Additional training requirements may be dictated by the regulatory agency that governs a particular business, or industry. For example, OSHA has its own specific training mandates for facilities that have a fire brigade, hazardous materials team, rescue team, or emergency medical response team.

Evaluate and Modify the Plan

A formal audit of the plan should be conducted at least once a year. Among the issues to consider in the annual audit are:

- Involvement of all levels of management in evaluating and updating the plan.

- Appropriate consideration of problem areas and resource shortfalls as identified in the vulnerability analysis.

- Relevance of training (i.e., does the training reflect the lessons learned from drills and actual events?).

- Disaster/emergency management group and response team understanding of their respective roles and responsibilities.

- Inclusion of new facility processes in the plan, as well as inclusion of any physical site changes in the plan.

- Current records of facility assets and photos of same.

- Attainment of training objectives.

- Changes in facility hazards.

- Roster of names/titles/emergency contact telephone numbers kept current.

- Incorporation of disaster/emergency management into other facility processes.

- Schedule of community agencies/organizations briefings and records of their involvement in plan evaluation.

Besides the annual audit, the plan should be evaluated and modified:

- After each training drill or exercise.
- After each real disaster and/or emergency.
- When personnel or their responsibilities change.
- When the layout or design of the facility changes.
- When policies or procedures change.

Sources

Federal Emergency Management Agency, *Emergency Management Guide for Business and Industry* by Thomas Wahle, Ogilvy Adams & Rinehart, and Gregg Beatty, Roy F. Weston, Inc., for the Federal Emergency Management Agency under FEMA Contract EMW-90-C-3348.

United States Department of Labor, Occupational Safety and Health Administration, *How to Prepare for Workplace Emergencies*, 2001, OSHA 3088 (Rev.).

United States Department of Labor, Occupational Safety and Health Administration, *Principal Emergency Response and Preparedness: Requirements and Guidelines*, OSHA 3122-06R, 2004.

Chapter 19

Managing the Disaster and Recovery Effort

Disasters, like emergencies, are unplanned events. Each event— whether it is considered a disaster or emergency—must be addressed within the context of its impact upon the company and the community. What is a nuisance to a large industrial complex could very well be considered a disaster at a smaller facility. Managing the disaster and recovery effort must be addressed from the perspective of emergency management.

EMERGENCY MANAGEMENT CONSIDERATIONS

Emergency management is the process of preparing for, mitigating, responding to and recovering from a disaster or emergency. It involves planning, training, conducting drills, inspecting and testing equipment and coordinating facility- and community-wide activities.

Management considerations describe certain core operational functions. These functions include:

• Direction and control.

• Communications.

• Life safety.

• Property protection.

- Community outreach.
- Recovery and restoration.
- Administration and logistics.

Direction and Control

The system for managing resources, analyzing information and making decisions in a disaster/emergency is called direction and control. While the direction and control system that is described assumes a facility of sufficient size, the principles described will still apply to the small facility that may require a less sophisticated systems approach.

The configuration of a particular system is contingent upon many factors. Larger industries may have their own fire team, emergency medical technicians, or hazardous materials team, while smaller entities may need to rely on mutual aid agreements. They may also be able to consolidate positions or combine responsibilities. Occupants/tenants of office buildings or industrial parks may be part of an emergency management program for the entire facility.

The Emergency Management Group—The emergency management group is the team responsible for the big picture. It controls all incident-related activities. The incident commander oversees the technical aspects of the response. The emergency management group supports the incident commander by allocating resources and by interfacing with the community, the media, outside response organizations and regulatory agencies. The emergency management group is headed by the Emergency Director, who should be the facility manager. The facility manager, as emergency director, is in command and control of all aspects of the disaster/emergency. Other emergency group members should be senior managers who have the authority to:

- Determine the short- and long-term effects of an emergency.
- Order the evacuation or shutdown of the facility.
- Interface with outside organizations and the media.
- Issue press releases.

The Incident Command System—The incident command system was developed specifically for the fire service, but its principles can be applied to all emergencies. The incident command system provides for coordinated response and a clear chain of command and safe operations.

The incident commander is responsible for front-line management of the incident, for tactical planning and execution, for determining whether outside assistance is needed and for relaying requests for internal resources or outside assistance through the emergency operations center.

The incident commander can be any employee, but a member of management with the authority to make decisions is usually the best choice. He/she must have both the capability and the authority to:

- Assume command.
- Assess the situation.
- Implement the emergency management plan.
- Determine response strategies.
- Activate resources.
- Order an evacuation.
- Oversee all incident response activities.
- Declare the disaster/emergency incident covered.

The Emergency Operations Center—The emergency operations center serves as a centralized management center for disaster/emergency operations. Here, decisions are made by the emergency management group based upon information provided by the incident commander and other personnel. Regardless of size or process, every facility should designate an area where decision makers can gather during a disaster or emergency.

The emergency operations center should be located in an area of the facility not likely to be involved in an incident, perhaps the security department, the manager's office, a conference room or the training center. An alternate operations center should be designated in the event that the primary location is not usable.

Each facility must determine its requirements for an emergency operations center based upon the functions to be performed and the number of people involved. Ideally, the center is a dedicated area equipped with communications equipment, reference materials, activity logs and all the tools necessary to respond quickly and appropriately to a disaster/emergency. Its resources should include:

- Communications equipment.
- A copy of the emergency management plan and procedures.
- Blueprints, maps, status boards.

- A list of emergency operations center personnel and descriptions of their duties.
- Technical information and data for advising responders.
- Building security system information.
- Information and data management capabilities.
- Telephone directories.
- Backup (emergency standby) power, communications and lighting.
- Emergency supplies.

Planning Considerations—In order to develop a direction and control system, several planning considerations must be addressed. In addition to defining the duties of personnel with an assigned role, procedures must be established for each position. Additionally, checklists for all procedures should be prepared. Procedures, as well as responsibilities for fire fighting, medical and health and engineering must also be defined. Lines of succession to ensure continuous leadership, authority and responsibility in key positions must also be determined. Finally, a determination of equipment and supply needs for each response function must be made.

At a minimum, all personnel should be assigned the responsibility for:

- Recognizing and reporting a disaster or emergency.
- Warning other employees/occupants in the area.
- Taking all necessary security and safety measures.
- Evacuating safely.
- Providing training.

Isolation of the incident scene must begin when the disaster/emergency is discovered. If possible, the person who discovers the incident should attempt to secure the scene and control access. However, no one should be placed in physical danger to perform any of these functions. The basic security measures include:

- Closing doors and windows.
- Establishing temporary barriers with furniture after people have safely evacuated.
- Dropping containment materials (absorbent pads, etc.) in the path of leaking materials.
- Closing file cabinets and desk drawers.

Only trained personnel should be allowed to perform any advanced security measures. Access to the facility, the emergency operations center and the incident scene should be limited to people directly involved in the response.

Coordination of Outside Response—In some cases, laws, codes, prior agreements, or the very nature of the emergency require the IC to turn operations over to an outside response organization. When this happens, the protocols established between the facility and outside response organizations are implemented. The facility's incident commander provides the community's own incident commander with a complete report on the situation.

The facility incident commander keeps track of which organizations are on-site and how the response is being coordinated. This helps increase personnel safety and accountability and prevents duplication of effort.

Communications

Communications are essential to any business operation. A communications failure can be a disaster in itself, cutting off vital business activities. Communications are needed to report emergencies, to warn personnel of the danger, to keep families and off-duty employees informed about what is happening at the facility to coordinate response actions and to keep in contact with customers and suppliers.

Contingency Planning—Planning for all possible contingencies, from a temporary or short-term disruption to a total communications failure, must be considered. The daily functions performed at a facility and the communications—both voice and data—used to support the functions, must be addressed. All facility communications must be prioritized in order to minimize the impact on business operations. Procedures for restoring communications systems must be established. Provisions for backup communications must be made for each business function. Options may include messengers, telephones, portable microwave, amateur radios, point-to-point private lines, satellite and high-frequency radio.

Emergency Communications—The functions that a facility may need to perform in a disaster and/or emergency must also be considered in terms of the communications systems needed to support them. Communications must be established between:

- Emergency responders.

- Responders and the incident commander.

- The incident commander and the emergency operations center.

- The incident commander and employees.

- The emergency operations center and outside response organizations, neighboring businesses, employees' families, customers and the media.

The various methods of communications may include:

- Messengers.
- Telephone.
- Two-way radio.
- Fax machines.
- Microwave.
- Satellite.
- Dial-up modems.
- Local area networks (LANs).
- Signals.

Family Communications—In a disaster, personnel will need to know whether their families are safe. Taking care of loved ones is always a first priority for people. In developing communications plans, it is important to consider how employees would communicate with their families in case they are separated from one another or are injured. Arrangements for an out-of-town contact for all family members to call in an emergency should be made. Additionally, a place should be designated to meet family members in case employees cannot get home during a disaster or an emergency situation.

Notification—Employee and occupant procedures for reporting disasters/emergencies should be established. Personnel should be informed of the procedures, and personnel who are assigned specific notification tasks should be trained. Emergency telephone numbers should be posted near each telephone, as well as on employee bulletin boards and in other prominent locations. An updated list of addresses and telephone and pager numbers of key emergency response personnel (internal and external) should be maintained.

Government agencies' notification requirements must be determined in advance. Notification must be made immediately to local government agencies when a disaster/emergency has the potential to affect public health and safety.

Warning—A system for warning personnel of an emergency should be established. The system should:

• Be audible or within view by all people within the facility.
• Have an auxiliary power supply.
• Have a distinct and recognizable signal.

Provisions for warning people with disabilities must be made. For instance, a flashing strobe light can be used to warn people who are hearing-impaired. Additionally, personnel should become familiar with the procedures for responding when the warning system is activated. Procedures for warning customers, contractors, visitors and others who may not be familiar with the facility's warning system must also be established.

Life Safety

Protecting the health and safety of everyone in the facility is the first priority during a disaster/emergency. For this reason, evacuation planning must be thorough and comprehensive. It should include:

• Designating evacuation routes and exits.
• Defining assembly areas and accountability procedures.
• Determining shelter locations.

Evacuation Planning—One common means of protection is evacuation. In the case of fire, an immediate evacuation to a predetermined area away from the facility may be necessary. In a hurricane, evacuation could involve the entire community and take place over a period of days. To develop an evacuation policy and procedure, the following points must be addressed:

1. Determine the conditions under which an evacuation would be necessary.

2. Establish a clear chain of command. Identify personnel with the authority to order an evacuation. Designate wardens to assist others and to account for personnel.

3. Establish specific evacuation procedures. Establish a system for accounting for personnel. Consider employees' transportation needs for community-wide evacuations.

4. Establish procedures for assisting people with disabilities and those who do not speak English.

5. Post evacuation procedures.

6. Designate personnel to continue or shut down critical operations while an evacuation is underway. They must be capable of recognizing when to abandon the operation and evacuate themselves.

7. Coordinate plans with the local emergency management office.

Evacuation Routes and Exits—Primary and secondary evacuation routes and exits must be designated. They should be clearly marked and well lit. Signs should be posted and emergency lighting should be installed in case a power outage occurs during an evacuation. In order to ensure the integrity and utility of the designated evacuation routes and exits, it may be necessary to have a non-facility professional determine if they are:

• Wide enough to accommodate the number of evacuating personnel.
• Clear and unobstructed at all times.
• Unlikely to expose evacuating personnel to additional hazards.

Assembly Areas and Accountability—Obtaining an accurate account of personnel after a site evacuation requires planning and practice. Therefore, assembly areas where personnel should gather after evacuating should be designated. A head count should be taken after the evacuation and the names and last known locations of personnel not accounted for should be determined and given to the EOC. (Confusion in the assembly areas can lead to unnecessary and dangerous search and rescue operations.) A method that accounts for non-employees/occupants, such as suppliers and customers, should also be established. In the event that the disaster/emergency incident expands, procedures for further evacuation should also be established. This may consist of sending employees/occupants home by normal means or providing them with transportation to an off-site location.

Shelter—In some emergencies, the best means of protection is to take shelter either within the facility or away from the facility in a public building. Shelter space within the facility and in the community should be identified and procedures for sending personnel to shelter should also be established (particularly important in the event of a tornado warning). Emergency supplies, including water, food and medical supplies, must also be determined. If appropriate, shelter managers should be designated and in all cases plans should be coordinated with local authorities.

Training and Information—All personnel should be trained in evacuation, shelter and other safety procedures. Training should be conducted at least annually or when:

- Employees are hired or new tenant-occupants locate within the facility.

- Evacuation wardens, shelter managers and others with special assignments are designated.

- New equipment, materials and processes are introduced.

- Procedures are updated or revised.

- Exercises show that employee performance must be improved.

Emergency information, including checklists and evacuation maps, should be provided, with evacuation maps posed in strategic and conspicuous locations. Information regarding evacuation and other safety procedures should also be provided to transient occupants.

Family Preparedness—The planning team should also consider various ways to help employees prepare their families for disasters/

emergencies. Not only will this help to increase the personal safety of employees, but it also helps the facility to get back up and running. Persons who are prepared at home will be better able to carry out their responsibilities at work.

Property Protection

Protecting facilities, equipment and vital records is essential to restoring operations once the disaster/emergency has occurred. The issues involved include planning considerations, protection systems, mitigation, facility shutdown and records preservation.

Planning Considerations—Planning considerations in protecting property include establishing procedures for:

- Fighting fires.
- Containing material spills.
- Shutting down equipment.
- Closing or barricading doors and windows.
- Covering or securing equipment.
- Moving equipment to a safe location.

In addition to identifying sources of backup equipment, supplies and parts, the materials that will be used to carry out protection procedures should be obtained. Personnel should be designated to authorize, supervise and perform a facility shutdown. Persons who are so designated should be trained to recognize when an effort should be abandoned.

Protection Systems—The various systems needed to detect abnormal situations, provide warning and protect property must be determined. These various systems include:

- Fire protection systems.
- Lightning protection systems.
- Water level monitoring systems.
- Overflow detection devices.
- Automatic shutoffs.
- Emergency standby power generation systems.

Mitigation—Consider ways to reduce the effects of disasters/ emergencies, such as moving or constructing facilities away from flood plains and fault zones. Also consider ways to reduce the chances of disasters/emergencies from occurring, such as changing processes or materials used to run the business.

Physical retrofitting measures should also be considered. Some of these measures include:

• Upgrading facilities to withstand the shaking of an earthquake or high winds.

• Floodproofing facilities by constructing flood walls or other flood protection devices.

• Installing fire sprinkler systems.

• Installing fire-resistant materials and furnishings.

• Installing storm shutters for all exterior windows and doors.

There are also non-structural mitigation measures to consider, including:

• Installing fire-resistant materials and furnishings.

• Securing light fixtures and other items that could fall or shake loose in an emergency.

• Moving heavy or breakable objects to low shelves.

• Attaching cabinets and files to low walls, or bolting them together.

• Placing Velcro strips under typewriters, tabletop computers and television monitors.

• Moving work stations away from large windows.

• Installing curtains or blinds that can be drawn over windows to prevent glass from shattering onto employees.

• Anchoring water heaters and bolting them to wall studs.

Additional mitigation measures can be determined through consultation with a structural engineer or architect, as well as the local community's building and zoning offices.

Facility Shutdown—Facility shutdown is generally a last resort but it is always a possibility. Improper or disorganized shutdown can result in confusion, injury and property damage. Some facilities require only simple actions such as turning off equipment, locking doors and activating alarms. Others require complex shutdown procedures. In working with department heads to establish shutdown procedures, information about when and how to shut off utilities should be included. The following issues should be identified:

- The conditions that could necessitate a shutdown.
- Who can order a shutdown.
- Who will carry out shutdown procedures.
- How a partial shutdown would affect other facility operations.
- The length of time required for shutdown and restarting.
- Training personnel in shutdown procedures.
- Posting shutdown procedures.

Records Preservation—A company's vital records may include the following documents:

- Financial and insurance information.
- Engineering plans and drawings.
- Product lists and specifications.
- Employee, customer and supplier databases.
- Formulas and trade secrets.
- Personnel files.

Preserving vital records is essential to the quick restoration of operations. Analyzing vital records involves:

- Classifying operations into functional categories, e.g., finance, production, sales, administration.

- Determining essential functions for keeping the business up and running, such as finance, production, sales, etc.

- Identifying the minimum information that must be readily accessible to perform essential functions—e.g., maintaining customer collections may require access to account statements.

- Identifying the records that contain the essential information and where they are located.

- Identifying the equipment and materials needed to access and use the information.

Next, procedures for protecting and accessing vital records must be established. Among the many approaches to consider are:

- Labeling vital records.
- Backing up computer systems.
- Making copies of records.
- Storing tapes and disks in insulated containers.
- Storing data off-site where they would not likely be damaged by an event affecting the facility.
- Increasing security of computer facilities.
- Arranging for evacuation of records to backup facilities.
- Backing up systems handled by service bureaus.
- Arranging for backup power.

Community Outreach

A facility's relationship with the community influences its ability to protect personnel and property and return to normal operations.

Involving the Community—Maintain a dialogue with community leaders, first responders, government agencies, community organizations and utilities, including:

- Appointed and elected leaders.
- Fire, police and emergency medical services personnel.
- Local Emergency Planning Committee (LEPC) members.
- Emergency management director.

- Public works department.
- American Red Cross.
- Hospitals.
- Telephone company.
- Electric utilities.
- Neighborhood groups.

Regular meetings with community emergency personnel to review emergency plans and procedures should be held. Discussions should center on what the facility is doing to prepare for and to prevent disasters/emergencies. Discussion should also focus on the facility's concern for the community's welfare and the ways that the facility could help in a community-wide disaster or emergency. Look for common interests and concerns. Opportunities for sharing resources and information should be identified. Additional community involvement methods include conducting confidence-building activities such as facility tours. Facility walk-throughs with community response groups provide an opportunity for these groups to become acquainted with the physical site. Also, community fire, police and emergency management personnel should be involved in the facility's drills and various exercises. Meeting with members of the community provides a basis for determining how mutual assistance can be provided in the event of disaster or emergency occurrences.

Mutual Aid Agreements—To avoid confusion and conflict in a disaster or emergency, mutual aid agreements with local response agencies and businesses should be established. These agreements should:

1. Define the type of assistance.
2. Identify the chain of command for activating the agreement.
3. Define communications procedures.

Mutual aid agreements can address any number of activities or resources that might be needed during a disaster/emergency, including:

- Providing for fire fighting and HAZMAT response.

- Providing shelter space, emergency storage, emergency supplies, medical support.

* Businesses allowing neighbors to use their property to account for personnel after an evacuation.

Community Service—In community-wide disasters/emergencies, business and industry are often needed to assist the community with:

* Personnel.
* Equipment.
* Shelter.
* Training.
* Storage.
* Feeding facilities.
* Emergency operations center facilities.
* Food, clothing, building materials.
* Funding.
* Transportation.

While there is no way to predict what demands will be placed on a company's resources, consideration should be given to how the community's needs might influence the company's corporate responsibilities in a disaster/emergency. Consideration should also be given to the various opportunities for community service before an actual disaster or emergency occurs.

Public Information—When site disasters/emergencies expand beyond the facility, the community will want to know the nature of the incident, whether the public's safety or health is in danger, what is being done to resolve the problem and what was done to prevent the situation from happening. Determining the various audiences that may be affected by a disaster and/or emergency is an essential step in identifying their respective information needs. The various audiences include the:

* Public.
* Media.
* Employees and retirees.
* Unions.
* Contractors and suppliers.

- Customers.
- Shareholders.
- Emergency response organizations.
- Regulatory agencies.
- Appointed and elected officials.
- Special interest groups.
- Neighbors.

Media Relations—In any disaster or emergency situation, the media is the most important link to the public. All companies should develop and maintain positive relations with local media outlets. Their needs and interest should be considered as well. Determining how to communicate important public information through the media in an emergency is a necessary component of disaster/emergency planning.

A trained spokesperson and an alternate spokesperson should be designated by the company. A media briefing area should be set up and security procedures should be established. These procedures should ensure that information is complete, accurate and approved for public release. An appropriate and useful way of communicating technical information should be determined. Background information about the facility should also be prepared.

In providing information to the media during a disaster or emergency, it is important to remember that:

- All media, including local and national media, should be given equal time and access to information.

- When appropriate, press briefings and interviews should be conducted.

- Media deadlines should be observed.

- Media representatives should always be escorted to ensure safety.

- Records of released information should be kept.

- Press releases should be provided when possible.

In working with the media, it is important to not speculate about the incident, or permit unauthorized personnel to release information.

Facts should never be covered up, nor should the media be misled. Finally, blame for the incident should never be placed.

Recovery and Restoration

Business recovery and restoration, or business resumption, goes right to a facility's bottom line: keeping people employed and the business running. Recovery and restoration issues include planning considerations, continuity of management, insurance and resumption of operations.

Planning Considerations—Planning considerations should include making contractual arrangements with vendors for such post-emergency services as records preservation, equipment repair, earth-moving or engineering. Meeting with insurance carriers to discuss property and business resumption policies is an additional consideration (photographing and/or videotaping the facility to document assets can be particularly helpful). Another consideration involves determining critical operations. Making plans for bringing systems back on-line must also be determined. The process may entail:

- Repairing or replacing equipment.
- Relocating operations to an alternate location.
- Contracting operations on a temporary basis.

Continuity of Management—Not every key person will be readily available or physically at the facility after a disaster/emergency. In order to ensure that recovery decisions can be made without any undue delay, it is particularly important to consult with legal counsel regarding laws and corporate bylaws that govern continuity of management.

To ensure continuity of management, it is necessary to establish procedures for:

- Assuring the chain of command.
- Maintaining lines of succession for key personnel.
- Moving to alternate headquarters.

Insurance—Most companies discover that they are not properly insured only after they have suffered a loss. Lack of appropriate insurance can be financially devastating. The following issues should be discussed with insurance carriers to determine the needs of a company or entity:

- Methods for valuing property.
- Coverage to include cost of required upgrades to code.
- Coverage requirements to preclude co-insurer status.
- Incidents covered.
- Deductibles.
- Policy holder requirements.
- Required records and documentation.
- Coverage for interruption of power (both on- and off-premises power interruption).
- Coverage for lost income due to plant shutdown, customer loss, etc.
- Emergency management program and rate adjustments.

Employee Support—Since employees are a company's most valuable asset, provision for their support should be made. Various services that could be provided to employees range from granting cash advances and/or salary continuation, to arranging flexible work hours/reduced work hours, as well as crisis counseling, assistance in temporary housing and day care.

Resuming Operations—Immediately after a disaster and/or emergency, the following steps should be taken to resume operations:

- Establish priorities.

- Continue to ensure the safety of personnel on the property. Assess remaining hazards and maintain security at the incident scene.

- Conduct an employee briefing.

- Keep detailed records. Consider audio recording all discussions. Take photographs of or videotape the damage.

- Account for all damage-related costs. Establish special job order numbers and charge codes for purchases and repair work.

- Follow notification procedures. Notify employees' families about the status of personnel on the property. Notify off-duty personnel about work status. Notify insurance carriers and appropriate government agencies.

- Protect undamaged property. Close up building openings. Remove smoke, water and debris. Protect equipment against moisture. Restore sprinkler systems. Physically secure the property. Restore power.

- Conduct an investigation. Coordinate actions with appropriate government agencies.

- Conduct salvage operations. Segregate damaged from undamaged property. Keep damaged goods on hand until an insurance adjuster has visited the premises, but move material outside if it is in the way or exposure to the elements would not make matters worse.

- Take an inventory of all damaged goods. This is usually done with the adjuster, or the adjuster's salvor if there is any appreciable amount of goods or value. If goods are released to the salvor, it is important to obtain a signed inventory stating the quantity and type of goods being removed.

- Restore equipment and property. For major repair work, review restoration plans with the insurance adjuster and appropriate government agencies.

- Assess the value of damaged property. Assess the impact of business interruption.

- Maintain contact with customers and suppliers.

Administration and Logistics

Maintaining complete and accurate records at all times is essential in ensuring an efficient disaster/emergency response and recovery. Certain records may also be required by regulation or by insurance carriers. Records can also prove invaluable in the event of any legal action that may be initiated following a disaster/emergency occurrence.

Administrative Actions—Administrative actions prior to a disaster or emergency include:

- Establishing and maintaining a written disaster/emergency management plan.
- Maintaining training records.
- Maintaining all written communications.
- Documenting drills and exercises and their critiques.
- Involving community emergency response organizations in planning activities.

Administrative actions during and after a disaster or emergency include:

- Maintaining telephone logs.
- Keeping a detailed record of events.
- Maintaining a record of injuries and follow-up actions.
- Accounting for personnel.
- Coordinating notification of family members.
- Issuing press releases.
- Maintaining sampling records.
- Managing finances.
- Coordinating personnel services.
- Documenting incident investigations and recovery operations.

Logistics—Before a disaster/emergency occurrence, logistics may entail the following actions:

- Acquiring equipment.
- Stockpiling supplies.
- Designating emergency facilities.
- Establishing training facilities.
- Establishing mutual aid agreements.
- Preparing a resource inventory.

During a disaster/emergency situation, logistics may entail the provision of:

- Providing utility maps to emergency responders.
- Providing material safety data sheets (MSDS) to employees.
- Moving backup equipment in place.
- Repairing parts.
- Arranging for medical support, food and transportation.
- Arranging for shelter facilities.
- Providing for backup power.
- Providing for backup communications.

Sources

Federal Emergency Management Agency, *Emergency Management Guide for Business and Industry* by Thomas Wahle, Ogilvy Adams & Rinehart, and Gregg Beatty, Roy F. Weston, Inc., for the Federal Emergency Management Agency under FEMA Contract EMW-90-C-3348.

United States Department of Labor, Occupational Safety and Health Administration, *How to Prepare for Workplace Emergencies*, 2001, OSHA 3088 (Rev.).

United States Department of Labor, Occupational Safety and Health Administration, *Principal Emergency Response and Preparedness: Requirements and Guidelines*, OSHA 3122-06R, 2004.

Appendix I

Sources of Assistance and Information

This section provides contact information for organizations that can offer help and information on natural disasters, bomb threats and disaster planning. Other sources of information are included in several of the chapters.

FEDERAL EMERGENCY MANAGEMENT AGENCY (FEMA) LOCATIONS

FEMA Headquarters
Federal Emergency Management Agency
500 C Street, SW
Washington, DC 20472
(800) 621-FEMA

FEMA Regional Offices
Region 1
Boston
(617) 223-9540

Region 2
New York
(212) 680-3600

Region 3
Philadelphia
(215) 931-5608

Region 4
Atlanta
(770) 220-5200

Region 5
Chicago
(312) 408-5500

Region 6
Denton, TX
(940) 898-5399

Region 7
Kansas City, MO
(816) 283-7061

Region 8
Denver
(303) 235-4800

Region 9
San Francisco
(570) 627-7100

Region 10
Bothell, WA
(425) 587-4600

STATE EMERGENCY MANAGEMENT AGENCIES

A
Alabama Emergency Management Agency
5898 County Road 41
P.O. Drawer 2160
Clanton, Alabama 35046-2160
(205) 280-2200
(205) 280-2495 FAX
ema.alabama.gov/

Alaska Division of Emergency Services
P.O. Box 5750
Fort Richardson, Alaska 99505-5750
(907) 428-7000
(907) 428-7009 FAX
www.ak-prepared.com

American Samoa Territorial Emergency Management Coordination (TEMCO)
American Samoa Government
P.O. Box 1086
Pago Pago, American Samoa 96799
(011)(684) 699-6415
(011)(684) 699-6414 FAX

Arizona Division of Emergency Management
5636 E. McDowell Rd
Phoenix, Arizona 85008
(602) 244-0504 or 1-800-411-2336
www.azdema.gov

Arkansas Department of Emergency Management
P.O. Box 758
Conway, Arkansas 72033
(501) 730-9750
(501) 730-9754 FAX
www.adem.state.ar.us

C
California Governor's Office of Emergency Services
3650 Schriever Ave.
Mather, CA 95655-4203
(916) 845-8510
(916) 845-8511 FAX
www.oes.ca.gov

Colorado Office of Emergency Management
Division of Local Government
Department of Local Affairs

9195 East Mineral Avenue
Suite 200
Centennial, Colorado 80112
(720) 852-6600
(720) 852-6750 Fax
www.dola.state.co.us/oem/oemindex.htm

Connecticut Office of Emergency Management
Military Department
360 Broad Street
Hartford, Connecticut 06105
(860) 566-3180
(860) 247-0664 FAX
www.mil.state.ct.us/OEM.htm

D
Delaware Emergency Management Agency
165 Brick Store Landing Road
Smyrna, Delaware 19977
(302) 659-3362
(302) 659-6855 FAX
www.state.de.us/dema/index.htm

District of Columbia Emergency Management Agency
2000 14th Street, NW, 8th Floor
Washington, D.C. 20009
(202) 727-6161
(202) 673-2290 FAX
dcema.dc.gov

F
Florida Division of Emergency Management
2555 Shumard Oak Blvd.
Tallahassee, Florida 32399-2100
(850) 413-9969
(850) 488-1016 FAX
floridadisaster.org

G
Georgia Emergency Management Agency
P.O. Box 18055
Atlanta, Georgia 30316-0055
(404) 635-7000
(404) 635-7205 FAX
www.State.Ga.US/GEMA

Office of Civil Defense
Government of Guam
P.O. Box 2877
Hagatna, Guam 96932
(011)(671) 475-9600
(011)(671) 477-3727 FAX
http://ns.gov.gu

Guam Homeland Security/Office of Civil Defense
221B Chalan Palasyo
Agana Heights, Guam 96910
Tel:(671)475-9600
Fax:(671)477-3727
www.guamhs.org

H
Hawaii State Civil Defense
3949 Diamond Head Road
Honolulu, Hawaii 96816-4495
(808) 733-4300
(808) 733-4287 FAX
www.scd.hawaii.gov

I
Idaho Bureau of Disaster Services
4040 Guard Street, Bldg. 600
Boise, Idaho 83705-5004
(208) 334-3460
(208) 334-2322 FAX
www2.state.id.us/bds

Illinois Emergency Management Agency
110 East Adams Street
Springfield, Illinois 62701
(217) 782-2700
(217) 524-7967 FAX
www.state.il.us/iema

Indiana State Emergency Management Agency
302 West Washington Street
Room E-208 A
Indianapolis, Indiana 46204-2767
(317) 232-3986
(317) 232-3895 FAX
www.ai.org/sema/index.html

Iowa Homeland Security & Emergency Management Division
Department of Public Defense
Hoover Office Building
Des Moines, Iowa 50319
(515) 281-3231
(515) 281-7539 FAX
Iowahomelandsecurity.org

K
Kansas Division of Emergency Management
2800 S.W. Topeka Boulevard
Topeka, Kansas 66611-1287
(785) 274-1401
(785) 274-1426 FAX
www.ink.org/public/kdem

Kentucky Emergency Management
EOC Building
100 Minuteman Parkway Bldg. 100
Frankfort, Kentucky 40601-6168
(502) 607-1682
(502) 607-1614 FAX
kyem.ky.gov

L
Louisiana Office of Emergency Preparedness
7667 Independence Blvd.
Baton Rouge, Louisiana 70806
(225) 925-7500
(225) 925-7501 FAX
www.ohsep.louisiana.gov

M
Maine Emergency Management Agency
45 Commerce Drive, Suite #2
#72 State House Station
Augusta, Maine 04333-0072
207-624-4400
207-287-3180 (FAX)
www.state.me.us/mema/memahome.htm

CNMI Emergency Management Office
Office of the Governor
Commonwealth of the Northern Mariana Islands
P.O. Box 10007
Saipan, Mariana Islands 96950
(670) 322-9529; (670) 322-7743 FAX
www.cnmiemo.org

National Disaster Management Office
Office of the Chief Secretary
P.O. Box 15
Majuro, Republic of the Marshall Islands 96960-0015
(011)(692) 625-5181
(011)(692) 625-6896 FAX

Maryland Emergency Management Agency
Camp Fretterd Military Reservation
5401 Rue Saint Lo Drive
Reistertown, Maryland 21136
(410) 517-3600
(877) 636-2872 Toll-Free
(410) 517-3610 FAX
www.mema.state.md.us

Massachusetts Emergency Management Agency
400 Worcester Road
Framingham, Massachusetts 01702-5399
(508) 820-2000
(508) 820-2030 FAX
www.state.ma.us/mema

Michigan Division of Emergency Management
4000 Collins Road
P.O. Box 30636
Lansing, Michigan 48909-8136
(517) 333-5042
(517) 333-4987 FAX
www.michigan.gov

National Disaster Control Officer
Federated States of Micronesia
P.O. Box PS-53
Kolonia, Pohnpei—Micronesia 96941
(011)(691) 320-8815
(001)(691) 320-2785 FAX

Minnesota Homeland Security and Emergency Management
Department of Public Safety
Suite 223
444 Cedar Street
St. Paul, Minnesota 55101-6223
(651) 296-2233
(651) 296-0459 FAX
www.hsem.state.mn.us

Mississippi Emergency Management Agency
P.O. Box 4501—Fondren Station
Jackson, Mississippi 39296-4501
(601) 352-9100
(800) 442-6362 Toll Free
(601) 352-8314 FAX
www.www.msema.org
www.msema.org/mitigate/mssaferoominit.htm

Missouri Emergency Management Agency
P.O. Box 116
2302 Militia Drive
Jefferson City, Missouri 65102
(573) 526-9100
(573) 634-7966 FAX
sema.dps.mo.gov

Montana Division of Disaster & Emergency Services
1900 Williams Street
Helena, Montana 59604-4789
(406) 841-3911
(406) 444-3965 FAX
dma.mt.gov/des

N
Nebraska Emergency Management Agency
1300 Military Road
Lincoln, Nebraska 68508-1090
(402) 471-7410
(402) 471-7433 FAX
www.nema.ne.gov

Nevada Division of Emergency Management
2525 South Carson Street
Carson City, Nevada 89711
(775) 687-4240
(775) 687-6788 FAX
dem.state.nv.us

Governor's Office of Emergency Management
State Office Park South
107 Pleasant Street
Concord, New Hampshire 03301
(603) 271-2231
(603) 225-7341 FAX
www.nhoem.state.nh.us

New Jersey Office of Emergency Management
Emergency Management Bureau
P.O. Box 7068
West Trenton, New Jersey 08628-0068
(609) 538-6050 Monday-Friday
(609) 882-2000 ext 6311 (24/7)
(609) 538-0345 FAX
www.state.nj.us/oem/county

New Mexico Department of Public Safety
Office of Emergency Management
P.O. Box 1628
13 Bataan Boulevard
Santa Fe, New Mexico 87505
(505) 476-9600
(505) 476-9635 Emergency
(505) 476-9695 FAX
www.dps.nm.org/emergency/index.htm

Emergency Management Bureau
Department of Public Safety
P.O. Box 1628
13 Bataan Boulevard
Santa Fe, New Mexico 87505
(505) 476-9606
(505) 476-9650
www.dps.nm.org/emc.htm

New York State Emergency Management Office
1220 Washington Avenue
Building 22, Suite 101
Albany, New York 12226-2251
(518) 457-2222
(518) 457-9995 FAX
www.nysemo.state.ny.us

North Carolina Division of Emergency Management
4713 Mail Service Center
Raleigh, NC 27699-4713

(919) 733-3867
(919) 733-5406 FAX
www.dem.dcc.state.nc.us/

North Dakota Division of Emergency Management
P.O. Box 5511
Bismarck, North Dakota 58506-5511
(701) 328-8100
(701) 328-8181 FAX
www.state.nd.us/dem

O
Ohio Emergency Management Agency
2855 W. Dublin Granville Road
Columbus, Ohio 43235-2206
(614) 889-7150
(614) 889-7183 FAX
www.state.oh.us/odps/division/ema

Office of Civil Emergency Management
Will Rogers Sequoia Tunnel 2401 N. Lincoln
Oklahoma City, Oklahoma 73152
(405) 521-2481
(405) 521-4053 FAX
www.odcem.state.ok.us

Oregon Emergency Management
Department of State Police
PO Box 14370
Salem, Oregon 97309-5062
(503) 378-2911
(503) 373-7833 FAX
egov.oregon.gov/OOHS/OEM

P
Palau NEMO Coordinator
Office of the President
P.O. Box 100
Koror, Republic of Palau 96940

(011)(680) 488-2422
(011)(680) 488-3312

Pennsylvania Emergency Management Agency
2605 Interstate Drive
Harrisburg PA 17110-9463
(717) 651-2001
(717) 651-2040 FAX
www.pema.state.pa.us

Puerto Rico Emergency Management Agency
P.O. Box 966597
San Juan, Puerto Rico 00906-6597
(787) 724-0124
(787) 725-4244 FAX

R
Rhode Island Emergency Management Agency
645 New London Ave
Cranston, Rhode Island 02920-3003
(401) 946-9996
(401) 944-1891 FAX
www.riema.ri.gov

S
South Carolina Emergency Management Division
2779 Fish Hatchery Road
West Columbia South Carolina 29172
(803) 737-8500
(803) 737-8570 FAX
www.scemd.org

South Dakota Division of Emergency Management
118 West Capitol
Pierre, South Dakota 57501
(605) 773-3231
(605) 773-3580 FAX
www.state.sd.us/dps/sddem/home.htm

T
Tennessee Emergency Management Agency
3041 Sidco Drive
Nashville, Tennessee 37204-1502
(615) 741-4332
(615) 242-9635 FAX
www.tnema.org

Texas Division of Emergency Management
5805 N. Lamar
Austin, Texas 78752
(512) 424-2138
(512) 424-2444 or 7160 FAX www.txdps.state.tx.us/dem/

U
Utah Division of Emergency Services and Homeland Security
1110 State Office Building
P.O. Box 141710
Salt Lake City, Utah 84114-1710
(801) 538-3400
(801) 538-3770 FAX
www.des.utah.gov

V
Vermont Emergency Management Agency
Department of Public Safety
Waterbury State Complex
103 South Main Street
Waterbury, Vermont 05671-2101
(802) 244-8721
(802) 244-8655 FAX
www.dps.state.vt.us

Virgin Islands Territorial Emergency Management—VITEMA
2-C Contant, A-Q Building
Virgin Islands 00820
(340) 774-2244
(340) 774-1491

Virginia Department of Emergency Management
10501 Trade Court
Richmond, VA 23236-3713
(804) 897-6502
(804) 897-6506
www.vdem.state.va.us

W

State of Washington Emergency Management Division
Building 20, M/S: TA-20
Camp Murray, Washington 98430-5122
(253) 512-7000
(253) 512-7200 FAX
www.emd.wa.gov

West Virginia Office of Emergency Services
Building 1, Room EB-80 1900 Kanawha Boulevard, East
Charleston, West Virginia 25305-0360
(304) 558-5380
(304) 344-4538 FAX
www.wvdhsem.gov

Wisconsin Emergency Management
2400 Wright Street
P.O. Box 7865
Madison, Wisconsin 53707-7865
(608) 242-3232
(608) 242-3247 FAX
emergencymanagement.wi.gov

Wyoming Office of Homeland Security
122 W. 25th Street
Cheyenne, Wyoming 82002
(307) 777-4900
(307) 635-6017 FAX
wyohomelandsecurity.state.wy.us

BUREAU OF ALCOHOL, TOBACCO AND FIREARMS (ATF) OFFICES

Bureau of Alcohol, Tobacco, Firearms and Explosives
Office of Field Operations Room 8100
650 Massachusetts Avenue, NW
Washington, D.C. 20226   (202)927-7970

Atlanta Field Division:	**404-417-2600**
Atlanta, GA (Group I)	404-417-1300
Atlanta, GA (Group II Arson)	404-417-1300
Atlanta, GA (Group III)	404-417-1300
Atlanta, GA (Group IV)	404-815-4400
Atlanta, GA (Group V—Industry Operations)	404-417-2670
Atlanta, GA (Group VI)	404-417-2600
Atlanta, GA (Group VII)	404-417-1300
Augusta, GA (Satellite Office)	706-724-9983
Columbus, GA (Satellite Office)	706-653-3545
Macon, GA	478-474-0477
Macon, GA (Group II—Industry Operations)	478-474-0477
Savannah, GA	912-790-8326
Baltimore Field Division:	**410-779-1700**
Baltimore, MD (Group I Arson)	410-779-1710
Baltimore, MD (Group II)	410-579-5011
Baltimore, MD (Group III)	410-779-1730
Baltimore, MD (Group IV)	410-779-1740
Baltimore, MD (Group V—Industry Operations)	410-779-1750
Hyattsville, MD	301-397-2640
Wilmington, DE (Criminal Enforcement)	302-252-0110
Wilmington, DE (Industry Operations)	302-252-0130
Boston Field Division:	**617-557-1200**
Boston, MA (Group I Arson)	617-557-1210
Boston, MA (Group II)	617-557-1220
Boston, MA (Group III)	617-557-1326
Boston, MA (Group IV)	617-557-1240
Boston, MA (Group V—Industry Operations)	617-557-1250
Burlington, VT	802-951-6593

Hartford, CT (Industry Operations)	860-240-3400
Manchester, NH	603-471-1283
New Haven, CT	203-773-2060
Portland, ME	207-780-3324
Providence, RI	401-528-4366
Providence, RI (Satellite Office—Industry Operations)	401-528-4366
Springfield, MA (Satellite Office)	413-785-0007
Worcester, MA	508-793-0240
Charlotte Field Division:	**704-716-1800**
Asheville, NC (Satellite Office)	828-271-4075/4076
Charleston, SC	843-763-3683
Charlotte, NC (Group I)	704-716-1810
Charlotte, NC (Group II)	704-716-1820
Charlotte, NC (Group III—Industry Operations)	704-716-1830
Charlotte, NC (Group IV)	704-716-1840
Charlotte, NC (Violent Crime Task Force)	704-716-1850
Columbia, SC	803-765-5723
Columbia, SC (Satellite Office—Industry Operations)	803-765-5722
Fayetteville, NC	910-483-3030
Fayetteville, NC (Satellite Office—Industry Operations)	910-483-3030
Florence, SC (Satellite Office)	843-292-0179
Greensboro, NC (Group I)	336-547-4224
Greensboro, NC (Group II—Industry Operations)	336-547-4150
Greenville, SC	864-282-2937
Greenville, SC (Satellite Office—Industry Operations)	864-282-2937
Raleigh, NC	919-856-4366
Wilmington, NC	910-343-6801
Chicago Field Division:	**312-846-7200**
Chicago, IL (Group I)	312-846-7230
Chicago, IL (Group II)	312-846-7250
Chicago, IL (Group III)	312-846-7270
Chicago, IL (Group IV)	312-846-8850
Chicago, IL (Group V)	312-846-8870
Fairview Heights, IL	618-632-9380
Fairview Heights, IL (Satellite Office—Industry Operations)	618-632-0704
Downers Grove, IL (Group I)	630-725-5220
Downers Grove, IL (Group II—Arson & Explosives)	630-725-5230

Downers Grove, IL (Group III—Industry Operations)	630-725-5290
Peoria, IL (Satellite Office—Industry Operations)	309-671-7108
Rockford, IL (Satellite Office)	815-987-4310
Rock Island, IL (Satellite Office)	309-732-0636
Springfield, IL (Group I—Criminal Enforcement)	217-547-3650
Springfield, IL (Group II—Industry Operations)	217-547-3675
Columbus Field Division:	**614-827-8400**
Cincinnati Field Office	513-684-3354
Cincinnati II IO Office	513-684-3351
Cleveland I Field Office	216-522-3080
Cleveland II Field Office	216-522-3786
Cleveland III IO Office	216-522-3374
Columbus I Field Office	614-827-8450
Columbus II Intel Group	614-827-8430
Columbus IO Satellite	614-827-8470
Fort Wayne Field Office	260-424-4440
Indianapolis I Field Office	317-226-7464
Indianapolis II IO Office	317-248-4002
Merrillville Field Office	219-755-6310
Toledo Field Office	419-259-7520
Youngstown Field Office	330-707-2300
Dallas Field Division:	**469-227-4300**
Dallas, TX (Group I)	469-227-4350
Dallas, TX (Group II Arson)	469-227-4370
Dallas, TX (Group III)	469-227-4395
Dallas, TX (Group IV)	972-915-9570
Dallas, TX (Group V—Industry Operations)	469-227-4415
El Paso, TX	915-534-6449
El Paso, TX (Satellite Office—Industry Operations)	915-534-6475
Fort Worth, TX	817-862-2800
Fort Worth, TX—Industry Operations	817-862-2850
Lubbock, TX (Group I)	806-798-1030
Lubbock, TX (Satellite Office—Industry Operations)	806-798-1030
Oklahoma City, OK (Group I—Industry Operations)	405-297-5073
Oklahoma City, OK (Group II)	405-297-5060
Tulsa, OK	918-581-7731
Tyler, TX	903-590-1475

Detroit Field Division:	**313-259-8050**
Ann Arbor	734-741-2456
Detroit, MI (Group I)	313-259-8110
Detroit, MI (Group II)	313-259-8120
Detroit, MI (Group III Arson)	313-259-8140
Detroit, MI (Group IV)	313-259-8320
Detroit, MI (Group V—Industry Operations)	313-259-8390
Detroit, MI (Group VI)	313-259-8760
Flint, MI	810 341-5710
Flint, MI (Satellite Office—Industry Operations)	810 341-5730
Grand Rapids, MI (Group I)	616-301-6100
Lansing, MI (Satellite Office)	517-337-6645
Grand Rapids, MI (Group II—Industry Operations)	616-301-6100
Houston Field Division:	**281-372-2900**
Austin, TX	512-349-4545
Beaumont, TX	409-835-0062
Beaumont, TX (Satellite Office—Industry Operations)	409-835-0062
Corpus Christi, TX	361-888-3392
Houston, TX (Group I)	281-372-2990
Houston, TX (Group II)	281-372-2960
Houston, TX (Group III Arson)	281-372-2930
Houston, TX (Group IV)	281-372-2980
Houston, TX (Group V)	281-372-3010
Houston, TX (Group VI—Industry Operations)	281-372-2950
McAllen, TX	956-687-5207
San Antonio, TX (Group I)	210-805-2727
San Antonio, TX (Group II—Industry Operations)	210-805-2777
Waco, TX (Satellite Office)	254-741-9900
Kansas City Field Division:	**816-559-0700**
Cape Girardeau, MO (Satellite Office)	573-331-7300
Cedar Rapids, IA	
(Satellite of the Des Moines Field Office)	319-393-6075
Davenport, IA (covered by Des Moines Field Office)	309-732-0636
Des Moines, IA	515-284-4372
Des Moines, IA (Satellite Office—Industry Operations)	515-284-4857
Kansas City, MO (Group I)	816-559-0710
Kansas City, MO (Group II)	816-559-0720

Kansas City, MO (Group III—Industry Operations)   816-559-0730
Kansas City, MO (Group IV)   816-746-4962
Kansas City, MO (Group V)   816-559-0850
Kansas City, MO (Group VI—Industry Operations)   816-559-0730
Omaha, NE   402-952-2605
Omaha, NE (Satellite Office—Industry Operations)   402-952-2635
Sioux City, IA (covered by Omaha, NE Field Office)   712-255-9128
Springfield, MO   417-837-2100
St. Louis, MO (Group I)   314-269-2200
St. Louis, MO (Group II)   314-269-2200
Wichita, KS   316-269-6229

Los Angeles Field Division: **213-534-2450**
Los Angeles, CA (Group I—Metro)   213-534-1050
St. Louis, MO (Group III—Industry Operations)   314-269-2250
Los Angeles, CA (Group II)   213-534-1070
Los Angeles, CA (Group III Arson)   213-534-6480
Los Angeles, CA (Group IV—Industry Operations)   213-534-2430
Los Angeles, CA (Group V)   213-534-5050
Riverside, CA   909-276-6031
San Diego, CA (Group I)   619-446-0700
San Diego, CA (Group II)   619-446-0720
San Diego, CA (Group III—Industry Operations)   619-446-0740
Santa Ana, CA (Group I)   714-246-8210
Santa Ana, CA (Group II—Industry Operations)   714-246-8252
Santa Maria, CA (Enforcement)   805-348-1820
Santa Maria, CA (Industry Operations)   805-348-0027
Van Nuys, CA   818-756-4350
Van Nuys, CA (Satellite Office—Industry Operations)   818-756-4364

Louisville Field Division: **502-753-3400**
Ashland, KY   606-329-8092
Bowling Green, KY   270-393-4755
Bowling Green, KY
    (Satellite Office—Industry Operations)   270-781-1757
Charleston, WV (Charleston I)   304-347-5249
Charleston, WV (Satellite Office—Industry Operations)   304-347-5172
Lexington, KY (Lexington I Field Office)   859-219-4500
Lexington, KY (Group II—Industry Operations)   859-219-4508

London, KY (Satellite Office)	606-878-3011/3012
Louisville, KY (Group I)	502-753-3450
Louisville, KY (Group II—Industry Operations)	502-753-3500
Louisville, KY (Group III)	502-753-3550
Wheeling, WV	304-232-4170
Wheeling, WV (Satellite Office—Industry Operations)	304-232-4170

Miami Field Division:

Fort Lauderdale, FL	**954-453-6001**
Fort Lauderdale, FL HIDTA	954-888-1661
Fort Pierce, FL (Satellite Office)	561-835-8878
San Juan, PR (Group I—HIDTA)	787-766-5084
San Juan, PR (Group II)	787-766-5084
San Juan, PR (Group III—Industry Operations)	787-766-5584
Mayaguez, PR (Satellite Office—Industry Operations)	787-344-8636
Miami, FL (Group I)	305-597-4910
Miami, FL (Group II)	305-597-4920
Miami, FL (Group III)	305-597-4930
Miami, FL (Group IV)	305-597-4940
Miami, FL (Group V—HIDTA)	305-597-2056
Miami, FL (Group VI—Industry Operations)	305-597-4960
St. Croix, VI (Satellite Office)	340-719-4799
St. Thomas, VI	340-774-2398
West Palm Beach, FL	561-835-8878

Nashville Field Division:

	615-565-1400
Birmingham, AL (Group I)	205-583-5920
Birmingham, AL (Group II—Industry Operations)	205-583-5950
Birmingham, AL (Group III)	205-583-5970
Chattanooga, TN	423-855-6422
Huntsville, AL (Satellite Office)	256-539-0623
Jackson, TN (Satellite Office)	731-265-4258
Johnson City, TN (Satellite Office)	423-283-7262/7104
Knoxville, TN	865-545-4505
Memphis, TN	901-544-0321
Mobile, AL	251-405-5000
Mobile, AL (Satellite Office—Industry Operations)	251-405-5000
Montgomery, AL	334-206-6050
Nashville, TN (Group I)	615-565-1400

Nashville, TN (Group II—Industry Operations)   615-565-1420
Nashville, TN (Group III)   615-565-1430

New Orleans Field Division: **985-246-7000**
Baton Rouge, LA   225-819-4314
Biloxi, MS   Phone Numbers Pending
Fort Smith, AR   501-709-0872
Jackson, MS   601-292-4000
Jackson, MS (Group II—Industry Operations)   601-292-4025
Little Rock, AR   501-324-6181
Little Rock, AR (Satellite Office—Industry Operations) 501-324-6457
New Orleans, LA (Group I)   985-246-7100
New Orleans, LA (Group II)   985-246-7140
New Orleans, LA (Group III—Industry Operations)   985-246-7120
New Orleans, LA (Group IV)   985-246-7160
New Orleans V (Arson/Explosives)   985 893-8333
Oxford, MS (Group I)   662-234-3751
Shreveport, LA   318-424-6850
Shreveport, LA (Satellite Office—Industry Operations) 318-424-6861

New York Field Division: **718-650-4000**
Albany, NY (Criminal)   518-431-4182
Albany, NY (Satellite Office)   518-431-4188
Bath, NY (Satellite Office—Industry Operations)   607-776-4549
Buffalo, NY (Group I—Criminal)   716-853-5070
Buffalo, NY (Group II—Industry Operations)   716-853-5160
Jersey City, NJ (Satellite Office)   201-547-6821
Long Island, NY (Satellite Office—Industry Operations) 631-694-8372
Mellville, NY   631-694-8372
New York, NY (Group I)   718-552-1610
New York, NY (Group II)   718-552-1620
New York, NY (Group III Arson)   718-896-6400
New York, NY (Group IV)   718-650-4040
New York, NY (Group V)   718-650-4050
New York, NY (Group VI—Industry Operations)   718-650-4060
New York, NY (Group VII)   718-650-4070
Rochester, NY (Satellite Office)   716-263-5720
Syracuse, NY (Criminal)   315-448-0889
Syracuse, NY (Satellite Office—Industry Operations)   315-448-0898

West Patterson, NJ (NJ Group I)   973-247-3010
West Patterson, NJ (NJ Group II Arson)   973-247-3020
West Patterson, NJ (NJ Group III—Industry Operations) 973-247-3030
White Plains, NY   914-682-6164
                                                                        215-717-4700
White Plains, NY (Satellite Office—Industry Operations) 914-682-6164

Philadelphia Field Division:
Atlantic City, NJ (Satellite Office)   **609-487-2110**
Camden, NJ   856-488-2520
Harrisburg, PA   717-221-3402
Lansdale, PA (Industry Operations)   215-362-1840
Philadelphia, PA (Group I—Violent Crime Impact Team)   215-446-9610
Philadelphia, PA (Group II Arson & Explosives)   215-446-7860
Philadelphia, PA (Group III)   215-446-9680
Philadelphia, PA (Group IV—Industry Operations)   215-446-7880
Philadelphia, PA (Group V—Intelligence Group)   215-446-7840
Philadelphia, PA (Group VI—Ceasefire)   215-446-9640
Philadelphia, PA (Group VII)   215-717-4710
Pittsburgh, PA (Group I and Group II Arson)   412-395-0540
Pittsburgh, PA (Group III—Industry Operations)   412-395-0600
Reading, PA   610-320-5222
Trenton, NJ (Arson and Explosives)   609-989-2155
Trenton, NJ (Satellite Office—Industry Operations)   609-989-2142
Wilkes-Barre, PA (Industry Operations)   570-826-6551

Phoenix Field Division: **602-776-5400**
Albuquerque, NM   505-346-6914
Albuquerque, NM (Satellite Office—Industry Operations) 505-346-6910
Cheyenne, WY   307-772-2346
Colorado Springs, CO   719-473-0166
Denver, CO (Group I)   303-844-7540
Denver, CO (Group II Arson)   303-844-7570
Denver, CO (Group III—Industry Operations)   303-844-7545
Phoenix, AZ (Group I)   602-776-5440
Phoenix, AZ (Group II)   602-776-5460
Phoenix, AZ (Group III—Industry Operations)   602-776-5480
Phoenix, AZ (Group IV)   602-776-5500
Salt Lake City, UT   801-524-7000

Salt Lake City, UT
(Satellite Office—Industry Operations)   801-524-7012
Tucson, AZ (Group I)   520-770-5100
Tucson, AZ (Group II)   520-770-5120
Tucson, AZ (Satellite Office—Industry Operations)   520-670-4804

San Francisco Field Division: **925-479-7500**
Bakersfield, CA (Satellite Office)   661-861-4420
Fresno, CA (Group I)   559-487-5393
Fresno, CA (Group II—Industry Operations)   559-487-5093
Las Vegas, NV   702-387-4600
Stockton, CA (Stockton I & Stockton II Satellite Office) 209-321-8878
Napa, CA (Satellite Office—Industry Operations)   707-224-7801
Oakland, CA (Group I)   510-267-2200
Oakland, CA (Satellite Office—Industry Operations)   925-479-7500
Redding, CA (Satellite Office)   530-224-1862
Reno, NV   775-784-5251
Sacramento, CA (Group I)   916-498-5100
Sacramento, CA (Group II—Industry Operations)   916-498-5095
San Francisco, CA (Group I)   415-436-8020
San Francisco, CA (Group II Arson)   925-479-7520
San Francisco, CA (Group III—Industry Operations)   925-479-7530
San Francisco, CA (Group IV)   925-479-7540
San Jose, CA (Group I)   408-535-5015
San Jose, CA (Group II—Industry Operations)   408-535-5538
Santa Rosa, CA (Industry Operations)   707-576-0184

Seattle Field Division: **206-389-5800**
Anchorage, AK   907-271-5701
Anchorage, AK (Satellite Office—Industry Operations) 907-271-5701
Boise, ID   208-334-1160
Boise, ID (Satellite Office—Industry Operations)   208-334-1164
Hawaii County, HI   809-933-8139
Honolulu, HI   808-541-2670
Honolulu, HI (Satellite Office—Industry Operations)   808-541-2670
Mongmong, Guam   671-472-7129
Portland, OR (Group I)   503-331-7810
Portland, OR (Group II)   503-331-7820
Portland, OR (Group III)   503-331-7830

Seattle, WA (Group I)	206-389-6860
Seattle, WA (Group II—Industry Operations)	206-389-6800
Seattle, WA (Group III—Arson & Explosives)	206-389-6830
Seattle, WA (Group IV)	206-389-5870
Spokane, WA (Group I)	509-324-7866
Spokane, WA (Group II—Industry Operations)	509-324-7881
Yakima, WA	509-454-4403

St. Paul Field Division:	**651-726-0200**
Billings, MT (Group I)	406-657-6886
Fargo, ND (Group I)	701-293-2860
Fargo, ND	
(Group II—Satellite Office, Industry Operations)	701-293-2880
Helena, MT (Group I)	406-441-1100
Helena, MT	
(Group II—Satellite Office, Industry Operations)	406-441-1100
Madison, WI (Group I Field Office)	608-441-5050
Milwaukee, WI (Group I)	414-727-6170
Milwaukee, WI (Group II—Industry Operations)	414-727-6200
Missoula, MT (Satellite Office)	406-721-2611
Rapid City, SD (Satellite Office)	605-343-3288
Sioux Falls, SD (Group I)	605-330-4368
St. Paul, MN (Group I)	651-726-0300
St. Paul, MN (Group II—Industry Operations)	651-726-0220
St. Paul, MN (Group III)	651-726-0230
St. Paul, MN (Group IV)	651-726-0260

Phoenix Field Division:	**602-776-5400**
Albuquerque, NM	505-346-6914
Albuquerque, NM (Satellite Office—Industry Operations)	505-346-6910
Cheyenne, WY	307-772-2346
Colorado Springs, CO	719-473-0166
Denver, CO (Group I)	303-844-7540
Denver, CO (Group II Arson)	303-844-7570
Denver, CO (Group III—Industry Operations)	303-844-7545
Phoenix, AZ (Group I)	602-776-5440
Phoenix, AZ (Group II)	602-776-5460
Phoenix, AZ (Group III—Industry Operations)	602-776-5480
Phoenix, AZ (Group IV)	602-776-5500

Salt Lake City, UT   801-524-7000
Salt Lake City, UT (Satellite Office—Industry Operations) 801-524-7012
Tucson, AZ (Group I)   520-770-5100
Tucson, AZ (Group II)   520-770-5120
Tucson, AZ (Satellite Office—Industry Operations)   520-670-4804

San Francisco Field Division: **925-479-7500**
Bakersfield, CA (Satellite Office)   661-861-4420
Fresno, CA (Group I)   559-487-5393
Fresno, CA (Group II—Industry Operations)   559-487-5093
Las Vegas, NV   702-387-4600
Stockton, CA (Stockton I & Stockton II Satellite Offices) 209-321-8878
Napa, CA (Satellite Office—Industry Operations)   707-224-7801
Oakland, CA (Group I)   510-267-2200
Oakland, CA (Satellite Office—Industry Operations) 925-479-7500
Redding, CA (Satellite Office)   530-224-1862
Reno, NV   775-784-5251
Sacramento, CA (Group I)   916-498-5100
Sacramento, CA (Group II—Industry Operations)   916-498-5095
San Francisco, CA (Group I)   415-436-8020
San Francisco, CA (Group II Arson)   925-479-7520
San Francisco, CA (Group III—Industry Operations) 925-479-7530
San Francisco, CA (Group IV)   925-479-7540
San Jose, CA (Group I)   408-535-5015
San Jose, CA (Group II—Industry Operations)   408-535-5538
Santa Rosa, CA (Industry Operations)   707-576-0184

Seattle Field Division: **206-389-5800**
Anchorage, AK   907-271-5701
Anchorage, AK (Satellite Office—Industry Operations) 907-271-5701
Boise, ID   208-334-1160
Boise, ID (Satellite Office—Industry Operations)   208-334-1164
Hawaii County, HI   809-933-8139
Honolulu, HI   808-541-2670
Honolulu, HI (Satellite Office—Industry Operations) 808-541-2670
Mongmong, Guam   671-472-7129
Portland, OR (Group I)   503-331-7810
Portland, OR (Group II)   503-331-7820
Portland, OR (Group III)   503-331-7830

Seattle, WA (Group I)	206-389-6860
Seattle, WA (Group II—Industry Operations)	206-389-6800
Seattle, WA (Group III—Arson & Explosives)	206-389-6830
Seattle, WA (Group IV)	206-389-5870
Spokane, WA (Group I)	509-324-7866
Spokane, WA (Group II—Industry Operations)	509-324-7881
Yakima, WA	509-454-4403
St. Paul Field Division:	**651-726-0200**
Billings, MT (Group I)	406-657-6886
Fargo, ND (Group I)	701-293-2860
Fargo, ND	
(Group II—Satellite Office, Industry Operations)	701-293-2880
Helena, MT (Group I)	406-441-1100
Helena, MT	
(Group II—Satellite Office, Industry Operations)	406-441-1100
Madison, WI (Group I Field Office)	608-441-5050
Milwaukee, WI (Group I)	414-727-6170
Milwaukee, WI (Group II—Industry Operations)	414-727-6200
Missoula, MT (Satellite Office)	406-721-2611
Rapid City, SD (Satellite Office)	605-343-3288
Sioux Falls, SD (Group I)	605-330-4368
St. Paul, MN (Group I)	651-726-0300
St. Paul, MN (Group II—Industry Operations)	651-726-0220
St. Paul, MN (Group III)	651-726-0230
St. Paul, MN (Group IV)	651-726-0260
Tampa Field Division:	**813-202-7300**
Fort Myers, FL (Group I Satellite Office)	239-334-8086
Fort Myers, FL	
(Group II Satellite Office—Industry Operations)	239-334-8086
Gainesville, FL (Satellite Office)	352-378-8017
Jacksonville, FL	904-380-5500
Jacksonville, FL (Satellite Office—Industry Operations)	904-380-5500
Orlando FL	407-384-2411
Orlando FL II (Industry Operations)	407-384-2420
Panama City, FL (Satellite Office)	850-769-0234
Pensacola, FL	850-435-8485
Tallahassee, FL	850-942-9660

Tampa, FL (Group I)	813-202-7310
Tampa, FL (Group II—Industry Operations)	813-202-7320
Tampa, FL (Group III)	813-301-3650

Washington Field Division:	**202-648-8010**
Bristol, VA	276-466-2727
Charlottesville, VA (Satellite Office)	434-970-3872
Falls Church, VA (Group I Arson)	703-287-1110
Falls Church, VA (Group II)	703-287-1120
Falls Church, VA (Group III—Industry Operations)	703-287-1130
Martinsburg, WV, LE	304-260-3400
Martinsburg, WV (Satellite Office—Industry Operations)	304-260-3400
Norfolk, VA	757-616-7400
Norfolk, VA (Satellite Office—Industry Operations)	757-441-3192
Richmond, VA (Group I)	804-200-4200
Richmond, VA (Group II—Industry Operations)	804-200-4141
Richmond, VA (Group III)	804-775-4200
Roanoke, VA	540-983-6920
Roanoke, VA (Satellite Office—Industry Operations)	540-983-6944
Washington, DC (Group I) (HIDTA)	202-305-8189
Washington, DC (Group II) (Firearms Trafficking)	202-648-8105
Washington, DC (Group III)	
(VCIT-Violent Crime Impact Team)	202-648-8090
Washington, DC (Group IV)	
(Intelligence/Regional Crime Gun Center)	202-648-8100

GENERAL INFORMATION SOURCES

American Meteorological Society
45 Beacon Street Boston, MA 02108-3693
(617) 227-2425
www.ametsoc.org

American Red Cross
Contact your local American Red Cross chapter. You will find them listed in your telephone directory under "A" for American Red Cross.

American Veterinary Medical Association
1931 North Meachan Road, #100
Schaumburg, Il 60173-4360 (847) 925-8070
www.amva.org

Humane Society of The United States
2100 L Street, NW
Washington, DC 20037
(202) 452-1100
www.hsus.org

National Academy of Engineering
500 Fifth Street, NW
Washington, DC 20001
(202) 334-3200
www.nae.edu

National Emergency Management Association
P.O. Box 11910Lexington, KY 40578
(859) 244-8000
www.nemaweb.org

National Oceanic and Atmospheric Administration (NOAA)
National Weather Service Warnings and Forecast Branch
1325 East West Highway
Silver Spring, MD 20910
(301) 713-0090
www.noaa.gov

High Plains Regional Climate Center
727 Hardin Hall, 3310 Holdredge Street
University of Nebraska-Lincoln
Lincoln, NE 6583-0997
(402) 472-6702
www.hprcc.unl.edu

Midwestern Climate Center
Illinois State Water Survey
2204 Griffith Drive

Champaign, IL 61820
(217) 244-8226
http://mcc.sws.uiuc.edu

Northeast Regional Climate Center
1123 Bradfield Hall
Cornell University
Ithaca, NY 14853
(607) 255-1751
www.nrcc.cornell.edu

Southeastern Regional Climate Center
1000 Assemble St., Suite 230
Columbia, SC 29201
(866) 845-1553
www.dnr.sc.gov/climate/sercc

Southern Regional Climate Center
E328 Howe-Russell Complex
Louisiana State University
Baton Rouge, LA 70803
(225) 578-5021
www.srcc.lsu.edu

Western Regional Climate Center
2215 Raggio Parkway
Reno, NV 89512
(775) 674-7010
www.wrcc.dri.edu

National Severe Storms Forecast Center (Forecasting)
Storm Prediction Center
1313 Halley Circle
Norman, OK 73069
(405) 579-0771
www.spc.noaa.gov

National Severe Storms Laboratory (Research)
1313 Halley Circle

Norman, OK 73069
(405) 360-3620
www.nssl.noaa.gov

National Safety Council
1121 Spring Lake Drive
Itasca, IL 60143-3201
(630) 285-1121
www.nsc.org

National Science Foundation
4201 Wilson Blvd.
Arlington, VA 22230
(703) 292-5111
(800) 281-8749
www.nsf.gov

Natural Hazards Research and Applications Information Center
482 UCB
Campus Box 482
University of Colorado
Boulder, CO 80309-0482
(303) 492-6818
www.colorado.edu/hazards

Oak Ridge National Laboratory, Hazard Management Group
Oak Ridge National Laboratory
P.O. Box 2008 MS6208
Oak Ridge, TN 37831-6206
9423 0 576-2716
www.ornl.gov
www.ngdc.noaa.gov

U.S. Geological Survey
National Center
12201 Sunrise Valley Drive
Reston, VA 20192
(703) 648-4000
www.usgs.gov

NATURAL DISASTER INFORMATION SOURCES

Hurricanes

National Hurricane Center
11691 S.W.17th St.
Miami, Fl 33165-2149
(305) 229-4470
www.nhc.noaa.gov

National Oceanic and Atmospheric Administration (NOAA)
National Weather Service Warnings and Forecast Branch
1325 East West Highway
Silver Spring, MD 20910
(301) 713-0090
www.noaa.gov

Storm Prediction Center (Forecasting)
1313 Halley Circle
Norman, OK 73069
www.spc.noaa.gov

National Severe Storms Laboratory (Research)
1313 Halley Circle
Norman, OK 73069
(405) 366-0427
www.nssl.noaa.gov

Earthquakes

Association of Bay Area Governments
P.O. Box 2050
Oakland, CA 94604
(510) 464-7900
www.abag.ca.gov

Building Seismic Safety Council
1090 Vermont Avenue, NW

Suite 700
Washington, DC 20005-4905
(202) 289-7800
www.bssconline.org

Central United States Earthquake Consortium
2630 East Holmes Road
Memphis, TN 38118
(901) 544-3570
www.cusec.org

Charleston Southern University, Earthquake Education Center
P.O. Box 11807
Charleston, SC 29423-8087
(843) 863-8090
www.csuniv.edu

Earthquake Engineering Research Institute
499-114th Street, Suite 320
Oakland, CA 94612-1934
(510) 451-0905
www.eeri.org

Memphis State University,
Center for Earthquake Research and Information
3890 Central
Memphis, TN 38152
(901) 678-2007
http://folkworm.ceri.memphis.edu

National Conference of States on Building Codes and Standards
505 Huntmar Park Drive, Suite 210
Herndon, VA 22070
(703) 437-0100
www.ngdc.noaa.gov

National Information Service for Earthquake Engineering
University of California—Berkeley
1301 South 46th St.

Richmond, CA 94804
(510) 665-3419
http://eerc.berkeley.edu

National Oceanic and Atmospheric Administration
National Geophysical Data Center
Code E/GC
325 Broadway
Builder, CO 80303-3228
(303) 497-6826
www.ngdc.noaa.gov

Seismological Society of America
201 Plaza Professional Building
El Cerrito, CA 94530
(510) 525-5474
www.seismosoc.org

University of Southern California,
Southern California Earthquake Center
3651 Trousdale Pkwy, Suite 169
Los Angeles, CA 90089-0742
(213) 740-5843
www.scec.org

U.S. Geological Survey
National Earthquake Information Center
P.O. Box 25046, MS-966
Denver Federal Center
Denver, CO 80225-0046
(303) 273-8500
http://earthquake.usgs.gov

Tornadoes

National Oceanic and Atmospheric Administration (NOAA)
National Weather Service
Warnings and Forecast Branch

1325 East West Highway
Silver Spring, MD 20910
(301) 713-0090
www.noaa.gov

National Severe Storms Forecast Center (Forecasting)
Storm Prediction Center
1313 Halley Circle
Norman, OK 73069
(405) 597-0771
www.spc.noaa.gov

National Severe Storms Laboratory (Research)
1313 Halley Circle
Norman, OK 73069
(405) 366-0427
www.nssl.noaa.gov

Texas Tech University
Institute for Disaster Research
Civil Engineering Department,
Box 41023
Lubbock, TX 79409-1023
(806) 742-3476
http://www.wind.ttu.edu

Tsunamis

Alaska Tsunami Warning Center
910 S. Felton Street
Palmer, AK 99645
(907) 745-4212
http://wcatwc.arh.noaa.gov

International Tsunami Information Center
737 Bishop St., No. 2200
Honolulu, HI 96813
(808) 541-1658
www.tsunamiwave.info

National Oceanic and Atmospheric Administration (NOAA)
National Weather Service
Warnings and Forecast Branch
1325 East West Highway
Silver Spring, MD 20910
(301) 713-0090
www.noaa.gov

National Severe Storms Forecast Center (Forecasting)
Storm Prediction Center
1313 Halley Circle
Norman, OK 73069
(405) 597-0771
www.spc.noaa.gov

National Severe Storms Laboratory (Research)
1313 Halley Circle
Norman, OK 73069
(405) 366-0427
www.nssl.noaa.gov

Pacific Tsunami Warning Center
91-270 Fort Weaver Road
Ewa Beach, HI 96706
(808) 689-8207
www.prh.noaa.gov/ptwc

Thunderstorms and Lightning

National Oceanic and Atmospheric Administration (NOAA)
National Weather Service
Warnings and Forecast Branch
1325 East West Highway
Silver Spring, MD 20910
(301) 713-0090
www.noaa.gov

National Severe Storms Forecast Center (Forecasting)
Storm Prediction Center
1313 Halley Circle
Norman, OK 73069
(405) 597-0771
www.spc.noaa.gov

National Severe Storms Laboratory (Research)
1313 Halley Circle
Norman, OK 73069
(405) 366-0427
www.nssl.noaa.gov

Floods and Flash Floods

Association of Dam Safety Officials, Inc.
450 Old Vine Street, Flr.2
Lexington, KY 40507-1544
(859) 257-5140
www.damsafety.org

Association of State Floodplain Managers
2809 Fish Hatchery Road
Madison, WI 53713
(608) 274-0123
www.floods.org

Association of State Wetlands Managers
P.O. Box 2463
Berne, NY 12023
(518) 872-1804
www.aswm.org

National Association of Flood and
Stormwater Management Agencies
1301 K Street, NW, Suite 800 East
Washington, DC 20005
(202) 218-4122
www.nafsma.org

National Oceanic and Atmospheric Administration (NOAA)
National Weather Service
Warnings and Forecast Branch
1325 East West Highway
Silver Spring, MD 20910
(301) 713-0090
www.noaa.gov

National Severe Storms Laboratory (Research)
1313 Halley Circle
Norman, OK 73069
(405) 366-0427
www.nssl.noaa.gov

Tennessee Valley Authority, Flood Risk Reduction Section
400 West Summit Hill Drive
Knoxville, TN 37902-1499
(865) 632-2101
www.tva.gov

U.S. Army Corps of Engineers
Floodplain Management Services and Coastal Resources
Branch 20
441 G Street NW
Washington, DC 20314
(202) 761-0099
www.usace.army.mil

Appendix II

Self-Inspection
Checklists

Source: Occupational Safety And Health Administration, U.S. Department of Labor.

Self-Inspection Checklists

These checklists are by no means all-inclusive. You should add to them or delete items that do not apply to your business; however, carefully consider each item and then make your decision. You should refer to OSHA standards for specific guidance that may apply to your work situation. (**Note:** These checklists are typical for general industry but not for construction or maritime industries.)

EMPLOYER POSTING

☐ Is the required OSHA Job Safety and Health Protection Poster displayed in a prominent location where all employees are likely to see it?

☐ Are emergency telephone numbers posted where they can be readily found in case of emergency?

☐ Where employees may be exposed to toxic substances or harmful physical agents, has appropriate information concerning employee access to medical and exposure records and Material Safety Data Sheets (MSDSs) been posted or otherwise made readily available to affected employees?

☐ Are signs concerning exit routes, room capacities, floor loading, biohazards, exposures to x-ray, microwave, or other harmful radiation or substances posted where appropriate?

☐ Is the Summary of Work-Related Injuries and Illnesses (OSHA Form 300A) posted during the months of February, March and April?

RECORDKEEPING

☐ Are occupational injuries or illnesses, except minor injuries requiring only first aid, recorded as required on the OSHA 300 log?

☐ Are employee medical records and records of employee exposure to hazardous substances or harmful physical agents up-to-date and in compliance with current OSHA standards?

☐ Are employee training records kept and accessible for review by employees, as required by OSHA standards?

☐ Have arrangements been made to retain records for the time period required for each specific type of record? (Some records must be maintained for at least 40 years.)

☐ Are operating permits and records up-to-date for items such as elevators, air pressure tanks, liquefied petroleum gas tanks, etc.?

SAFETY AND HEALTH PROGRAM

☐ Do you have an active safety and health program in operation that includes general safety and health program elements as well as the management of hazards specific to your worksite?

☐ Is one person clearly responsible for the safety and health program?

☐ Do you have a safety committee or group made up of management and labor representatives that meets regularly and reports in writing on its activities?

☐ Do you have a working procedure to handle in-house employee complaints regarding safety and health?

☐ Are your employees advised of efforts and accomplishments of the safety and health program made to ensure they will have a workplace that is safe and healthful?

☐ Have you considered incentives for employees or workgroups who excel in reducing workplace injury/illnesses?

MEDICAL SERVICES AND FIRST AID

☐ Is there a hospital, clinic, or infirmary for medical care near your workplace or is at least one employee on each shift currently qualified to render first aid?

☐ Have all employees who are expected to respond to medical emergencies as part of their job responsibilities received first aid training; had hepatitis B vaccination made available to them; had appropriate training on procedures to protect them from bloodborne pathogens, including universal precautions; and have available and understand how to use appropriate PPE to protect against exposure to bloodborne diseases?*

*Pursuant to an OSHA memorandum of July 1, 1992, employees who render first aid only as a collateral duty do not have to be offered pre-exposure hepatitis B vaccine only if the employer includes and implements the following requirements in his/her exposure control plan: (1) the employer must record all first aid incidents involving the presence of blood or other potentially infectious materials before the end of the work shift during which the first aid incident occurred; (2) the employer must comply with post-exposure evaluation, prophylaxis and follow-up requirements of the Bloodborne Pathogens standard with respect to "exposure incidents," as defined by the standard; (3) the employer must train designated first aid providers about the reporting procedure; (4) the employer must offer to initiate the hepatitis B vaccination series within 24 hours to all unvaccinated first aid providers who have rendered assistance in any situation involving the presence of blood or other potentially infectious materials.

☐ If employees have had an exposure incident involving bloodborne pathogens, was an immediate post-exposure medical evaluation and follow-up provided?

☐ Are medical personnel readily available for advice and consultation on matters of employees' health?

☐ Are emergency phone numbers posted?

☐ Are fully supplied first aid kits easily accessible to each work area, periodically inspected and replenished as needed?

☐ Have first aid kits and supplies been approved by a physician, indicating that they are adequate for a particular area or operation?

☐ Is there an eye-wash station or sink available for quick drenching or flushing of the eyes and body in areas where corrosive liquids or materials are handled?

FIRE PROTECTION

☐ Is your local fire department familiar with your facility, its location and specific hazards?

☐ If you have a fire alarm system, is it certified as required and tested annually?

☐ If you have interior standpipes and valves, are they inspected regularly?

☐ If you have outside private fire hydrants, are they flushed at least once a year and on a routine preventive maintenance schedule?

☐ Are fire doors and shutters in good operating condition?

☐ Are fire doors and shutters unobstructed and protected against obstructions, including their counterweights?

☐ Are fire door and shutter fusible links in place?

☐ Are automatic sprinkler system water control valves, air and water pressure checked periodically as required?

☐ Is the maintenance of automatic sprinkler systems assigned to responsible persons or to a sprinkler contractor?

☐ Are sprinkler heads protected by metal guards if exposed to potential physical damage?

☐ Is proper clearance maintained below sprinkler heads?

☐ Are portable fire extinguishers provided in adequate number and type and mounted in readily accessible locations?

☐ Are fire extinguishers recharged regularly with this noted on the inspection tag?

☐ Are employees periodically instructed in the use of fire extinguishers and fire protection procedures?

PERSONAL PROTECTIVE EQUIPMENT AND CLOTHING

☐ Has the employer determined whether hazards that require the use of PPE (e.g., head, eye, face, hand, or foot protection) are present or are likely to be present?

☐ If hazards or the likelihood of hazards are found, are employers selecting appropriate and properly fitted PPE suitable for protection from these hazards and ensuring that affected employees use it?

☐ Have both the employer and the employees been trained on PPE procedures, i.e., what PPE is necessary for job tasks, when workers need it, and how to properly wear and adjust it?

☐ Are protective goggles or face shields provided and worn where there is any danger of flying particles or corrosive materials?

☐ Are approved safety glasses required to be worn at all times in areas where there is a risk of eye injuries such as punctures, abrasions, contusions, or burns?

☐ Are employees who wear corrective lenses (glasses or contacts) in workplaces with harmful exposures required to wear *only* approved safety glasses, protective goggles, or use other medically approved precautionary procedures?

☐ Are protective gloves, aprons, shields, or other means provided and required where employees could be cut or where there is reasonably anticipated exposure to corrosive liquids, chemicals, blood, or other potentially infectious materials? See the OSHA Bloodborne

Pathogens standard, 29 CFR 1910.1030(b), for the definition of "other potentially infectious materials."

☐ Are hard hats required, provided and worn where danger of falling objects exists?

☐ Are hard hats periodically inspected for damage to the shell and suspension system?

☐ Is appropriate foot protection required where there is the risk of foot injuries from hot, corrosive, or poisonous substances, falling objects, crushing, or penetrating actions?

☐ Are approved respirators provided when needed? (See 29 CFR 1910.134 for detailed information on respirators or check OSHA's website at www.osha.gov).

☐ Is all PPE maintained in a sanitary condition and ready for use?

☐ Are food or beverages consumed only in areas where there is no exposure to toxic material, blood, or other potentially infectious materials?

☐ Is protection against the effects of occupational noise provided when sound levels exceed those of the OSHA Noise standard?

☐ Are adequate work procedures, PPE and other equipment provided and used when cleaning up spilled hazardous materials?

☐ Are appropriate procedures in place to dispose of or decontaminate PPE contaminated with, or reasonably anticipated to be contaminated with, blood or other potentially infectious materials?

GENERAL WORK ENVIRONMENT

☐ Are all worksites clean, sanitary and orderly?

☐ Are work surfaces kept dry and appropriate means taken to assure the surfaces are slip-resistant?

☐ Are all spilled hazardous materials or liquids, including blood and other potentially infectious materials, cleaned up immediately and according to proper procedures?

☐ Is combustible scrap, debris and waste stored safely and removed from the worksite promptly?

☐ Is all regulated waste, as defined in the OSHA Bloodborne Pathogens standard (29 CFR 1910.1030), discarded according to Federal, state and local regulations?

☐ Are accumulations of combustible dust routinely removed from elevated surfaces including the overhead structure of buildings, etc.?

☐ Is combustible dust cleaned up with a vacuum system to prevent suspension of dust particles in the environment?

☐ Is metallic or conductive dust prevented from entering or accumulating on or around electrical enclosures or equipment?

☐ Are covered metal waste cans used for oily or paint-soaked waste?

☐ Are all oil and gas-fired devices equipped with flame failure controls to prevent flow of fuel if pilots or main burners are not working?

☐ Are paint spray booths, dip tanks, etc., cleaned regularly?

☐ Are the minimum number of toilets and washing facilities provided and maintained in a clean and sanitary fashion?

☐ Are all work areas adequately illuminated?

☐ Are pits and floor openings covered or otherwise guarded?

☐ Have all confined spaces been evaluated for compliance with 29 CFR 1910.146? (Permit-required confined spaces.)

WALKWAYS

☐ Are aisles and passageways kept clear and marked as appropriate?

☐ Are wet surfaces covered with non-slip materials?

☐ Are holes in the floor, sidewalk, or other walking surface repaired properly, covered, or otherwise made safe?

☐ Is there safe clearance for walking in aisles where motorized or mechanical handling equipment is operating?

☐ Are materials or equipment stored in such a way that sharp projections will not interfere with the walkway?

☐ Are spilled materials cleaned up immediately?

☐ Are changes of direction or elevations readily identifiable?

☐ Are aisles or walkways that pass near moving or operating machinery, welding operations, or similar operations arranged so employees will not be subjected to potential hazards?

☐ Is adequate headroom provided for the entire length of any aisle or walkway?

☐ Are standard guardrails provided wherever aisle or walkway surfaces are elevated more than 30 inches (76.20 centimeters) above any adjacent floor or the ground?

☐ Are bridges provided over conveyors and similar hazards?

FLOOR AND WALL OPENINGS

☐ Are floor openings guarded by a cover, a guardrail, or equivalent on all sides (except at stairways or ladder entrances)?

☐ Are toeboards installed around the edges of permanent floor openings where persons may pass below the opening?

☐ Are skylight screens able to withstand a load of at least 200 pounds (90.7 kilograms)?

☐ Is the glass in windows, doors, glass walls, etc., subject to possible human impact, of sufficient thickness and type for the condition of use?

☐ Are grates or similar type covers over floor openings such as floor drains designed to allow unimpeded foot traffic or rolling equipment?

☐ Are unused portions of service pits and pits not in use either covered or protected by guardrails or equivalent?

☐ Are manhole covers, trench covers and similar covers, and their supports designed to carry a truck rear axle load of at least 20,000 pounds (9,072 kilograms) when located in roadways and subject to vehicle traffic?

☐ Are floor or wall openings in fire-resistant construction provided with doors or covers compatible with the fire rating of the structure and provided with a self-closing feature when appropriate?

STAIRS AND STAIRWAYS

☐ Do standard stair rails or handrails on all stairways have at least four risers?

☐ Are all stairways at least 22 inches (55.88 centimeters) wide?

☐ Do stairs have landing platforms not less than 30 inches (76.20 centimeters) in the direction of travel and extend 22 inches (55.88 centimeters) in width at every 12 feet (3.6576 meters) or less of vertical rise?

☐ Do stairs angle no more than 50 and no less than 30 degrees?

☐ Are stairs of hollow-pan type treads and landings filled to the top edge of the pan with solid material?

☐ Are step risers on stairs uniform from top to bottom?

☐ Are steps slip-resistant?

☐ Are stairway handrails located between 30 inches (76.20 centimeters) and 34 inches (86.36 centimeters) above the leading edge of stair treads?

☐ Do stairway handrails have at least 3 inches (7.62 centimeters) of clearance between the handrails and the wall or surface they are mounted on?

☐ Where doors or gates open directly on a stairway, is a platform provided so the swing of the door does not reduce the width of the platform to less than 21 inches (53.34 centimeters)?

☐ Are stairway handrails capable of withstanding a load of 200 pounds (90.7 kilograms), applied within 2 inches (5.08 centimeters) of the top edge in any downward or outward direction?

☐ Where stairs or stairways exit directly into any area where vehicles may be operated, are adequate barriers and warnings provided to prevent employees from stepping into the path of traffic?

☐ Do stairway landings have a dimension measured in the direction of travel at least equal to the width of the stairway?

☐ Is the vertical distance between stairway landings limited to 12 feet (3.6576 meters) or less?

ELEVATED SURFACES

☐ Are signs posted, when appropriate, showing the elevated surface load capacity?

☐ Are surfaces that are elevated more than 30 inches (76.20 centimeters) provided with standard guardrails?

☐ Are all elevated surfaces beneath which people or machinery could be exposed to falling objects provided with standard 4-inch (10.16-centimeter) toeboards?

☐ Is a permanent means of access and egress provided to elevated storage and work surfaces?

☐ Is required headroom provided where necessary?

☐ Is material on elevated surfaces piled, stacked, or racked in a manner to prevent it from tipping, falling, collapsing, rolling, or spreading?

☐ Are dock boards or bridge plates used when transferring materials between docks and trucks or railcars?

EXITING OR EGRESS - EVACUATION

☐ Are all exits marked with an exit sign and illuminated by a reliable light source?

☐ Are the directions to exits, when not immediately apparent, marked with visible signs?

☐ Are doors, passageways or stairways that are neither exits nor access to exits, but could be mistaken for exits, appropriately marked "NOT AN EXIT," "TO BASEMENT," "STOREROOM," etc.?

☐ Are exit signs labeled with the word "EXIT" in lettering at least 5 inches (12.70 centimeters) high and the stroke of the lettering at least 1/2-inch (1.2700 centimeters) wide?

☐ Are exit doors side-hinged?

☐ Are all exits kept free of obstructions?

☐ Are at least two means of egress provided from elevated platforms, pits, or rooms where the absence of a second exit would increase the risk of injury from hot, poisonous, corrosive, suffocating, flammable, or explosive substances?

☐ Are there sufficient exits to permit prompt escape in case of emergency?

☐ Are special precautions taken to protect employees during construction and repair operations?

☐ Is the number of exits from each floor of a building and the number of exits from the building itself appropriate for the building occupancy load?

☐ Are exit stairways that are required to be separated from other parts of a building enclosed by at least 2-hour fire-resistive construction in buildings more than four stories in height, and not less than 1-hour fire-resistive construction elsewhere?

☐ Where ramps are used as part of required exiting from a building, is the ramp slope limited to 1 foot (0.3048 meter) vertical and 12 feet (3.6576 meters) horizontal?

☐ Where exiting will be through frameless glass doors, glass exit doors, storm doors, etc., are the doors fully tempered and meet the safety requirements for human impact?

EXIT DOORS

☐ Are doors that are required to serve as exits designed and constructed so that the path of exit travel is obvious and direct?

☐ Are windows that could be mistaken for exit doors made inaccessible by means of barriers or railings?

☐ Are exit doors able to be opened from the direction of exit travel without the use of a key or any special knowledge or effort when the building is occupied?

☐ Is a revolving, sliding, or overhead door prohibited from serving as a required exit door?

☐ Where panic hardware is installed on a required exit door, will it allow the door to open by applying a force of 15 pounds (6.80 kilograms) or less in the direction of the exit traffic?

☐ Are doors on cold storage rooms provided with an inside release mechanism that will release the latch and open the door even if the door is padlocked or otherwise locked on the outside?

☐ Where exit doors open directly onto any street, alley, or other area where vehicles may be operated, are adequate barriers and warnings provided to prevent employees from stepping into the path of traffic?

☐ Are doors that swing in both directions and are located between rooms where there is frequent traffic provided with viewing panels in each door?

PORTABLE LADDERS

☐ Are all ladders maintained in good condition, joints between steps and side rails tight, all hardware and fittings securely attached, and moveable parts operating freely without binding or undue play?

☐ Are non-slip safety feet provided on each metal or rung ladder, and are ladder rungs and steps free of grease and oil?

☐ Are employees prohibited from placing a ladder in front of doors opening toward the ladder unless the door is blocked open, locked, or guarded?

☐ Are employees prohibited from placing ladders on boxes, barrels, or other unstable bases to obtain additional height?

☐ Are employees required to face the ladder when ascending or descending?

☐ Are employees prohibited from using ladders that are broken, have missing steps, rungs, or cleats, broken side rails, or other faulty equipment?

☐ Are employees instructed not to use the top step of ordinary stepladders as a step?

☐ When portable rung ladders are used to gain access to elevated platforms, roofs, etc., does the ladder always extend at least 3 feet (0.9144 meters) above the elevated surface?

☐ Are employees required to secure the base of a portable rung or cleat type ladder to prevent slipping, or otherwise lash or hold it in place?

☐ Are portable metal ladders legibly marked with signs reading "CAUTION - Do Not Use Around Electrical Equipment" or equivalent wording?

☐ Are employees prohibited from using ladders as guys, braces, skids, gin poles, or for other than their intended purposes?

☐ Are employees instructed to only adjust extension ladders while standing at a base (not while standing on the ladder or from a position above the ladder)?

☐ Are metal ladders inspected for damage?

☐ Are the rungs of ladders uniformly spaced at 12 inches (30.48 centimeters) center to center?

HAND TOOLS AND EQUIPMENT

☐ Are all tools and equipment (both company and employee-owned) used at the workplace in good condition?

☐ Are hand tools, such as chisels, punches, etc., which develop mushroomed heads during use, reconditioned or replaced as necessary?

☐ Are broken or fractured handles on hammers, axes and similar equipment replaced promptly?

☐ Are worn or bent wrenches replaced?

☐ Are appropriate handles used on files and similar tools?

☐ Are employees aware of hazards caused by faulty or improperly used hand tools?

☐ Are appropriate safety glasses, face shields, etc., used while using hand tools or equipment that might produce flying materials or be subject to breakage?

☐ Are jacks checked periodically to ensure they are in good operating condition?

☐ Are tool handles wedged tightly into the heads of all tools?

☐ Are tool cutting edges kept sharp so the tool will move smoothly without binding or skipping?

☐ Are tools stored in a dry, secure location where they cannot be tampered with?

☐ Is eye and face protection used when driving hardened or tempered studs or nails?

PORTABLE (POWER OPERATED) TOOLS AND EQUIPMENT

☐ Are grinders, saws and similar equipment provided with appropriate safety guards?

☐ Are power tools used with proper shields, guards, or attachments, as recommended by the manufacturer?

☐ Are portable circular saws equipped with guards above and below the base shoe?

☐ Are circular saw guards checked to ensure that they are not wedged up, leaving the lower portion of the blade unguarded?

☐ Are rotating or moving parts of equipment guarded to prevent physical contact?

☐ Are all cord-connected, electrically operated tools and equipment effectively grounded or of the approved double insulated type?

☐ Are effective guards in place over belts, pulleys, chains and sprockets on equipment such as concrete mixers, air compressors, etc.?

☐ Are portable fans provided with full guards or screens having openings 1/2 inch (1.2700 centimeters) or less?

☐ Is hoisting equipment available and used for lifting heavy objects, and are hoist ratings and characteristics appropriate for the task?

☐ Are ground-fault circuit interrupters provided on all temporary electrical 15 and 20 ampere circuits used during periods of construction?

☐ Are pneumatic and hydraulic hoses on power-operated tools checked regularly for deterioration or damage?

ABRASIVE WHEEL EQUIPMENT GRINDERS

☐ Is the work rest used and kept adjusted to within 1/8 inch (0.3175 centimeter) of the wheel?

☐ Is the adjustable tongue on the top side of the grinder used and kept adjusted to within 1/4 inch (0.6350 centimeters) of the wheel?

☐ Do side guards cover the spindle, nut and flange and 75 percent of the wheel diameter?

☐ Are bench and pedestal grinders permanently mounted?

☐ Are goggles or face shields always worn when grinding?

☐ Is the maximum revolutions per minute (rpm) rating of each abrasive wheel compatible with the rpm rating of the grinder motor?

☐ Are fixed or permanently mounted grinders connected to their electrical supply system with metallic conduit or other permanent wiring method?

☐ Does each grinder have an individual on and off control switch?

☐ Is each electrically operated grinder effectively grounded?

☐ Are new abrasive wheels visually inspected and ring tested before they are mounted?

☐ Are dust collectors and powered exhausts provided on grinders used in operations that produce large amounts of dust?

☐ Are splash guards mounted on grinders that use coolant to prevent the coolant from reaching employees?

☐ Is cleanliness maintained around grinders?

POWER-ACTUATED TOOLS

☐ Are employees who operate power-actuated tools trained in their use and required to carry a valid operator's card?

☐ Is each power-actuated tool stored in its own locked container when not being used?

☐ Is a sign at least 7 inches (17.78 centimeters) by 10 inches (25.40 centimeters) with bold face type reading "POWER-ACTUATED TOOL IN USE" conspicuously posted when the tool is being used?

☐ Are power-actuated tools left unloaded until they are ready to be used?

☐ Are power-actuated tools inspected for obstructions or defects each day before use?

☐ Do power-actuated tool operators have and use appropriate PPE such as hard hats, safety goggles, safety shoes and ear protectors?

MACHINE GUARDING

☐ Is there a training program to instruct employees on safe methods of machine operation?

☐ Is there adequate supervision to ensure that employees are following safe machine operating procedures?

☐ Is there a regular program of safety inspection of machinery and equipment?

☐ Is all machinery and equipment kept clean and properly maintained?

☐ Is sufficient clearance provided around and between machines to allow for safe operations, set up and servicing, material handling and waste removal?

☐ Is equipment and machinery securely placed and anchored to prevent tipping or other movement that could result in personal injury?

☐ Is there a power shut-off switch within reach of the operator's position at each machine?

☐ Can electric power to each machine be locked out for maintenance, repair, or security?

☐ Are the noncurrent-carrying metal parts of electrically operated machines bonded and grounded?

☐ Are foot-operated switches guarded or arranged to prevent accidental actuation by personnel or falling objects?

☐ Are manually operated valves and switches controlling the operation of equipment and machines clearly identified and readily accessible?

☐ Are all emergency stop buttons colored red?

☐ Are all pulleys and belts within 7 feet (2.1336 meters) of the floor or working level properly guarded?

☐ Are all moving chains and gears properly guarded?

☐ Are splash guards mounted on machines that use coolant to prevent the coolant from reaching employees?

☐ Are methods provided to protect the operator and other employees in the machine area from hazards created at the point of operation, ingoing nip points, rotating parts, flying chips and sparks?

☐ Are machine guards secure and arranged so they do not cause a hazard while in use?

☐ If special hand tools are used for placing and removing material, do they protect the operator's hands?

☐ Are revolving drums, barrels and containers guarded by an enclosure that is interlocked with the drive mechanism so that revolution cannot occur unless the guard enclosure is in place?

☐ Do arbors and mandrels have firm and secure bearings, and are they free from play?

☐ Are provisions made to prevent machines from automatically starting when power is restored after a power failure or shutdown?

☐ Are machines constructed so as to be free from excessive vibration when the largest size tool is mounted and run at full speed?

☐ If machinery is cleaned with compressed air, is air pressure controlled and PPE or other safeguards utilized to protect operators and other workers from eye and body injury?

☐ Are fan blades protected with a guard having openings no larger than I/2 inch (1.2700 centimeters) when operating within 7 feet (2.1336 meters) of the floor?

☐ Are saws used for ripping equipped with anti-kickback devices and spreaders?

☐ Are radial arm saws so arranged that the cutting head will gently return to the back of the table when released?

LOCKOUT/TAGOUT PROCEDURES

☐ Is all machinery or equipment capable of movement required to be de-energized or disengaged and blocked or locked out during cleaning, servicing, adjusting, or setting up operations?

☐ If the power disconnect for equipment does not also disconnect the electrical control circuit, are the appropriate electrical enclosures identified and is a means provided to ensure that the control circuit can also be disconnected and locked out?

☐ Is the locking out of control circuits instead of locking out main power disconnects prohibited?

☐ Are all equipment control valve handles provided with a means for locking out?

☐ Does the lockout procedure require that stored energy (mechanical, hydraulic, air, etc.) be released or blocked before equipment is locked out for repairs?

☐ Are appropriate employees provided with individually keyed personal safety locks?

☐ Are employees required to keep personal control of their key(s) while they have safety locks in use?

☐ Is it required that only the employee exposed to the hazard can place or remove the safety lock?

☐ Is it required that employees check the safety of the lockout by attempting a startup after making sure no one is exposed?

☐ Are employees instructed to always push the control circuit stop button prior to re-energizing the main power switch?

☐ Is there a means provided to identify any or all employees who are working on locked-out equipment by their locks or accompanying tags?

☐ Are a sufficient number of accident prevention signs or tags and safety padlocks provided for any reasonably foreseeable repair emergency?

☐ When machine operations, configuration, or size require an operator to leave the control station and part of the machine could move if accidentally activated, is the part required to be separately locked out or blocked?

☐ If equipment or lines cannot be shut down, locked out and tagged, is a safe job procedure established and rigidly followed?

WELDING, CUTTING AND BRAZING

☐ Are only authorized and trained personnel permitted to use welding, cutting, or brazing equipment?

☐ Does each operator have a copy of and follow the appropriate operating instructions?

☐ Are compressed gas cylinders regularly examined for obvious signs of defects, deep rusting, or leakage?

☐ Is care used in handling and storage of cylinders, safety valves, relief valves, etc., to prevent damage?

☐ Are precautions taken to prevent the mixture of air or oxygen with flammable gases, except at a burner or in a standard torch?

☐ Are only approved apparatuses (torches, regulators, pressure reducing valves, acetylene generators, manifolds) used?

☐ Are cylinders kept away from sources of heat and elevators, stairs, or gangways?

☐ Is it prohibited to use cylinders as rollers or supports?

☐ Are empty cylinders appropriately marked and their valves closed?

☐ Are signs posted reading "DANGER, NO SMOKING, MATCHES, OR OPEN LIGHTS," or the equivalent?

☐ Are cylinders, cylinder valves, couplings, regulators, hoses and apparatuses kept free of oily or greasy substances?

☐ Is care taken not to drop or strike cylinders?

☐ Are regulators removed and valve-protection caps put in place before moving cylinders, unless they are secured on special trucks?

☐ Do cylinders without fixed wheels have keys, handles, or non-adjustable wrenches on stem valves when in service?

☐ Are liquefied gases stored and shipped valve-end up with valve covers in place?

☐ Are employees trained never to crack a fuel gas cylinder valve near sources of ignition?

☐ Before a regulator is removed, is the valve closed and gas released?

☐ Is red used to identify the acetylene (and other fuel-gas) hose, green for the oxygen hose and black for inert gas and air hoses?

☐ Are pressure-reducing regulators used only for the gas and pressures for which they are intended?

☐ Is open circuit (no-load) voltage of arc welding and cutting machines as low as possible and not in excess of the recommended limits?

☐ Under wet conditions, are automatic controls for reducing no-load voltage used?

☐ Is grounding of the machine frame and safety ground connections of portable machines checked periodically?

☐ Are electrodes removed from the holders when not in use?

☐ Is it required that electric power to the welder be shut off when no one is in attendance?

☐ Is suitable fire extinguishing equipment available for immediate use?

☐ Is the welder forbidden to coil or loop welding electrode cable around his body?

☐ Are wet machines thoroughly dried and tested before use?

☐ Are work and electrode lead cables frequently inspected for wear and damage, and replaced when needed?

☐ Are cable connectors adequately insulated?

☐ When the object to be welded cannot be moved and fire hazards cannot be removed, are shields used to confine heat, sparks and slag?

☐ Are fire watchers assigned when welding or cutting is performed in locations where a serious fire might develop?

☐ Are combustible floors kept wet, covered with damp sand, or protected by fire-resistant shields?

☐ Are personnel protected from possible electrical shock when floors are wet?

☐ Are precautions taken to protect combustibles on the other side of metal walls when welding is underway?

☐ Are used drums, barrels, tanks and other containers thoroughly cleaned of substances that could explode, ignite, or produce toxic vapors before hot work begins?

☐ Do eye protection, helmets, hand shields and goggles meet appropriate standards?

☐ Are employees exposed to the hazards created by welding, cutting, or brazing operations protected with PPE and clothing?

☐ Is a check made for adequate ventilation in and where welding or cutting is performed?

☐ When working in confined places, are environmental monitoring tests done and means provided for quick removal of welders in case of an emergency?

COMPRESSORS AND COMPRESSED AIR

☐ Are compressors equipped with pressure relief valves and pressure gauges?

☐ Are compressor air intakes installed and equipped so as to ensure that only clean, uncontaminated air enters the compressor?

☐ Are air filters installed on the compressor intake?

☐ Are compressors operated and lubricated in accordance with the manufacturer's recommendations?

☐ Are safety devices on compressed air systems checked frequently?

☐ Before a compressor's pressure system is repaired, is the pressure bled off and the system locked out?

☐ Are signs posted to warn of the automatic starting feature of the compressors?

☐ Is the belt drive system totally enclosed to provide protection for the front, back, top and sides?

☐ Are employees strictly prohibited from directing compressed air towards a person?

☐ Are employees prohibited from using highly compressed air for cleaning purposes?

☐ When compressed air is used to clean clothing, are employees trained to reduce the pressure to less than 10 pounds per square inch (psi)?

☐ When using compressed air for cleaning, do employees wear protective chip guarding and PPE?

☐ Are safety chains or other suitable locking devices used at couplings of high-pressure hose lines where a connection failure would create a hazard?

☐ Before compressed air is used to empty containers of liquid, is the safe working pressure of the container checked?

☐ When compressed air is used with abrasive blast cleaning equipment, is the operating valve a type that must be held open manually?

☐ When compressed air is used to inflate auto tires, are a clip-on chuck and an inline regulator preset to 40 psi required?

☐ Are employees prohibited from using compressed air to clean up or move combustible dust if such action could cause the dust to be suspended in the air and cause a fire or explosion hazard?

COMPRESSORS/AIR RECEIVERS

☐ Is every receiver equipped with a pressure gauge and one or more automatic, spring-loaded safety valves?

☐ Is the total relieving capacity of the safety valve able to prevent pressure in the receiver from exceeding the maximum allowable working pressure of the receiver by more than 10 percent?

☐ Is every air receiver provided with a drain pipe and valve at the lowest point for the removal of accumulated oil and water?

☐ Are compressed air receivers periodically drained of moisture and oil?

☐ Are all safety valves tested at regular intervals to determine whether they are in good operating condition?

☐ Is there a current operating permit?

☐ Is the inlet of air receivers and piping systems kept free of accumulated oil and carbonaceous materials?

COMPRESSED GAS CYLINDERS

☐ Are cylinders with a water weight capacity over 30 pounds (13.6 kilograms) equipped with a means to connect a valve protector device, or with a collar or recess to protect the valve?

☐ Are cylinders legibly marked to clearly identify the type of gas?

☐ Are compressed gas cylinders stored in areas protected from external heat sources such as flame impingement, intense radiant heat, electric arcs, or high-temperature lines?

☐ Are cylinders located or stored in areas where they will not be damaged by passing or falling objects or subject to tampering by unauthorized persons?

☐ Are cylinders stored or transported in a manner to prevent them from creating a hazard by tipping, falling, or rolling?

☐ Are cylinders containing liquefied fuel gas stored or transported in a position so that the safety relief device is always in direct contact with the vapor space in the cylinder?

☐ Are valve protectors always placed on cylinders when the cylinders are not in use or connected for use?

☐ Are all valves closed off before a cylinder is moved, when the cylinder is empty and at the completion of each job?

☐ Are low-pressure fuel gas cylinders checked periodically for corrosion, general distortion, cracks, or any other defect that might indicate a weakness or render them unfit for service?

☐ Does the periodic check of low-pressure fuel gas cylinders include a close inspection of the cylinders' bottoms?

HOIST AND AUXILIARY EQUIPMENT

☐ Is each overhead electric hoist equipped with a limit device to stop the hook at its highest and lowest point of safe travel?

☐ Will each hoist automatically stop and hold any load up to 125 percent of its rated load if its actuating force is removed?

☐ Is the rated load of each hoist legibly marked and visible to the operator?

☐ Are stops provided at the safe limits of travel for trolley hoists?

☐ Are the controls of hoists plainly marked to indicate the direction of travel or motion?

☐ Is each cage-controlled hoist equipped with an effective warning device?

☐ Are close-fitting guards or other suitable devices installed on each hoist to ensure that hoist ropes will be maintained in the sheave grooves?

☐ Are all hoist chains or ropes long enough to handle the full range of movement of the application while maintaining two full wraps around the drum at all times?

☐ Are guards provided for nip points or contact points between hoist ropes and sheaves permanently located within 7 feet (2.1336 meters) of the floor, ground, or working platform?

☐ Are employees prohibited from using chains or rope slings that are kinked or twisted and prohibited from using the hoist rope or chain wrapped around the load as a substitute for a sling?

☐ Is the operator instructed to avoid carrying loads above people?

INDUSTRIAL TRUCKS - FORKLIFTS

☐ Are employees properly trained in the use of the type of industrial truck they operate?

☐ Are only trained personnel allowed to operate industrial trucks?

☐ Is substantial overhead protective equipment provided on high lift rider equipment?

☐ Are the required lift truck operating rules posted and enforced?

☐ Is directional lighting provided on each industrial truck that operates in an area with less than 2 footcandles per square foot of general lighting?

☐ Does each industrial truck have a warning horn, whistle, gong, or other device that can be clearly heard above normal noise in the areas where it is operated?

☐ Are the brakes on each industrial truck capable of bringing the vehicle to a complete and safe stop when fully loaded?

☐ Does the parking brake of the industrial truck prevent the vehicle from moving when unattended?

☐ Are industrial trucks that operate where flammable gases, vapors, combustible dust, or ignitable fibers may be present approved for such locations?

☐ Are motorized hand and hand/rider trucks designed so that the brakes are applied and power to the drive motor shuts off when the operator releases his or her grip on the device that controls the truck's travel?

☐ Are industrial trucks with internal combustion engines that are operated in buildings or enclosed areas carefully checked to ensure that such operations do not cause harmful concentrations of dangerous gases or fumes?

☐ Are safe distances maintained from the edges of elevated ramps and platforms?

☐ Are employees prohibited from standing or passing under elevated portions of trucks, whether loaded or empty?

☐ Are unauthorized employees prohibited from riding on trucks?

☐ Are operators prohibited from driving up to anyone standing in front of a fixed object?

☐ Are arms and legs kept inside the running lines of the truck?

☐ Are loads handled only within the rated capacity of the truck?

☐ Are trucks in need of repair removed from service immediately?

SPRAYING OPERATIONS

☐ Is adequate ventilation provided before spraying operations are started?

☐ Is mechanical ventilation provided when spraying operations are performed in enclosed areas?

☐ When mechanical ventilation is provided during spraying operations, is it so arranged that it will not circulate the contaminated air?

☐ Is the spray area free of hot surfaces and at least 20 feet (6.096 meters) from flames, sparks, operating electrical motors and other ignition sources?

☐ Are portable lamps used to illuminate spray areas suitable for use in a hazardous location?

☐ Is approved respiratory equipment provided and used when appropriate during spraying operations?

☐ Do solvents used for cleaning have a flash point to 100 degrees Fahrenheit (deg. F) or more?

☐ Are fire control sprinkler heads kept clean?

☐ Are "NO SMOKING" signs posted in spray areas, paint rooms, paint booths and paint storage areas?

☐ Is the spray area kept clean of combustible residue?

☐ Are spray booths constructed of metal, masonry, or other substantial noncombustible material?

☐ Are spray booth floors and baffles noncombustible and easily cleaned?

☐ Is infrared drying apparatus kept out of the spray area during spraying operations and is the spray booth completely ventilated before using the drying apparatus?

☐ Is the electric drying apparatus properly grounded?

☐ Are lighting fixtures for spray booths located outside the booth with the interior lighted through sealed clear panels?

☐ Are the electric motors for exhaust fans placed outside booths or ducts?

☐ Are belts and pulleys inside the booth fully enclosed?

☐ Do ducts have access doors to allow cleaning?

☐ Do all drying spaces have adequate ventilation?

ENTERING CONFINED SPACES

☐ Are confined spaces thoroughly emptied of any corrosive or hazardous substances, such as acids or caustics, before entry?

☐ Are all lines to a confined space that contain inert, toxic, flammable, or corrosive materials valved off and blanked or disconnected and separated before entry?

☐ Are all impellers, agitators, or other moving parts and equipment inside confined spaces locked out if they present a hazard?

☐ Is either natural or mechanical ventilation provided prior to confined space entry?

☐ Are appropriate atmospheric tests performed to check for oxygen deficiency, toxic substances and explosive concentrations in the confined space before entry?

☐ Is adequate illumination provided for the work to be performed in the confined space?

☐ Is the atmosphere inside the confined space frequently tested or continuously monitored during work?

☐ Is there a trained and equipped standby employee positioned outside the confined space, whose sole responsibility is to watch the work in progress, sound an alarm if necessary and render assistance?

☐ Is the standby employee appropriately trained and equipped to handle an emergency?

☐ Are employees prohibited from entering the confined space without lifelines and respiratory equipment if there is any question as to the cause of an emergency?

☐ Is approved respiratory equipment required if the atmosphere inside the confined space cannot be made acceptable?

☐ Is all portable electrical equipment used inside confined spaces either grounded and insulated or equipped with ground fault protection?

☐ Are compressed gas bottles forbidden inside the confined space?

☐ Before gas welding or burning is started in a confined space, are hoses checked for leaks, torches lighted only outside the confined area and the confined area tested for an explosive atmosphere each time before a lighted torch is taken into the confined space?

☐ If employees will be using oxygen-consuming equipment such as salamanders, torches, naces, etc., in a confined space, is sufficie provided to assure combustion without re ing the oxygen concentration of the atmo phere below 19.5 percent by volume?

☐ Whenever combustion-type equipment is in a confined space, are provisions made ensure the exhaust gases are vented outs of the enclosure?

☐ Is each confined space checked for decayi vegetation or animal matter which may p duce methane?

☐ Is the confined space checked for possible industrial waste which could contain toxic properties?

☐ If the confined space is below ground and near areas where motor vehicles will be c ating, is it possible for vehicle exhaust or bon monoxide to enter the space?

ENVIRONMENTAL CONTROLS

☐ Are all work areas properly illuminated?

☐ Are employees instructed in proper first and other emergency procedures?

☐ Are hazardous substances, blood and oth potentially infectious materials, which ma cause harm by inhalation, ingestion, or sk absorption or contact, identified?

☐ Are employees aware of the hazards invo with the various chemicals they may be e posed to in their work environment, such ammonia, chlorine, epoxies, caustics, etc.

☐ Is employee exposure to chemicals in the workplace kept within acceptable levels?

☐ Can a less harmful method or product be used?

☐ Is the work area ventilation system appro ate for the work performed?

☐ Are spray painting operations performed spray rooms or booths equipped with an appropriate exhaust system?

☐ Is employee exposure to welding fumes c trolled by ventilation, use of respirators, e sure time limits, or other means?

☐ Are welders and other nearby workers provided with flash shields during welding operations?

☐ If forklifts and other vehicles are used in buildings or other enclosed areas, are the carbon monoxide levels kept below maximum acceptable concentration?

☐ Has there been a determination that noise levels in the facilities are within acceptable levels?

☐ Are steps being taken to use engineering controls to reduce excessive noise levels?

☐ Are proper precautions being taken when handling asbestos and other fibrous materials?

☐ Are caution labels and signs used to warn of hazardous substances (e.g., asbestos) and biohazards (e.g., bloodborne pathogens)?

☐ Are wet methods used, when practicable, to prevent the emission of airborne asbestos fibers, silica dust and similar hazardous materials?

☐ Are engineering controls examined and maintained or replaced on a scheduled basis?

☐ Is vacuuming with appropriate equipment used whenever possible rather than blowing or sweeping dust?

☐ Are grinders, saws and other machines that produce respirable dusts vented to an industrial collector or central exhaust system?

☐ Are all local exhaust ventilation systems designed to provide sufficient air flow and volume for the application, and are ducts not plugged and belts not slipping?

☐ Is PPE provided, used and maintained wherever required?

☐ Are there written standard operating procedures for the selection and use of respirators where needed?

☐ Are restrooms and washrooms kept clean and sanitary?

☐ Is all water provided for drinking, washing and cooking potable?

☐ Are all outlets for water that is not suitable for drinking clearly identified?

☐ Are employees' physical capacities assessed before they are assigned to jobs requiring heavy work?

☐ Are employees instructed in the proper manner for lifting heavy objects?

☐ Where heat is a problem, have all fixed work areas been provided with spot cooling or air conditioning?

☐ Are employees screened before assignment to areas of high heat to determine if their health might make them more susceptible to having an adverse reaction?

☐ Are employees working on streets and roadways who are exposed to the hazards of traffic required to wear bright colored (traffic orange) warning vests?

☐ Are exhaust stacks and air intakes located so that nearby contaminated air will not be re-circulated within a building or other enclosed area?

☐ Is equipment producing ultraviolet radiation properly shielded?

☐ Are universal precautions observed where occupational exposure to blood or other potentially infectious materials can occur and in all instances where differentiation of types of body fluids or potentially infectious materials is difficult or impossible?

FLAMMABLE AND COMBUSTIBLE MATERIALS

☐ Are combustible scrap, debris and waste materials (oily rags, etc.) stored in covered metal receptacles and promptly removed from the worksite?

☐ Is proper storage practiced to minimize the risk of fire, including spontaneous combustion?

☐ Are approved containers and tanks used to store and handle flammable and combustible liquids?

☐ Are all connections on drums and combustible liquid piping, vapor and liquid tight?

☐ Are all flammable liquids kept in closed containers when not in use (e.g., parts cleaning tanks, pans, etc.)?

☐ Are bulk drums of flammable liquids grounded and bonded to containers during dispensing?

☐ Do storage rooms for flammable and combustible liquids have explosion-proof lights and mechanical or gravity ventilation?

☐ Is liquefied petroleum gas stored, handled and used in accordance with safe practices and standards?

☐ Are "NO SMOKING" signs posted on liquefied petroleum gas tanks and in areas where flammable or combustible materials are used or stored?

☐ Are liquefied petroleum storage tanks guarded to prevent damage from vehicles?

☐ Are all solvent wastes and flammable liquids kept in fire-resistant, covered containers until they are removed from the worksite?

☐ Is vacuuming used whenever possible rather than blowing or sweeping combustible dust?

☐ Are firm separators placed between containers of combustibles or flammables that are stacked one upon another to ensure their support and stability?

☐ Are fuel gas cylinders and oxygen cylinders separated by distance and fire-resistant barriers while in storage?

☐ Are fire extinguishers selected and provided for the types of materials in the areas where they are to be used?

Class A - Ordinary combustible material fires.

Class B - Flammable liquid, gas or grease fires.

Class C - Energized-electrical equipment fires.

☐ Are appropriate fire extinguishers mounted within 75 feet (22.86 meters) of outside areas containing flammable liquids and within 10 feet (3.048 meters) of any inside storage area for such materials?

☐ Are extinguishers free from obstructions or blockage?

☐ Are all extinguishers serviced, maintained and tagged at intervals not to exceed one year?

☐ Are all extinguishers fully charged and in their designated places?

☐ Where sprinkler systems are permanently installed, are the nozzle heads so directed arranged that water will not be sprayed in operating electrical switchboards and equ ment?

☐ Are safety cans used for dispensing flamr or combustible liquids at the point of use'

☐ Are all spills of flammable or combustible uids cleaned up promptly?

☐ Are storage tanks adequately vented to p vent the development of excessive vacuu pressure as a result of filling, emptying, c atmosphere temperature changes?

☐ Are storage tanks equipped with emerger venting that will relieve excessive interna pressure caused by fire exposure?

☐ Are rules enforced in areas involving stor and use of hazardous materials?

HAZARDOUS CHEMICAL EXPOSURE

☐ Are employees aware of the potential haz and trained in safe handling practices for ations involving various chemicals stored used in the workplace such as acids, base caustics, epoxies, phenols, etc.?

☐ Is employee exposure to chemicals kept v acceptable levels?

☐ Are eye-wash fountains and safety showe provided in areas where corrosive chemic are handled?

☐ Are all containers, such as vats, storage t. etc., labeled as to their contents, e.g., "C/ TICS"?

☐ Are all employees required to use person protective clothing and equipment when dling chemicals (gloves, eye protection, re rators, etc.)?

☐ Are flammable or toxic chemicals kept in closed containers when not in use?

☐ Are chemical piping systems clearly mark to their content?

☐ Where corrosive liquids are frequently han in open containers or drawn from storage ' sels or pipelines, are adequate means read available for neutralizing or disposing of spills or overflows and performed properly and safely?

☐ Are standard operating procedures established and are they being followed when cleaning up chemical spills?

☐ Are respirators stored in a convenient, clean and sanitary location, and are they adequate for emergencies?

☐ Are employees prohibited from eating in areas where hazardous chemicals are present?

☐ Is PPE used and maintained whenever necessary?

☐ Are there written standard operating procedures for the selection and use of respirators where needed?

☐ If you have a respirator protection program, are your employees instructed on the correct usage and limitations of the respirators? Are the respirators National Institute for Occupational Safety and Health (NIOSH)-approved for this particular application? Are they regularly inspected, cleaned, sanitized and maintained?

☐ If hazardous substances are used in your processes, do you have a medical or biological monitoring system in operation?

☐ Are you familiar with the threshold limit values or permissible exposure limits of airborne contaminants and physical agents used in your workplace?

☐ Have appropriate control procedures been instituted for hazardous materials, including safe handling practices and the use of respirators and ventilation systems?

☐ Whenever possible, are hazardous substances handled in properly designed and exhausted booths or similar locations?

☐ Do you use general dilution or local exhaust ventilation systems to control dusts, vapors, gases, fumes, smoke, solvents, or mists that may be generated in your workplace?

☐ Is operational ventilation equipment provided for removal of contaminants from production grinding, buffing, spray painting, and/or vapor degreasing?

☐ Do employees complain about dizziness, headaches, nausea, irritation, or other factors of discomfort when they use solvents or other chemicals?

☐ Is there a dermatitis problem? Do employees complain about dryness, irritation, or sensitization of the skin?

☐ Have you considered having an industrial hygienist or environmental health specialist evaluate your operation?

☐ If internal combustion engines are used, is carbon monoxide kept within acceptable levels?

☐ Is vacuuming used rather than blowing or sweeping dust whenever possible for cleanup?

☐ Are materials that give off toxic, asphyxiant, suffocating, or anesthetic fumes stored in remote or isolated locations when not in use?

HAZARDOUS SUBSTANCES COMMUNICATION

☐ Is there a list of hazardous substances used in your workplace and an MSDS readily available for each hazardous substance used?

☐ Is there a current written exposure control plan for occupational exposure to bloodborne pathogens and other potentially infectious materials, where applicable?

☐ Is there a written hazard communication program dealing with MSDSs, labeling and employee training?

☐ Is each container for a hazardous substance (i.e., vats, bottles, storage tanks, etc.) labeled with product identity and a hazard warning (communication of the specific health hazards and physical hazards)?

☐ Is there an employee training program for hazardous substances that includes:

• an explanation of what an MSDS is and how to use and obtain one;

• MSDS contents for each hazardous substance or class of substances;

• explanation of "A Right to Know";

- identification of where an employee can see the written hazard communication program;

- location of physical and health hazards in particular work areas and the specific protective measures to be used; and

- details of the hazard communication program, including how to use the labeling system and MSDSs.

☐ Does the employee training program on the bloodborne pathogens standard contain the following elements:

- an accessible copy of the standard and an explanation of its contents;

- a general explanation of the epidemiology and symptoms of bloodborne diseases;

- an explanation of the modes of transmission of Bloodborne Pathogens;

- an explanation of the employer's exposure control plan and the means by which employees can obtain a copy of the written plan;

- an explanation of the appropriate methods for recognizing tasks and the other activities that may involve exposure to blood and other potentially infectious materials;

- an explanation of the use and limitations of methods that will prevent or reduce exposure, including appropriate engineering controls, work practices and PPE;

- information on the types, proper use, location, removal, handling, decontamination and disposal of PPE;

- an explanation of the basis for selection of PPE;

- information on the hepatitis B vaccine;

- information on the appropriate actions to take and persons to contact in an emergency involving blood or other potentially infectious materials;

- an explanation of the procedure to follow if an exposure incident occurs, including the methods of reporting the incident and the medical

follow-up that will be made available;

- information on post-exposure evaluations and follow-up; and

- an explanation of signs, labels and color coding.

☐ Are employees trained in:

- how to recognize tasks that might result in occupational exposure;

- how to use work practice, engineering controls and PPE, and their limitations;

- how to obtain information on the types, selection, proper use, location, removal, handling, decontamination and disposal of PPE; and

- who to contact and what to do in an emergency.

ELECTRICAL

☐ Do you require compliance with OSHA standards for all contract electrical work?

☐ Are all employees required to report any obvious hazard to life or property in connection with electrical equipment or lines as soon as possible?

☐ Are employees instructed to make preliminary inspections and/or appropriate tests to determine conditions before starting work on electrical equipment or lines?

☐ When electrical equipment or lines are to be serviced, maintained, or adjusted, are necessary switches opened, locked out or tagged, whenever possible?

☐ Are portable electrical tools and equipment grounded or of the double insulated type?

☐ Are electrical appliances such as vacuum cleaners, polishers, vending machines, etc., grounded?

☐ Do extension cords have a grounding conductor?

☐ Are multiple plug adaptors prohibited?

☐ Are ground-fault circuit interrupters installed on each temporary 15 or 20 ampere, 120 volt alternating current (AC) circuit at locations where construction, demolition, modifications, alterations, or excavations are being performed?

☐ Are all temporary circuits protected by suitable disconnecting switches or plug connectors at the junction with permanent wiring?

☐ Do you have electrical installations in hazardous dust or vapor areas? If so, do they meet the National Electrical Code (NEC) for hazardous locations?

☐ Are exposed wiring and cords with frayed or deteriorated insulation repaired or replaced promptly?

☐ Are flexible cords and cables free of splices or taps?

☐ Are clamps or other securing means provided on flexible cords or cables at plugs, receptacles, tools, equipment, etc., and is the cord jacket securely held in place?

☐ Are all cord, cable and raceway connections intact and secure?

☐ In wet or damp locations, are electrical tools and equipment appropriate for the use or location or otherwise protected?

☐ Is the location of electrical power lines and cables (overhead, underground, under floor, other side of walls, etc.) determined before digging, drilling, or similar work is begun?

☐ Are metal measuring tapes, ropes, hand-lines or similar devices with metallic thread woven into the fabric prohibited where they could come in contact with energized parts of equipment or circuit conductors?

☐ Is the use of metal ladders prohibited where the ladder or the person using the ladder could come in contact with energized parts of equipment, fixtures, or circuit conductors?

☐ Are all disconnecting switches and circuit breakers labeled to indicate their use or equipment served?

☐ Are disconnecting means always opened before fuses are replaced?

☐ Do all interior wiring systems include provisions for grounding metal parts of electrical raceways, equipment and enclosures?

☐ Are all electrical raceways and enclosures securely fastened in place?

☐ Are all energized parts of electrical circuits and equipment guarded against accidental contact by approved cabinets or enclosures?

☐ Is sufficient access and working space provided and maintained around all electrical equipment to permit ready and safe operations and maintenance?

☐ Are all unused openings (including conduit knockouts) in electrical enclosures and fittings closed with appropriate covers, plugs, or plates?

☐ Are electrical enclosures such as switches, receptacles, junction boxes, etc., provided with tight-fitting covers or plates?

☐ Are disconnecting switches for electrical motors in excess of two horsepower able to open the circuit when the motor is stalled without exploding? (Switches must be horsepower rated equal to or in excess of the motor rating.)

☐ Is low voltage protection provided in the control device of motors driving machines or equipment that could cause injury from inadvertent starting?

☐ Is each motor disconnecting switch or circuit breaker located within sight of the motor control device?

☐ Is each motor located within sight of its controller or is the controller disconnecting means able to be locked open or is a separate disconnecting means installed in the circuit within sight of the motor?

☐ Is the controller for each motor that exceeds two horsepower rated equal to or above the rating of the motor it serves?

☐ Are employees who regularly work on or around energized electrical equipment or lines instructed in cardiopulmonary resuscitation (CPR)?

☐ Are employees prohibited from working alone on energized lines or equipment over 600 volts?

NOISE

☐ Are there areas in the workplace where continuous noise levels exceed 85 decibels?

☐ Is there an ongoing preventive health program to educate employees in safe levels of noise, exposures, effects of noise on their health and the use of personal protection?

☐ Have work areas where noise levels make voice communication between employees difficult been identified and posted?

☐ Are noise levels measured with a sound level meter or an octave band analyzer and are records being kept?

☐ Have engineering controls been used to reduce excessive noise levels? Where engineering controls are determined to be infeasible, are administrative controls (i.e., worker rotation) being used to minimize individual employee exposure to noise?

☐ Is approved hearing protective equipment (noise attenuating devices) available to every employee working in noisy areas?

☐ Have you tried isolating noisy machinery from the rest of your operation?

☐ If you use ear protectors, are employees properly fitted and instructed in their use?

☐ Are employees in high noise areas given periodic audiometric testing to ensure that you have an effective hearing protection system?

FUELING

☐ Are employees prohibited from fueling an internal combustion engine with a flammable liquid while the engine is running?

☐ Are fueling operations performed to minimize spillage?

☐ When spillage occurs during fueling operations, is the spilled fuel washed away completely, evaporated, or are other measures taken to control vapors before restarting the engine?

☐ Are fuel tank caps replaced and secured before starting the engine?

☐ In fueling operations, is there always metal contact between the container and the fuel tank?

☐ Are fueling hoses designed to handle the specific type of fuel?

☐ Are employees prohibited from handling or transferring gasoline in open containers?

☐ Are open lights, open flames, sparking, or arcing equipment prohibited near fueling or transfer of fuel operations?

☐ Is smoking prohibited in the vicinity of fueling operations?

☐ Are fueling operations prohibited in buildings or other enclosed areas that are not specifically ventilated for this purpose?

☐ Where fueling or transfer of fuel is done through a gravity flow system, are the nozzles self-closing?

IDENTIFICATION OF PIPING SYSTEMS

☐ When nonpotable water is piped through a facility, are outlets or taps posted to alert employees that the water is unsafe and not to be used for drinking, washing, or other personal use?

☐ When hazardous substances are transported through above-ground piping, is each pipeline identified at points where confusion could introduce hazards to employees?

☐ When pipelines are identified by color painted bands or tapes, are the bands or tapes located at reasonable intervals and at each outlet, valve, or connection, and are all visible parts of the line so identified?

☐ When pipelines are identified by color, is the color code posted at all locations where confusion could introduce hazards to employees?

☐ When the contents of pipelines are identified by name or name abbreviation, is the information readily visible on the pipe near each valve or outlet?

☐ When pipelines carrying hazardous substances are identified by tags, are the tags constructed of durable materials, the message printed clearly and permanently, and are tags installed at each valve or outlet?

☐ When pipelines are heated by electricity, steam, or other external source, are suitable warning signs or tags placed at unions, valves, or other serviceable parts of the system?

MATERIALS HANDLING

☐ Is there safe clearance for equipment through aisles and doorways?

☐ Are aisleways permanently marked and kept clear to allow unhindered passage?

☐ Are motorized vehicles and mechanized equipment inspected daily or prior to use?

☐ Are vehicles shut off and brakes set prior to loading or unloading?

☐ Are containers of liquid combustibles or flammables, when stacked while being moved, always protected by dunnage (packing material) sufficient to provide stability?

☐ Are dock boards (bridge plates) used when loading or unloading operations are taking place between vehicles and docks?

☐ Are trucks and trailers secured from movement during loading and unloading operations?

☐ Are dock plates and loading ramps constructed and maintained with sufficient strength to support imposed loading?

☐ Are hand trucks maintained in safe operating condition?

☐ Are chutes equipped with sideboards of sufficient height to prevent the materials being handled from falling off?

☐ Are chutes and gravity roller sections firmly placed or secured to prevent displacement?

☐ Are provisions made to brake the movement of the handled materials at the delivery end of rollers or chutes?

☐ Are pallets usually inspected before being loaded or moved?

☐ Are safety latches and other devices being used to prevent slippage of materials off of hoisting hooks?

☐ Are securing chains, ropes, chockers, or slings adequate for the job?

☐ Are provisions made to ensure that no one is below when hoisting material or equipment?

☐ Are MSDSs available to employees handling hazardous substances?

TRANSPORTING EMPLOYEES AND MATERIALS

☐ Do employees who operate vehicles on public thoroughfares have valid operator's licenses?

☐ When seven or more employees are regularly transported in a van, bus, or truck, is the operator's license appropriate for the class of vehicle being driven and are there enough seats?

☐ Are vehicles used to transport employees equipped with lamps, brakes, horns, mirrors, windshields and turn signals, and are they in good repair?

☐ Are transport vehicles provided with handrails, steps, stirrups, or similar devices, placed and arranged to allow employees to safely mount or dismount?

☐ Are employee transport vehicles equipped at all times with at least two reflective-type flares?

☐ Is a fully charged fire extinguisher, in good condition, with at least a 4 B:C rating maintained in each employee transport vehicle?

☐ When cutting tools or tools with sharp edges are carried in passenger compartments of employee transport vehicles, are they placed in closed boxes or containers that are secured in place?

☐ Are employees prohibited from riding on top of any load that could shift, topple, or otherwise become unstable?

CONTROL OF HARMFUL SUBSTANCES BY VENTILATION

☐ Is the volume and velocity of air in each exhaust system sufficient to gather the dusts, fumes, mists, vapors, or gases to be controlled, and to convey them to a suitable point of disposal?

☐ Are exhaust inlets, ducts and plenums designed, constructed and supported to prevent collapse or failure of any part of the system?

☐ Are clean-out ports or doors provided at intervals not to exceed 12 feet (3.6576 meters) in all horizontal runs of exhaust ducts?

☐ Where two or more different operations are being controlled through the same exhaust system, could the combination of substances involved create a fire, explosion, or chemical reaction hazard in the duct?

☐ Is adequate makeup air provided to areas where exhaust systems are operating?

☐ Is the source point for makeup air located so that only clean, fresh air, free of contaminants will enter the work environment?

☐ Where two or more ventilation systems serve a work area, is their operation such that one will not offset the functions of the other?

SANITIZING EQUIPMENT AND CLOTHING

☐ Is required personal protective clothing or equipment able to be cleaned and disinfected easily?

☐ Are employees prohibited from interchanging personal protective clothing or equipment, unless it has been properly cleaned?

☐ Are machines and equipment that process, handle, or apply materials that could injure employees cleaned and/or decontaminated before being overhauled or placed in storage?

☐ Are employees prohibited from smoking or eating in any area where contaminants are present that could be injurious if ingested?

☐ When employees are required to change from street clothing into protective clothing, is a clean change room with a separate storage facility for street and protective clothing provided?

☐ Are employees required to shower and wash their hair as soon as possible after a known contact with a carcinogen has occurred?

☐ When equipment, materials, or other items are taken into or removed from a carcinogen-regulated area, is it done in a manner that will not contaminate non-regulated areas or the external environment?

TIRE INFLATION

☐ Where tires are mounted and/or inflated on drop center wheels or on wheels with split rims and/or retainer rings, is a safe practice procedure posted and enforced?

☐ Does each tire inflation hose have a clip-on chuck with at least 2.54 inches (6.45 centimeters) of hose between the chuck and an in-line hand valve and gauge?

☐ Does the tire inflation control valve automatically shut off the air flow when the valve is released?

☐ Is a tire restraining device such as a cage, rack, or other effective means used while inflating tires mounted on split rims or rims using retainer rings?

☐ Are employees prohibited from standing directly over or in front of a tire while it is being inflated?

Appendix III

Mitigation Plan
Worksheets

The following worksheets from the Federal Emergency Management Agency (FEMA) are provided as a guideline to aid in the mitigation plan. The worksheets are to be used as guides in planning. The facility manager, or appointed designee, should modify the format as necessary to meet with the company's requirements and internal policies. The worksheets, designed for state and local governments, are not comprehensive and should be modified to meet specific organizational considerations.

Source

Federal Emergency Management Agency, *State and Local Mitigation Planning—How to Guides. Understanding our Risks—Identifying Hazards and Estimating Losses.* FEMA 386-1. August, 2001.

Worksheet #1   Identify the Hazards   step 1

Date: *What kinds of natural hazards can affect you?*

Task A. List the hazards that may occur.

1. *Research newspapers and other historical records.*
2. *Review existing plans and reports.*
3. *Talk to the experts in your community, state, or region.*
4. *Gather information on Internet Websites.*
5. *Next to the hazard list below, put a check mark in the Task A boxes beside all hazards that may occur in your community or state.*

Task B. Focus on the most prevalent hazards in your community or state.

1. *Go to hazard Websites.*
2. *Locate your community or state on the Website map.*
3. *Determine whether you are in a high-risk area. Get more localized information if necessary.*
4. *Next to the hazard list below, put a check mark in the Task B boxes beside all hazards that pose a significant threat.*

Use this space to record information you find for each of the hazards you will be researching. Attach additional pages as necessary.

Hazard	Task A	Task B
Avalanche	☐	☐
Coastal Erosion	☐	☐
Coastal Storm	☐	☐
Dam Failure	☐	☐
Drought	☐	☐
Earthquake	☐	☐
Expansive Soils	☐	☐
Extreme Heat	☐	☐
Flood	☐	☐
Hailstorm	☐	☐
Hurricane	☐	☐
Land Subsidence	☐	☐
Landslide	☐	☐
Severe Winter Storm	☐	☐
Tornado	☐	☐
Tsunami	☐	☐
Volcano	☐	☐
Wildfire	☐	☐
Windstorm	☐	☐
Other_____	☐	☐
Other_____	☐	☐
Other_____	☐	☐

Hazard or Event Description (type of hazard, date of event, number of injuries, cost and types of damage, etc.)	Source of Information	Map Available for this Hazard?	Scale of Map

Worksheet #2   Profile Hazard Events   step 2

Date: *How Bad Can It Get?*

Task A. Obtain or create a base map.

You can use existing maps from:

* Road maps
* USGS topographic maps or Digital Orthophoto Quarter Quads (DOQQ)
* Topographic and/or planimetric maps from other agencies
* Aerial topographic and/or planimetric maps

OR you can create a base map using:

* Field surveys
* GIS software
* CADD software
* Digitized paper maps

Title of Map	Scale	Date

Flood
- [ ] 1. Get a copy of your FIRM. _____
- [ ] 2. Verify the FIRM is up-to-date and complete. _____

- [ ] 1. Transfer the boundaries from your FIRM onto your base map (floodway, 100-yr flood, 500-yr flood).
- [ ] 2. Transfer the BFEs onto your base map.

Earthquake
- [ ] 1. Go to the http://geohazards.cr.usgs.gov Website.
- [ ] 2. Locate your planning area on the map.
- [ ] 3. Determine your PGA.

- [ ] 1. Record your PGA: _____
- [ ] 2. If you have more than one PGA print, download or order your PGA map.

Tsunami
- [ ] 1. Get a copy of your tsunami inundation zone map. _____

- [ ] 1. Copy the boundary of your tsunami inundation zone onto your base map.

Tornado
- [ ] 1. Find your design wind speed. _____

- [ ] 1. Record your design wind speed: _____
- [ ] 2. If you have more than one design wind speed, print, download, or copy your design wind speed zones, copy the boundary of your design wind speed zones on your base map, then record the design wind speed zones on your base map.

Coastal Storm
- [ ] 1. Get a copy of your FIRM. _____
- [ ] 2. Verify that the FIRM is up-to-date and complete.
- [ ] 3. Determine the annual rate of coastal erosion.
- [ ] 4. Find your design wind speed.

- [ ] 1. Transfer the boundaries of your coastal storm hazard areas onto your base map.
- [ ] 2. Transfer the BFEs onto your base map.
- [ ] 3. Record the erosion rates on your base map:
- [ ] 4. Record the design wind speed here and on your base map: _____

Landslide
- [ ] 1. Map location of previous landslides. _____
- [ ] 2. Map the topography. _____
- [ ] 3. Map the geology. _____
- [ ] 4. Identify the high-hazard areas on your map. _____

- [ ] 1. Mark the areas susceptible to landslides onto your base map.

Wildfire
- [ ] 1. Map the fuel models located within the urban-wildland interface areas. _____
- [ ] 2. Map the topography. _____
- [ ] 3. Determine your critical fire weather frequency. _____
- [ ] 4. Determine your fire hazard severity. _____

- [ ] 1. Draw the boundaries of your wildfire hazard areas onto your base map.

Other
- [ ] 1. Map the hazard. _____

- [ ] 1. Record hazard event info on your base map.

Worksheet #3a   **Inventory Assets**   **step** 3

Date: *What will be affected by the hazard event?*

Task A. Determine the proportion of buildings, the value of buildings, and the population in your community or state that are located in hazard areas.

Hazard _____

Type of Structure (Occupancy Class)	Number of Structures			Value of Structures			Number of People		
	# in Community or State	# in Hazard Area	% in Hazard Area	$ in Community or State	$ in Hazard Area	% in Hazard Area	# in Community or State	# in Hazard Area	% in Hazard Area
Residential									
Commercial									
Industrial									
Agricultural									
Religious/ Non-profit									
Government									
Education									
Utilities									
Total									

Task B. Determine whether (and where) you want to collect additional inventory data.

	Y	N
1. Do you know where your greatest damages may occur in your hazard areas?	____	____
2. Do you know whether your critical facilities will be operational after a hazard event?	____	____
3. Is there enough data to determine which assets are subject to the greatest potential damages?	____	____
4. Is there enough data to determine whether significant elements of the community are vulnerable to potential hazards?	____	____
5. Is there enough data to determine whether certain areas of historic, environmental, political, or cultural significance are vulnerable to potential hazards?	____	____
6. Is there concern about a particular hazard because of its severity, repetitiveness, or likelihood of occurrence?	____	____
7. Is additional data needed to justify the expenditure of community or state funds for mitigation initiatives?	____	____

Worksheet #3b **Inventory Assets** step **3**

Date: *What will be affected by the hazard event?*

Task C. Compile a detailed inventory of what can be damaged by a hazard event.

Inventory the assets (critical facilities, businesses, historic, cultural, and natural resource areas, and areas of special consideration), that can be damaged by a hazard event.

Hazard _____

Name or Description of Asset	Sources of Information	Critical Facility	Vulnerable Populations	Economic Assets	Special Considerations	Historic/Other Considerations	Size of Building (sq ft)	Replacement Value ($)	Contents Value ($)	Function Use or Value ($)	Displacement Cost ($ per day)	Occupancy or Capacity (#)	Other Hazard Specific Information
		✓	✓	✓	✓	✓							

page 2 of 2

Worksheet #4   Estimate Losses   step 4

Date: *How will these hazards affect you?*

Hazard _____

	Structure Loss (Task A.1.)					Contents Loss (Task A.2.)				
Name/ Description of Structure	Structure Replacement Value (Step 3) ($)	x	Percent Damage (Step 4) (%)	=	Loss to Structure ($)	Replacement Value of Contents (Step 3) ($)	x	Percent Damage (Step 4) (%)	=	Loss to Contents ($)
		x		=			x		=	
		x		=			x		=	
		x		=			x		=	
		x		=			x		=	
		x		=			x		=	
		x		=			x		=	
		x		=			x		=	
		x		=			x		=	
	Total Loss to Structure					Total Loss to Contents				

	Structure Use and Function Loss (Task A.3.)									Structure Loss + Content Loss + Function Loss ($)
Name/ Description of Structure	Average Daily Operating Budget (Step 3) ($)	x	Functional Downtime (Step 4) (# of days)	+	Displacement Cost per Day (Step 3) ($)	x	Displacement Time (Step 4) ($)	=	Structure Use & Function Loss ($)	
		x		+		x		=		
		x		+		x		=		
		x		+		x		=		
		x		+		x		=		
		x		+		x		=		
		x		+		x		=		
		x		+		x		=		
		x		+		x		=		
	Total Loss to Structure Use & Function									Total Loss for Hazard Event (Task B.2.)

Appendix IV

Building Vulnerability Assessment Screening

Appendix IV provides a tool for a comprehensive assessment of terrorism vulnerability in buildings. It contains a list of questions that provide the basis for identifying the physical and operational vulnerability of the building.

Table A: Site

Item	Vulnerability Question	Vulnerability estimate	Detailed assessment	Visual inspection	Document review	Org/Mgmt procedure	Moving vehicle	Stationary vehicle	Covert entry	Mail	Supplies	Blast effects	Airborne (contamination)	Waterborne (contamination)
		Characterization					**Terrorist Tactics**							
		Type		Collection			Delivery Methods				Mechanisms			
Site.1a	What major structures surround the facility?	•		•	•									
Site.1b	What critical infrastructure, government, military, or recreation facilities are in the local area that impact transportation, utilities, and collateral damage (attack at this facility impacting the other major structures or attack on the major structures impacting this facility)?	•		•	•	•								
Site.1c	What are the adjacent land uses immediately outside the perimeter of this facility?	•		•	•									
Site.1d	Do future development plans change these land uses outside the facility perimeter?		•	•	•									
Site.2	Does the terrain place the building in a depression or low area?		•	•										
Site.3	In dense, urban areas, does curb lane parking place uncontrolled parked vehicles unacceptably close to a facility in public rights-of-way?	•	•			•	•					•		
Site.4	Is a perimeter fence or other types of barrier controls in place?	•	•				•		•					
Site.5	What are the site access points to the facility?	•		•			•		•					
Site.6	Is vehicle traffic separated from pedestrian traffic on the site?	•	•			•	•		•					
Site.7	Is there vehicle and pedestrian access control at the perimeter of the site?	•	•			•	•		•					
Site.8a	Is there space for inspection at the curb line or outside the protected perimeter?	•	•						•					
Site.8b	What is the minimum distance from the inspection location to the building?	•	•				•		•			•		
Site.9	Is there any potential access to the site or facility through utility paths or water runoff?	•		•	•				•					
Site.10a	What are the existing types of vehicle anti-ram devices for the facility?	•	•						•					
Site.10b	Are these devices at the property boundary or at the building?	•	•						•					
Site.11	What is the anti-ram buffer zone standoff distance from the building to unscreened vehicles or parking?	•	•						•			•		

Source: Federal Emergency Management Agency (FEMA)

Table A: Site (continued)

Item	Vulnerability Question	Vulnerability estimate	Detailed assessment	Visual inspection	Document review	Org/Mgmt procedure	Moving vehicle	Stationary vehicle	Covert entry	Mail	Supplies	Blast effects	Airborne (contamination)	Waterborne (contamination)
		Type		Collection			Delivery Methods					Mechanisms		
Site.12a	Are perimeter barriers capable of stopping vehicles?	●		●	●		●							
Site.12b	Will the perimeter and facility barriers for protection against vehicles maintain access for emergency responders, including large fire apparatus?		●			●								
Site.13	Does site circulation prevent high-speed approaches by vehicles?	●		●			●							
Site.14	Are there offsetting vehicle entrances from the direction of a vehicle's approach to force a reduction of speed?	●	●				●							
Site.15	Is there a minimum setback distance between the building and parked vehicles?	●		●					●			●		
Site.16	Does adjacent surface parking maintain a minimum standoff distance?	●		●					●			●		
Site.17	Do stand-alone, above ground parking facilities provide adequate visibility across as well as into and out of the parking facility?	●	●						●	●				
Site.18	Are garage or service area entrances for employee-permitted vehicles protected by suitable anti-ram devices?	●	●			●	●							
Site.19	Do site landscaping and street furniture provide hiding places?	●		●					●					
Site.20a	Is the site lighting adequate from a security perspective in roadway access and parking areas?	●	●						●					
Site.20b	Are line-of-sight perspectives from outside the secured boundary to the building and on the property along pedestrian and vehicle routes integrated with landscaping and green space?	●	●			●								
Site.21	Do signs provide control of vehicles and people?	●	●											
Site.22	Are all existing fire hydrants on the site accessible?	●	●											

Source: Federal Emergency Management Agency (FEMA)

Table B: Architectural

Item	Vulnerability Question	Characterization — Type: Vulnerability estimate	Detailed assessment	Characterization — Collection: Visual inspection	Document review	Org/Mgmt procedure	Terrorist Tactics — Delivery Methods: Moving vehicle	Stationary vehicle	Covert entry	Mail	Supplies	Terrorist Tactics — Mechanisms: Blast effects	Airborne (contamination)	Waterborne (contamination)
Arch.1	Does the site and architectural design incorporate strategies from a Crime Prevention Through Environmental Design (CPTED) perspective?	•	•				•	•						
Arch.2	Is it a mixed-tenant facility?	•		•	•	•								
Arch.3	Are pedestrian paths planned to concentrate activity to aid in detection?	•	•						•					
Arch.4	Are there trash receptacles and mailboxes in close proximity to the facility that can be used to hide explosive devices?	•	•									•		
Arch.5	Do entrances avoid significant queuing?	•		•		•								
Arch.6a	Does security screening cover all public and private areas?	•	•	•					•					
Arch.6b	Are public and private activities separated?	•		•		•								
Arch.6c	Are public toilets, service spaces, or access to stairs or elevators located in any non-secure areas, including the queuing area before screening at the public entrance?	•	•						•					
Arch.7	Is access control provided through main entrance points for employees and visitors? (lobby receptionist, sign-in, staff escorts, issue of visitor badges, checking forms of personal identification, electronic access control systems)	•	•		•				•					
Arch.8	Is access to private and public space or restricted area space clearly defined through the design of the space, signage, use of electronic security devices, etc.?	•	•		•				•					
Arch.9	Is access to elevators distinguished as to those that are designated only for employees and visitors?	•	•		•				•					
Arch.10	Do public and employee entrances include space for possible future installation of access control and screening equipment?	•	•		•				•					
Arch.11	Do foyers have reinforced concrete walls and offset interior and exterior doors from each other?	•	•									•		
Arch.12	Do doors and walls along the line of security screening meet requirements of UL752 "Standard for Safety: Bullet-Resisting Equipment"?	•	•	•										

Source: Federal Emergency Management Agency (FEMA)

Table B: Architectural (continued)

Item	Vulnerability Question	Vulnerability estimate	Detailed assessment	Visual inspection	Document review	Org/Mgmt procedure	Moving vehicle	Stationary vehicle	Covert entry	Mail	Supplies	Blast effects	Airborne (contamination)	Waterborne (contamination)
				Characterization					Terrorist Tactics					
		Type		Collection			Delivery Methods					Mechanisms		
Arch.13	Do circulation routes have unobstructed views of people approaching controlled access points?	•		•					•					
Arch.14	Is roof access limited to authorized personnel by means of locking mechanisms?			•		•			•					
Arch.15a	Are critical assets (people, activities, building systems and components) located close to any main entrance, vehicle circulation, parking, maintenance area, loading dock, or interior parking?	•		•	•	•	•	•	•			•		
Arch.15b	Are the critical building systems and components hardened?			•	•	•						•		
Arch.16	Are high-value or critical assets located as far into the interior of the building as possible and separated from the public areas of the building?	•		•	•	•						•		
Arch.17	Is high visitor activity away from critical assets?	•				•			•					
Arch.18a	Are critical assets located in spaces that are occupied 24 hours per day?	•				•								
Arch.18b	Are assets located in areas where they are visible to more than one person?	•				•								
Arch.19	Are loading docks and receiving and shipping areas separated in any direction from utility rooms, utility mains, and service entrances including electrical, telephone/data, fire detection/alarm systems, fire suppression water mains, cooling and heating mains, etc.?	•	•								•	•	•	•
Arch.20a	Are mailrooms located away from facility main entrances, areas containing critical services, utilities, distribution systems, and important assets?	•	•							•				
Arch.20b	Is the mailroom located near the loading dock?	•	•							•	•	•	•	•
Arch.21	Does the mailroom have adequate space available for equipment to examine incoming packages and for an explosive disposal container?	•	•							•		•	•	•
Arch.22	Are areas of refuge identified, with special consideration given to egress?	•	•	•	•									

Source: Federal Emergency Management Agency (FEMA)

Table B: Architectural (continued)

Item	Vulnerability Question	Vulnerability estimate	Detailed assessment	Visual inspection	Document review	Org/Mgmt procedure	Moving vehicle	Stationary vehicle	Covert entry	Mail	Supplies	Blast effects	Airborne (contamination)	Waterborne (contamination)
		Characterization					**Terrorist Tactics**							
		Type		Collection			Delivery Methods					Mechanisms		
Arch.23a	Are stairwells required for emergency egress located as remotely as possible from high-risk areas where blast events might occur?	•	•									•		
Arch.23b	Are stairways maintained with positive pressure or are there other smoke control systems?	•	•	•									•	
Arch.24	Are enclosures for emergency egress hardened to limit the extent of debris that might otherwise impede safe passage and reduce the flow of evacuees?	•		•								•		
Arch.25	Do interior barriers differentiate level of security within a facility?	•		•	•	•								
Arch.26	Are emergency systems located away from high-risk areas?	•		•	•	•						•		
Arch.27a	Is interior glazing near high-threat areas minimized?		•	•								•		
Arch.27b	Is interior glazing in other areas shatter resistant?		•	•								•		

Source: Federal Emergency Management Agency (FEMA)

Table C: Structural Systems

Item	Vulnerability Question	Vulnerability estimate	Detailed assessment	Visual inspection	Document review	Org/Mgmt procedure	Moving vehicle	Stationary vehicle	Covert entry	Mail	Supplies	Blast effects	Airborne (contamination)	Waterborne (contamination)
		Characterization					**Terrorist Tactics**							
		Type		Collection			Delivery Methods					Mechanisms		
StrucSys.1a	What type of construction?	●		●	●							●		
StrucSys.1b	What type of concrete & reinforcing steel?		●	●								●		
StrucSys.1c	What type of steel?		●	●								●		
StrucSys.1d	What type of foundation?		●	●								●		
StrucSys.2a	Do the reinforced concrete structures contain symmetric steel reinforcement (positive and negative faces) in all floor slabs, roof slabs, walls, beams and girders that may be subjected to rebound, uplift and suction pressures?		●	●								●		
StrucSys.2b	Do the lap splices fully develop the capacity of the reinforcement?		●	●								●		
StrucSys.2c	Are lap splices and other discontinuities staggered?		●	●								●		
StrucSys.2d	Do the connections possess ductile details?		●	●								●		
StrucSys.2e	Is special shear reinforcement, including ties and stirrups, available to allow large post-elastic behavior?		●	●								●		
StrucSys.3a	Are the steel frame connections moment connections?		●	●	●							●		
StrucSys.3b	Is the column spacing minimized so that reasonably sized members will resist the design loads and increase the redundancy of the system?	●		●	●							●		
StrucSys.3c	What are the floor-to-floor heights?	●		●	●							●		
StrucSys.4	Are critical elements vulnerable to failure?		●		●							●		
StrucSys.5	Will the structure suffer an unacceptable level of damage resulting from the postulated threat (blast loading or weapon impact)?		●		●							●		
StrucSys.6a	Is the structure vulnerable to progressive collapse?	●		●	●							●		
StrucSys.6b	Is the facility capable of sustaining the removal of a column for one floor above grade at the building perimeter without progressive collapse?		●	●								●		

Source: Federal Emergency Management Agency (FEMA)

Table C: Structural Systems (continued)

Item	Vulnerability Question	Vulnerability estimate	Detailed assessment	Visual inspection	Document review	Org/Mgmt procedure	Moving vehicle	Stationary vehicle	Covert entry	Mail	Supplies	Blast effects	Airborne (contamination)	Waterborne (contamination)
		Characterization					**Terrorist Tactics**							
		Type		*Collection*			*Delivery Methods*					*Mechanisms*		
StrucSys.6c	In the event of an internal explosion in an uncontrolled public ground floor area does the design prevent progressive collapse due to the loss of one primary column?		●	●								●		
StrucSys.6d	Do architectural or structural features provide a minimum 6-inch standoff to the internal columns?		●	●	●							●		
StrucSys.6e	Are the columns in the unscreened internal spaces designed for an unbraced length equal to two floors, or three floors where there are two levels of parking?		●	●								●		
StrucSys.7	Are there adequate redundant load paths in the structure?	●		●								●		
StrucSys.8	Are there transfer girders supported by columns within unscreened public spaces or at the exterior of the building?		●	●								●		
StrucSys.9	Will the loading dock design limit damage to adjacent areas and vent explosive force to the exterior of the building?		●	●	●							●		
StrucSys.10	Are mailrooms, where packages are received and opened for inspection, and unscreened retail spaces designed to mitigate the effects of a blast on primary vertical or lateral bracing members?		●		●	●						●		

Source: Federal Emergency Management Agency (FEMA)

Table D: Building Envelope

Item	Vulnerability Question	Characterization — Type — Vulnerability estimate	Detailed assessment	Collection — Visual inspection	Document review	Org/Mgmt procedure	Terrorist Tactics — Delivery Methods — Moving vehicle	Stationary vehicle	Covert entry	Mail	Supplies	Mechanisms — Blast effects	Airborne (contamination)	Waterborne (contamination)
BldgEnv.1	What is the designed or estimated protection level of the exterior walls against the postulated explosive threat?	•		•								•		
BldgEnv.2a	Is there less than 40 % fenestration openings per structural bay?	•	•									•		
BldgEnv.2b	Is the window system design on the exterior façade balanced to mitigate the hazardous effects of flying glazing following an explosive event? (glazing, frames, anchorage to supporting walls, etc.)	•	•	•								•		
BldgEnv.2c	Do the glazing systems with a ½-inch bite contain an application of structural silicone?	•	•	•								•		
BldgEnv.2d	Is the glazing laminated or is it protected with an anti-shatter film?	•	•	•								•		
BldgEnv.2e	If an anti-shatter film is used, is it a minimum of a 7-mil thick film, or specially manufactured 4-mil thick film?	•	•	•								•		
BldgEnv.3a	Do the walls, anchorage, and window framing fully develop the capacity of the glazing material selected?	•	•									•		
BldgEnv.3b	Are the walls capable of withstanding the dynamic reactions from the windows?	•	•									•		
BldgEnv.3c	Will the anchorage remain attached to the walls of the facility during an explosive event without failure?	•	•									•		
BldgEnv.3d	Is the façade connected to back-up block or to the structural frame?	•	•	•								•		
BldgEnv.3e	Are non-bearing masonry walls reinforced?	•	•	•								•		
BldgEnv.4a	Does the facility contain ballistic glazing?	•	•	•								•		
BldgEnv.4b	Does the ballistic glazing meet the requirements of UL 752 Bullet-Resistant Glazing?	•	•	•										
BldgEnv.4c	Does the facility contain security-glazing?	•	•	•					•					
BldgEnv.4d	Does the security-glazing meet the requirements of ASTM F1233 or UL 972, Burglary Resistant Glazing Material?	•	•	•					•					
BldgEnv.4e	Do the window assemblies containing forced entry resistant glazing (excluding the glazing) meet the requirements of ASTM F 588?	•	•	•					•					
BldgEnv.5	Do non-window openings, such as mechanical vents and exposed plenums, provide the same level of protection required for the exterior wall?	•	•	•									•	•

Source: Federal Emergency Management Agency (FEMA)

Table E: Utility Systems

Item	Vulnerability Question	Characterization					Terrorist Tactics							
		Type		Collection			Delivery Methods					Mechanisms		
		Vulnerability estimate	Detailed assessment	Visual inspection	Document review	Org/Mgmt procedure	Moving vehicle	Stationary vehicle	Covert entry	Mail	Supplies	Blast effects	Airborne (contamination)	Waterborne (contamination)
UtilSys.1a	What is the source of domestic water? (utility, municipal, wells, lake, river, storage tank)	•		•	•									•
UtilSys.1b	Is there a secure alternate drinking water supply?		•	•	•	•								•
UtilSys.2	Are there multiple entry points for the water supply?		•	•	•									•
UtilSys.3	Is the incoming water supply in a secure location?		•	•	•	•								•
UtilSys.4a	Does the facility have storage capacity for domestic water?		•	•	•									•
UtilSys.4b	How many gallons and how long will it allow operations to continue?	•		•	•	•								•
UtilSys.5a	What is the source of water for the fire suppression system? (local utility company lines, storage tanks with utility company backup, lake, or river)	•		•	•									
UtilSys.5b	Are there alternate water supplies for fire suppression?	•		•	•	•								
UtilSys.6	Is the fire suppression system adequate, code-compliant, and protected (secure location)?		•	•	•									
UtilSys.7a	Do the sprinkler/standpipe interior controls (risers) have fire- and blast-resistant separation?		•	•								•		
UtilSys.7b	Are the sprinkler and standpipe connections adequate and redundant?	•		•	•									
UtilSys.7c	Are there fire hydrant and water supply connections near the sprinkler/standpipe connections?		•	•										
UtilSys.8a	Are there redundant fire water pumps (e.g., one electric, one diesel)?		•	•		•								
UtilSys.8b	Are the pumps located apart from each other?		•	•										
UtilSys.9a	Are sewer systems accessible?		•	•	•	•								
UtilSys.9b	Are they protected or secured?		•	•	•									
UtilSys.10	What fuel supplies do the facility rely upon for critical operation?	•		•	•	•								
UtilSys.11a	How much fuel is stored on the site or at the facility and how long can this quantity support critical operations?		•	•		•								

Source: Federal Emergency Management Agency (FEMA)

Table E: Utility Systems (continued)

Item	Vulnerability Question	Vulnerability estimate	Detailed assessment	Visual inspection	Document review	Org/Mgmt procedure	Moving vehicle	Stationary vehicle	Covert entry	Mail	Supplies	Blast effects	Airborne (contamination)	Waterborne (contamination)
UtilSys.11b	How is it (fuel) stored?		●	●										
UtilSys.11c	How is it (fuel) secured?		●	●		●								
UtilSys.12a	Where is the fuel supply obtained?	●				●								
UtilSys.12b	How is it (fuel) delivered?		●			●								
UtilSys.13a	Are there alternate sources of fuel?	●				●								
UtilSys.13a	Are there alternate sources of fuel?	●				●								
UtilSys.13b	Can alternate fuels be used?	●			●	●								
UtilSys.14	What is the normal source of electrical service for the facility?	●			●	●								
UtilSys.15a	Is there a redundant electrical service source?		●		●	●								
UtilSys.15b	Can the facilities be fed from more than one utility substation?		●			●								
UtilSys.16	How may service entry points does the facility have for electricity?		●	●	●									
UtilSys.17	Is the incoming electric service to the building secure?		●	●		●								
UtilSys.18a	What provisions for emergency power exist? What systems receive emergency power and have capacity requirements been tested?	●		●	●	●								
UtilSys.18b	Is the emergency power co-located with the commercial electric service?		●	●										
UtilSys.18c	Is there an exterior connection for emergency power?		●	●										
UtilSys.19	By what means does the main telephone and data communications interface the facility?	●		●	●	●								
UtilSys.20	Are there multiple or redundant locations for the telephone and communication service?		●	●	●	●								
UtilSys.21a	Does the fire alarm system require communication with external sources?		●		●	●								
UtilSys.21b	By what method is the alarm signal sent to the responding agency: telephone, radio, etc?		●		●	●								
UtilSys.21c	Is there an intermediary alarm monitoring center?		●		●	●								
UtilSys.22	Are utility lifelines aboveground, underground, or direct buried?		●	●	●									

Source: Federal Emergency Management Agency (FEMA)

Table F: Mechanical Systems (Including Chemical, Biological, and Radiological Systems)

| Item | Vulnerability Question | Characterization | | | | | Terrorist Tactics | | | | | | | |
| | | Type | | Collection | | | Delivery Methods | | | | | Mechanisms | | |
		Vulnerability estimate	Detailed assessment	Visual inspection	Document review	Org/Mgmt procedure	Moving vehicle	Stationary vehicle	Covert entry	Mail	Supplies	Blast effects	Airborne (contamination)	Waterborne (contamination)
MechSys.1a	Where are the air intakes and exhaust louvers for the building? (low, high, or midpoint of the building structure)	•		•	•								•	
MechSys.1b	Are the intakes accessible to the public?		•	•		•							•	
MechSys.2	Are there multiple air intake locations?	•		•	•								•	
MechSys.3a	What are the types of air filtration? Include the efficiency and number of filter modules for each of the main air handling systems.		•		•								•	
MechSys.3b	Is there any collective protection for chemical, biological, and radiological contamination designed into the facility?	•	•	•	•								•	
MechSys.4	Is there space for larger filter assemblies on critical air handling systems?	•		•	•								•	
MechSys.5	Are there provisions for air monitors or sensors for chemical or biological agents?	•		•	•								•	
MechSys.6	By what method are air intakes closed when not operational?	•				•							•	
MechSys.7a	How are air handling systems zoned?	•		•	•								•	
MechSys.7b	What areas and functions do each of the primary air handling systems serve?	•			•								•	
MechSys.8	Are there large central air handling units or are there multiple units serving separate zones?	•			•								•	
MechSys.9a	Are there any redundancies in the air handling system?	•		•	•								•	
MechSys.9b	Can critical areas be served from other units if a major system is disabled?		•	•	•								•	
MechSys.10	Is the air supply to critical areas compartmentalized?		•	•	•								•	
MechSys.11	Are supply and exhaust air systems for critical areas secure?		•	•	•								•	
MechSys.12a	What is the method of temperature and humidity control?		•	•	•	•							•	
MechSys.12b	Is it (temp. control) localized or centralized?		•	•	•	•								
MechSys.13a	Where are the building automation control centers and cabinets located?		•	•	•									

Source: Federal Emergency Management Agency (FEMA)

Table F: Mechanical Systems (Including Chemical, Biological, and Radiological Systems) (continued)

| | | Characterization | | | | | Terrorist Tactics | | | | | | | |
| | | Type | | Collection | | | Delivery Methods | | | | | Mechanisms | | |
Item	Vulnerability Question	Vulnerability estimate	Detailed assessment	Visual inspection	Document review	Org/Mgmt procedure	Moving vehicle	Stationary vehicle	Covert entry	Mail	Supplies	Blast effects	Airborne (contamination)	Waterborne (contamination)
MechSys.13b	Are they in secure areas?		●	●	●	●								
MechSys.13c	How is the control wiring routed?		●	●	●									
MechSys.14	Does the control of air handling systems support plans for sheltering in place?		●		●	●								
MechSys.15	Where is roof-mounted equipment located on the roof?(near perimeter, at center of roof)	●		●										
MechSys.16	Are fire dampers installed at all fire barriers?		●	●	●									
MechSys.17	Do fire walls and fire doors maintain their integrity?		●	●	●									
MechSys.18	Do elevators have recall capability and elevator emergency message capability?		●	●	●	●								

Table G: Plumbing and Gas Systems

| | | Characterization | | | | | Terrorist Tactics | | | | | | | |
| | | Type | | Collection | | | Delivery Methods | | | | | Mechanisms | | |
Item	Vulnerability Question	Vulnerability estimate	Detailed assessment	Visual inspection	Document review	Org/Mgmt procedure	Moving vehicle	Stationary vehicle	Covert entry	Mail	Supplies	Blast effects	Airborne (contamination)	Waterborne (contamination)
PlumbGas.1	What is the method of water distribution?	●			●									●
PlumbGas.2	What is the method of gas distribution?, (heating, cooking, medical, process)	●			●									
PlumbGas.3	Is there redundancy to the main piping distribution?		●		●									
PlumbGas.4a	What is the method of heating domestic water?	●		●	●	●								
PlumbGas.4b	What fuel(s) is used?		●	●	●	●								
PlumbGas.5a	Where are gas storage tanks located? (heating, cooking, medical, process)		●	●										
PlumbGas.5b	How are they (gas tanks) piped to the distribution system?(above or below ground)		●	●	●									
PlumbGas.6	Are there reserve supplies of critical gases?	●			●	●								

Source: Federal Emergency Management Agency (FEMA)

Table H: Electrical Systems

| | | Characterization | | | | | Terrorist Tactics | | | | | | | |
| | | Type | | Collection | | | Delivery Methods | | | | | Mechanisms | | |
Item	Vulnerability Question	Vulnerability estimate	Detailed assessment	Visual inspection	Document review	Org/Mgmt procedure	Moving vehicle	Stationary vehicle	Covert entry	Mail	Supplies	Blast effects	Airborne (contamination)	Waterborne (contamination)
ElectSys.1a	Are there any transformers or switchgears located outside the building or accessible from the building exterior?	●		●										
ElectSys.1b	Are they (transformers or switchgears) vulnerable to public access?	●		●		●								
ElectSys.1c	Are they (transformers or switchgears) secured?		●	●		●								
ElectSys.2	What is the extent of the external facility lighting in utility and service areas and at normal entryways used by the building occupants?			●	●									
ElectSys.3	How are the electrical rooms secured and where are they located relative to other higher risk areas, starting with the main electrical distribution room at the service entrance?		●	●	●	●								
ElectSys.4a	Are critical electrical systems co-located with other building systems?		●	●										
ElectSys.4b	Are critical electrical systems located in areas outside of secured electrical areas?	●		●	●	●								
ElectSys.4c	Is security system wiring located separately from electrical and other service systems?		●	●	●									
ElectSys.5	How are electrical distribution panels serving branch circuits secured or are they in secure locations?		●	●	●	●								
ElectSys.6a	Does emergency backup power exist for all areas within the facility or for critical areas only?	●		●	●									
ElectSys.6b	How is the emergency power distributed?		●		●	●								
ElectSys.6c	Is the emergency power system independent from the normal electrical service, particularly in critical areas?		●		●									
ElectSys.7a	How is the primary electrical system wiring distributed?		●		●	●								
ElectSys.7b	Is it co-located with other major utilities?		●	●	●									
ElectSys.7c	Is there redundancy of distribution to critical areas?		●	●	●	●								

Source: Federal Emergency Management Agency (FEMA)

Table I: Fire Alarm Systems

| | | Characterization | | | | | Terrorist Tactics | | | | | | | |
| | | Type | | Collection | | | Delivery Methods | | | | | Mechanisms | | |
Item	Vulnerability Question	Vulnerability estimate	Detailed assessment	Visual inspection	Document review	Org/Mgmt procedure	Moving vehicle	Stationary vehicle	Covert entry	Mail	Supplies	Blast effects	Airborne (contamination)	Waterborne (contamination)
FireAlarm.1a	Is the facility fire alarm system centralized or localized?		●	●	●									
FireAlarm.1b	How are alarms annunciated, both locally and centrally?		●	●	●	●								
FireAlarm.1c	Are critical documents and control systems located in a secure yet accessible location?		●	●		●								
FireAlarm.2a	Where are the fire alarm panels located?		●	●										
FireAlarm.2b	Are they allow access to unauthorized personnel?		●	●		●								
FireAlarm.3a	Is the fire alarm system stand-alone or integrated with other functions such as security and environmental or building management systems?	●			●	●								
FireAlarm.3b	What is the interface?			●	●	●								
FireAlarm.4	Do key fire alarm system components have fire- and blast-resistant separation?		●	●	●							●		
FireAlarm.5	Is there redundant off-premises fire alarm reporting?	●			●	●								

Source: Federal Emergency Management Agency (FEMA)

Table J: Communications and IT Systems

		Characterization					Terrorist Tactics							
		Type		Collection			Delivery Methods					Mechanisms		
Item	Vulnerability Question	Vulnerability estimate	Detailed assessment	Visual inspection	Document review	Org/Mgmt procedure	Moving vehicle	Stationary vehicle	Covert entry	Mail	Supplies	Blast effects	Airborne (contamination)	Waterborne (contamination)
CommIT.1a	Where is the main telephone distribution room and where is it in relation to higher risk areas?	•		•	•	•								
CommIT.1b	Is the main telephone distribution room secure?		•	•		•								
CommIT.2a	Does the telephone system have an UPS (uninterruptible power supply)?		•		•	•								
CommIT.2b	What is its (ups) type, power rating, operational duration under load, and location? (battery, on-line, filtered)		•	•										
CommIT.3a	Where are communication systems wiring closets located? (voice, data, signal, alarm)	•		•	•									
CommIT.3b	Are they (communication closets) co-located with other utilities?		•	•	•									
CommIT.3c	Are they (communication closets) in secure areas?		•	•	•	•								
CommIT.4	How is communications system wiring distributed? (secure chases and risers, accessible public areas)		•	•	•									
CommIT.5	Are there redundant communications systems available?		•		•	•								
CommIT.6a	Where are the main distribution facility, data centers, routers, firewalls, and servers located?		•		•									
CommIT.6b	Where are the secondary and/or intermediate (IT) distribution facilities?		•		•									
CommIT.7	What type and where are the WAN (wide area network) connections?		•	•	•									
CommIT.8a	What type, power rating, and location of the UPS (uninterruptible power supply)? (battery, on-line, filtered)		•	•	•									
CommIT.8b	Are the UPS also connected to emergency power?		•	•	•									
CommIT.9	What type of LAN (local area network) cabling and physical topology is used? (Category(Cat) 5, Gigabit Ethernet, Ethernet, Token Ring)		•	•	•									
CommIT.10	For installed radio/wireless systems, what are their types and where are they located? (RF (radio frequency), HF (high frequency), VHF (very high frequency), MW (medium wave)		•	•	•									

Source: Federal Emergency Management Agency (FEMA)

Table J: Communications and IT Systems (continued)

Item	Vulnerability Question	Vulnerability estimate	Detailed assessment	Visual inspection	Document review	Org/Mgmt procedure	Moving vehicle	Stationary vehicle	Covert entry	Mail	Supplies	Blast effects	Airborne (contamination)	Waterborne (contamination)
		Characterization					Terrorist Tactics							
		Type		Collection			Delivery Methods					Mechanisms		
CommIT.11	Do the IT (Information Technology - computer) systems meet requirements of confidentiality, integrity, and availability?	•			•	•								
CommIT.12	Where is the disaster recovery/mirroring site?	•			•	•								
CommIT.13	Where is the back-up tape/file storage site and what is the type of safe environment? (safe, vault, underground)Is there redundant refrigeration in the (backup IT storage) site?	•			•	•								
CommIT.14	Are there any SATCOM (satellite communications) links? (location, power, UPS, emergency power, spare capacity/capability)	•	•	•										
CommIT.15a	Is there a mass notification system that reaches all building occupants? (public address, pager, cell phone, computer override, etc.)	•			•									
CommIT.15b	Will one or more of these systems be operational under hazard conditions? (UPS, emergency power)	•			•	•								
CommIT.16a	Do control centers and their designated alternate locations have equivalent or reduced capability for voice, data, mass notification, etc.? (emergency operations, security, fire alarms, building automation)	•			•	•								
CommIT.16b	Do the alternate locations also have access to backup systems, including emergency power?	•			•									

Source: Federal Emergency Management Agency (FEMA)

Table K: Equipment Operations and Maintenance

Item	Vulnerability Question	Vulnerability estimate	Detailed assessment	Visual inspection	Document review	Org/Mgmt procedure	Moving vehicle	Stationary vehicle	Covert entry	Mail	Supplies	Blast effects	Airborne (contamination)	Waterborne (contamination)
EquipOM.1a	Are there composite drawings indicating location and capacities of major systems and are they current? (electrical, mechanical, and fire protection; and date of last update)	•		•										
EquipOM.1b	Do updated O&M (operation and maintenance) manuals exist?	•		•										
EquipOM.2a	Have critical air systems been rebalanced?	•			•	•								
EquipOM.2b	If so, when and how often?	•				•								
EquipOM.3	Is air pressurization monitored regularly?	•				•								
EquipOM.4	Does the facility have a policy or procedure for periodic recommissioning of major Mechanical/Electrical/Plumbing systems?	•				•								
EquipOM.5	Is there an adequate operations and maintenance program including training of facilities management staff?	•				•								
EquipOM.6	What maintenance and service agreements exist for M/E/P systems?	•			•									
EquipOM.7	Are backup power systems periodically tested under load?	•				•								
EquipOM.8	Is stairway and exit sign lighting operational?	•	•											

Characterization: Type / Collection — Terrorist Tactics: Delivery Methods / Mechanisms

Source: Federal Emergency Management Agency (FEMA)

Table L: Security Systems

Item	Vulnerability Question	Vulnerability estimate	Detailed assessment	Visual inspection	Document review	Org/Mgmt procedure	Moving vehicle	Stationary vehicle	Covert entry	Mail	Supplies	Blast effects	Airborne (contamination)	Waterborne (contamination)
		Characterization					Terrorist Tactics							
		Type		Collection			Delivery Methods					Mechanisms		
SecPerim.1a	Are black/white or color CCTV (closed circuit television) cameras used?	●	●				●		●					
SecPerim.1b	Are they monitored and recorded 24 hours/7 days a week? By whom?	●			●	●		●	●					
SecPerim.1c	Are they analog or digital by design?	●		●			●		●					
SecPerim.1d	What are the number of fixed, wireless and pan-tilt-zoom cameras used?	●	●	●			●		●					
SecPerim.1e	Who are the manufacturers of the CCTV cameras?	●	●	●			●		●					
SecPerim.1f	What is the age of the CCTV cameras in use?	●		●	●		●		●					
SecPerim.2a	Are the cameras programmed to respond automatically to perimeter building alarm events?	●			●	●		●	●					
SecPerim.2b	Do they have built-in video motion capabilities?	●		●			●		●					
SecPerim.3	What type of camera housings are used and are they environmental in design to protect against exposure to heat and cold weather elements?	●	●	●			●		●					
SecPerim.4	Are panic/duress alarm buttons or sensors used, where are they located and are they hardwired or portable?	●	●				●		●					
SecPerim.5	Are intercom call boxes used in parking areas or along the building perimeter?	●	●		●		●		●					
SecPerim.6	What is the transmission media used to transmit camera video signals: fiber, wire line, telephone wire, coaxial, wireless?	●	●	●				●	●					
SecPerim.7	Who monitors the CCTV system?	●			●	●		●	●					
SecPerim.8a	What is the quality of video images both during the day and hours of darkness?	●	●		●		●		●					
SecPerim.8b	Are infrared camera illuminators used?	●	●		●		●		●					
SecPerim.9	Are the perimeter cameras supported by an uninterruptible power supply, battery, or building emergency power?	●		●			●		●					
SecPerim.10	What type of exterior IDS sensors are used: electromagnetic, fiber optic, active infrared, bistatic microwave, seismic, photoelectric, ground, fence, glass break (vibration/shock), single, double and roll-up door magnetic contacts or switches.	●	●	●			●		●					

Source: Federal Emergency Management Agency (FEMA)

Table L: Security Systems (continued)

| | | Characterization | | | | | Terrorist Tactics | | | | | | | |
| | | Type | | Collection | | | Delivery Methods | | | | | Mechanisms | | |
Item	Vulnerability Question	Vulnerability estimate	Detailed assessment	Visual inspection	Document review	Org/Mgmt procedure	Moving vehicle	Stationary vehicle	Covert entry	Mail	Supplies	Blast effects	Airborne (contamination)	Waterborne (contamination)
SecPerim.11	Is a global positioning satellite system (GPS) used to monitor vehicles and asset movements?	●		●	●	●	●							
SecInter.12a	Are black/white or color CCTV (closed circuit television) cameras used?	●	●						●					
SecInter.12b	Are they monitored and recorded 24 hours/7 days a week? By whom?	●			●				●					
SecInter.12c	Are they analog or digital by design?	●		●					●					
SecInter.12d	What are the number of fixed, wireless and pan-tilt-zoom cameras used?	●	●	●					●					
SecInter.12e	Who are the manufacturers of the CCTV cameras?	●	●	●					●					
SecInter.12f	What is the age of the CCTV cameras in use?	●			●	●			●					
SecInter.13a	Are the cameras programmed to respond automatically to perimeter building alarm events?	●			●				●					
SecInter.13b	Do they have built-in video motion capabilities?	●			●				●					
SecInter.14	What type of camera housings are used and are they designed to protect against exposure or tampering?	●	●	●					●					
SecInter.15	Are the camera lenses used of the proper specifications, especially distance viewing and clarity?	●			●	●			●					
SecInter.16	What is the transmission media used to transmit camera video signals: fiber, wire line, telephone wire, coaxial, wireless?	●	●	●					●					
SecInter.17	Is the quality in interior camera video images of good visual and recording quality?	●	●			●			●					
SecInter.18	Are the interior cameras supported by an uninterruptible power supply source, battery, or building emergency power?	●	●						●					
SecInter.19	What are the first costs and maintenance costs associated with the interior cameras?	●			●	●			●					
SecInter.20a	What type of security access control system is used?	●				●			●					
SecInter.20b	Are these same devices used for physical security also used (integrated) with providing access control to security computer networks (e.g. in place of or in combination with user ID and system passwords)?	●			●	●			●					

Source: Federal Emergency Management Agency (FEMA)

Table L: Security Systems (continued)

Item	Vulnerability Question	Characterization — Type: Vulnerability estimate	Detailed assessment	Collection: Visual inspection	Document review	Org/Mgmt procedure	Terrorist Tactics — Delivery Methods: Moving vehicle	Stationary vehicle	Covert entry	Mail	Supplies	Mechanisms: Blast effects	Airborne (contamination)	Waterborne (contamination)
SecInter.23b	How old are the systems and what are the related first and maintenance service costs?	●		●	●				●					
SecInter.24	Are there panic/duress alarm sensors used, where are they located and are they hardwired or portable?	●	●	●					●					
SecInter.25	Are intercom call-boxes or building intercom system used throughout the facility?	●	●	●	●				●					
SecInter.26	Are magnetometers (metal detectors) and x-ray equipment used and at what locations within the facility?	●	●						●					
SecInter.27	What type of interior IDS sensors are used: electromagnetic, fiber optic, active infrared-motion detector, photoelectric, glass break (vibration/shock), single, double and roll-up door magnetic contacts or switches?	●		●	●				●					
SecInter.28	Are mechanical, electrical, medical gas, power supply, radiological material storage, voice/data telecommunication system nodes, security system panels, elevator and critical system panels, and other sensitive rooms continuously locked, under electronic security CCTV camera and intrusion alarm systems surveillance?	●				●			●					
SecInter.29	What types of locking hardware are used throughout the facility? Are manual and electromagnetic cipher, keypad, pushbutton, panic bar, door strikes and related hardware and software used?	●	●						●					
SecInter.30	Are any potentially hazardous chemicals, combustible or toxic materials stored on-site in non-secure and non-monitored areas?	●				●								
SecInter.31	What security controls are in place to handle the processing of mail and protect against potential biological, explosive or other threatening exposures?	●				●								
SecInter.32a	Is there a designated security control room and console in place to monitor security, fire alarm and possibly other building systems?	●	●						●					
SecInter.32b	Is there a backup control center designated and equipped?	●	●	●					●					

Source: Federal Emergency Management Agency (FEMA)

Table L: Security Systems (continued)

Item	Vulnerability Question	Vulnerability estimate	Detailed assessment	Visual inspection	Document review	Org/Mgmt procedure	Moving vehicle	Stationary vehicle	Covert entry	Mail	Supplies	Blast effects	Airborne (contamination)	Waterborne (contamination)
		Characterization					Terrorist Tactics							
		Type		Collection			Delivery Methods					Mechanisms		
SecInter.32c	Is there off-site 24-hour monitoring of intrusion detection systems?	•		•					•					
SecInter.33	Is the security console and control room adequate in size, provide room for expansion, have adequate environment controls (e.g. a/c, lighting, heating, air circulation, backup power, etc,) and is ergonomically designed?	•	•											
SecInter.34	Is the location of the security room in a secure area with limited, controlled and restricted access controls in place?	•	•		•									
SecInter.35a	What are the means by which facility and security personnel can communicate with one another: portable radio, pager, cell phone, personal data assistants (PDA's), etc)?	•			•									
SecInter.35b	What problems have been experienced with these and other electronic security systems?	•			•									
SecInter.36	Is there a computerized security incident reporting system used to prepare reports and track security incident trends and patterns?	•			•									
SecInter.37	Does the present security force have access to use a computerized guard tour system?	•			•									
SecInter.38a	Are vaults or safes in the facility?	•	•											
SecInter.38b	Where are they located?	•	•											
SecDocs.39	Are security system as-built drawings been generated and ready for review?	•		•										
SecDocs.40	Have security system design and drawing standards been developed?	•		•										
SecDocs.41	Are security equipment selection criteria defined?	•		•										
SecDocs.42	What contingency plans have been developed or are in place to deal with security control center redundancy and backup operations?	•			•									
SecDocs.43	Have security system construction specification documents been prepared and standardized?	•		•										
SecDocs.44	Are all security system documents to include as-built drawings current?	•		•										

Source: Federal Emergency Management Agency (FEMA)

Table L: Security Systems (continued)

| | | Characterization | | | | | Terrorist Tactics | | | | | | | |
| | | Type | Collection | | | | Delivery Methods | | | | Mechanisms | | | |
Item	Vulnerability Question	Vulnerability estimate	Detailed assessment	Visual inspection	Document review	Org/Mgmt procedure	Moving vehicle	Stationary vehicle	Covert entry	Mail	Supplies	Blast effects	Airborne (contamination)	Waterborne (contamination)
SecDocs.45	Have qualifications been determined in using security consultants, system designers and engineers, installation vendors, and contractors?	●			●									
SecDocs.46	Are security systems decentralized, centralized, integrated, and operate over existing IT network or standalone method of operation?	●		●	●									
SecDocs.47	What security systems manuals are available?	●		●										
SecDocs.48	What maintenance or service agreements exist for security systems?	●		●										

Source: Federal Emergency Management Agency (FEMA)

Table M: Security Master Plan

Item	Vulnerability Question	Vulnerability estimate	Detailed assessment	Visual inspection	Document review	Org/Mgmt procedure	Moving vehicle	Stationary vehicle	Covert entry	Mail	Supplies	Blast effects	Airborne (contamination)	Waterborne (contamination)
		Characterization					**Terrorist Tactics**							
		Type		Collection			Delivery Methods					Mechanisms		
SecPlan.1a	Does a written security plan exist for this facility?	●		●										
SecPlan.1b	When was the initial security plan written and last revised?	●		●										
SecPlan.1c	Who is responsible for preparing and reviewing the security plan?	●			●									
SecPlan.2	Has the security plan been communicated and disseminated to key management personnel and departments?	●			●									
SecPlan.3	Has the security plan been benchmarked or compared against related organizations and operational entities?	●			●									
SecPlan.4	Has the security plan ever been tested and evaluated from a cost-benefit and operational efficiency and effectiveness perspective?	●			●									
SecPlan.5	Does it define mission, vision, short-long term security program goals and objectives?	●			●									
SecPlan.6	Are threats, vulnerabilities, risks adequately defined and security countermeasures addressed and prioritized relevant to their criticality and probability of occurrence?	●			●									
SecPlan.7	Has a security implementation schedule been established to address recommended security solutions?	●			●									
SecPlan.8	Have security operating and capital budgets been addressed, approved and established to support the plan?	●			●	●								
SecPlan.9	What regulatory or industry guidelines/standards were followed in the preparation of the security plan?	●			●	●								
SecPlan.10	Does the security plan address existing security conditions from an administrative, operational, managerial and technical security systems perspective?	●			●	●								
SecPlan.11	Does the security plan address the protection of people, property, assets, and information?	●			●	●								
SecPlan.12	Does the security plan address the following major components: access control, surveillance, response, building hardening and protection against biological, chemical, radiological and cyber-network attacks?	●			●	●								

Source: Federal Emergency Management Agency (FEMA)

Table M: Security Master Plan (continued)

| | | Characterization | | | | | Terrorist Tactics | | | | | | | |
| | | Type | | Collection | | | Delivery Methods | | | | | Mechanisms | | |
Item	Vulnerability Question	Vulnerability estimate	Detailed assessment	Visual inspection	Document review	Org/Mgmt procedure	Moving vehicle	Stationary vehicle	Covert entry	Mail	Supplies	Blast effects	Airborne (contamination)	Waterborne (contamination)
SecPlan.13	Has the level of risk been identified and communicated in the security plan through the performance of a physical security assessment?	●		●	●									
SecPlan.14a	When was the last security assessment performed?	●		●	●									
SecPlan.14b	Who performed the security risk assessment?	●		●	●									
SecPlan.15a	Were the following areas of security analysis addressed in the security master plan: Asset Analysis: Does the security plan identify and prioritize the assets to be protected in accordance to their location, control, current value, and replacement value?	●			●									
SecPlan.15b	Threat Analysis: Does the security plan address potential threats; causes of potential harm in the form of death, injury, destruction, disclosure, interruption of operations, or denial of services? (possible criminal acts (documented and review of police/security incident reports) associated with forced entry, bombs, ballistic assault, biochemical and related terrorist tactics, attacks against utility systems infrastructure and buildings)	●			●									
SecPlan.15c	Vulnerability Analysis: Does the security plan address other areas and anything else associated with a facility and it's operations that can be taken advantage of to carry out a threat? (architectural design and construction of new and existing facilities, technological support systems (e.g. heating, air conditioning, power, lighting and security systems, etc.) and operational procedures, policies and controls)	●			●									
SecPlan.15d	Risk Analysis: Does the security plan address the findings from the asset, threat, and vulnerability analyses to develop, recommend and consider implementation of appropriate security countermeasures?	●			●									

Source: Federal Emergency Management Agency (FEMA)

Glossary

CHEMICAL TERMS

acetylcholinesterase. An enzyme that hydrolyzes the neurotransmitter acetylcholine. The action of this enzyme is inhibited by nerve agents.

aerosol. Fine liquid or solid particles suspended in a gas; for example, fog or smoke.

atropine. A compound used as an antidote for nerve agents.

blister agents. Substances that cause blistering of the skin. Exposure is through liquid or vapor contact with any exposed tissue (eyes, skin, lungs).

blood agents. Substances that injure a person by interfering with cell respiration (the exchange of oxygen and carbon dioxide between blood and tissues).

casualty (toxic) agents. Produce incapacitation, serious injury, or death. They can be used to incapacitate or kill victims. These agents are the choking, blister, nerve, and blood agents. See also **choking agents; blister agents; nerve agents; blood agents.**

central nervous system depressants. Compounds that have the predominant effect of depressing or blocking the activity of the central nervous system. The primary mental effects include the disruption of the ability to think, sedation, and lack of motivation.

central nervous system stimulants. Compounds that have the predominant effect of flooding the brain with too much information. The primary mental effect is loss of concentration, causing indecisiveness and the inability to act in a sustained, purposeful manner.

choking agents. Substances that cause physical injury to the lungs. Exposure is through inhalation. In extreme cases, membranes swell and lungs become filled with liquid. Death results from lack of oxygen; hence, the victim is "choked."

chemical agents. A chemical substance that is intended for use in military operations to kill, seriously injure, or incapacitate people through its physiological effects. Excluded from consideration are riot control agents, and smoke and flame materials. The agent may appear as a vapor, aerosol, or liquid; it can be either a casualty/toxic agent or an incapacitating agent.

cutaneous. Pertaining to the skin.

decontamination. The process of making any person, object, or area safe by absorbing, destroying, neutralizing, making harmless, or removing the hazardous material.

G-series nerve agents. Chemical agents of moderate to high toxicity developed in the 1930s. Examples are tabun (GA), sarin (GB), soman (GD), and GF.

incapacitating agents. Produce temporary physiological and/or mental effects via action on the central nervous system. Effects may persist for hours or days, but victims usually do not require medical treatment. However, such treatment speeds recovery. See also **vomiting agents; tear (riot control) agents; central nervous system depressants; central nervous system stimulants.**

industrial agents. Chemicals developed or manufactured for use in industrial operations or research by industry, government, or academia. These chemicals are not primarily manufactured for the specific purpose of producing human casualties or rendering equipment, facilities, or areas dangerous for use by man. Hydrogen cyanide, cyanogen chloride, phosgene, chloropicrin and many herbicides and pesticides are industrial chemicals that also can be chemical agents.

liquid agent. A chemical agent that appears to be an oily film or droplets. The color ranges from clear to brownish amber.

nerve agents. Substances that interfere with the central nervous system. Exposure is primarily through contact with the liquid (skin and eyes) and secondarily through inhalation of the vapor. Three distinct symptoms associated with nerve agents are: pin-point pupils, an extreme headache, and severe tightness in the chest.

nonpersistent agent. An agent that upon release loses its ability to cause casualties after 10 to 15 minutes. It has a high evaporation rate and is lighter than air and will disperse rapidly. It is considered to be a short-term hazard. However, in small unventilated areas, the agent will be more persistent.

organophosphorous compound. A compound, containing the elements phosphorus and carbon, whose physiological effects include inhibition of acetylcholinesterase. Many pesticides (malathione and parathion) and virtually all nerve agents are organophosphorous compounds.

percutaneous agents. Able to be absorbed by the body through the skin.

persistent agent. An agent that upon release retains its casualty-producing effects for an extended period of time, usually anywhere from 30 minutes to several days. A persistent agent usually has a low evaporation rate and its vapor is heavier than air. Therefore, its vapor cloud tends to hug the ground. It is considered to be a long-term hazard. Although inhalation hazards are still a concern, extreme caution should be taken to avoid skin contact as well.

protection. Any means by which an individual protects his body. Measures include masks, self-contained breathing apparatuses, clothing, structures such as buildings, and vehicles.

tear (riot control) agents. Produce irritating or disabling effects that rapidly disappear within minutes after exposure ceases.

V-series nerve agents. Chemical agents of moderate to high toxicity developed in the 1950s. They are generally persistent. Examples are VE, VG, VM, VS, and VX.

vapor agent. A gaseous form of a chemical agent. If heavier than air, the cloud will be close to the ground. If lighter than air, the cloud will rise and disperse more quickly.

volatility. A measure of how readily a substance will vaporize

vomiting agents. Produce nausea and vomiting effects, can also cause coughing, sneezing, pain in the nose and throat, nasal discharge, and tears.

BIOLOGICAL TERMS

aerosol. Fine liquid or solid particles suspended in a gas; for example, fog or smoke.

antibiotic. A substance that inhibits the growth of or kills microorganisms.

antisera. The liquid part of blood containing antibodies that react against disease causing agents.

bacteria. Single-celled organisms that multiply by cell division and that can cause disease in humans, plants, or animals.

biochemicals. The chemicals that make up or are produced by living things.

biological warfare. The intentional use of biological agents as weapons to kill or injure humans, animals, or plants, or to damage equipment.

biological warfare agents. Living organisms or the materials derived from them that cause disease in or harm to humans, animals, or plants, or cause deterioration of material. Biological agents may be used as liquid droplets, aerosols, or dry powders.

bioregulators. Biochemicals that regulate bodily functions. Bioregulators that are produced by the body are termed "endogenous." Some of these same bioregulators can be chemically synthesized.

causative agent. The organism or toxin that is responsible for causing a specific disease or harmful effect.

contagious. Capable of being transmitted from one person to another.

culture. A population of micro-organisms grown in a medium.

decontamination. The process of making people, objects, or areas safe by absorbing, destroying, neutralizing, making harmless, or removing the hazardous material.

fungi. Any of a group of plants mainly characterized by the absence of chlorophyll, the green colored compound found in other plants. Fungi range from microscopic single-celled plants (such as molds and mildews) to large plants (such as mushrooms).

host. An animal or plant that harbors or nourishes another organism.

incapacitating agent. Agents that produce physical or psychological effects, or both, that may persist for hours or days after exposure, rendering victims incapable of performing normal physical and mental tasks.

infectious agents. Biological agents capable of causing disease in a susceptible host.

infectivity. (1) The ability of an organism to spread. (2) The number of organisms required to cause an infection to secondary hosts. (3) The capability of an organism to spread out from the site of infection and cause disease in the host organism. Infectivity also can be viewed as the number of organisms required to cause an infection.

line-source delivery system. A delivery system in which the biological agent is dispersed from a moving ground or air vehicle in a line perpendicular to the direction of the prevailing wind. See also **point-source delivery system**.

microorganism. Any organism, such as bacteria, viruses, and some fungi that can be seen only with a microscope.

mycotoxin. A toxin produced by fungi.

nebulizer. A device for producing a fine spray or aerosol.

organism. Any individual living thing, whether animal or plant.

parasite. Any organism that lives in or on another organism without providing benefit in return.

pathogen. Any organism (usually living) capable of producing serious disease or death, such as bacteria, fungi, and viruses.

pathogenic agents. Biological agents capable of causing serious disease.

point-source delivery system. A delivery system in which the biological agent is dispersed from a stationary position. This delivery method results in coverage over a smaller area than with the line-source system. See also **line-source delivery system.**

route of exposure (entry). The path by which a person comes into contact with an agent or organism; for example, through breathing, digestion, or skin contact.

single-cell protein. Protein-rich material obtained from cultured algae, fungi, protein and bacteria, and often used as food or animal feed.

spore. A reproductive form some micro-organisms can take to become resistant to environmental conditions, such as extreme heat or cold, while in a "resting stage."

toxicity. A measure of the harmful effect produced by a given amount of a toxin on a living organism. The relative toxicity of an agent can be expressed in milligrams of toxin needed per kilogram of body weight to kill experimental animals.

toxins. Poisonous substances produced by living organisms.

vaccine. A preparation of killed or weakened microorganism products used to artificially induce immunity against a disease.

vector. An agent, such as an insect or rat, capable of transferring a pathogen from one organism to another.

venom. A poison produced in the glands of some animals; for example, snakes, scorpions, or bees.

virus. An infectious micro-organism that exists as a particle rather than as a complete cell. Particle sizes range from 20 to 400 manometers (one-billionth of a meter). Viruses . are not capable of reproducing outside of a host cell.

RADIOLOGICAL TERMS

acute radiation syndrome. Consists of three levels of effects: Hematopoietic (blood cells, most sensitive); Gastrointestinal (GI cells, very sensitive); and Central Nervous System (brain/muscle cells, insensitive). The initial signs and symptoms are nausea, vomiting, fatigue, and loss of appetite. Below about 200 rems, these symptoms may be the only indication of radiation exposure.

alpha particle. The alpha particle has a very short range in air and a very low ability to penetrate other materials, but it has a strong ability to ionize materials. Alpha particles are unable to penetrate even the thin layer of dead cells of human skin and consequently are not an external radiation hazard. Alpha-emitting nuclides inside the body as a result of inhalation or ingestion are a considerable internal radiation hazard.

beta particles. High-energy electrons emitted from the nucleus of an atom during radioactive decay. They normally can be stopped by the skin or a very thin sheet of metal.

Cesium-137 (Cs-137). A strong gamma ray source and can contaminate property, entailing extensive clean-up. It is commonly used in industrial measurement gauges and for irradiation of material. Half-life is 30.2 years.

Cobalt-60 (Co-60). A strong gamma ray source, and is extensively used as a radio therapeutic for treating cancer, food and material irradiation, gamma radiography, and industrial measurement gauges. Half-life is 5.27 years.

curie (Ci). A unit of radioactive decay rate defined as 3.7×10^{10} disintegrations per second.

decay. The process by which an unstable element is changed to another isotope or another element by the spontaneous emission of radiation from its nucleus. This process can be measured by using radiation detectors such as Geiger counters.

decontamination. The process of making people, objects, or areas safe by absorbing, destroying, neutralizing, making harmless, or removing the hazardous material.

dose. A general term for the amount of radiation absorbed over a period of time.

dosimeter. A portable instrument for measuring and registering the total accumulated dose to ionizing radiation.

gamma rays. High-energy photons emitted from the nucleus of atoms; similar to x rays. They can penetrate deeply into body tissue and many materials. Cobalt-60 and Cesium-137 are both strong g-emitters. Shielding against gamma radiation requires thick layers of dense materials, such as lead. Gamma rays are potentially lethal to humans.

half-life. The amount of time needed for half of the atoms of a radioactive material to decay.

highly enriched uranium (HEU). Uranium that is enriched to above 20% Uranium-235 (U-235). Weapons-grade HEU is enriched to above 90% in U-235.

ionize. To split off one or more electrons from an atom, thus leaving it with a positive electric charge. The electrons usually attach to one of the atoms or molecules, giving them a negative charge.

Iridium-192. A gamma-ray emitting radioisotope used for gamma-radiography. The half-life is 73, 83 days.

isotope. A specific element always has the same number of protons in the nucleus. That same element may, however, appear in forms that have different numbers of neutrons in the nucleus. These different forms are referred to as "isotopes" of the element. For example, deuterium (2H) and tritium (3H) are isotopes of ordinary hydrogen (H).

lethal dose (50/30). The dose of radiation expected to cause death within 30 days to 50% of those exposed without medical treatment. The generally accepted range from 400-500 rem received over a short period of time.

nuclear reactor. A device in which a controlled, self-sustaining nuclear chain reaction can be maintained with the use of cooling to remove generated heat.

plutonium-239 (Pu-239). A metallic element used for nuclear weapons. The half-life is 24,110 years.

rad. A unit of absorbed dose of radiation defined as deposition of 100 ergs of energy per gram of tissue. It amounts to approximately one ionization per cubic micron.

radiation. High energy alpha or beta particles or gamma rays that are emitted by an atom as the substance undergoes radioactive decay.

radiation sickness. High energy alpha or beta particles or gamma rays that are emitted by an atom as the substance undergoes radioactive decay.

radioactive waste. Disposable, radioactive materials resulting from nuclear operations. Wastes are generally classified into two categories, high-level and low-level waste.

radiological dispersal device (RDD). A device (weapon or equipment), other than a nuclear explosive device, designed to disseminate radioactive material in order to cause destruction, damage, or injury by means of the radiation produced by the decay of such material.

radioluminescence. The luminescence produced by particles emitted during radioactive decay.

rem. A roentgen man equivalent is a unit of absorbed dose that takes into account the relative effectiveness of radiation that harms human health.

shielding. Materials (lead, concrete, etc.) used to block or attenuate radiation for protection of equipment, materials, or people.

Special Nuclear Material (SNM). Plutonium and uranium enriched in the isotope Uranium-233 or Uranium 235.

uranium 235 (U-235). Naturally occurring uranium U-235 is found at 0.72% enrichment. U-235 is used as an reactor fuel or for weapons; however, weapons typically use U-235 enriched to 90%. The half-life is 7.04×10^8 years.

x-ray. An invisible, highly penetrating electromagnetic radiation of much shorter wavelength (higher frequency) than visible light. Very similar to gamma-rays.

Source: CIA

EARTHQUAKE HAZARD TERMS

aftershock. An earthquake of similar or lesser intensity that follows the main earthquake.

earthquake. A sudden slipping or movement of a portion of the earth's crust, accompanied and followed by a series of vibrations.

epicenter. The place on the earth's surface directly above the point on the fault where the earthquake rupture began. Once fault slippage begins, it expands along the fault during the earthquake and can extend hundreds of miles before stopping.

fault. The fracture across which displacement has occurred during an earthquake. The slippage may range from less than an inch to more than 10 yards in a severe earthquake.

magnitude. The amount of energy released during an earthquake, which is computed from the amplitude of the seismic waves. A magnitude of 7.0 on the Richter Scale indicates an extremely strong earthquake. Each whole number on the scale represents an increase of about 30 times more energy released than the previous whole number represents. Therefore, an earthquake measuring 6.0 is about 30 times more powerful than one measuring 5.0.

seismic waves. Vibrations that travel outward from the earthquake fault at speeds of several miles per second. Although fault slippage directly under a structure can cause considerable damage, the vibrations of seismic waves cause most of the destruction during earthquakes.

Source: FEMA

Index